THE INDEX
OF
PROHIBITED
BOOKS

THE INDEX OF PROHIBITED BOOKS

ROBIN VOSE

FOUR CENTURIES OF STRUGGLE OVER WORD AND IMAGE FOR THE GREATER GLORY OF GOD

REAKTION BOOKS

*For Milo Robin Carlos Gomes Jones,
in celebration of his third year of lightening our hearts*

Published by Reaktion Books Ltd
Unit 32, Waterside
44–48 Wharf Road
London N1 7UX, UK
www.reaktionbooks.co.uk

First published 2022
Copyright © Robin Vose 2022

All rights reserved

No part of this publication may be reproduced, stored in a retrieval system, or transmitted, in any form or by any means, electronic, mechanical, photocopying, recording or otherwise, without the prior permission of the publishers

Printed and bound in Great Britain
by TJ Books Ltd, Padstow, Cornwall

A catalogue record for this book is available from the British Library

ISBN 978 1 78914 657 8

CONTENTS

INTRODUCTION 7

PART I

1 CENSORSHIP BEFORE THE INDEX 27

2 INVENTING THE INDEX 46

3 EXPANDING THE INDEX 69

4 HOW TO BAN A BOOK 100

PART II

5 CENSORED SCRIPTURES 125

6 CENSORED MAGIC AND SCIENCE 155

7 CENSORED SEX, FAITH AND THE ARTS 179

8 CENSORSHIP AND MODERNITY 204

CONCLUSION 227

ABBREVIATIONS AND BIBLIOGRAPHICAL NOTES 247
REFERENCES 249
FURTHER READING 265
ACKNOWLEDGEMENTS 287
PHOTO ACKNOWLEDGEMENTS 289
INDEX 290

INTRODUCTION

This book is a study of a very particular institution, first established in the sixteenth century of the Common Era (CE) as a means of preventing the spread of objectionable religious ideas within the Roman Catholic communities of Europe. That institution, the *Index librorum prohibitorum* or Index of Prohibited Books, primarily took the form of printed lists of books and authors that Church officials wanted to keep away from all but the most carefully selected and qualified expert readers.[1] It was thus essentially a tool, a technology of censorship, designed to achieve a certain goal in a specific context. Like all tools, it maintained certain basic characteristics while also being modified over time to better serve its purpose(s). This was especially true as the objectives and circumstances of its wielders evolved and spread to new lands. Such shifts and continuities, the very stuff of which history is made, are fascinating in and of themselves.

No further justification is needed to write a book. My task in the chapters that follow is therefore in some ways quite simple: to tell the story of how and why, over a period of almost exactly four centuries, Catholic authorities designed and deployed various forms of Index as a means of enforcing one particular system for the censorship of words and images.

But this is also a very complicated undertaking, since we are talking about arguably the most important, longest-lived and least understood institutional exercise in censorship that has ever been attempted. At some times and in some places, it did incalculable harm to the history of human creativity. It was also in many ways a failure – right from its awkward beginnings to its surprisingly late end. And it was never *only* a means of persecuting those who had been identified as enemies of the Church; nor was it ever simply the blunt instrument of anti-intellectualism, aimed at the generalized suppression of all forms of free thought, that it is sometimes depicted as in caricature. It could even be argued that the Index served as a positive force in some contexts, or at least a well-intentioned effort, for the honest discernment of good from bad spiritual, intellectual, literary and cultural productions – in modern terms, by distinguishing between art and trash, debunking 'junk' science and charlatans, muting 'fake news' and so on. At its best, when directed by some of the world's most brilliant scholars, this censorship was in fact much less arbitrary or heavy-handed than is often supposed. In such instances it was not really all that far from (and perhaps even more transparent than) modern practices of academic peer review, or the many ways in which our own media experiences are dictated by Internet algorithms.

Whatever our final modern judgements may be, the legacy of the Index of Prohibited Books is richly deserving of close critical scrutiny so that we can better understand precisely *what* actually happened over its long history, and *how* it happened and *why*. Hopefully we can learn from some of the mistakes and excesses of the past in this regard – especially as we contemplate how best to navigate the far more effective, ubiquitous, and insidious systems of digital-era censorship that already envelop us.

BEFORE EMBARKING ON an exploration of just what the Index was (or rather what the many different Indexes were, along with the complex institutional frameworks, policies and supplementary documentation that supported them), it might also be helpful to explain some of the limits to this study. Like all historical phenomena, the Index existed in a context that shaped its development and the ways in which it was perceived by contemporaries. This wider context must be acknowledged as much as possible, but obviously not everything can be covered in a single book. For example, while it is important to recognize that the Catholic Church was far from unique in its censorship efforts (which extended beyond the Index itself), I will not attempt to fully explore the equally fascinating and complex details of parallel censorship by *secular* authorities. In each of the countries in which it operated, the Church's ability (and perceived 'need') to censor materials was limited to a greater or lesser extent by royal, parliamentary or other secular jurisdictions that similarly sought to prevent the circulation of offensive writings or images. We should therefore not assume that just because a text failed to appear on the Index, it had free rein in every kingdom; in fact, some texts never reached the Index compilers precisely because they had previously been suppressed by order of a king or queen, or by their ministers and agents.

Similarly, this book will not focus much attention on contemporary Protestant or non-Christian censorship. Of course such censorship did exist, and it could be fierce: Calvinist judges famously burned the anti-Trinitarian Michael Servetus on a bonfire of his own books in 1553, while Elizabeth I of England was notorious for her censorship of Catholic and Protestant recusants alike. In 1656 – the same year that Quaker books belonging to Mary Fisher and Ann Austin were burned by Protestant authorities in Boston's Market Square – the philosopher Baruch Spinoza was being punished with expulsion by his own Jewish community in Amsterdam, which also placed a permanent ban on all his writings.[2] Across the non-European and non-Christian world, different forms of censorship certainly existed and these could at times become entwined with the history of the Catholic Church itself (as when Jesuit missionaries' books were burned by Chinese authorities in the later eighteenth and early nineteenth centuries).[3] For the most part, however, these long and knotty histories range far beyond the scope of the present book.

Strictly speaking, the term 'Index of Prohibited Books' is used here to designate only those published and formally recognized censorship lists that were duly authorized as such by an established hierarchy of the Roman Catholic Church. Their exact title could vary: sometimes simply *Cathalogus librorum* (Spain, 1559), sometimes *Index et catalogus librorum prohibitorum* (Spain, 1583); or even *Index auctorum, et librorum, qui tanquam haeretici, aut suspecti, aut perniciosi, ab officio sancta Romanae inquisitionis reprobatur, et in universa Christiana republica interdicuntur* ('Index of Authors, and Books, which have been Condemned by the Holy Office of the Roman Inquisition and Forbidden in all Christendom as Either Heretical, or Suspicious or Pernicious', Rome, 1557). They might be compiled and issued by various branches or representatives of the Church, including not only popes and regional inquisitions but bishops and university departments of theology. These collections of titles and authors' names were also supplemented from time to time by singular edicts banning one or more author, written work or image. And while books were their main focus, other forms of writing were also occasionally addressed, so that later Index literature included consideration of newspapers, magazines and pamphlets as well. Certain types of images were banned on a regular basis, and ancillary documentation prepared by the various inquisitions or papal offices could eventually condemn everything from paintings to musical compositions to motion pictures (and in the twenty-first century, though no longer technically falling under the purview of an 'Index of Prohibited Books', the papacy continues to legislate on the proper use of communication technologies).[4] But overall the Indexes comprise a fairly homogeneous set of printed lists, primarily targeting written works.[5]

My challenge will be to coherently examine all these disparate yet related documents as a whole phenomenon, in order to fully understand how the Catholic Church sought to achieve a totalizing goal that ultimately had to be abandoned as overly ambitious: absolute control over the spiritual and ideological content of written and other forms of communication that audiences of the faithful might be exposed to throughout their lives.

Our story runs from the first localized 'Indexes' of the 1540s to the final abolition of the 'universal' papal Index in 1966. But its antecedents begin earlier, and its echoes continue down to the present. And it extends from the heartlands of Catholic Europe to colonized territories of the Americas, Africa and Asia as well, stretching at times even beyond the confines of the Index proper to consider more 'irregular' (but still related) forms of Church censorship. This is a lot to cover, and many gaps will necessarily remain. It is to be hoped that such lacunae will inspire interested readers to go on with further research of their own, continuing to explore the ever-challenging problems of censorship and its discontents, throughout history and around the world. Because this is a story that matters a great deal; one that reveals just how fundamentally important the use and abuse of words and images has so often been to human societies.

The Power of Words and Images

'In the beginning was the Word, and the Word was with God, and the Word was God.' This memorable opening line from the New Testament's Gospel of John goes a long way towards establishing the importance of *words* in Christian tradition. For many believers, it is to be understood above all as relating to the divinity of Christ, whom they associate with the divine Word (Greek: *logos*). But if we look more closely at the full Vulgate Latin text of this passage and those immediately following it, as medieval and early modern Catholic exegetes most certainly did, a further significance soon becomes evident.

In principio erat verbum, et verbum erat apud deum, et deus erat verbum.
In the beginning was the Word, and the Word was with God, and the **Word** was God [or rather, 'God was the Word'].

Hoc erat in principio apud deum.
This [the Word] was in the beginning with God.

Omnia per ipsum facta sunt: et sine ipso factum est nihil quod factum est.
All things were made by it [the Word]: and without it nothing was made that was made.

In ipso vita erat, et vita erat lux hominum:
In it [the Word] was life, and life was the light of men.

Et lux in tenebris lucet, et tenebrae eam non comprehenderunt.
And light shines in darkness, and darkness did not overcome it.[6]

Let's take a moment to reflect on the precise function of 'the Word' itself in this foundational text, so familiar yet for that very reason so easily overlooked. In the Vulgate Latin reading of John 1:2–5 it is the Word (or rather *verbum*, with its subsequent pronominal forms *hoc*, *ipsum* and *ipso*) that immediately emerges as the true focal point – as opposed to the personified God/Christ figure that modern English translations generally insert in its place, through a subtle adjustment of pronouns. Both the Catholic Douay-Rheims and the Protestant King James versions of the Bible (both of which played a major part in the history of Index censorship, as we will examine at greater length later on) use the masculine 'He' and 'Him', instead of the neuter 'it', as pronouns to replace the neuter word *verbum* (and so shift our attention back to a masculine Christ).[7] Yet in the understanding of medieval readers such as Thomas Aquinas, whose interpretation was authoritative for most inquisitors and censors of the early modern Catholic Church, the Gospel here clearly teaches that *the Word* itself, signifier of Christ though it might be, was both *with and equivalent* to God from the first; that through the *Word* all was made, and done; and that in this *Word* was constituted both *life (vita)* and the *light (lux)* that sustains humankind through darkness. The *Word* is thus fundamentally divine; it is omnipotent; it is the essential root of all things.

Theologians such as Aquinas taught and passed on to their flocks a strong belief that words do matter a great deal. Words are of radically divine origin, and they have a real impact on the created world. Of course such thinkers also recognized that words can sometimes be uttered in less consequential ways, flitting about as mere 'vibrations in the air' in the words of St Augustine.[8] For his part, Aquinas himself distinguished between divine, angelic and human words. The first comprises an existentially fundamental reality beyond our comprehension (as in God's creation of primordial light by means of a speech act, in Genesis 1:5), while the second is a simultaneously communicative and transcendental mediation between worlds (as in the angel's speech on behalf of God in Zechariah 1:9). Human words by contrast are essentially imperfect, above all in their failure to completely describe, invoke or express reality. Unlike the singular divine Word that creates and sustains the universe, human words must be clumsily multiplied in an inevitably imprecise effort to convey meaning. Worse, in their imperfect striving such floods of human words are liable to be misunderstood – and thereby to deceive.[9] Power and danger reside simultaneously in words. In the Christian tradition, therefore, they always have at least the potential to matter a great deal.

Concern over the power – and hence the danger – of words is not, of course, unique to Aquinas or to Christianity. As the Jesuit scholar Walter J. Ong notes, the ascription of what he calls 'magical potency' to words, or their characterization as in some way 'power-driven', may indeed be universal.[10] Certainly the Hebrew language, in which the first books of the Jewish Bible were originally composed, contains and mingles the intricately related meanings of 'word, utterance, speech' as well as 'order, command, action' (and even the very concept of 'thing') within the root D-B-R.[11] Derivatives of this root appear over 2,500 times in the Hebrew Bible (what Christians call the Old Testament) alone. When God first *speaks* to Abraham in Genesis 15:1 He is identified as *DBaR-Yahweh* (translated by St Jerome in the Christian Vulgate as *sermo domini*, or 'the Word of the Lord'), whereas when He *subjugates* the enemies of David in Psalm 18:48 the phrase used is *yaDBeR amim*.[12] The Ten Commandments themselves, in Hebrew, are known as the Ten Words (*aseret haDeBaRim*), while the similarly legislative Book of Deuteronomy was also originally called *DeBaRim* (from its opening passage, 'These are the *words* which Moses spoke'). Word and deed, speech and act, symbol and consequence, even creation and subjugation, are thus all deeply rooted in widely shared linguistic as well as cultural and religious pasts.

=✠=

IMAGES TOO have long come in for special scrutiny by biblically minded folks, at the very least since Moses received God's Ten Commandments at Sinai. The first of these (using the Catholic numbering) includes the following admonition:

Non facies tibi sculptile, neque omnem similitudinem quae est in coelo desuper,
Thou shalt not make to thyself a graven thing, nor the likeness of any thing that is in heaven above,

et quae in terra deorsum, nec eorum quae sunt in aquis sub terra.
or in the earth beneath, nor of those things that are in the waters under the earth.[13]

Here we have an apparently clear warning against human creation of sculpted, carved or graven objects (*sculptile*), and indeed of any representation or likeness (*similitudinem*) drawn from the natural world. The fuller text of this First Commandment (Exodus 20:3–6) includes a prefatory order to have no other gods, before continuing with what seems to be an explanatory admonishment not to 'bow down to' or 'serve' images as this would displease the jealous and punishing God of Abraham. Of course, for many monotheists (including most Muslims, Jews and some Christians) this could mean a fairly strict ban on any type of veneration before images, and especially before depictions of human or animal forms, which might be (mis)taken for a divinity. For Catholic Christians, however, an important distinction was made early on (and reinforced in the wake of struggles over iconoclasm in the eighth, ninth and sixteenth centuries) between the wholly unacceptable worship of false idols (*idolatria*), and legitimate veneration of holy beings, including saints and angels, which could be accomplished through such practices as the spiritual contemplation of holy images (*iconodulia*). Furthermore, most

Christians accept that some images can be spiritually neutral, if they do not involve any potential for worship (though they can still be morally or intellectually offensive). These were, and remain, difficult points of theology as well as of cultural politics. But again, they underline two key points: much like words, images are potentially very powerful, and also very dangerous if misunderstood or abused.

Even in non-religious contexts, it is hard to overestimate the importance – and potential danger – of words and images as communicative instruments in human society. Without words, or some other means of expressing complex thought, can we even imagine truly functioning as humans? They may not have magical or cosmic powers, but they do permit us to share information, to develop relationships and to inspire those around us. Without the ability to put concepts into words, we lose the power not only to pass on ideas to others but, perhaps, to pursue certain lines of thought in our own minds – as George Orwell suggested with his nightmarish invention of 'Newspeak', in which subversive words are altogether purged from a future vocabulary.[14]

Censorship of Words and Images

Orwell's dystopic vision came about as a result of his meditations on the secular totalitarian experiences of mid-twentieth-century Nazi Germany and Stalinist Russia. These modern, 'advanced' states sought to manipulate their citizens by strictly controlling the words they could read, write or utter (as well as the images they could see, and even the music they could hear). Censorship, book burnings and torture at the hands of secret police awaited those who sought to defy that control, because such regimes understood that the spread of dissenting opinions threatened their monopoly on power. Yet fear of dangerous words and images is of course far from unique to totalitarian dictatorships in the secular world; strict censorship and state propaganda rules were just as carefully developed by the Nazis' 'democratic' Allied opponents, and the lessons of wartime media control have not been lost on post-war leaders of global corporate capitalism. Censorship continues today under many guises, from many quarters and for many reasons: from bans on offensive works such as Hitler's *Mein Kampf* or cartoons depicting the Prophet Muhammad, to anti-pornography laws, to the litigious sorts of 'brand protection' activities undertaken by The Walt Disney Company or the International Olympic Committee, to name but a few.[15] It is therefore not very difficult to agree that *communication* – whether by words, images or otherwise – is (and probably always has been) both vitally important to human society and liable to restriction by those who oppose the messages being conveyed.

It is perhaps equally easy to agree that, as a general rule, communication is good and censorship is bad. Like most university professors dedicated to supporting the principles of free expression and academic freedom, I myself would tend to hold these views; only in extreme cases would I agree that certain writings or images are so repulsive and potentially harmful (as for example in cases of threatening 'hate speech', libel or misrepresentation) that they should be excised entirely from the public sphere and their authors sanctioned. Even then, I would hope that such communications could be made available under more or less controlled circumstances for the purposes of bona fide critical research (such as research into the propagation of racist ideologies, or deceptive conspiracy theories). But the fact remains that, if pressed for an opinion, I would indeed accept a degree of censorship for some types of communications. I suspect many readers of this book, no matter how libertarian their views, would similarly concede that society is probably better off if certain works are banned altogether, with others subjected to at least some sort of limit on their circulation. Even if a written or artistic work is permitted to exist, that doesn't mean that everyone should *have* to be exposed to it. Whether offensive, uninteresting or objectionable for other reasons, some communications may well be voluntarily shunned by any number of potential audiences, without the need for imposition of any censorship at all.

Not all communications are of equal value. Again, as a university professor, I have read more than my share of badly written essays (by both students *and* by fellow academics, including myself) that should probably never have seen the light of day – or, at the very least, which do not deserve broad publication. The same could be said of bad conference presentations, along with the multitude of bad literature, bad art, bad theatre and bad music that we all tend to come across in the course of our lives. Sometimes it is more than a question of poor taste, as in cases where actual falsification or misinterpretation of evidence can have serious repercussions. Current debates over the safety of vaccines, the social impacts of immigration or the reality of human-induced climate change are just a few examples of hot-button issues in which the dissemination of erroneous findings can have life-and-death consequences. Surely, then, a certain degree of oversight and discrimination can be justified to ensure that in some cases audiences are at least advised of whether or not a publication enjoys the approval of respected experts. This is the function of peer review, of accreditation panels and of award-granting committees: to discern the worthy from the unworthy, the legitimate from the deceptive, the useful from the counter-productive.[16]

Such discernment is all the more important if a communication is liable to be reproduced and stored for future generations by means of writing, drawing, painting, sculpting or scoring – and above all by means of the mechanical mass-reproduction technologies of print, engraving, audiovisual recording or digitalization. Ephemeral comments and embarrassing performances can fade into memory and so disappear over time, but as every user of the Internet knows (or should know), *recorded* words and images can have an unfortunate tendency to come back and haunt us through reproduction.

⸻✢⸻

EXPERT DISCERNMENT is one thing; coercive censorship, though potentially related, is quite another. In the former case, judgements are made and communications *about* a production are offered to a potential audience. Whether or not audiences choose to accept those judgements depends upon the perceived authority and reliability of the judges in question. But if there is no coercion involved, then presumably the production remains available and audience members may choose to accept, reject or ignore whatever they have been told about it. They may also choose to take the experts' opinions 'under advisement', while still going on to judge matters for themselves. In such situations, critical discussion results in more communication, not less. Nothing has been banned, even if some things end up being discouraged – perhaps even quite strongly.

Power makes all the difference. In situations where access to special resources is necessary to produce a communication – to publish a printed book, for example, to carve an expensive stone monument, to stage an opera or film a movie – then the negative judgements of wealthy patrons or granting agencies may indeed result in a certain degree of silencing. Similarly, blacklisting and boycotts can have a censorious impact on the success of an attempted communication. But things really ramp up when powerful forces align to ensure the actual *eradication* of certain communications, through the imposition of more thoroughgoing forms of censorship. These can still vary: from the utter destruction of all written works by means of violent state book burnings as depicted in Ray Bradbury's *Fahrenheit 451* (1953) to Orwell's imagined state in which masses of low-quality and bowdlerized 'prolefeed' books, pamphlets and electronic media are actually churned out by a so-called Ministry of Truth (along with the violent suppression of unauthorized productions, and their consignment to a fiery 'memory hole'). Generalized destruction, or excessive diffusion with the intent of drowning out all contrary voices: both are potential forms of totalitarian censorship, when carried out by powerful enforcement agents.

Yet, as noted above, not all censorship is totalitarian. Even relatively open and liberal societies may decide to impose limited forms of censorship on certain types of writing, performance and art that they deem unacceptable (as sometimes occurs nowadays both in so-called 'cancel culture', and in widespread efforts to 'reform' school curricula). Nor is all censorship consistent. As we will see throughout this book, censorship is frequently episodic, sometimes incoherent and at times contradictory. It is also generally political. Above all, it varies over time and from place to place depending on context. Understanding this sort of variation is, of course, the essence of history. By studying those variations, those specificities of how censorship actually manifested across changes in time and space, we can learn a great deal about not only the history of censorship but the history of communication itself: the history of how, and why, certain words and images became so imbued with significance that they attracted the attention, and sometimes the persecutory interventions, of powerful forces in a given society.

Censorship and Persecution

'Persecution' lies at the heart of the most troubling forms of censorship, so it is also important to be clear about just what this term actually signifies. In its vaguest sense, persecution can mean any set of actions taken by one group (or individual) to negatively impact another.

More specifically, it refers to the *unfair* or *unjustified* singling out of a target for some sort of harmful treatment over a sustained period. It can thus be separated from the notion of legitimate 'prosecution', which is (at least in theory) a fair and justifiable response – including censorship in some cases – to some sort of criminalized transgression. It is also to be distinguished from occasional minor outbursts of conflict, as well as from instances of economic competition or warfare (at least when these latter are conducted according to established rules and involve combatants who are more or less equal in power). True persecution is thus an inherently objectionable activity, a wicked practice that deserves to be better understood in order to seek ways of diminishing or preventing it.

But the concept of persecution is also inherently relative and contestable. Persecutors rarely see themselves as such, for they find ways to justify their actions as either fair or necessary, or both. Frequently, their justification takes the form of understanding *themselves* to be the true victims of persecution (whether actual or potential) in any given situation, while painting their targeted enemies as genuine threats to be defended against. In so doing, attacks and restrictions imposed against others can be redefined as perfectly legitimate gestures in the service of a greater good. Roman pagans who had Christians thrown to the lions presumably thought they were helping to preserve the integrity of their Empire from a morally dubious and politically threatening new sect; centuries later, descendants of those early Christian martyrs put unorthodox Christians, Jews, Muslims and pagan Indigenous peoples to equally gruesome deaths for having somehow 'persecuted' the Church with their insubordination or infidelity. Even the latest crop of fascistic White Supremacists claim that they are right to hate and violently attack racialized minorities because these represent some sort of ill-defined and imaginary demographic threat to an equally nebulous fantasy of 'European Civilization'. So too, the Catholic theologians with whom we are most centrally concerned in this book saw themselves as doing God's work by censoring the damnable works of heretics and liars – in order to save true believers from falling into the diabolical Enemy's carefully laid traps, and joining the rest of those wicked 'persecutors' of Christian Truth in the eternal persecution of Hellfire.

Persecution, then, is a rhetorically charged form of selective aggression that systematically and unfairly targets specific victims for severe ill-treatment. Hypocritical and delusional usage aside, it has traditionally been associated primarily with deliberate and organized attacks by an objectively more powerful group against other groups that are defined by their racialized, ethno-linguistic, gendered, sexual or other form of bodily difference, as well as against those whose defining category of 'difference' is rather religious, political or otherwise ideological. Often these categories overlap, as with the phenomenon of modern-day European Islamophobes who 'fear' (or rather hate) and therefore seek to persecute not only actual Muslims of all sorts, but veiled women, turbaned men, foreigners, those who speak with a certain accent and dark-skinned peoples in general – whether these happen to be Muslim believers or not – without ever fully understanding who or what these categories really encompass. At its root persecution is all about drawing lines (however shaky) between an 'us' and a 'them' . . . and then finding ways to make 'them' suffer. Depending on its virulence, that suffering can extend anywhere from simple humiliation or economic exploitation, to political disempowerment, to full-blown murderous genocide.

Persecutory censorship thus derives from a desire to harm and potentially eliminate an identifiable enemy. It may lie closer to the 'disempowerment' side of the persecutory spectrum in some cases, but its consequences can also be downright bloody if authors or readers are subjected to corporal penalties – as did happen, sometimes horrifically, in the period covered by this book. Censorship can also have secondary persecutory consequences, as when a group's literature or other forms of cultural expression are banned as part of a larger campaign of forced assimilation, ethnic cleansing or genocidal eradication. We will see examples of this as well in the chapters that follow.

Such targeted persecutions may be distinguished from more legitimately 'prosecutory' approaches to the suppression of objectionable words and images. In the latter cases, communications are judged according to pre-established and more or less universally applied codes of propriety; they are also dealt with by means of more or less impartial rules of procedure. For example, a book or painting might be evaluated and condemned because of its genuinely misleading or offensive contents, rather than simply as a means of harming the work's creators on account of their membership in a despised group. Ideally, such determinations would only be made by qualified and fair-minded judges, following accepted jurisprudential norms and using objective measures that are generally reflective of current professional or social values. This was certainly how most medieval, early modern and even modern inquisitorial censors would have seen their own efforts.

The problem remains, however, that any distinctions between unjustifiable censorship stemming from *persecution*, and justifiable instances of censorship that result from legitimate *prosecution*, are always subjective. One believer's orthodoxy is another's heresy; one reader's masterpiece is another's travesty; one viewer's pornography is another's celebration of the human body. We tend to approve acts of censorship against communications that we don't like, while deriding censorship of those we accept. In earlier times it was no different: Protestants attacked the Catholic Church for its vicious censorship of what they took to be 'Christian truth', even as those same Protestants destroyed the works of Catholics, non-Christians and rival Protestants. Regimes of all sorts have sought to erase, re-write or condemn the political writings of their opponents. And creative works judged offensive by one generation have frequently been celebrated by the next (and vice versa). In all these cases, different groups of contemporaries found the censorship of their own era, and their own like-minded community, to be more or less justified. It is a complicated and often troubling history, but one well worth investigating beyond the level of simple assumptions, generalizations and stereotypes.

⸻ ✠ ⸻

WE WILL APPROACH this history from a number of angles. In Chapter One, a whirlwind summary of ancient and medieval censorship provides a background against which later events will take place, culminating with the composition of what was arguably the first ever (manuscript) list of banned books to be widely distributed among inquisitors. This is followed in Chapter Two by an account of how Church officials by the mid-sixteenth century gradually came to craft the first real Index(es) of Prohibited Books. This innovation was triggered by three interrelated developments: the invention of print, the advent of a Protestant Reformation and the institution of new types of inquisitorial tribunals above all in Spain, Portugal and Italy. In Chapter Three, the story continues as early prototypical forms of the Index give way to later (often much bigger, and more complex) publications from the late sixteenth to the eighteenth centuries. This succession of Index editions, each with their own style and organizing devices as well as ever-shifting contents, itself provides a fascinating angle from which to examine the histories of early modern book production, in addition to shedding important light on such matters as the evolution of attitudes towards heresy and censorship – and the sometimes bitter internal conflicts that made each new version of the Index into a test of the Church's own levels of doctrinal cohesion.

Chapter Four marks something of a transition from more or less chronological to thematic analysis. Here we pause to consider some of the processes by which books were normally banned and placed on the Indexes of the early modern Catholic world. Case studies of how two particular works by the medieval author Ramon Llull were later treated (in two very different contexts) will demonstrate some of the circuitous routes by which individual books and their authors could in fact come to be banned – or not. These processes were complicated in their own right, as rules and expectations continued to evolve from one iteration of the Index to the next, but they could also be further complicated by jurisdictional struggles between different censorial bodies such as the Spanish, Portuguese, Roman and other Italian Inquisitions, as well as the separate Congregation of the Index after its foundation in 1571.

Chapters Five through to Seven focus on specific types of censored books. The first examines how censors dealt with books that clearly had spiritual value for their intended audiences, but might also harbour hidden dangers if their contents were not scrupulously combed for potentially misleading turns of phrase. This category would include many editions and translations of the Bible itself, from late medieval to early modern times. Even when written or printed by pious Christian authors with all the best intentions, the very centrality of such works to Christian spiritual life made their careful vetting all the more 'necessary' in the eyes of Church officials. Non-Christian religious works of potential spiritual interest to Christians, such as the Jewish Talmud and Kabbalistic texts, or the Muslim Qur'an, were also subjected to rigorous scrutiny by Catholic censors, lest they accidentally seduce good Christians into deviating from the true path.

In Chapter Six, we turn to what can loosely be called 'scientific' books. Though not strictly an initial focus of the Index, censors were increasingly pressured to react against both the 'ancient' arts of magic, astrology and demon-summoning, and the sometimes still more challenging assertions of 'modern' scientific research – above all when these threatened to undermine traditional teachings of the established Church. The trials of Giordano Bruno and Galileo Galilei are only two of the more notorious instances of 'scientific' persecution to have taken place in the age of the Index, and it is worth noting that Catholic censors continually went to great lengths to suppress what they considered to be bad, or at least dangerous, scientific research (which were sometimes, but not always, the same thing) throughout the Enlightenment and right into modern times.

Chapter Seven looks more closely at how inquisitors and Index compilers dealt with the equally complicated subjects of objectionable (often sexual, but also religious and political) content in literature and the visual or performing arts. Though again not really a matter of serious concern to early inquisitors, changes in social mores and the evolution of new readership interests led Catholic authorities to be increasingly prudish about depictions of human sexuality from the later Renaissance to the modern period. Artistic productions were also targeted in some instances for the threats they were deemed to pose to other aspects of Christian spiritual life, such as reverence for the divine or proper veneration of the saints. The age of political absolutism also naturally lent itself to increasingly close scrutiny of anything from social critique and satire to outright calls for reform, revolution and tyrannicide. This led to problematic censorship of some Greek and Roman classic literature, as well as more modern compositions of all sorts.

Finally, Chapter Eight provides an opportunity to bring our story up to the modern day. Upheavals of the late eighteenth and early nineteenth centuries led to dissolution of the Spanish and Portuguese Inquisitions, and significantly weakened the Church's ability to enforce its decisions throughout much of the world. Nevertheless, papal oversight of censorship continued to engage with those modern phenomena it took to be most threatening to Catholic values; indeed in many ways censorship reached new peaks in this period as conservative 'ultramontane' forces within the Church successfully advocated for the doctrine of papal infallibility. Targets included Freemasonry, materialism, atheism and anticlericalism as well as certain types of socialism, fascism and feminism.

At the same time, Church censorship became increasingly susceptible to mockery and charges of irrelevance, even as it was eclipsed by modern state, corporate and academic forms of censorship. By 1917 the Congregation of the Index was folded into the Holy Office of the Roman Inquisition, and in 1966 the Index of Prohibited Books was formally terminated. Nevertheless, through the ongoing vigilance of the Holy Office (now known as the Congregation for the Doctrine of the Faith), papal bureaucracy continues to impose its decisions on spiritually acceptable and unacceptable forms of expression right up to the present day.

⸺✞⸺

THROUGHOUT, THIS is a tale of tragedy when we consider just how much harm was in fact caused to those whose writings and other creative productions were prohibited, or may never have been undertaken in the first place out of fear of persecution. The loss caused by inquisitorial and other forms of censorship to human thought and artistic expression over the centuries is truly incalculable. There are also moments when the story turns to comedy, however, as the misguided, contradictory and at times downright silly efforts of Index compilers are brought to light. But there is still another important dimension to the story. The perhaps uncomfortable fact remains that many of the Church's highly trained theologians, lawyers, inquisitors and expert consultants – who contributed tens of thousands of hours of their time to evaluating and then either endorsing, suppressing or 'improving' suspect works – were in fact among the greatest minds of their age (and some were also later declared saints). When they approached their tasks with seriousness of purpose, and a clear determination to weed out only those compositions that actually posed real offences to the deity, or threats to human salvation as they understood it, they were also performing creative work – and they were acting for what they quite literally took to be the Greater Glory of God. They may have significantly limited the spiritual, intellectual and cultural legacies of the modern age, but they also shaped and in some ways positively contributed to making that age into what it eventually became. We can certainly lament these facts, but fact they remain nonetheless – and understanding just how, and why, such human efforts ended up taking the forms that they did is the true work of historical study.

Looking back over the centuries, it is indeed tempting to lament (and at times to poke fun at) past instances of censorship that now strike us as wholly unfair and unjustified. I myself fully intend to do so from time to time in this book. However, condemnations and dismissals of historical 'errors' should never prevent us from also taking serious stock of precisely what actually happened in the past, how it happened and why. That is the function of history: to examine and learn from past experiences. And that is why I now invite you to delve into the fascinating history of the Catholic Church's most important, and centuries-long, series of censorial experiments. It is a history full of complexity and insights into the religious, intellectual and artistic past, at times on a global scale. It is a history that is at times shocking; at times tragic; and not infrequently amusing as well. I hope you will both enjoy and learn from it.

PART I

1 CENSORSHIP BEFORE THE INDEX

Gazing down from the walls of his palace at Tell el-Amarna, the great pharaoh Akhenaten may well have smiled as gangs of workers set about ripping the names and images of Egypt's traditional deities from their temples and stelae. Within a matter of weeks he had managed to eradicate most traces of all gods but one: his own patron, the sun-disc Aten. This first recorded act of wholesale censorship has been traced to the origins of monotheism itself, with the suggestion that exclusivist religions such as Judaism, and later Christianity and Islam, may actually have inherited something of their intolerance for the worship of other gods from Akhenaten's great act of suppression. Moses and his followers certainly do seem to have come from an Egyptian context and brought notions of zealous monotheism with them to the new Holy Land of Canaan shortly after Akhenaten's fall. The connections that can be drawn between strictly monotheistic religion and exclusionary censorship are intriguing, but should not be exaggerated. Any powerful regime or organization can choose to silence its opposing voices, no matter how many gods, goddesses or guiding principles they may invoke in the process.

Akhenaten's suppression of the cults of Amon-Ra and the rest was in fact short-lived, and memories of his regime were soon wiped clean in their turn by rival polytheistic forces. This later work of erasure was so effective that the true nature and extent of the Aten experiment remain unclear today, while Akhenaten himself was only restored to the king-lists 3,000 years after his passing. Such is the power of censorship when applied with determination by a dominant group; and above all when there is little potential for the proscribed names, images and ideas to be spread by alternative means of communication. In ancient Egypt, only priests and pharaohs had access to the resources necessary for fixing such communications in lasting form, whether on papyrus scrolls or on monumental stone walls. Peasants undoubtedly muttered among themselves whatever they liked about Aten and his partisans, whether positive or negative. But peasants' words are rarely if ever recorded, and such ephemeral 'vibrations in the air', passed down from mouth to ear, were eventually lost to the shifting sands and floods of the Nile valley.

State and religious rulers' concern with censorship of undesirable messaging, whether by applying revisions to official king-lists (as regularly practised in ancient Egypt, as well as neighbouring Assyria) or by putting whole generations of suspect intellectuals to a swift and often gruesome death (as was notoriously said to have been done in Qin China to over four hundred Confucian scholars), seems to have existed for as long as have the very records those rulers sought to control. Yet the ubiquity of pre-modern censorship should also not be exaggerated. Where literary and artistic production was rare, and literacy (or exposure to wrought images) even more so, the stakes of censorship were relatively low. Thus Egyptian, Assyrian and Chinese officials may have ensured that official records were cleansed of objectionable dynastic claims or philosophical concepts from time to time, to guarantee a minimum of resistance in court circles; but they would generally not have thought it necessary to wander about the countryside checking on the thoughts or graffiti scrawls of common herdsmen, farmers and villagers. The idea of maintaining lists of banned writings would have been even more absurd: in a context where written works generally existed in single copies, rarely had titles and were seldom passed down for more than one generation, such an endeavour would have been impossible as well as a thorough waste of time.

In ancient Greece, we see some signs of a broadening intellectual culture that might eventually make words – especially in their written form – more dangerous and therefore liable to suppression. The execution of Socrates (*c.* 399 BCE) is perhaps the best known early instance of an intellectual being put to death for his teachings, though if the influential later distribution of Socratic ideas by his student Plato is anything to go by then it would seem that the Athenians were not overly concerned about effectively censoring his words per se. Indeed, within a generation of Socrates' death, his dialogues could be found on shelves of the newly established Library of Alexandria, one of the best-known (though not the first) research libraries to have been established with public funds. The ultimate fate of the Alexandrian library, and many lesser institutions once scattered across the Greek world, remains controversial. It seems to have been subjected to a purge under Ptolemy VIII Physcon around

145 BCE, resulting in the exile and perhaps death of its chief librarian Aristarchus of Samothrace, but the institution itself remained an active part of the larger *Museion* complex until at least the third century CE. It certainly lost books due to wars, accidental fires and other mishaps from time to time, but in the end it seems to have died from bureaucratic neglect rather than by censorial decree.

Greek rulers were eager to destroy books they saw as subversive in other contexts, however, even while permitting them to exist within the confines of scholarly libraries. Thus we learn from the biblical story of Maccabees that the Seleucid rulers of Judea (who boasted at least one richly stocked library in Antioch) sought to destroy all copies of religious texts that could be found among their subject Jewish populations: 'The books of the law that they found they tore to pieces and burned with fire. Anyone found possessing the book of the covenant, or anyone who adhered to the law, was condemned to death by decree of the king' (1 Maccabees 1:56–7). This draconian measure was cut short by the Jewish revolt of the Hasmonean Maccabees, who ousted the Seleucid Greeks in 167 BCE and destroyed numerous Greek altars (no doubt along with some Greek writings and images) in the process.

Censorship was in all these cases episodic, unsystematic and inspired by a desire to persecute religio-political enemies in the context of a war or civil crisis. It was carried out by brutal yet simple means: by expelling or killing intellectual authors, or by ripping, burning and otherwise destroying texts seized from a targeted building or population. No permanent institution was created to surveil or suppress the production and dissemination of words (though presumably librarians such as Aristarchus had the power to choose which books would enter or be culled from their collections, just as intellectuals including Socrates, and later Plato and his student Aristotle, could pick and choose which contemporaries were worthy of engagement in philosophical debate). Books, or rather papyrus scrolls and other written media, were still rare and valuable. The challenge was more to generate lists of what actually survived, rather than lists of what should be censored or destroyed.

Ancient Romans, for their part, did have an office of 'censor', but it was not primarily concerned with suppression of words or images. Instead, Roman censors acted as overseers of the census. They also had the power of *regimen morum*, by which they were empowered to pass judgement on the morality of individual citizens in certain cases, but there is no evidence to suggest that they were particularly upset by scandalous writings or drawings (such as the many instances of quite graphic sexual imagery discovered at archeological sites like Pompeii). Indeed, the most notorious case of Roman literary censorship is intriguing more for its apparent limits than for its severity. In 8 CE Augustus Caesar famously exiled the poet Ovid, and it seems that access to the latter's *Ars amatoria* (Art of Love) may have subsequently been limited in some public libraries. It remains unlikely, however, that either action was in fact taken because the emperor was offended by the sexually 'immoral' elements of the book; political fallout from some now-obscure court intrigue seems a more convincing explanation. Either way, Ovid's other works continued to circulate, and the *Ars amatoria* too remained available to interested readers from its initial composition right up to the present day. Indeed, it is interesting to note that the first clear suggestion that Ovid's *Ars* actually fell victim to Augustan censorship comes not from a contemporary Roman source but from a medieval copyist, writing in an age when book censorship was finally becoming a much more normative (if still episodic) fact of life than it had ever been in ancient times.[1]

Censorship in the Early Church

It was the Roman Empire's conversion to Christianity which seems to have begun a slow shift from entirely sporadic episodes of censorship to more generalized concerns about the dangers of objectionable writing. Already in the times of the apostles, as depicted in the biblical book of Acts, converts to Christianity seem to have felt that burning books associated with their former beliefs was a praiseworthy expression of religious zeal: 'And many of them who had followed curious arts [*eis qui fuerant curiosa sectati*], brought together their books, and burnt them before all; and counting the price of them, they found the money to be fifty thousand pieces of silver [*pecuniam denariorum*]' (Acts 19:19).[2] Similar attitudes likely explain some of the disturbances in which Christians attacked Alexandrian pagan intellectuals such as the philosopher Hypatia (d. 415 CE), while others participated in the mass-destruction of pagan books at the royal library of Antioch (363 CE).

Such destructive events could still be chalked up to isolated incidents of mob violence or political reaction, triggered by now-forgotten local pressures and leaving little more than traces of memory behind them. Nor is it clear whether books themselves, or writings of any kind, were at the heart of these conflicts; rather they tended to suffer collateral damage. But Christianity is an inherently logocentric religion, as previously discussed, and words clearly mattered more to early Christians than they had to their pagan ancestors. Particularly when written down as texts dealing with spiritual matters, words could be very powerful means of communicating new ideas about God, His expectations of humankind and our prospects for salvation. It was therefore vital to many believers that 'true' religious writings be carefully set down and studied by those qualified to do so, while 'false' writings should be consigned to oblivion. And as the Church began to take on the form of a more permanent institutional structure after the fourth century, its power to ensure that this was in fact done began to grow dramatically.

A first concern was thus to establish the canonical texts of Christianity itself. Christians had of course inherited the Hebrew Bible of Judaism, but to this 'Old' Testament they soon added new writings that gradually took on the character of an entirely 'New' Testament. This was, however, far from being a simple or uncontroversial process. As early as 150 CE, as Christians increasingly began to circulate texts of the Gospels, Acts and Letters of the Apostles, disputes began to arise about which of these should be considered authoritative, which innocuous but not particularly holy and which spurious – if not altogether dangerous. The latter categories, some later known as either *apocrypha* (literally, 'hidden') or *pseudepigrapha* (false writings), were subjected to different treatments over time. The Acts of Paul, for example, were denounced by Tertullian for their apparent advocacy of female preaching and ministry; they eventually ceased to be copied, although fragments on the martyrdom of Paul may have been incorporated into the final text of the canonical book of Acts.[3] Other texts such as the Gospels of Thomas, Judas and Mary Magdalene were quickly abandoned by most Christians and relegated to small communities of so-called Gnostics, whose traces have only recently been unearthed in desert regions of Egypt, Palestine and Syria. Still, it was not until the conversion of Roman Emperor Constantine, and his consequent legalization of Christianity in the fourth century, that concerted efforts could begin to establish an authoritative and widely agreed-upon set of books to be included in the Church's 'official' Bible.

Debates over which books to include, and which to exclude, from a scriptural canon provide fascinating glimpses into the evolution of any religion. In the Christian case, such debates would be revived over a thousand years later during the Reformation, when Protestants and other critics began to challenge and alter that canon once more. But even in the earliest phases of Roman Church history, disputes over the canon also left a written legacy that would later set important precedents for Catholic book censorship. Chief among these was the so-called *Decretum Gelasianum*, or Decree of Gelasius. This was a formal position statement attributed to Pope Gelasius I (r. 492–6), in which a number of lists are given. Some of these involve Christological dogmas, while others give details about which books should be considered part of the Old and New Testaments. Yet another list gives qualified opinions about the acceptability of several texts that are *not* to be considered canonical. Some of these are still said to be worthy of close study (including the works of Church Fathers such as Sts Augustine and Jerome), while others are considered 'questionable' (such as a letter of Pope Leo to Flavian, the writings of Origen or 'the laborious work of Iuvencus [which] we nevertheless do not spurn but are amazed by').[4]

Most interesting for our purposes, however, is the final list in this decree, which most likely dates to a time slightly after Gelasius in the mid-sixth century and should therefore be called 'pseudo-Gelasian'. It is a list of more than sixty books and 35 authors 'to be avoided by all Catholics'; it further counsels avoidance of 'all amulets [*pilacteria omnia*] which are compiled not in the name of angels as they pretend, but are written in the names of great demons'. Here we have what could arguably be considered the first official list of banned writings (and amuletic works of art) in the Catholic tradition. It would have a long reach, as will be seen below, above all because of its inclusion in Gratian's *Decretum* and thence in the influential work of the medieval inquisitor Nicholas Eymeric.[5]

Amulet (*pilacterium*) depicting an angel, Byzantine, 6th century CE, bronze.

Censored Knowledge

The pseudo-Gelasian decree listed several authors whose interpretations of Christian doctrine had been found to be heretical – that is, they deviated from the 'orthodox' or 'right-thinking' interpretations of the now-established Roman Church hierarchy. Any texts that fixed such 'heterodox' opinions in writing (and thus threatened to preserve and further disseminate them) were therefore to be avoided. No further mechanisms by which to identify or destroy such writings were mentioned in the decree, however, because they did not exist and were not really needed. Though the writings of heretics such as Valentinus, Arius, Nestorius, Pelagius and others would continue to be copied in minority contexts on the fringes or beyond the borders of the Roman Empire, they did not constitute much of an existential threat to the now-Imperial Church. Once their core arguments had been polemically refuted by Catholic theologians such as Augustine, moreover, they could more or less safely be relegated to the realm of academic curiosity. With no institutional apparatus by which sympathizers could reproduce or teach their writings on a large scale, such heresies all but disappeared from Roman territories by the end of the sixth or seventh centuries at least.[6]

An institutional apparatus for sympathetically reproducing and teaching older *pagan* wisdom did exist in the early centuries of Christian Rome, but it too soon withered and disappeared. As we have already seen, the great libraries of Alexandria, Antioch and other cities were ultimately dissolved due to a fatal combination of hostility and neglect. Long-established academies and schools closed their doors for the same reasons: their classes in Graeco-Roman science and philosophy were no longer favoured by governmental or Church authorities, and elite students increasingly found that better career prospects could be accessed by studying Christian curricula with private tutors, or in schools associated with monasteries or other Church institutions. Justinian's closure of the Athenian Academy in 529 was one of the final nails in the European coffin of Greek philosophical education, though there were others too.[7] Studies of pagan philosophy continued in an attenuated fashion for several more centuries, especially in the urban East of the Empire and then in regions falling under Islamic rule, but those philosophical and scientific texts that remained in circulation in the Latin West were often subject to simplification or abridgement, as performed by Christian scholars such as Boethius (d. 524 CE).

⸻✛⸻

THE STORY OF how Islamic cultures ultimately preserved and re-transmitted ancient Greek knowledge to European Christians has often been told. At first many Christian intellectuals of the so-called 'Renaissance of the Twelfth Century' were excited about the possibility of accessing long-lost original texts by Plato, Aristotle and many others, now brought forth for the first time in centuries, thanks to a wave of translations from Arabic manuscripts. Some of these scholars had purely scientific interests, but others saw the potential for using old Greek (along with newer Arab) logic and insights into the natural world as a means of deepening their comprehension of the most challenging aspects of Christian doctrine. Theologians such as Peter Abelard (d. 1142) were thus among the first to embrace newly translated books from the Islamic world, and they put them to good use in transforming some of the ways that medieval Christian students could be taught about the true meaning of biblical texts.

Abelard's teaching took place for the most part in monastic settings, but he also famously took on private students. Unfortunately his relationship with one of these, the brilliant Heloise, caused Abelard to be castrated by his lover's relatives after she became pregnant. Yet this sexual impropriety was not the cause of Peter Abelard's eventual run-ins with Christian censorship; on the contrary, both Abelard and Heloise were perfectly willing to write at some length about their affair, and manuscripts of their collected correspondence were quite popular in the later Middle Ages.[8] Instead, it was his use of rational argumentation, bolstered by Aristotelian logic, that led to the burning of Abelard's *Theologia summi boni* (Theology of the Greatest Good) by order of the Council of Soissons in 1121.[9] Some years later, he was further subjected to accusations of heresy by Bernard of Clairvaux at the Council of Sens (1141). Not surprisingly, Abelard at one point lamented his treatment and expressed a wish that he could travel to the lands of Islam, where one could study philosophy without facing persecution as a result.[10]

Abelard was far from being the only medieval scholar to see the potential value of Aristotelian and other pagan knowledge as a means of enriching Christian thought. But opponents of this sort of innovation soon came forward to ban inappropriate studies of Aristotle at the University of Paris, and the propriety of such studies for students of the powerful new Dominican and Franciscan Orders was also much discussed. Eventually, intellectual friars such as the Dominicans Albertus Magnus and Thomas Aquinas, as well as Franciscans such as Bonaventure and Duns Scotus, established a place for Aristotelianism in the scholastic curricula of later medieval universities and religious Orders. But it was slow going, and as late as 1277 some 219 philosophical propositions (including several of Aquinas's own teachings) were solemnly condemned and forbidden to students by the bishop of Paris, Stephen Tempier.

Aristotelian texts were not the only ones to cause consternation among conservative Churchmen in the thirteenth century. As medieval universities began to attract more and more students, some of the best of whom were more than eager to delve into all available aspects of learning that might enrich their comprehension of the Bible and its many secrets, warnings began to be heard about the dangers of Jewish books as well. With their traditions of Bible interpretation long pre-dating those of Christianity, and their expertise in Hebrew (the original biblical language), Jewish scholars had already been sought out for consultation by the Victorine canons of Paris and other monastic intellectuals in the twelfth century. Yet in 1233, Dominicans in Montpellier burned the writings of Moses Maimonides, perhaps the greatest Jewish scholar of the age, in response to fears that he had inappropriately mixed Aristotelian knowledge with traditional Jewish learning in his *Guide for the Perplexed*. Then, in 1236, a Franciscan friar (and convert from Judaism) known as Nicholas Donin denounced the Jewish Talmud for its supposed inclusion of anti-Christian blasphemies, 'absurd' tales and alleged distortions of God's teachings to the Jews. After a trial by a panel of Paris theologians (including several university professors, as well as representatives from local bishops and the Dominican and Franciscan Orders), the Talmud was also condemned and burned in 1242. In the years that followed, many more manuscript copies of both the Talmud and Maimonides's writings would be seized and subjected to strict censorship, if not complete destruction, by Christian authorities.

Muslim religious books, for their part, were less frequently subjected to Church censorship at first (likely because they posed less of a challenge for Christian biblical studies). They also generated less interest among Christian readers, and translations of the Qur'an, for example, were extremely rare. Nevertheless, like the Talmud and other Jewish books, a wide variety of writings in Arabic would eventually find their way onto the Index of Prohibited Books – as will be further discussed in Chapters Two and Five.

Censored Heresies

The Church's concerns about impacts of ancient Greek scientific knowledge on orthodox understandings of Christian dogma, as well as the possibility of Jewish (or other non-Christian) knowledge similarly offending or misleading Christian souls, were not resolved in the Middle Ages. Attitudes varied widely among leading Churchmen about the best ways to deal with books containing such knowledge, and positions were reversed or refined many times. Despite occasional book burnings, the Talmud and works of scholars like Abelard and Maimonides continued to be read; even the bans of 1277 had limited long-term effects on teaching in the universities. These episodes would, however, leave an important legacy of documentation and precedents that would eventually impact future censorship campaigns.

Pedro Berruguete, *Saint Dominic and the Albigenses* (depiction of Cathar books being tried by fire *c.* 1203), late 15th century, oil on panel.

More strenuous (and in many ways successful) efforts were deployed to combat what was widely seen as a much more direct and serious threat to the unity of the Catholic Church than any proliferation of non-Christian books: the rise of Christian theological heresies, above all from the twelfth century on. Much remains unclear about exactly how and why these heresies emerged, or how organized they really were. But what is certain is that many Christians of the high and later Middle Ages were increasingly concerned with spiritual issues, and increasingly critical of some of the ways in which the traditional Church handled them. Critiques of excessive Church wealth and materialism, in particular, became a common focal point, and a number of different writers and movements soon began to voice calls for spiritual reform – or even revolution.

Perhaps the best-known and longest-lived of these movements was that of Peter Waldo (d. 1205), a Lyonnais merchant who gave up his rich lifestyle and began a campaign of preaching the Gospel to communities that had previously been under-served by the existing pastoral system. This usurpation of traditional priestly functions, by a layman who lacked specialized training, was naturally ill-received by many local clergymen; however papal officers were willing to grant Waldo limited authority to preach so long as he was entirely submissive to the dictates of Church hierarchs. After a while, the compromise broke down and rebellious 'Waldensians' began to spread to numerous parts of Christendom, without authorization, from the twelfth to the sixteenth centuries and beyond. Their disobedience clearly marked them as heretics in the eyes of many; but of course these 'Poor Men of Lyons' saw themselves as sincere Christian believers who were simply trying to follow the directions they read in the Gospel itself. Their earnest, spiritual and avowedly 'apostolic' way of life threatened to put the mainstream Church to shame.

Around the same time, another more extreme heresy was alleged to have arisen in southern France. 'Catharism' (also known as Albigensianism, from its base in the town of Albi) is said by some to have been a revival of ancient Manichean dualism, organized into a hierarchical counter-Church; others argue that it was likely never more than a loose set of unorthodox beliefs, grounded in spiritual readings of the Bible but never constituting much of an actual movement. Either way, it was perceived by contemporary Churchmen as a dire threat to orthodox Catholicism, and severely persecuted as a consequence. By the 1230s papal inquisitors had been deputed to interrogate and punish suspected Cathars as well as Waldensians; a crusade of French troops was also sent to put down local resistance in the region of Languedoc. Isolated pockets of Catharism still apparently existed in the early decades of the fourteenth century, but the heretics themselves left few written records and their religious teachings were scarcely more than a memory by the end of the Middle Ages.

Overlapping with the Waldensian and Cathar heresies were other forms of spiritual opposition to the established Church. Building upon the prophecies of a Cistercian abbot named Joachim of Fiore (d. 1202), some members of the Franciscan Order believed in the coming of a new age in which true Spiritual Christians would take over from a corrupted papacy; the influential writings of later Franciscan scholars such as Peter John Olivi (d. 1298) and Angelo of Clareno (d. 1337) confirmed and reinforced such apocalypticism. Their example spread among the laity, including the numerous spiritual Christians known as Beguins or Beghards, some of whom authored treatises explaining their beliefs. The intellectual Catalan lay author Arnold of Villanova (d. 1311) was similarly impressed with the radical Franciscans' critique of traditional Catholicism, and contemporary mystics such as Marguerite Porete (d. 1310) and Ramon Llull (d. 1316) brought forth both oral and written claims of direct divine inspiration for troubled times. Some of these reforming or prophetic figures managed to obtain official Church recognition and approval for their preaching and writing, as did the Dominican future saints Catherine of Siena (d. 1380) and Vincent Ferrer (d. 1419). But others were condemned as heretics in no uncertain terms. Their books could be seized and burned, and they personally ran the risk of torture and death if caught.

⹂✠⹃

MEANWHILE, other Christians continued to turn to alternative sources of support. As will be further examined in Chapter Six, practices that we might now see as 'magic' were not necessarily frowned upon in medieval times; some (such as the medicinal use of special herbs and stones) were considered to have scientific merits. Astrology, too, if properly practised, was widely considered to be a legitimate field of study. Those who understood how to effectively use magical words and charms for good purposes (a continuation of the amuletic tradition mentioned in the pseudo-Gelasian *Decretum*) might be valued members of mainstream society, and many were themselves members of the clergy. Harmful magic, on the other hand – using poisons or curses to negatively impact others – was strictly forbidden and punishable by death. And by the turn of the fourteenth century, attitudes towards the use of all forms of 'magic' had begun to harden in some circles. Pope John XXII asserted that many magical practitioners necessarily relied upon the assistance of demons to achieve supernatural results, whether for good or evil, and that such reliance constituted de facto betrayal or even renunciation of Christ. Sorcerors of this type were therefore guilty of an act of apostasy, which was itself a form of heresy, and so subject to inquisitorial investigation and punishment. Texts dealing with magic and demon-summoning therefore became increasingly important targets in the struggle to censor harmful writings, and by 1290 Church officials had formally agreed that books on demonic magic posed a major threat to Christian society.[11]

Technologies of Medieval Censorship: The Inquisition

Gazing out from the doorway of St Stephen's cathedral in the southern French city of Toulouse, the Dominican inquisitor Bernard Gui may well have smiled as royal officials set about preparing bonfires to burn yet another cartload of Jewish and heretical books in the summer of 1321. Or he may have wept; we really don't know his mood, though some of his writings on the subject do indicate that he took pains to at least appear sympathetic to his victims.[12] Either way, Gui was engaged in what he took to be important work: the protection of Christian society from dangerous words and the ideas they expressed – words and ideas that were sometimes bound up within books, which might seduce innocent readers with their promises of hidden wisdom.

Gui was part of what had by 1321 become something of an institution in the Catholic Church, though it was still far less organized or stable than it would be two centuries later: the *inquisitio haereticae pravitatis* (inquisition against heretical depravity).[13] *Inquisitio* was simply a form of investigative procedure in pre-Christian Roman law; it had been adopted for various uses by an increasingly legalistic Church hierarchy by the eighth or ninth century at least, but came to be applied above all in certain cases of suspected heresy by the end of the twelfth.[14] With constantly evolving rules and practices, inquisitions against heretics were generally conducted on an ad hoc basis by bishops and their theological advisors. Then, in 1233, Pope Gregory IX took a further step by deputing members of the Dominican and Franciscan Orders to conduct more or less permanent heresy inquisitions in especially volatile regions of southern France, northern Italy and parts of Germany. Henceforth the 'inquisition' can be said to have existed as an established, if not yet particularly regularized, institutional force.

With assistance from royal or other secular men-at-arms, and local offices staffed by scribes and notaries, friar-inquisitors began

Manuscript illumination of Ramon Llull in the *Breviculum* of Thomas le Myesier, 14th century.

to conduct trials, impose sentences and keep records of their proceedings from the thirteenth century on. In some cases, including that of Bernard Gui in Toulouse, their records have at least partially survived. They show an increasingly efficient and powerful bureaucracy at work – though generally not yet one that was focused on book censorship. Bernard Gui himself did supervise burnings of the Talmud, and made note of several heretical books in his inquisitor's manual (the *Practica inquisitionis*); these included the Beguins' carefully guarded short treatise on the memory of Peter John Olivi, entitled *Transitus sancti Patris*.[15] But Gui compiled no actual list of such books, and his mentions of them in the *Practica* are always incidental. At the time of his writing it seems that inquisitors saw heretical books merely as clues indicating the possibility of their owners' heretical beliefs. Books were to be destroyed after a trial, perhaps, but not necessarily pursued as targets of inquisition in their own right. Thus when Pope Urban v first issued the influential disciplinary bull *Coena domini* in 1363, it focused primarily on excommunicating and anathematizing a list of heresies; it would be more than two hundred years before a subsequent pope would revise its text by adding the key censorial phrase: 'and their books'.[16]

Nevertheless, the creation of medieval heresy inquisitions did establish precedents that would have important consequences for the later history of the Index of Prohibited Books. In particular, it is worth noting that the Catalan inquisitor Nicholas Eymeric's *Directorium inquisitorum* – a manual written in 1376, some fifty years after Bernard Gui's – includes an entire section in its second part, eight short chapters in all, devoted to listing heretical books that should be prohibited to the faithful and destroyed wherever possible. These eight *quaestiones* arguably constitute the first known formal list of banned books to be assembled by a member of the clergy since the days of pseudo-Gelasius. And as we will see, the reprinting of Eymeric's treatise after 1578 (with extensive glosses) would make it one of the most influential medieval sources to impact the conduct of inquisitorial book censorship in the early modern period.

It is therefore worth quickly summarizing the contents of Eymeric's list: in *quaestio* 23 he reproduces pseudo-Gelasius' entire list of ancient heretical books and authors. In *quaestio* 24 he skips nearly six centuries, to Pope Innocent III's 1215 ban on a single book by Joachim of Fiore. Next comes an extended discussion of allegedly heretical writings by Franciscan and related 'Spiritual' authors such as Michael of Cesena, Peter John Olivi and Dolcino of Novara in *quaestiones* 25, 26 and 29 respectively. *Quaestio* 26 also contains what was for Eymeric perhaps the most important condemnation of all (in a case that we will revisit repeatedly over the course of this book): his personal condemnation of writings by the Catalan mystic Ramon Llull. In *quaestio* 28 Eymeric turns his attention to several other lay authors, including the celebrated Arnold of Villanova as well as the more obscure Bartholomew of Genoa, Nicholas of Calabria and a pseudo-prophet named Gundisalvus (Gonsalvo). Finally, scattered throughout *quaestiones* 27–9, he lists several books allegedly connected to the invocation of demons – as well as writings by one Dominican author, a mysterious 'Raymundus Neophytus', who seems to have dabbled in demon-summoning.[17]

This list, though extensive, is obviously far from exhaustive. There is no mention, for example, of the previous burnings of Peter Abelard's works at the Councils of Sens or Soissons, or of authors who were actually executed for the content of their writings, such as Marguerite Porete.[18] Nor does Eymeric bother to forbid any Aristotelian texts, despite having previously identified dozens of 'errors' contained in the writings of Aristotle and of Muslim and Jewish philosophers such as al-Ghazālī, Averroes and Maimonides.[19] He was surely aware of the 1277 Paris condemnations, and subsequent controversies around similar 'errors' that continued to appear in the writings of Christian philosophers, yet there is no mention of these either. The Talmud is nowhere discussed at all in the *Directorium*, nor is the Qur'an, though Eymeric was certainly quite concerned about what he took to be Jewish and Islamic threats to Christian orthodoxy in other contexts.[20] He was also surprisingly silent about some of the most recent controversial writings to have been condemned by popes, bishops and councils during the course of his own lifetime: those of John of Jandun (d. 1328), Master Eckhart (d. 1328) or Nicholas of Autrecourt (d. 1369), for example, or of anti-papal partisans such as Dante (d. 1321), Marsilius of Padua (d. 1342), William of Ockham (d. 1347) and John Wyclif (d. 1384).[21]

Significant though it may have been at the time of its writing, and influential as it would later become in expanded print formats during the Reformation era, the *Directorium inquisitorum* actually faded into relative obscurity for nearly two centuries after its initial composition at the papal court in Avignon. And for the rest of the Middle Ages, even with the continued proliferation of Wycliffite and then Hussite writings after their definitive condemnation at the Council of Constance in 1415, heresy inquisitors continued to deal with book censorship very much on an episodic ad hoc basis. Manuscripts dealing with heretical ideas, magic and demon-summoning were undoubtedly seized and destroyed from time to time. The Talmud was also repeatedly condemned: in 1409 by anti-Pope Alexander v, in 1415 by anti-Pope Benedict xiii and in 1433 by Pope Eugenius iv to name just a few episodes. But it is important to remember that the Middle Ages remained a time of manuscript book copying until at least the 1450s, with hand-copying still normative for several decades after the advent of print. As a result, controversial books were quite rare; they were expensive, and therefore unlikely to be found in the hands of any but the most well-educated elites (and even then in only minimal quantities). Stated simply, they were not a serious enough threat to warrant special measures aimed at their total elimination. Instead, they were perceived as merely part of a larger problem posed by heretical behaviours, and by the existence of heretical communities. Any censorship that occurred thus tended to be conducted as part of larger projects of anti-heretical persecution. No lists of banned books were really needed, and as far as we know none were composed in any formal sense for use by inquisitors – aside from the very few manuscript copies of Eymeric's *Directorium* in circulation after 1376, which were themselves often abridged in ways that suggest copyists did not find its *quaestiones* about book censorship to be particularly worth the effort of reproduction.[22]

⸻✠⸻

ANCIENT AND MEDIEVAL censorship thus took many forms without ever becoming fully regularized or institutionalized. It undoubtedly had a terrible impact over the centuries, causing serious losses and distortions in some cases. We will never know what wisdom and creativity would have been passed on if the rulers, mobs and 'experts' of past ages had not taken it upon themselves to purge the records and libraries of their day. The increased concern of medieval Churchmen with controlling circulation of intellectual or spiritual reading materials in a time of growing literacy and university studies is particularly unfortunate, and many innovative minds were never allowed to pass along the full extent of their insights as a result. The unprecedented emergence of more or less permanent heresy inquisitions provided at least the potential for a new institutional base, and welcome new resources, for would-be burners of books towards the end of the Middle Ages. The production of allegedly heretical manuscripts had evidently also reached enough of an intensity to make at least one of those inquisitors begin to think about listing books that would make good candidates for the pyres. It would, however, take two further developments – the consolidation of mass print technologies and the near-simultaneous emergence of yet another deeply challenging series of heretical movements – to inspire the next logical step in that move towards greater degrees of censorship: the creation of a formal and authoritative Index of Prohibited Books.

2

INVENTING THE INDEX

In the year 1515, while presiding at the Fifth Lateran Council in Rome, Pope Leo x issued a bull entitled *Inter sollicitudines*. This was by no means the first papal pronouncement on the need to censor printing, but it was meant to be definitive: from now on, all printed books should be examined and cleared by Church authorities before publication.[1]

Leo's bull also acknowledged that printing could be a very good thing, and in particular a valuable means of getting spiritually beneficial reading materials into the hands of more people. The inventor Johannes Gutenberg's first printed edition, a Latin Bible produced in 1450 in Mainz, had already set an early precedent for the mechanical diffusion of important Christian texts. Since then several more Bibles and other pious books had appeared in print without any raising of alarms from Church officials. And Leo was no anti-intellectual thug. A refined scion of the great Florentine Medici family, he was in fact the very epitome of a Renaissance pope. He patronized artists such as Raphael and enlarged what would later become the Sapienza University of Rome; he supported Daniel Bomberg's groundbreaking publication of a printed Babylonian Talmud; and he even founded his own printing press for the copying of Greek books.

But the historical times in which Leo moved were challenging. Fears of heresy lingered, with ongoing conflicts between Catholics and Waldensians in the Alpine regions, Wycliffite Lollards in England and Hussites in Bohemia. In Spain, allegations of unfaithfulness were being levelled against that country's large population of converted Jews (the so-called *conversos* or 'New Christians'), and against ever-increasing numbers of converted Muslims (known as *moriscos*), who were believed to retain a primary loyalty to their former religion. The resulting waves of paranoia among 'Old Christians' had already led in 1478 to the establishment of a greatly expanded, coordinated and permanent new form of royally controlled Spanish *Inquisición contra la heretica pravedad* ('Inquisition against heretical depravity', referred to hereafter as the Spanish Inquisition). This was followed by expulsion of all remaining unconverted Jews from Spain in 1492; Portugal followed suit five years later. Meanwhile more traditional heresy inquisitors continued to operate against alleged heretics and witches in many German, French and Italian regions. Radical preachers roamed the land, and as a young man in his native Florence the future Pope Leo had personally witnessed upheavals caused by a fiery Dominican named Girolamo Savonarola, who called for Church reforms and expelled the Medici altogether before being excommunicated for his defiance of papal authority and finally executed in 1498. Things were far from harmonious in Christendom. The Fifth Lateran Council was itself called by Leo's predecessor Julius II (r. 1503–13) in a context of imminent war and lingering conciliar threats to papal power.

The potential for unruly words like Savonarola's to cause still further disruptions among the faithful – especially when amplified by mass distribution through the printing press – was confirmed in the years after 1517 as a German priest named Martin Luther sprang into the religious spotlight, and effectively initiated what would come to be known as the Protestant Reformation. Luther's stinging critiques of contemporary Church doctrines and practices quickly found their way into print and spread across Europe, long before papally assigned evaluators (including the inquisitor Prierias, and papal legate Thomas de Vio Cajetan) had a chance to determine whether or not they were in fact fully orthodox. Unauthorized dissemination of such writings was in clear defiance of the sort of prior censorship demanded by *Inter sollicitudines*, and matters only got worse in 1522 when Luther again ignored the rules and published his unauthorized German translation of the New Testament. The fact that this version introduced subtle changes to the 'traditional' text by tailoring key phrases to align with Luther's teachings (such as adding the word 'alone' after 'faith' in Romans 3:28), compounded by the fact that its author was excommunicate and a condemned heretic, deeply worried Church officials who were already concerned by the success of unapproved vernacular Bibles previously circulating among Waldensians and Lollards.[2]

Luther's books and pamphlets were widely blamed for subversions of Church authority, with outright insurrectionary violence sometimes the result. By 1525, Lutheran-inspired participants in the bloody German Peasants' War were also using the power of print to spread their own anti-establishment message. Meanwhile new reformers such as Jean Calvin, Huldrych Zwingli and the Anabaptist

Menno Simons continued to emerge in Luther's wake, at times arguing with him and taking his 'Protestant' movement in directions its founder had never envisioned. As their followers consolidated political control over regions stretching from Switzerland and parts of what is now Germany to the Dutch Netherlands, Scandinavia and various territories in central Europe, the number and variety of written materials escaping the Church's pre-censorship regime naturally continued to multiply.

For secular as well as religious leaders the writing could now literally be seen on the wall – as the French King Francis I discovered when he woke up on the morning of 17 October 1534, to find that anti-Catholic placards had been posted on his bedchamber door as well as in public squares across his realm. It was becoming increasingly clear that Protestantism would be no passing fad, a fact made all the more unmistakable just two weeks later when King Henry VIII of England solidified his own break with the Catholic Church by issuing the first Act of Supremacy. Henceforth not only rebellious peasants, priests and barons but kings were in open defiance of Rome, and increasingly, they had access to printing presses to help them let everyone else know why.

New Tools for Old Problems

If authors and printers could simply ignore the demands of papal bulls like *Inter sollicitudines*, as Luther had, and if, like him, they also lived in regions where Catholic authorities no longer had any real power to discipline them, then it was evident that further actions needed to be taken if book censorship was ever to stem the new tide of 'heretical' writings unleashed by the Protestant Reformation. One of these measures was the issuance of public notices specifically banning particular printed books, or short lists of book titles, that were known to have been illicitly printed. If they could not be cut off at the source, there was at least a hope that such books could be prevented from circulating openly or widely in Catholic communities, and that they could be seized if ever they did come to light. Secular officials took the lead in this matter at first, with the assistance of local theological experts, by identifying particularly subversive texts and alerting citizens to the dangers of reading them. Thus in Spain, France and the Low Countries, edicts and placards

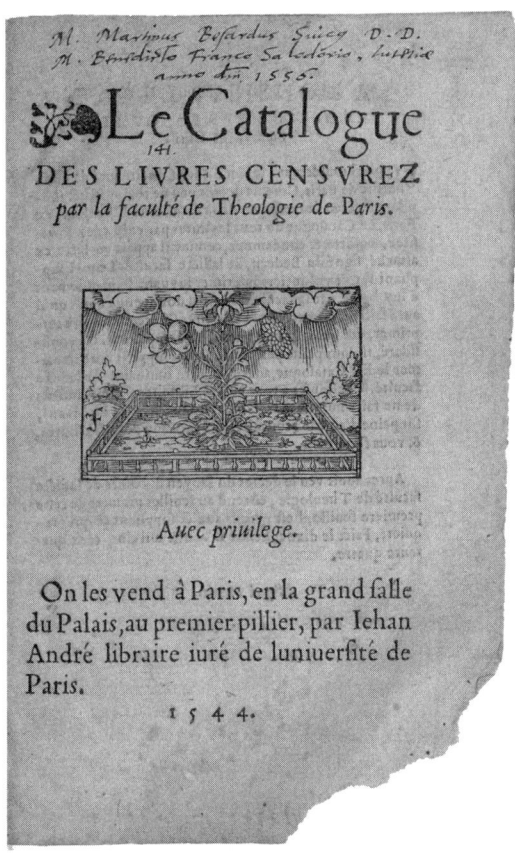

Title page for the Parisian Index, 1544.

denouncing suspect authors and their books were promulgated by royal, episcopal or inquisitorial authority in churches and town squares on a somewhat regular basis in the second quarter of the sixteenth century. In the various independent regions of Italy, different jurisdictions handled book censorship in widely divergent ways, while in Paris university and parlement officials also asserted their rights to issue independent judgements against books they considered to be heretical – causing no small degree of confusion when their decisions contradicted those of the king. Henry VIII of England, for his part, published a list of eighteen forbidden works in 1526, which would be expanded to 85 titles three years later while he was still a loyal son of the Church. Demands for prior censorship and licensing of all printed books, along with inspections of printers' and booksellers' inventories, continued to be heard from clergy and kings alike, but when it came to censoring those books that had already found their way into print, certainty was hard to come by and loopholes could often be found.

Early sixteenth-century efforts to control book production thus tended to be rather localized and uncoordinated ad hoc approaches to publishing threats that were still seen as more or less episodic. So long as rulers felt they could afford to consult with their experts and react to new publications on a case-by-case basis, such measures might be deemed sufficient. But by the 1540s it was evident that more resources would have to be found to effectively manage the increasingly onerous and complex business of book censorship. Edicts and placards began to evolve into regularized lists and catalogues, so that by mid-century the phenomenon of the 'Index of Prohibited Books' had started to take on its first definitive form. An important step was taken in 1544 when theology professors at the University of Paris were authorized by King Francis I to publish a list of 'heretical' books that were, in their professional judgement, unsuitable for scholastic use or indeed for reading by any faithful Christian. Lightly revised editions of this alphabetical Parisian list, entitled *Le Catalogue des Livres Examinez et Censurez par la Faculté de Theologie de l'Université de Paris*, followed in 1545 and again in 1547 – correcting typographical errors and adding a few new entries each time. Further revised versions followed in 1551 and 1556, during the reign of Francis's successor Henry II. These prototypical lists were not very extensive, with just over a hundred titles listed in 1544; even the expanded edition of 1556 stretched only to sixty printed folios in a small octavo format (about the size of a slim modern paperback). Each edition's contents were arranged alphabetically, by last name of author, in two sections divided by language: the first being entirely devoted to Latin works, followed by another in French (with some Italian as well). Anonymous works appeared in yet another set of more or less alphabetical lists, arranged by title and by language, and in the edition of 1551 futher lists were appended to include banned scriptural texts and the Italian writings of Bernardino Ochino – whom we shall meet again shortly. These catalogues of prohibited books were intended primarily for local use in Paris or other French intellectual centres, and they were hardly exhaustive, focusing almost exclusively on recent Protestant theological works as opposed to earlier heresies or morally suspect compositions. But they were the start of a tradition that would last, and grow, for a very long time.

Not to be outdone by their French counterparts, theology professors at the University of Leuven (in the Belgian territories controlled by Emperor Charles v, who was also King Charles I of Spain and the ruler of many German, Italian and New World territories besides) published their own Index of Prohibited Books in 1546. The Leuven Index, printed as an 'Index of Books, which the Theologians of Leuven by Order of His Caesarean Majesty Diligently Examined and Censored as Forbidden' (*Librorum, quos ad Caesareae Maiestatis iussum Theologi Lovanienses diligenter examinatos censuerunt interdicendos, index*) differed slightly from the Parisian in terms of the books it prohibited, but also in its organization. After several pages of prefatory exortations, its first section focused entirely on banned editions of the Bible, organized by language (Latin, Greek, German and French). This was followed by an alphabetical list of 'other' Latin works, again organized at first by last name of author, before turning to non-alphabetical collections of German, Dutch and French titles (the first two set off in a different typeface). Like the Paris *Catalogue*, the Leuven Index would be re-issued in lightly expanded form in 1550 (though no longer alphabetized by surname), and then again in 1558, first with the approval of Emperor Charles's designated Low Countries representative Mary of Hungary, and then with that of his Spanish successor King Philip II.

These Paris and Leuven censorship lists are noteworthy for being the work of university professors, acting with royal authority and oversight (though not always full agreement). Far from entertaining modern notions of academic freedom, many early modern professors took it as their professional responsibility to discern which books made acceptable contributions to the 'truth' of Catholic theology, and which were dangerously misguided – and therefore misleading, and worthy of suppression. In this sense faculty acted in a sort of 'peer review' capacity, but they were also essentially serving as heresy inquisitors.[3] Many of the *targeted* writers on the university Indexes were also professors of theology, including some colleagues of the censors themselves, infusing the whole process with more than a whiff of internal score-settling. Among the names proscribed by the first Paris Index of 1544, for example, we find prominent French humanist scholars such as Jacques Lefèvre d'Étaples, Guillaume Farel and François Vatable, all enemies of a dominant professorial faction previously led by Noël Beda. Even the university's rector,

Claude d'Espence, was denounced in certain extant copies of the 1556 Paris Index, though ongoing conflicts over his orthodoxy were made evident by the fact that his name was removed in time for an alternative press run in that same year.[4] Notorious Protestant theologians such as Luther and his allies Philip Melanchthon, Johannes Brenz and Andreas Osiander were of course prominent in both the Paris and the Leuven lists, as were their more extreme rivals. But clear divisions between rebellious Protestants on the one hand, and loyal Catholic advocates of reform on the other, remained difficult to draw in many cases. Desiderius Erasmus of Rotterdam (d. 1536, and not to be confused with the Lutheran Erasmus Sarcerii, who was also named on the Index) provides perhaps the most important example of this. Much ink was spilled as university censors wavered back and forth debating precisely whether, when and how he might have crossed over into heterodox theological territory in his many published works. In the end, a dozen of his writings were posthumously placed on the Parisian Index of 1544, yet it took the censors at Leuven (where the celebrated scholar had formerly lectured) another fourteen years to decide against even a single Erasmian text. Censorship of Erasmus' books would continue to remain a live issue for Catholic censors throughout the subsequent history of the Index.[5]

The Parisian and Leuvenian university professors' lists were soon copied for use by actual heresy inquisitors elsewhere in Europe as well. Though Spanish censorship edicts had already been issued on a sporadic basis for years, it was only in 1551 that a printed list of banned books was formally produced and distributed by the Spanish Inquisition under the title *Catalogus librorum reprobatorum ex iudicio Academiae Lovaniensis* (Catalogue of Books Rejected by Judgement of the University of Leuven). This early effort was, as its title suggests, almost entirely copied from the 1550 Leuven Index, though Inquisitor-General Fernando de Valdés did add a few titles of more 'local' interest, such as entries focused on Islamic writings. He also decided on a particularly 'Spanish' prohibition against four books by Erasmus, whose favoured status under Emperor Charles waned significantly in the years leading up to the accession of Philip II (r. 1556–98). In 1554 a further step was taken when a special Spanish list of banned Bibles was published, to highlight growing concerns about the import of Protestant texts across the Pyrenees. But for the most part Spanish inquisitors were happy at this point to

Hans Holbein the Younger, *Erasmus of Rotterdam*, 1523, oil on panel.

follow the lead of their Flemish compatriots in the matter of book censorship.

Meanwhile to the west, the Portuguese Inquisition (which had been established along similar lines to the Spanish in 1536) compiled its own first, brief handwritten *Prohibição dos Livros Defesos* as a guide to book censorship in 1547. This was largely a reproduction of both the Paris and Leuven lists, printed copies of which were evidently in local circulation among the Portuguese clergy, but it also augmented those entries with further Spanish and Portuguese content. Such additions effectively established Portugal as the most extensively censored kingdom of the day, with a truly international scope to its list of banned books. This initial collection would subsequently be expanded and printed in 1551 as a *Rol dos Livros Defesos*, containing nearly five hundred entries (including a new high of sixteen works written by Desiderius Erasmus).

Several jurisdictions in Italy were also experimenting with censorial edicts and short lists of banned books in the 1530s and '40s. In 1549, Venice went a step further by publishing a slightly longer printed list of approximately 150 entries, under a rather flowery title that can roughly be translated as 'Catalogue of Various Works, Compositions and Books, which as Heretical, Suspect, Impious and Scandalous are to be Damned and Prohibited in This Glorious City of Venice, and in All the Illustrious Venetian Dominions, Both of Sea and Land' (*Catalogo di diverse opere, compositioni, et libri; li quale come heretici, spospetti, impii, & scandalosi si dichiarano dannati, & prohibiti in questa inclita citta di Vinegia, & in tutto l'illustrissimo dominio Vinitiano, sì da mare, come da terra*). Though similar in size to the Paris Indexes on which it was partly modelled, this catalogue provoked an uproar among the influential printers and booksellers of the Most Serene Republic, as well as its traditionally tolerant intellectual class. It was soon recalled as a result of that opposition, but there was ultimately no denying the mood of the times. By 1554 a still more comprehensive Venetian Index was in circulation, along with a similar version specially printed for the Spanish-dominated Duchy of Milan. These new Indexes prohibited nearly seven hundred authors and titles (though Erasmus was all but ignored), including several that had never been listed before and which seem to have been drawn from an ominous new source: the medieval *Directorium inquisitorum* of Nicholas Eymeric, which was poised to enjoy something of a revival.[6]

Thus by the mid-1550s, a series of fairly brief, quite focused and expertly compiled Indexes (or Catalogues, or Rolls) of prohibited books had been produced for the protection and guidance of faithful readers in most of the Catholic regions of Europe. Often comparing notes, if not directly copying from one another, Church censors had clearly identified Protestant spiritual writings as the main challenge standing in the way of their efforts to prevent the circulation of dangerous texts. University professors led the way in this, in large part due to their vested interest in controlling the legitimacy of textual curricula for the training of future theologians. Inquisitors did similar work in the Iberian territories of Spain and Portugal, where permanent heresy Inquisitions (though not originally intended to focus on book censorship) provided a ready-made infrastructure for all sorts of ideological control. The work of censorship was thus divided along national lines, which allowed political enemies such as Valois France, the Habsburg Empire (including Spain) and the independent Republic of Venice to police their own internal book markets without acknowledging any authority of censors working for a rival state. Uniformity was impossible given such divisions, which naturally led to inconsistencies when it came to the condemnation of individual authors such as Erasmus, or of regionally specific concerns such as the spread of Islamic literature in Iberia. For the most part, Catholics could agree on the need to censor Protestant attacks against their core religious loyalties and beliefs, but this agreement proved impossible to sustain as soon as censorship agendas started to expand.

It would ultimately fall to the main centralizing authority of the Roman Catholic Church, the papacy, to attempt to bring a greater degree of order to these varying agendas. But preliminary attempts to impose even partial uniformity would take several more years to come to fruition, and more than two centuries later the goal remained incomplete. Rome's belated engagement with Index censorship lists, coming as it did more than forty years after *Inter sollicitudines* and well over a decade after the creation of a regular Roman Inquisition, was both long overdue and frequently ambivalent. But once established, it would permanently change the face of Catholic censorship around the world.

The Plot Thickens

The papal Curia in Rome was in fact rather more seriously divided by the problem of censoring Protestant and other 'heretical' books than were the opinionated professorial factions dominant in leading northern universities at mid-century. Roman-based theologians such as Cajetan and Prierias had of course been among the first to reject Luther's ideas, and Pope Leo x had consequently not hesitated to anathematize Luther and his followers as heretics in 1521. But as the Protestant challenge continued to evolve and grow (and as some Catholic theologians took the time to read Protestant writings more carefully, despite the best efforts of Church censors), influential voices within the hierarchy also called for compromise and a more measured response. Some saw a degree of merit in Protestant critiques of the Church's corruption, and alleged deviations from its original apostolic mission; others felt that certain new theological ideas (such as 'justification by faith alone') might indeed have religious value, and could therefore be incorporated withing the existing system of Catholic thought. Some were even willing to challenge the papacy's increasingly exclusive claims to power, though ultimately papal authority remained in many ways the fundamental dividing line between Catholics and all types of Protestants. The decades between the 1530s and 1550s were thus crucial, as different tendencies and factions lined up to see whether recent rifts between Christian believers in the Latin West could somehow be mended.

Precisely at the same time that their colleagues were attempting to compile definitive lists of prohibited heretics and their books in other parts of Italy, France, Spain, Portugal and the Holy Roman Empire, then, moderates in Rome itself were hoping to be able to reform the Church from within and so perhaps achieve a degree of rapprochement with those very same heretics. Such moderates included some of the highest-ranking clerical elites, including the papal notary and diplomat Pietro Carnesecchi (himself a Medici and protégé of Pope Clement VII); Bernardino Ochino, vicar-general of the Capuchin Order; the abbot and preacher Pietro Martire Vermigli; the papal nuncio Pier Paolo Vergerio; and cardinals Giovanni Morone, Pietro Bembo and Reginald Pole. Together with influential humanist scholars like Juan de Valdés and Marcantonio Flaminio, and noble lay patrons such as Giulia Gonzaga and Vittoria Colonna, these comprised an important faction of Catholic reformers who believed the Church was badly in need of change, even if this meant exploring some of the same paths that Protestants had recently travelled. And for a while it looked as though they might prevail. In 1536, Pope Paul III appointed a Council for the Reform of the Church (*Consilium de Emendanda Ecclesia*), which included Pole and seven others. Their report was completed the following year and would have gone a long way towards correcting many abuses (chiefly financial) if it had been acted on.

At the same time, pressure was building to call a new general Council that would address both internal and Protestant criticisms against the Church. This would eventually lead to the convocation of the Council of Trent (1545–63), though political difficulties long delayed both its opening and its conclusion. And, while waiting for such a universal solution to take place, some began to experiment with new forms of Catholic religious organization on their own. Ochino's Capuchins, a reformed Order derived from the Franciscans, were one example of this, established in 1525. Another was the Jesuit Order, also known as the Society of Jesus, newly constituted in 1541 under the leadership of Ignatius Loyola (a Basque ex-soldier with close ties to Cardinal Pole). Founded as a devoutly Catholic religious Order whose goals were summed up in its motto 'for the greater glory of God and the salvation of man' (*ad maiorem Dei gloriam inque hominum salutem*), the Jesuits soon became known for their creativity and pragmatism as they sought to overcome the challenges of an increasingly divided Christendom.

A less open-minded faction was also hard at work in Rome. Led by Cardinal Gian Pietro Carafa (himself a member of the new Theatine religious Order, who had grudgingly worked with Pole on the *Consilium de Emendanda Ecclesia*), these individuals wanted nothing to do with Protestant ideas, which they shunned as irredeemably heretical. Bowing to their pressure, Paul III authorized the establishment of a special papal heresy inquisition for Rome, whose main focus was to be the prosecution of Protestants, by means of the bull *Licet ab initio* in 1542. Carafa was nominated to serve on this new body, and quickly became its dominant force along with his loyal ally Michele Ghislieri. Like the Spanish and Portuguese Inquisitions, theirs was to be a permanent and centrally directed tribunal (in contrast with medieval heresy inquisitions, which had tended to operate more or less sporadically with very little oversight and few resources, whenever and wherever their presence was thought to be necessary).[7] The Roman Inquisition thus promised to give the fight against Protestant 'heresy' new teeth, and new scope for action.

Within a matter of weeks Carafa was using this new authority to summon his respected colleague Bernardino Ochino for questioning on the subject of Ochino's *Dialogues*, which had aroused suspicions of Lutheran sympathy ever since their appearance in print in 1539. Tipped off that he would never leave Rome alive if he submitted, Ochino fled first to Calvinist Geneva and later to England, where he received asylum from the Protestant King Edward VI. Frustrated, the Roman inquisitors next turned (having first found Ochino guilty in absentia and burned him in effigy) to the arrest of Pietro Carnesecchi in 1546. Again, their efforts were at first in vain since Carnesecchi enjoyed the protection of both Paul III and Cardinal Pole. But they bided their time and continued to compile a growing dossier on Carnesecchi even after his release – along with files on all his friends

Anon., 'Pope Paul IV (Gian Pietro Carafa)', engraving in Onofrio Panvinio, XXVII *Pontificum Maximorum elogia et imagines* (1568).

and supporters. In 1549, after the death of Paul III, the inquisitors' work bore preliminary fruit as Carafa was able to use allegations of possible heretical tendencies to ensure that the popular English reformer Reginald Pole did not become the next pope.⁸ Carafa's hardline allies would not have too long to wait before further victories would also be theirs.

After the short 'compromise' reigns of Julius III (r. 1550–55) and Marcellus II (r. 1555), it was finally Cardinal Carafa's own turn to rise to the papal throne as Paul IV (r. 1555–9). The results were dramatic. First, the new pope turned his hostile gaze to the Jews, who had already suffered renewed attacks on the Talmud under Julius III. Those living in Rome were now ordered into ghettos, and the Talmud was yet again subjected to censorship and threats of destruction.⁹ Second, Carnesecchi was re-arrested, as was Cardinal Morone in 1557. Pole too was denounced but died while visiting Queen Mary I's newly Catholicized English court, in 1558. Others (including Valdés, Bembo, Colonna and Flaminio) had already died; Ochino and Vermigli were in exile. The tables also now turned for Bartolomé de Carranza, the highly respected reforming Spanish archbishop of Toledo, who had recently worked with Pole in England as Mary's confessor from 1554 to 1557, and served Emperor Charles V at his deathbed in September 1558.¹⁰ In a striking reversal, Charles's heir Philip II – who found himself at the head of an unprecedented, though ultimately short-lived, Anglo-Dutch-Spanish-Italian Catholic alliance through his paternal inheritance and his marriage to Mary Tudor – authorized Carranza's sudden arrest on charges of heresy in 1559. Patiently laid traps had thus been sprung, and the now elderly Carafa pope could be confident that he had finally outlasted practically all of his enemies when he died in August 1559.

During his short but effective papacy, Paul IV also continued the project of book censorship that had long been dear to his heart. As a founding member of the Roman Inquisition, he had ensured that book censorship and oversight of printing presses were among its original duties, and he helped to weed out what he judged to be offensive texts (such as Ochino's *Dialogues*, and several works by Juan de Valdés) whenever he could. By 1555, he knew well enough that formal catalogues and indexes of prohibited books had previously been produced by authorities in France, Spain, Portugal and the Empire as well as in nearby Venice and Milan. What was still lacking was an Index of Prohibited Books for the papal territories, authorized by Rome and of potentially universal application to all who recognized the power of the papacy. If he could achieve this aim, such an Index would give Paul IV the opportunity to cement his doctrinal victory and definitively place the names and books of his enemies among those of the hated Protestants and heresiarchs of old – where they belonged. In the end this was to prove too ambitious, and compromises had to be made on a number of points, but completion of the first authoritative Roman Index of Prohibited Books would still be one of Gian Pietro Carafa's most important legacies.

The plan, like so many of Paul's projects, had been maturing for a long time. A preliminary short list of condemned authors was already prepared as early as 1545.[11] After this, the difficulty of achieving consensus on new condemnations led to a decision to use the existing university Indexes in Rome until circumstances should prove more amenable; thus a minimally adjusted version of the 1545 Parisian Index was reprinted for use at Rome in 1549.[12] Meanwhile, a shadowy commission for banned books, led by the Inquisition's commissary-general Michele Ghislieri, continued to compile further notes and bide its time. Then, in 1550, two Dominicans were assigned to begin work on the development of a prospective new Roman Index. Their efforts were deemed sufficiently sound to be shared with colleagues in Florence, Venice and Milan, and the contents of the prototypical new Roman list thus influenced the 1554 Indexes published in those cities (including their use of Eymeric). But with the possibility of Protestant reconciliation still on the agenda at the Council of Trent, publication of such an Index in Rome itself was not yet possible.

Political changes, including above all Carafa's election to the papacy, cleared the way most dramatically after 1555. By 1557, an ambitious first draft of the new Index was ready. Building upon previous lists, Paul sought to ensure that his would be more exhaustive than any that had appeared before; and whenever there was doubt about the orthodoxy of a given text, he was quick to err on the side of a guilty verdict. As a result, many new books and authors that had never before been formally denounced now found their way onto his list. Paul and his advisors certainly had a copy of Eymeric's *Directorium inquisitorum* to hand (though they may also have consulted Bernard of Luxemburg's 1522 *Catalogus haereticorum*, which borrowed substantially from the *Directorium* without attribution),

Title page for the Roman Index, 1559.

since all of the titles previously censored in that old medieval text now appeared in print once more. This included names such as Arnold of Villanova and Ramon Llull, the 'heretical' status of whose books had been disputed by several orthodox theologians and whose cause was powerfully supported by none other than Philip II of Spain.[13] In other cases, such as with the obscure authors 'Gondissalvus' and 'Raimundus Neophitus', Paul's Index compilers were evidently copying from the *Directorium* quite mechanically, since by this time no traces remained of any book written by either. There were other controversial inclusions as well, including so many popular (and lucrative) books and authors that the booksellers of Italy threatened to revolt if the list were not emended. Boccaccio's *Decameron*, Ariosto's *Orlando*, Machiavelli's *Prince*, the complete works of Erasmus and ancient Roman classics such as Lucian were all among those now being threatened with oblivion.

After much debate, a revision to the draft Roman Index was finally undertaken. Necessary cuts (nearly one-fifth of the total) were made under the direction of Cardinal Bernardino Scottus in 1558, though new additions were also made so that the final number of prohibitions still remained at over 1,100. The resulting 1559 Roman Index of Prohibited Books was thus longer than its predecessors from other countries but still quite compact, covering only about 35 unpaginated folios (or seventy pages) in all. It was more moderate than its first edition (all copies of which were, ironically, recalled and thus effectively censored), but nevertheless remained extremely onerous, especially in its proscription of entire categories of books that might in fact have no heretical content whatsoever. For example, all books written by heretics, all books printed without an author's name, date, publisher or place of publication and all books produced by any printer who had ever published a heretical book in the past, were now to be forbidden no matter what their actual contents. Most entries continued to fall under a single alphabetical list (with three subdivisions under each letter for completely banned authors, partially banned authors and anonymous works listed by title), but additional lists of prohibited Bibles and even banned printers were also appended. Printers and booksellers remained suitably outraged, and scandalized bibliophiles were among the many who celebrated the pope's death later that same year. Paul had lived long enough to approve the final release of his long-anticipated Index, but not long enough to enjoy watching it take full effect.

The Inquisitions of Spain and Portugal also soon issued their own newly revised Indexes (in 1559 and 1561 respectively); these bodies were still considered to be independent of Rome, but their censors were aware of and closely followed Paul's lead in many cases. The Portuguese in particular agreed to the total condemnation of all books by Erasmus. While not going quite that far, the Spanish Index also now expanded its reach to include a prohibition against sixteen Erasmian texts (most, but not all, the same ones that had been banned in Portugal since 1551). Censorship of Ramon Llull was not so easily accepted in Iberia once Philip II had made his feelings known on the matter, but otherwise Paul was remarkably successful in advancing his version of harsh censorship to a position of new prominence throughout the Catholic Church. And this extended beyond books: as we will see further in Chapter Seven, Paul IV also despised what he saw as 'immoral' art, ordering alterations to cover up the nudity of figures in the Sistine Chapel as well as other masterpieces.

Having alienated so many with his rigid intransigence, however, some aspects of Paul IV's achievements were in fact erased or reversed as soon as his iron grip ceased to hold. At his death, Roman mobs gathered to loot his quarters and deface his monuments. Soon they also turned their anger to the palace of the Inquisition, which was ransacked and put to the torch. Decades of carefully assembled files on all the suspected heretics of Rome and its territories went up in smoke. And shortly thereafter a new and more pragmatic pope, Pius IV, was on the throne (r. 1559–65). Both Carnesecchi and Morone were released from prison (though Carranza remained behind bars in Spain). Carafa was no more, but serious damage had been done, and precedents had been set. There was no going back for the now powerfully established institutions of papal Inquisition and papal censorship.

Title page for the Spanish Index, 1559.

A New Normal: The Index of Trent

With dividing lines between Protestants and Catholics appearing more stark than ever, the best that Pope Pius IV could hope for was to at least bring a certain sense of closure to some of the controversies that had so long torn at the internal unity of the Church. With England once more under Protestant rule after the accession of Elizabeth I in 1558, and both France and the Netherlands increasingly threatened by the prospect of fratricidal civil wars of religion, Pius worked hard to bring the Council of Trent to a long-overdue conclusion in hopes that it would provide clarity and perhaps some compromises to satisfy faithful Catholics and tepid Protestants alike. As soon as that was settled, in 1563, he turned to the task of revising Paul IV's still rather draconian (and not entirely well-organized) Index of Prohibited Books. Taking advantage of advice from leading theologians who remained in Italy at the close of the Council, as well as the easy availability of previous Index editions, Pius soon rushed through a new 'Tridentine' version of the Index which was ready for publication in 1564.

Thorough yet relatively balanced, the Tridentine Index managed to gain approval from the still-conflicted but exhausted parties who cared most about such things: various theological factions within the papal court, the mutually antagonistic Spanish and French royal envoys and the ever-vigilant booksellers of Italy. It also included an important new innovation: a set of ten more or less clear and simple printed 'Rules' (*Regulae*), which laid out general guidelines for any future censorship, as well as for disputed cases. Overall, its number of entries was roughly comparable to that of the 1559 Pauline Index, and both were similarly organized not only alphabetically (now generally using first or 'Christian' names rather than surnames, except in the case of notorious heresiarchs who sometimes appeared under more than one heading) but in terms of subdivision into three categories. Those who were completely forbidden would henceforth be known as 'Class One' authors (*auctores primae classis*); these were then followed by individual prohibited works by named authors (whose other writings could be accepted by default); and then by anonymous banned works, listed alphabetically by title. Thus under 'I', one could find not only 'Ioan. Calvinus' (for Joannes or Jean Calvin, who also appears under 'C') as a Class One heretic, but selected works

Elia Naurizio, *General Congregation of the Council of Trent in Santa Maria Maggiore*, 1633, oil on canvas.

by 'Iacobi Fabri' (Latin for Jacques Lefèvre d'Étaples, including his commentaries on the Gospels and Pauline epistles) and finally titles beginning with 'I', such as the *Instructio visitationis Saxonicae*. The final product remained physically unremarkable. Like its predecessors, this Index was generally printed in a handy pocket-sized format, about the size of a small novella or chapbook, with a length of only about 25–35 double-sided folios (depending on the edition). It was easy to carry, easy to consult and meant to be used far beyond the confines of Rome itself.

Copies of this new Roman Index, along with other documents issued by the Council of Trent, were promptly shipped all over the Catholic world and licensed for further reprinting. Dozens of slight variants of the Tridentine Index can therefore be found in modern collections, having been printed as far afield as Cologne, Liège and Lisbon as well as in Rome, Venice, Milan and Bologna.[14] It represented something of a new standard in censorship practice, to be respected in principle by all Catholics, even though local secular and Church authorities continued to challenge the applicability of such a Roman Index for particular cases from time to time. The French monarchy initially rejected the Tridentine Index's authority over its own clergy, for example, and the Spanish Inquisition (as will be seen in later chapters of this book) long continued to produce its own more or less independent Indexes, sometimes in open defiance of Roman opinion. Yet Pius and the theologians at Trent had undeniably achieved another major milestone in the history of Church censorship. All that remained was to see how long this papally directed project would last, in a world of constantly evolving theological debates and ever-more diverse book cultures.

The pendulum swung once more in 1566, when Pius IV was succeeded by none other than Michele Ghislieri – Carafa's inquisitorial colleague and fellow hardliner, who had played a leading role in the preparation of the 1559 Index. Taking the name of Pius V (r. 1566–72), Ghislieri may have been signalling that he would opt for a certain degree of continuity rather than yet another destabilizing reversal of papal policy in matters of doctrine and censorship. And well he might be concerned about avoiding unnecessary further disruptions; after all, conflicts with Protestants continued to worsen in France (where the St Bartholomew's Day massacre would kill thousands of Huguenots in 1572) and in the Low Countries (where the Duke of Alba unleashed a devastating campaign of terror against Protestant rebels from 1567 to 1573). The Tridentine Index of Prohibited Books was seen as a useful tool to regulate and regularize book censorship in such fraught contexts. New editions specially designed for circulation in the Low Countries were therefore printed at Antwerp in 1569, 1570 and 1571.

These Antwerp Indexes, though explicitly based on the Tridentine model and deferential to its authority, had necessarily to deal with a multitude of anti-Catholic, anti-papal and anti-Habsburg texts that had continued to appear on the market since 1564. Efforts to keep up with these sorts of recent publications were led in the Low Countries by the Spanish theologian and bibliophile Benito Arias Montano, who also spent much his remaining time working on editions of Hebrew texts as well as an ambitious new Polyglot Bible project (and suffered his own brushes with suspicious inquisitors as a result). But even a genius like Montano was hard-pressed to keep up with five tumultuous years of heterodox book publishing. It was evident to all, including Pius v, that further resources would need to be committed on a regular basis if the Index was not to continually fall behind the times. It was therefore decided to place responsibility for all future book censorship in the hands of an entirely new Roman institution: the Congregation of the Index. This was in some ways the last stage in the rationalization of papally directed censorship: moving beyond the sporadic (and often contested) efforts of individual popes and their advisors to come up with new Indexes as needed, this new committee was intended to proactively examine any and all contentious books that might come to its attention in the future, while also providing a permanent advisory body to keep the papacy informed with regard to censorship matters in general.

By 1572, the year of Pius v's death, the new Congregation was fully staffed and operational. As we will see in the next chapter, however, it would fall into a certain torpor in the first years of his successor's reign, and it would never completely free itself from the threat of domination by the Roman Inquisition (whose evaluative and censorial powers continued to overlap with those of the Congregation from 1571 right up to the latter's suppression in 1917). Confusion and contradiction thus continued to plague Church efforts to mount a common front against the spread of heretical books. Nevertheless, the creation of a specialized office charged with the maintenance of future editions of the papal Index of Prohibited Books went a long way towards ensuring that its lists would only grow in size and complexity. Bureaucracies by their very nature tend to justify their continued existence by constantly seeking new fields of activity, and 'mission creep' was certainly a factor for Index compilers of the seventeenth and later centuries. No more would the fight against Protestants and medieval heresies be sufficient; science and art, politics and literature, history and morality, as well as internal theological disputes among Catholics, would all become fair game for the ever-broadening scope of the censors' interests.

⸻ ✠ ⸻

THUS, OVER THE COURSE of much of the sixteenth century, Catholic authorities responded to threats posed by the new Protestant 'heresies', especially as these were spread by means of new print technologies, with their own innovative use and regulation of printed texts. They listed and limited the spread of heretical or otherwise 'bad' books, disputed and inconsistent though these categories sometimes were. Their efforts were aided by new, permanent Inquisitions established not only in Spain and Portugal but finally in Rome itself, and eventually also by a specialized agency known as the Congregation of the Index, entirely dedicated to the ideal of centralized papal book censorship. In the wake of the Council of Trent, Indexes of Prohibited Books became increasingly standardized and broadly available for the use of Catholics all over the world, with the promise of expert updates to those lists being provided on a regular basis thereafter. The Index was by now a sophisticated fixture of Catholic intellectual life, and it was there to stay. At least that was the theory; we will see in the chapters that follow how history, as always, was rather more complicated in practice.

3 EXPANDING THE INDEX

Francisco Peña (1540–1612) was an ambitious young canon lawyer in the year 1572. Born in a small Aragonese village in what is now eastern Spain, he had been trained at some of the best schools in his field – first at Valencia and then Bologna. Now, after years of diligent study, he was finally in the Eternal City of Rome and looking to make a spectacular career for himself.

He arrived at a good time. In May, Pius V died and was immediately replaced by Ugo Boncompagni, himself a Bolognese canon lawyer who ascended the papal throne as Gregory XIII (r. 1572–85). This new pope was a serious intellectual, famous to posterity as the founder of a reformed 'Gregorian' calendar, and he was also interested in a number of other projects involving both book censorship and the revision of key Catholic doctrinal texts. Francesco Pegna (as he would become known in Italian), with his specialized legal training and growing passion for inquisitorial work, would turn out to be a perfect candidate to take part in several of these.

Pegna got right down to business. Between 1573 and 1575 he completed a series of journeyman essays on jurisprudence, including an extensive but unfinished work on the punishment of heretics that survives only in manuscript form (*De poenis haereticorum*). His interest in inquisitorial procedure increased as he followed the case of Bartolomé de Carranza, the reform-minded archbishop of Toledo who had been transferred to Rome in 1567 after awaiting trial in a Spanish prison for eight years. Carranza was finally exonerated and released by Pope Gregory in 1576, just one week before the archbishop's death, leaving many unresolved questions about the propriety of his treatment. Reflecting on this and other problems, Pegna continued to write, and in 1578 he brought his first major work into print: a two-volume annotated re-edition of Nicholas Eymeric's medieval inquisition manual, the *Directorium inquisitorum*. This text, which would be revised and re-issued with significantly larger annotated sections in 1585 and 1587 (along with further reprints of the 1587 edition in 1595 and 1607) was eventually to make Pegna's reputation and had a major impact on all aspects of inquisition law.

As previously noted, the *Directorium* was also a groundbreaking manual for inquisitors in terms of its unusual focus on book censorship. After nearly two centuries of general neglect, its lists of banned books had finally been copied into the earliest Venetian and Roman Indexes thanks to the zeal of Gian Pietro Carafa and his allies; now the full weight of Eymeric's inquisitorial vision (as interpreted by Pegna) would also be made available to a much wider clerical audience.

At the same time, Pegna worked to complete a more focused short treatise specifically 'On the Expurgation of Books by Legal Experts, and the Abolition of Their False Dogmas' (*De expurgandis iuris consultorum libris abolendisque falsis eorum dogmatibus*). This was a fairly obvious piece of self-promotion, privately circulated in manuscript rather than print, and intended above all for the eyes of Cardinal Guglielmo Sirleto, then director of both the Vatican Library and the Congregation of the Index. Pegna's emphasis on 'expurgation', by which he meant the selective cutting of dubious passages from otherwise orthodox books (as opposed to simply placing them on an Index and banning them altogether), was very much a sign of the times and intended to demonstrate that he understood the challenges facing Index compilers at the end of the sixteenth century. Paul IV's sort of take-no-prisoners approach to censorship was increasingly seen as counter-productive as well as heavy-handed, even by hardliners, and ever since Trent there had been talk of supplementing the existing Spanish, Portuguese and Roman Indexes with new expurgatory ones.

Sirleto, a dedicated linguist and bibliophile, was undoubtedly sympathetic to the expurgatory project and duly impressed with Pegna's potential to contribute to it. The eager canonist from Aragon was finally permitted to serve as a consultor to the Congregation in 1584, and there he distinguished himself by clashing with more moderate colleagues such as the Jesuit scholar (and later cardinal, now saint) Robert Bellarmine. Revelling in his newfound powers, Pegna offered a particularly audacious critical assessment and extensive revision of the autobiographical *Commentaries* written by Enea Silvio Piccolomini (before he became Pope Pius II, r. 1458–64). Yet other Church censors had already begun to get bogged down under their heavy workloads by the end of the 1570s, and their collective efforts to complete a new post-Tridentine Index would grind to a total halt in the months leading up to Gregory XIII's death in 1585.

Scipione Pulzone, *Cardinal Guglielmo Sirleto*, 1568–73, oil on canvas.

The Congregation of the Index ceased meeting altogether soon after, and no further evaluations would be performed until 1587, under the new Pope Sixtus v. But when its work resumed, Pegna was right there at the front of the class, waiting to take up his censor's pen once more. He would assist with the compilation of expanded papal Indexes for both Sixtus v and Clement viii, and spent the rest of his long life fighting to make both the Congregation of the Index and that of the Roman Inquisition (reorganized by Sixtus v as the 'Supreme Sacred Congregation of the Roman and Universal Inquisition' in 1588) into truly formidable forces for the preservation of Christian orthodoxy.

Pegna's career was in many ways unique, but it provides a glimpse into key aspects of the changes that were to transform the Index of Prohibited Books, and Catholic censorship generally, for several generations after the closure of the Council of Trent. Under the direction of men like Sirleto, Pegna, Bellarmine and many others, the Congregation of the Index would become an increasingly sophisticated and specialized intellectual project. Though Protestant books could still simply be listed and condemned without any further need for close evaluation due to the 'heretical' identity of their producers (and Roman censors often simply used sales catalogues from the annual Frankfurt book fairs for precisely this purpose), expansion of Index censorship after the last decade of the sixteenth century increasingly required expert readers capable of discerning orthodox from heterodox (or morally objectionable) content – even in books by devout Catholics. Careful analysis and professional judgement were essential if sufficiently fine lines were to be laid out and maintained between pernicious works to be banned, perfectly acceptable works that could be permitted and an ever-expanding intermediate category of works that were for the most part valuable, yet noticeably marred by infelicities of style or substance.

Expurgation was to become an important feature of this work, at least theoretically, with Index Congregation members and invited specialists all weighing in on which portions of a text might require selective cutting, rewriting or other forms of editorial intervention before it could be cleared for broader circulation. But the continued exponential growth of the publishing industry, in Protestant as well as Catholic countries, ensured that the Congregation's personnel were regularly overwhelmed by the magnitude and complexity of their tasks. Cardinals like Agostino Valier were well aware of the problem and lamented the constant flow of new books to be censored. In his 1588 *Opusculum de cautione adhibenda in edendis libris* (Treatise on the Caution to be Applied in Editing Books), Valier wondering if it would *ever* be possible to stem the resulting tide of dangerous literature from overwhelming the best efforts of good Catholic censors, unless a total moratorium on book publishing could be imposed.

Pegna's experiences also demonstrate the inevitable overlap of offices that complicated Index management, especially in Rome. Heresy suppression (and thus censorship) remained a duty shared by members of the Congregation of the Inquisition as well as the

Congregation of the Index, and it was unclear which should predominate in cases of disagreement. Then there was the master of the sacred palace, the chief papal theologian, traditionally a Dominican, who had been entrusted with personal responsibility for subjecting all books printed at Rome to pre-publication review since at least 1515, long before the formation of either of the Congregations (which he now sat on *ex officio*). Popes themselves might also weigh in with strong opinions on which texts should be banned or expurgated, as could their favourites and protégés, along with many other Roman bureaucrats (such as Vatican librarians) who claimed expertise and therefore potential authority over the use of books. Jurisdiction over the discipline and judgement of the faithful was similarly held not only by the pope himself, and the Inquisition after 1542, but by religious tribunals such as the Rota court, where the seemingly ubiquitous Pegna sat as a judge (*auditor*) after 1588. With vitally important and complex issues at stake, this volatile assemblage of opinions, personalities and ambitions could (and did) easily turn into a perfect recipe for renewed eruptions of factionalism and bureaucratic infighting.

Under such circumstances it was hardly surprising that the intellectual Gregory XIII and his immediate successors, the stern Franciscan Sixtus V (r. 1585–90) and three other short-lived pontiffs (Urban VII, Gregory XIV and Innocent IX, together r. 1590–91), all failed to issue any new Indexes. A first attempt came to naught in 1584, a full twenty years after Trent, in part because Sirleto's draft was simply too long and complicated to be fully digested before the process was interrupted by a papal election and then the cardinal's own death in 1585. Sixtus' still more ambitious plans for a revised Index were similarly thwarted by his death five years later, but even if they had not it would have taken a lot of political pressure to force through his radical overhaul of the Tridentine Rules (which, according to his scheme, would have been expanded to a whopping 22 instead of the original ten). Sixtus' draconian prohibitions against the writings of many respected Catholic authors – including Robert Bellarmine himself, as well as the great Spanish legal scholar Francisco de Vitoria (d. 1546) – were also deeply unpopular. It would only be thanks to careful diplomacy and many compromises that a subsequent pope, Clement VIII (r. 1592–1605), was able to finally bring about substantial updates to the Tridentine Index in 1593 and 1596, effectively doubling the number of books explicitly prohibited by Roman authority, and adding a series of prefatory *Observationes* and *Instructiones* to clarify the Tridentine Rules. It would take nearly seventy years before another major revision to the Roman Index could be effected, ensuring that Clement's still rather modest little Index (less than a hundred pages in all, including appendices) would remain a more or less standard manual of Catholic censorship throughout the first two-thirds of the tumultuous seventeenth century.

Purging and Growing

Expurgation remained a daunting task at Rome, even after the Clementine Indexes were finally passed. Though mandated in the Rules of Trent, reinforced by Pius v's bull *Licet alias* in 1570 and successfully assayed at a local level by the Antwerp expurgatory Index of 1571, the Congregation of the Index simply failed to recruit and organize the sizeable cohorts of experts that would have been needed to properly fulfill this mandate throughout the first two decades of its existence. And when experts did finally start to weigh in on their assigned readings, the Congregation proved incapable of marshalling their varied opinions into a consistent and useable list of recommended edits. Yet the need for such a list was more urgent than ever. Comprehensive bans on all writings by Protestants, whether they touched on religious subjects or not, continued to generate widespread dissatisfaction since they deprived Catholic readers of access to important scientific innovations – even when experts could agree that the texts in question posed no real spiritual threat. Expurgation was also seen as a means of finally resolving problems such as the mingling of a few bad passages with many more good ones in the works of loyal Catholics such as Niccolò Machiavelli and Desiderius Erasmus, not to mention Pope Pius II. Some sort of expurgatory Index, devoted to providing guidelines for the correction rather than the total eradication of books, needed to be produced as soon as possible. Pope Clement recognized this, and provisions for such a future Index of expurgation were duly included in a new series of instructions 'On the Correction of Books', printed just after the Tridentine Rules in all copies of the Clementine and subsequent Roman Indexes.

But if it was difficult to achieve consensus on which books should be included in updated versions of the existing prohibitory Index, it ultimately proved impossible for Roman censors to do so when it came to the complicated task of poring over and suggesting emendations to thousands of pages of dense typescripts (mostly written in Latin, and mostly on intricate points of theology). Precedents from earlier expurgatory efforts in the Low Countries, Portugal and Spain were consulted, and scholars all over Italy and beyond were invited to assist in the thankless (and generally unpaid) work even as power struggles continued to fester between (and within) the Congregations of the Inquisition and the Index. But it still took time for contributions to be submitted, and when they finally arrived they were of varying quality and thoroughness. Moreover, they sometimes contradicted one another, or fell into what members of the Congregation believed to be errors of their own. And then there was the fact that different editions and varying paginations of the same text might make it impossible for readers to accurately locate the precise passages they were supposed to expurgate. Far from bringing truth and order to the world of scholarly writing, this new exercise in collaborative 'peer review' ran a strong risk of devolving into a chaotic morass of cross-purposes and one-upmanship.

Finally, in December of 1604, a decision was made to delegate oversight of the whole Roman expurgatory project to the current master of the sacred palace, Friar Giovanni Maria Guanzelli (also known by his place of origin, 'Brisighella'). Three years later, in 1607, he was satisfied with the expurgation of only fifty works – the results of which were drafted into a preliminary *Tomus primus indicis librorum expurgandorum* of over 740 pages. As its title indicates, this was intended to be just the first volume of an ongoing project that would dwarf all the comparatively slender Indexes that had been printed to date. But disagreements arose immediately, above all with the Index Congregation's secretary, Cardinal Paolo Pico, who thought that Guanzelli's edits still left too many problematic passages undisturbed. Although efforts were made to broker a settlement by which the *Index librorum expurgandorum* could be revised and brought out in a new format, Guanzelli had had enough and promptly left to become bishop of a peaceful seaside town in Apulia. His *Tomus primus* was twice printed, in 1607 and 1608, but never enjoyed official authority as a manual for the rehabilitation of proscribed books. Roman Indexes would continue to list books that were to be prohibited only 'until corrected' (*donec corrigatur*), on the presumption that an expurgatory index would someday clarify what corrections were in fact required, but no more formal papal guides to expurgation were ever produced. Emendations were instead performed on a case-by-case basis, with instructions often archived in Rome but difficult to access elsewhere, further complicating the history of Roman censorship in the early modern period.

This did not mean that the goal of regular textual expurgation was abandoned by any means; in Iberia especially, it flourished. In Portugal the Index of 1581, a relatively slender volume at less than a hundred pages, contained numerous expurgatory sections in its second half. In Spain too, centralization of censorship powers in the hands of an all-powerful inquisitor-general (ideally working in concert with an advisory council known as the *Suprema*) tended to make decision-making somewhat easier than in Rome. Inquisitor-General Gaspar de Quiroga thus managed to orchestrate publication of an entirely revised Spanish Index of Prohibited Books in two substantial volumes, one prohibitive, the other expurgatory, in 1583 and 1584 respectively. The first was a traditional but much expanded update to the Spanish Index of 1559, in a larger quarto format and weighing in at over two hundred printed pages compared to a previous 72. Its companion expurgatory volume was nearly double that length, with detailed 'corrections' to nearly a hundred books stretching across almost four hundred pages. These Portuguese and Spanish expurgatory Indexes were liable to criticism by other experts and they were certainly not adopted in Rome, but they had the virtue of actually being finished, and they long enjoyed official status in the Iberian territories and their colonies.

Quiroga's achievement set a new standard for future Spanish Indexes, while also ensuring that the Spanish and Roman Index traditions would continue to remain separate. An even larger folio-sized Spanish *Index librorum prohibitorum et expurgatorum* was published by Inquisitor-General Sandoval in 1612, this time combining over a hundred pages of prohibitions with 739 pages of expurgations (plus significant unpaginated ancillary material). Twenty years later (after publishing an initial addendum to Sandoval in 1628) it was Inquisitor-General Zapata's turn to oversee a *Novus index librorum prohibitorum et expurgatorum* that ran to well over 1,000 pages. In 1640 Inquisitor-General Sotomayor continued the trend with an even larger volume, and by 1667 the Spanish Index had reached a truly gargantuan scale at over 1,400 pages in length – all set in multiple, often tiny, fonts and typefaces. Meanwhile the Portuguese Inquisition had dropped out of the race in 1624 (having similarly attained over 1,000 pages), and Portuguese censors would thenceforth rely solely upon Roman Indexes for censorship purposes rather than crafting their own.

New Targets

Such attempts at expanding and refining the various Indexes (prohibitory and expurgatory, Roman and Iberian) occurred in parallel with other developments in censorship policy throughout the seventeenth century. Despite the frustration of figures such as Valier over the seemingly endless and ever-expanding backlog of books to be evaluated and censored (or purged), there were always those who wanted to add still more grist to the mill of censorship; sometimes presumably because of genuine outrage over the contents of a publication, but likely just as often also to impress clerical superiors with the strictness of their orthodoxy and thoroughness of their erudition. Once book censorship had become an accepted and (in official Catholic circles at least) respected endeavour, it was inevitable that new denunciations would continually be forthcoming, and that those tasked with performing the censor's work would be motivated to broaden the scope of their investigations. This was especially true once the dedicated full-time censorial bureaucracy of the Congregation of the Index had been put in place. Soon it was no longer sufficient to weed out Protestant theological errors, and new targets beckoned. Several important new categories of texts (and images) were eventually banned as a result, as will be examined at greater length in the second half of this book.

Yet even if we remain for now strictly focused on the sorts of problematic theological writings that first gave rise to the Indexes of Prohibited Books, this phenomenon of broadened censorship can easily be observed. Thus at the end of the sixteenth century, outright Protestant 'heresies' (which were in any case subject to a general ban under the Rules of Trent, and so no longer needed to be individually listed) were increasingly joined by more subtle and therefore troubling debates over orthodox doctrine withing the ranks of the Catholic clergy itself. In terms of sheer volume of documentation produced, for example, it is quite possible that the otherwise rather obscure *De auxiliis* controversy caused more work for consultants to the papacy, the various Inquisitions and the Congregation of the Index than any other single issue in the whole long history of the Index. This was a complex question, or series of questions, about the role of free will and grace in aiding (that is, providing *auxilium* to) human salvation. Luther had previously made the concept of salvation 'by grace alone' (*sola gratia*) a cornerstone of Protestant theology, as did Calvin and other Reformation leaders – to the point of arguing that one's prospects for salvation are all but predetermined (salvific faith being a gift of God, one either has it by God's grace or one does not). Catholics, for their part, tended to insist on the constant importance of free will and personal efforts to obtain salvation by the performance of 'good works' (including financial gifts to the Church), although they generally accepted that divine grace was also necessary in some form. But in this new iteration of the controversy, the disputants on both sides were all fervent Catholics. As a result the differences between their positions were subtle indeed; so subtle that popes Clement VIII and Paul V (r. 1605–21) both ultimately declared themselves unable to take a side in the debate, instead ordering everyone involved to simply stop arguing. Their equivocal decisions took years to arrive at, however, and a great deal of censorial ink was spilled in the meantime.

Trouble began with the teachings of Luis de Molina (d. 1600), a Spanish Jesuit whose emphasis on free will (as opposed to divine grace) became associated with a school of theology known as Molinism. His four-volume *De liberi arbitrii cum gratiae donis, divina praescientia, providentia, praedestinatione et reprobatione concordia* (On the Concordance of Free Choice with the Gifts of Grace, Divine Foreknowledge, Providence, Predestination and Condemnation) was published in 1588, and immediately caused consternation among Spanish Dominicans in particular. For most Dominicans, their medieval confrère Thomas Aquinas had already established an authoritative doctrine on the questions of grace and free will – orthodox doctrine that had served the Church well in its defence against Protestant heresies – and no fine-tuning was required. Furthermore, they worried that overly extreme trust in free will and personal good works could imply that ethical non-Catholics (and even 'good' non-Christians) might be able to go to heaven without benefit of formal membership in Christ's True Church. Pre-existing rivalries between Jesuits and Dominicans did not help matters. The pope soon became involved, and after much discussion Clement VIII at first despaired of a solution. By 1594 he had called for a moratorium on *De auxiliis* debates, at least for Spain.

Silence was not easily held, however, and in 1598 Clement was obliged to realize that further action was needed. Indeed such was the difficulty of the *De auxiliis* problem that, rather than turning to his own inquisitors or master of the sacred palace for an opinion, he actually convoked an entirely new Roman office, known as the Congregation on the Assistance of Grace (*Congregatio de auxiliis gratiae*), which would be devoted to holding learned examinations of the question. Among its participants was none other than Francesco Pegna, who left copious handwritten notes on the meetings, as well as the celebrated theological writers Tomás de Lemos and Diego Álvarez.[1] Yet after nearly ten years of arguments, and thousands of pages of writing, the parties were no nearer to resolution. After Clement's death another truce was called by the new pope, Paul V, in 1607. The Congregation was disbanded and in 1611 a formal ban on any further mention of the matter was imposed. In this case, the Church had actually decided to censor *itself*, and future issues of the Index would continually remind Catholics of this prohibition on an entire field of theological speculation.

⁓✢⁓

DEBATES INEVITABLY continued, sometimes in print form, not only on the *De auxiliis* question but on various other scientific and moral issues as well. The problem was, again, how best to approach the Sisyphean task of keeping track of books on an ever-expanding range of topics, and censoring them when necessary. Having essentially given up on the expurgatory project, the Congregation of the Index and its Roman allies therefore adopted a two-fold approach in the seventeenth century. It was expected that new Indexes would continue to appear at somewhat regular intervals, though perhaps not as regularly as in Spain, and that they would grow periodically as new authors and titles were added (but no longer with any pretence at trying to provide universal guidance for their detailed correction). A bewildering variety of printed Roman Indexes were produced as a result, with new and slowly expanding versions appearing in 1607,

1611, 1614, 1618, 1620, 1627, 1632, 1640, 1644, 1649, 1653, 1657, 1664, 1665, 1667, 1670, 1677, 1681, 1683 and 1685 (eventually reaching over five hundred pages in length). At first these were still simply re-editions of the Clementine Index of 1596, augmented from time to time by a few new prohibitions, and sometimes bound together with the canons of the Council of Trent. Some, such as the Krakow 1603 Index and various other versions produced in France and Germany, were specially issued for local use but still very much based on the Clementine model. It was not until 1664, the centennial anniversary of the Tridentine Index, that a real new effort was made to revise and improve the Roman Index of Prohibited Books as a practical tool for ongoing censorship.

The 1664 'Alexandrine' Index, named for its patron Pope Alexander VII (r. 1655–67), finally eliminated the confusing practice of nesting multiple alphabetical lists under each letter (Class One authors, partially censored authors and anonymous works listed by title), which had previously made searching for particular works on the Index quite an unreasonably time-consuming task. From now on prohibited authors (still listed by Christian or first names) and prohibited book titles would all be alphabetically listed in a continuous series; details regarding their date of first censorship were also provided in many cases. Noting that there had been no formal revision of the Index for several decades, but rather a hotch-potch of provisional updates sprinkled with incomplete appendices listing more recent bans, Alexander also announced that his new version would incorporate all the latest Roman censorship decisions. Yet the ambitious nature of this 1664 Index also led to other problems. Having grown to over four hundred pages in length, and with new condemnations appearing almost yearly, it proved impossible to alphabetically integrate all the new listings with the old; therefore not one but three separate alphabetical lists (the second two dealing with more recent additions) would ultimately be included in the Alexandrine Index, all bound up in a hefty quarto format. To this were added further appendices, a full reprint of the old Trent Index and copies of Roman censorship decrees that had been issued over nearly a century by popes, inquisitors, Index Congregation members and masters of the sacred palace.

While it was thus perhaps slightly easier to use the Alexandrine than previous Roman Indexes, once one became accustomed to its various components, it was no longer a handy pocket-volume. The 1664 Index, like the hugely complex Spanish Indexes that were also being produced in this same period, was meant primarily as a reference text, to be kept in an office along with other works of canon law and scrutinized by experts who might need access to full texts of censorship decrees and other supporting documents (rather than just lists of names and titles). It had thus evolved from a rather blunt-edged simple tool, carried by enforcers raiding bookshops or inspecting ships' cargos for Protestant contraband, into a sophisticated resource for the sorts of elite scholars who were now being tasked with the oversight and maintenance of Catholic censorship in a bewildering age of constant intellectual ferment.

Giovanni Battista Gaulli, *Pope Alexander VII (Fabio Chigi)*, 17th century, oil on canvas.

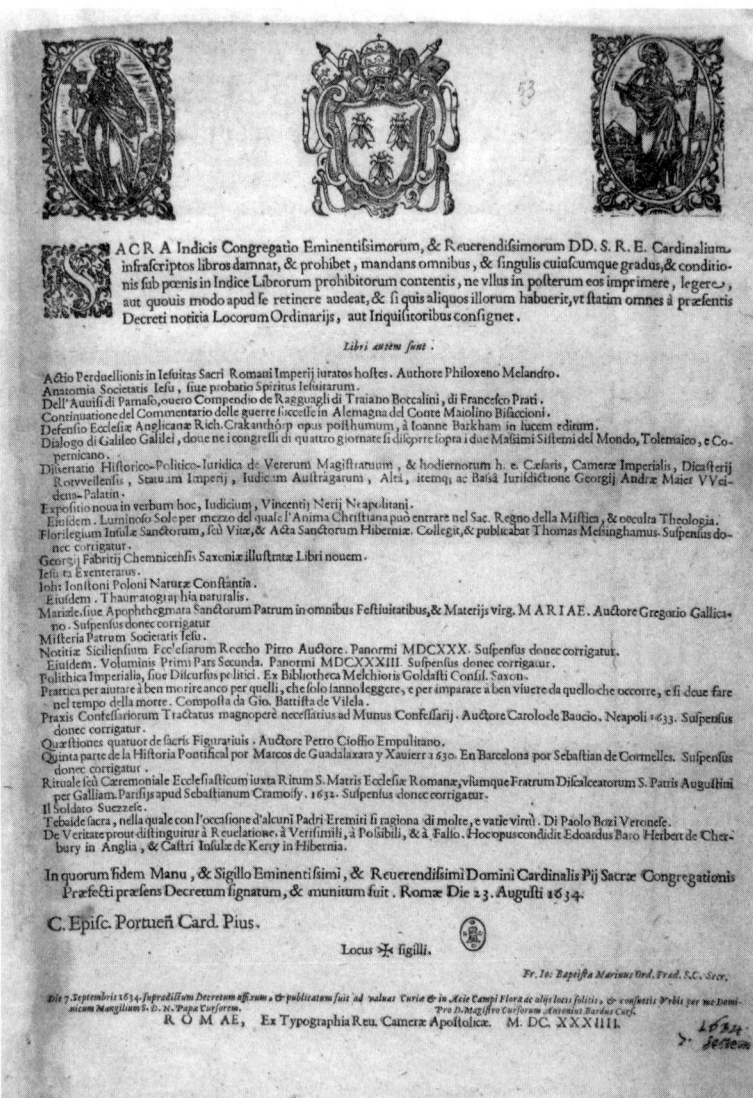

Censorship decree banning several books including Galileo's *Dialogo*, Rome, 1634.

The dozens of censorship decrees printed at the end of the 1664 Alexandrine Index represent a second means by which Roman authorities went about keeping their prohibitions up-to-date in the Baroque era. Rather than waiting for revisions to appear in a new Index, book prohibitions were posted as they became available in the form of special decrees issued by the Congregation of the Index; similar edicts could also be issued directly by the Congregation of the Inquisition, by the pope, by the master of the sacred palace and in a handful of cases by other Curial officers. These were simply announcements that a certain work or set of works had been banned. Signed, sealed, dated and sometimes (but not always) giving at least some indication of the issues that led to the prohibition, notices were also printed in large quantities as single-sheet broadsides suitable for reading out in public and posting on church doors or walls, as well as being archived (and reprinted in subsequent Indexes after 1664). Their distribution could thus be extremely wide, with individual copies sent as far away as the New World with instructions for subsequent reprinting and continued redistribution.[2] Such ephemeral posted copies were unlikely to survive for very long once exposed to the elements, however, and may not always have reached a wide audience as a result, soon becoming in many cases nothing more than an easily ignored backdrop of tattered and semi-legible old posters for parishioners to file past on their way to Mass. But they would presumably have at least drawn the attention of those most interested in book culture: those literate elites, clergy, students and intellectuals who were indeed anxious to know about the latest condemnations.

For specific examples of such edicts, and a sense of their importance, one can again look at how echoes of the *De auxiliis* debates continued to provoke both writing and censorship in the later decades of the seventeenth century. After a short period of resentful silence, controversy once more broke forth in the form of the so-called 'Jansenist' conflict. Cornelius Jansen, the theologian who started it all, was a Catholic bishop in the Spanish Netherlands who also taught at the University of Leuven until his death in 1638. He left a posthumous manuscript entitled *Augustinus*, in which he interpreted St Augustine's writings on Original Sin and the need for divine grace as strong endorsement for an anti-Molinist theology of predestination; that is, only those chosen by God would be saved, and God's primordial choice was unaffected by human decisions to do good works by means of free will. However, as a faithful son of the Church, Jansen was clear in his dying wish that he in no way wanted to deviate from the orthodox views of Rome. His book was to be subjected to scrutiny from expert Catholic theologians, and he submitted in advance to any changes that might be ordered by the Holy See. In other words, he literally *invited* censorship.

As it happened, publication of the *Augustinus* in 1640 poured new fuel on the smouldering embers of hard feelings that remained between Jesuits, Dominicans and other pious theologians with a stake in the *De auxiliis* issue. Jansen's friend and supporter Jean Duvergier had already been imprisoned by Cardinal Richelieu of France for his inflammatory preaching on the matter, and other influential writers such as the mathematician Blaise Pascal soon also entered the fray. The *Augustinus* enjoyed approval from the theology faculty at the University of Paris as well as Jansen's former colleagues in Leuven, but by 1642 (after an investigation by the Roman Holy Office) Pope Urban VIII intervened with a formal bull of condemnation entitled *In eminenti*. Without getting into the details of the theological issues at stake, Urban declared that Jansen's text violated the terms of Paul V's previous ban on continued *De auxiliis* discussions. Yet it took another 22 years for Cornelius Jansen to finally be placed on the revised Roman Index of 1664 (in list 1, under 'C'), along with Jean Duvergier (in list 2, under 'I' for *Ioannes*). During that intervening time, the prohibitions against Jansen would only have been known to those who were informed by means of either Urban's bull itself, or through further condemnations issued during the pontificate of Innocent X (r. 1644–55). One of these, a decree published by the Roman Inquisition in April 1654, covers three quarto pages as reprinted at the end of the Alexandrine Index. Curial authorities were clearly doing all they could to ensure that their basic message was received by good Catholic readers, even those who could no longer fully recall Clement VIII's sixty-year-old ban on *De auxiliis* debates: 'stop talking about Original Sin and predestination, and above all, stop reading books like Jansen's *Augustinus*.' But the Index itself was only one of their means of (rather belatedly) doing so; posted edicts were essential for more immediate results.

Suppression of Jansenist writings ultimately proved to be a long and frustrating process, as Jansen's supporters continued to ignore or reject the judgements of Clement, Urban, Innocent and their inquisitors. Pascal's *Provincial Letters* on the subject were pseudonymously published in 1656, and duly condemned for their pro-Jansenist arguments in yet another inquisitorial decree of 1657. This decree was widely circulated and later copied into the 1664 Index, and while Pascal was not named, his *Lettres* were indeed listed for prohibition

Benoît Farjat, 'Cardinal Enrico (Henry) Noris', engraving in Mario Guarnacci, *Vitae, et res gestae Pontificum Romanorum et s.r.e. Cardinalium*, vol. 1 (1751).

on the Alexandrine Index under 'E' (for their Latin title, *Epistolae decem & octo Gallico idiomate inscribantur*). Meanwhile, French royal censors also stepped in and ordered all copies of the *Lettres* to be destroyed by 1660. Then, in 1673, an Irish Italian cardinal named Henry (Enrico) Noris dropped another bombshell with publication of his *Historia Pelagiana* – a not-so-veiled attack on the

Molinists, whom he considered too close to the free-will assertions of the ancient heretic Pelagius. By now, things had changed in Roman theological circles. Pope Clement X (r. 1670–76) ultimately accepted Noris's arguments, after receiving him in personal audience. Far from being banned, Noris was instead named a *qualificator* of the Roman Inquisition; he was also assigned to serve as court theologian to Grand Duke Cosimo III of Tuscany, and later made a Vatican librarian. But as it turns out the anti-Jansenist Spanish Inquisition was less sympathetic, and though his name did not yet appear on the Spanish Index of Prohibited Books, a general consensus soon spread that Noris's writings were to be considered anathema by Spanish Catholics. Conflicts over Jansen's and Noris's orthodoxy (or lack thereof) would continue to rage – and generate new writings, including several flurries of edicts issued by both the Spanish and Roman Inquisitions, for decades to come.

Over the course of the seventeenth century, then, Catholic book censorship became an increasingly ambitious, sophisticated and wide-ranging enterprise that occupied the attentions of vast numbers of the Church's best and brightest minds. Far from just being an exercise in filtering out dangerous writings by medieval and Protestant heretics, as originally envisioned by kings and popes in the pre-Tridentine era, the compilation of new Indexes of Prohibited (and, at least in Spain, expurgated) Books had become an entire field of intellectual activity in which everything from Bibles, scientific treatises and novels (as we will soon see), to convoluted essays on the niceties of Catholic doctrine, could all be evaluated and wrestled over ad nauseam. Censorship efforts now overflowed the bounds even of the printed Indexes themselves, with formal decrees and broadside edicts being posted to church walls (and, undoubtedly, gathering dust in priests' offices) with increased regularity. These contributed to the Church's universal goal of tracking and accounting for every possible instance of objectionable writing. Yet for all that, confusion and misunderstanding remained. If even popes and inquisitors could not agree on the orthodoxy of books like Noris's *Historia Pelagiana*, instead issuing mixed messages and contradictory verdicts, then what were pious Catholic readers to do?

Piracy and Criticism

In fact, the complexities and inevitable shortcomings of global censorship were obvious to all involved, and critics were quick to lampoon the Catholic Index of Prohibited Books or put it to subversive use. Pirated editions of the Index were already being produced in the sixteenth century, in order to publicize and condemn the Catholic Church's censorship of what for Protestants were in fact perfectly 'good' books.³ Pier Paolo Vergerio raised the alarm as early as 1549, before the Venetian Index of that same year had even appeared, with a smuggled version of his own that was published by the Landolphi press in the remote Swiss village of Poschiavo; he later issued annotated 'Protestant' copies of other Index editions, including the rigid Pauline Roman Index of 1559, for the same purpose. Then, in 1586, a copy of the 1571 Antwerp expurgatory Index was published at Heidelberg along with a dedication to the Lutheran Duke John Casimir of Saxe-Coburg, and an introductory letter by the Calvinist theology professor Francis Junius (François du Jon) the Elder. This false Index would later be reprinted in Strasbourg (1599 and 1609), and Hanau (1611). The Saumur printer Thomas Portau similarly produced an unauthorized version of Quiroga's 1584 Spanish expurgatory Index in 1601, complete with his own introductory essay drawing attention to the sorts of harmless or trivial passages it sought to suppress. Another Protestant imprint, this time reproducing the 1612 Spanish Sandoval Index, was published at Geneva in 1619. Dedicated to the Palatine Elector Frederick v (grandfather to King George I of England), this edition featured an introductory letter by the prominent Genevan theology professor Bénédict Turrettini (d. 1631). None of these pirate editions seem to have resorted to falsification or extravagant reformatting to score their polemical points; simply providing Protestant readers with genuine copies of Spanish or Roman Indexes, along with prefatory letters of explanation, was evidently deemed to be damning enough.

The value of the Catholic Indexes of Prohibited Books for Protestant use went still further, beyond the fields of religious controversy. Thus in 1627 the first head of the Bodleian Library at Oxford University, Thomas James, obtained and reprinted his own version of the Catholic Index as a bibliographical resource. Noting that Index compilers had in fact done rather a good job over the years of listing

Gilbert Jackson (attrib.), *Thomas James*, 17th century, oil on canvas.

all the greatest works of Protestant scholarship, James urged his fellow librarians to use such efforts as a collector's guide – a wish list, as it were, of all the very best in contemporary theological writing. James's edition is actually a somewhat eclectic mix of Catholic Indexes, drawing on both Spanish and Roman exemplars, and combining their entries into a simplified alphabetical order. He also took pains to be as up-to-date as possible, even accessing Roman edicts that had not yet been incorporated into the official Index itself, the better to flesh out his plans for a theological research collection at Oxford.[4] In some ways, therefore, this Anglican co-optation of Catholic religious censorship actually anticipated some of the organizational reforms that would later make their way into the Alexandrine Index.

Roman Catholic officials were sensitive to such Protestant abuse of the Index, and they did all they could to prevent these sorts of embarrassing critiques of their (admittedly imperfect) censorship efforts. Pirated editions of the Index were, naturally, themselves banned – as a Spanish Inquisitorial edict of 1677 makes clear regarding yet another 1667 reprint of Turrettini's Geneva Index. But problematic editions printed for bona fide Catholic use also needed to be suppressed. As we have already seen with the failures of Roman Index production in 1557, and then again with the abortive Sistine Index of 1590 (not to mention the expurgatory fiasco of 1607), Church authorities had no qualms about quietly censoring their own Indexes whenever it was determined that these might cause scandal or other problems among the faithful. An unauthorized attempt in 1655 by the French Jesuit Thomas de Augustinis to publish a helpful digest entitled *Librorum omnium in sacrae indicis congregationis decretis prohibitorum ab anno 1636 usque ad annum 1655 elenchus ordine alphabetico digestus* (A List of All the Prohibited Books in Decrees of the Sacred Congregation of the Index from the Years 1636 to 1655, in Alphabetical Order) was thus banned by a decree of the Index Congregation in 1658 (and subsequently named in the 1664 Roman Index) on the grounds that it was, in fact, incomplete.

The above account is itself far from a complete summary of the many ways in which Indexes of Prohibited Books sometimes ended up embarrassing the Church rather than furthering its objectives of total control over religious and intellectual discourse. As the limits and challenges of global censorship continuously made themselves evident in the seventeenth and eighteenth centuries, and the errors and infelicities to be found in various Index editions continued to pile up, it was clear to many on all sides of the religious divide that the idea of seeking to control all forms of human writing, even if grounded in good intentions, smacked of hubris and absurdity. Shortened versions such as Augustinis's ill-fated work, or the more successful French Recollect Jean-Baptiste Hannot's handy *Index librorum prohibitorum ex magno indice Romano et appendice unica fideliter excerptus* (1714) continued to be published as informal efforts to make the Index more effective for local officials who lacked the elite training and resources of a Curial theologian. But it often must

OS LOS INQVISIDORES
APOSTOLICOS CONTRA LA HERETICA PRAVEDAD,

y Apoſtaſia, en la Ciudad, Reyno, y Arçobiſpado de Toledo, con los Obiſpados de Auila, Segouia, y Siguença, de los Puertos aca, por autoridad Apoſtolica, y ordinaria, &c. A todas, y qualeſquier perſonas de qualquier eſtado, grado, condicion, y preeminencia, ò dignidad que ſean, exemptos, ò no exemptos, vezinos, y moradores, eſtantes, y habitantes en eſta Ciudad de Toledo, y en todas las demás Ciudades, villas, y lugares del dicho nueſtro diſtrito, y a cada vno de vos, ſalud en nueſtro Señor Ieſu Chriſto, que es verdadera ſalud, y a los nueſtros mandamientos, q̃ mas verdaderamẽte ſon dichos Apoſtolicos, firmemente obedecer, y cumplir: ſabed que a nueſtra noticia ha venido vn libro de a folio, impreſſo en papel mas largo que lo ordinario, cuyo titulo es: *Index librorum prohibitorum, & expurgandorum, nouiſsimus pro Catholicis Hiſpaniarũ Regnis Philippi Quarti Regis Catholici, impreſſo Matriti ex Typographo Didaci Diaz, anno 1667, en 992. paginas, ſin las reglas generales, advertencias, y mandatos, è indice vniuerſal de Autores, que no tienen folios; por eſtar impreſſo ſin nombre de Autor, y ſin licẽcia del Excelentiſsimo ſeñor Inquiſidor general, y auerſe impreſſo fuera del Reyno, ſuponiendoſe falſamente eſtarlo en Madrid por Diego Diaz, año de 1667 y eſtar mandado en el indice expurgatorio del año de 1640. debaxo de graues penas, que ſin preceder expreſſamente licencia, no ſe pueda imprimir, ni traer impreſſo de fuera de eſtos Reynos, ni vſar de las tales impreſsiones eſtrangeras. Y la prefacion que eſta al principio del dicho libro Indice, impreſſo el dicho año de 1667 en ſeis hojas, que tiene por titulo, *Benedicti Turretini Sacrarum literarum profeſſoris, præfatio in Indicem, editæ anno 1619 in formæ Cathalogi D. Bernardi de Sandoual, Archiepiſcopi Toletani, Inquiſitoris Generalis*; porque en el dicho Indice expurgatorio del dicho año de 1640. el dicho Author con el nombre de Benedicto Turretino, eſtá prohibido por Herege Caluiniſta en la primera claſſe, ſin exceptuar obra ninguna ſuya, y la dicha ſu prefacion es vn libelo infamatorio, lleno de calumnias falſas, de mentiras, y de injurias contra los Tribunales del Santo Oficio de la Inquiſicion, y injurioſa a la Sede Apoſtolica, y al Santo Concilio de Trento, y toda ella es erronea, proxima hæreſi, ſediciola, eſcandaloſa, y piarum aurium ofenſiua. Y el prologo pequeño que eſtá antes de la dicha prefacion, y es ſu titulo, *Lectori ſalutem*; por ſer alabança del dicho Benedict. Turretino, y en aprouacion de lo que contiene dicha ſu prefacion. Y la que deſpues de ella ſe ſigue, cuyo titulo es, *Ex Franciſci Iunij præfatione in Indicem expurgatorij, cenſorum Velgij*; por ſer el dicho Franciſco Iunio Author condenado, herege Caluiniſta, y lo que refiere, ſobre ſer falſo, es injurioſo. Y el teſtimonio que eſtá conſiguiẽte a la dicha prefacion de Franciſco Iunio, que es ſu titulo, *Ex Dauidis Blondelli epiſtola præfixa libello, quo examinatur quæſtio de Ioanna Papiſſa, p.3. editionis Gallicæ, anni 1647*. y concluye diziendo, *Andreas Ribetus id ipſum confirmat, Clauaij S. Almaſij teſtimonio*; por ſer falſa la hiſtoria que refiere, y el apoyarla es injurioſo a la Sede Apoſtolica, y eſcandaloſo, y ſer el dicho Andres Ribero Author condenado, herege Caluiniſta; como tambien lo es el dicho Claudio Salmaſio. Y lo ſiguiente al dicho teſtimonio, que tiene por titulo, *Speciminis ergo ſubijcimus eorum quæ Inquiſitorum iuſſu delenda ſunt exempla*; por ſer lo que refiere falſo, y injurioſo al Santo Oficio de la Inquiſicion, eſcandaloſo, y temerario; el qual libro con lo referido, prohibimos in totum.

Iaſsimiſmo prohibimos in totum vn librito pequeño de a octauo en 44 hojas, eſcrito con letras Hebreas, impreſſo (ſegun parece de eſtar) in Venecia, M. DC. LXXIV. nella ſtamparia Bragadina, por Chriſtoforo Ambroſini, con lic. de Sup. Por eſtar impreſſo para el vſo de los Iudaizantes, y no poder tener otro vſo entre los Catholicos, y ſer lo que cõtiene vna inſtruccion de los puntos principales, en que conſiſte el Iudaiſmo, cortando el libro de la Sagrada Eſcriptura, y truncandola, por ſer ſu impreſsion en Venecia, donde ay Sinagoga.

Por tanto mandamos, que ninguna perſona de qualquier eſtado, calidad, ò condicion, ò dignidad que ſea, los pueda tener, leer, ò vender, manuſcriptos, ò impreſſos, aſsi de las dichas, como de otras qualeſquier impreſsiones, ni imprimirlos de nueuo, pena de excomunion mayor latæ ſententiæ, y de docientos ducados para gaſtos del Santo Oficio, con apercibimiento, que ſe procedera contra los inobedientes. Y mandamos, que de dia que eſta nueſtra carta fuere leida, y publicada, ò como de lla ſupieredes, en qualquier manera, haſta ſeis dias luego ſiguientes; los quales os damos, y aſignamos por tres terminos, y el vltimo por peremptorio, traigais, exibais, y preſenteis ante Nos, ò ante los Comiſſarios de eſte Santo Oficio, q̃ reſiden en los lugares de nueſtro diſtrito, para que nos remitan todos los dichos libros, y papeles arriba declarados, que aſsi tuuieredes, y manifeſteis los que otras perſonas tuuieren, y ocultaren. Y lo cõtrario haziendo, el dicho termino paſſado, los que contumazes, y rebeldes fueredes en no hazer, y cumplir lo ſuſodicho; hechas, y repetidas las dichas Canonicas moniciones en derecho premiſſas: Nos de aora que entonces, y de entonces para aora, ponemos, y promulgamos en vos, y en cada vno de vos las dichas perſonas, la dicha ſentencia de excomunion mayor, y os hauemos por incurſos en las dichas cenſuras, y penas, y os apercibimos, que procederemos contra vos a execucion de ellas, y como por derecho hallaremos. En teſtimonio de lo qual mandamos dar eſta nueſtra carta, firmada de nueſtros nombres, ſellada con el ſello de eſte Santo Oficio, y refrendada por vno de los Secretarios del, en la Sala de nueſtra Audiencia del Santo Oficio de la Inquiſicion de Toledo à _____ dias del mes de _____ de mil y ſeiſcientos y ſetenta y ſiete años.

Por mandado del Santo Oficio de la Inquiſicion de Toledo]

Nadie le quite, pena de Excomunion mayor.

Censorship edict regarding banned works (including a false imprint of the Index), Inquisición de Toledo (Spain), 1677.

have seemed a losing battle, and many inquisitors and censors likely approached their seemingly limitless and ever-growing responsibilities with a mingled sense of both awe and resignation. The mockery didn't help either. Change, once more, would be required if the Index project was to survive.

Enlightening the Index

By the early decades of the eighteenth century, Index reform was taking on a new urgency in Rome and elsewhere. While Protestant authors laughed, and Catholic censors struggled to find what they needed amid the seemingly endless processions of names, titles and appendices cluttering up their ever-growing Index and edict collections, European book culture itself was also rapidly changing. Such challenges would again require new approaches to censorship list management.

Encouraged and empowered by the continued spread of print technology, that double-edged sword that was both the greatest fear and the greatest weapon of inquisitorial censors, European intellectuals had reached new heights of prestige, influence and confidence by the turn of the eighteenth century. An emerging 'Republic of Letters' by now transcended national, linguistic and even (at times) religious borders, such that scholars writing in Paris, Madrid or Rome were often keenly aware of and deeply interested in the latest achievements of their colleagues in London, Amsterdam or Leipzig; not to mention new insights daily emerging from explorers and savants working in the Americas, Africa and Asia. Catholic scholars took part in many aspects of these developments, participating fully in the drive towards ever-greater reliance on human reason that was to define the 'Enlightenment', even while some of their colleagues decried what they took to be a faithless modern neglect of divine revelation. For the latter, new fads of physical experimentation and rational observation were all well and good until they threatened to undermine truths that should already be accepted on the simple authority of Church tradition.

Such concerns naturally impacted the evolution of the Index of Prohibited Books, whose Roman and Spanish series both continued to be updated and printed throughout the eighteenth century. There was a great deal of continuity, given the conservative views of many

Giuseppe Maria Crespi, *Pope Benedict XIV (Prospero Lambertini, 1675–1758)*, 1740, oil on canvas.

censors who felt that severity and comprehensiveness were required now more than ever. In Spain, the Indexes of 1707 and 1747 thus remained massive two-volume affairs, each well over 1,000 pages in length. Yet the advent of a modernizing Bourbon monarchy eventually forced extensive reorganization of the Spanish Inquisition's offices and procedures. The Spanish Index was significantly shortened and made easier to use in a three-hundred-page 1790 edition that was somewhat ominously titled the *Indice ultimo de los libros prohibidos* (Final Index of Prohibited Books), and it was clear that many at court would have preferred it if this were indeed the last such list to ever be produced. Meanwhile in Rome, the Congregation of the Index reached a new peak of its activity, issuing fresh editions of the Index in 1704, 1711, 1714, 1717, 1726, 1744, 1747 and 1752. Most of these were again merely reprints of previous editions. But they were also accompanied by ceaseless waves of bulls and edicts, publicizing and clarifying the papacy's concerns about all sorts of new texts and authors whenever these emerged from the presses of Europe and its colonies.

A first priority remained, as ever, the preservation of Catholic theological orthodoxy, and thus throughout the Enlightenment period echoes of past controversies continued to be heard. Pope Clement XI (r. 1700–1721) attempted to impose yet another resolution to the Jansenist debate with his 1713 bull *Unigenitus*, again enjoining silence on all parties for the good of Christian unity. The following year, Clement's new Index was unequivocal in its ban on several of the most important Jansenist and anti-Jansenist texts to have emerged over the course of the last century – apart from those by Henry Noris, who remained untouchable. In 1747, however, in the Spanish Inquisition's most ambitious Index to date, Inquisitor-General Pérez de Prado took the provocative step of condemning Cardinal Noris's *Historia Pelagiana* as a work of 'Class One' heresy. This was not the first time Rome and Madrid had differed on the need to censor a book written by a high-ranking Catholic leader (papal Indexes had long ceased to prohibit Archbishop Carranza's writings on the catechism, for example, while vindictive inquisitorial politics ensured that this disgraced prelate's name would never be removed from the Spanish Index).[5] But it was a bold move nonetheless. What remained to be seen was whether Pope Benedict XIV (r. 1740–58), would take the bait and once more re-open the seemingly endless Jansenist feud.

Benedict, born Prospero Lambertini in 1675, was in many ways a model pope of the Enlightenment. He was a lover of books who initiated cataloguing of the Vatican's huge collection of Oriental manuscripts, adding another 3,300 of his own volumes to its holdings over the course of his career. He also read Protestant books, and corresponded with 'enlightened' *philosophes* such as Montesquieu. As Benedict XIV, he granted a licence to print the collected works of Galileo in 1741, and subsequently removed the long-standing general prohibition against any publications dealing with the Copernican theories of heliocentrism (thus setting in motion events leading to Galileo's full rehabilitation by Church authorities in the nineteenth century). He opposed the enslavement of Indigenous peoples in the Americas (though his treatment of Jews and Africans was less favourable), and sought to reform many aspects of Christian life. But for all that he was also a stern theologian, devoted to traditional Thomism and fully convinced of the value of inquisitorial censorship. He had been trained as a canon lawyer and served at both the Rota court and the Roman Inquisition as a *consultor*. He also supported the canonization of Michele Ghislieri, the notorious inquisitor-pope Pius V, in 1712, and his correspondence makes it very clear that he had no patience for Spanish defiance of papal authority in the Noris case.

Censorship, for Benedict, was to be taken seriously and conducted with coordination and discipline – it must not be used as a means of scoring cheap political points, especially when these threatened to foster divisions within the Church. When Spanish inquisitors ignored his orders, the pope therefore had no qualms about going directly to the Bourbon king Ferdinand VI with an ultimatum. Ferdinand acquiesced, likely welcoming the opportunity to rein in some of his own more intransigent inquisitors, and knuckles were duly rapped. Noris's name would never again appear on any Index, and Spanish inquisitors quickly set to work scrubbing it from all copies of the 1747 Index. Once again, Catholic censors found themselves censoring their own work as well as that of others.

Benedict XIV subsequently devoted several years of his pontificate to a thorough reorganization of the Congregation of the Index. Proposing an entirely new constitution in his 1753 bull *Sollicita ac provida*, he identified abuses by Cardinal Passionei (whom he called a 'prideful despot' in censorship cases) and instead named Cardinal Querini as the new prefect for the Congregation.[6] The fruits of his reforms were evident in the innovative Index of Prohibited Books that was published to great fanfare in 1758. In a bid for greater efficiency and consistency, authors listed on this papal Index would appear for the first time since the 1550s in alphabetical order by surname (a practice also taken up in the Spanish Index of 1790). More importantly, Benedict added a series of new guidelines for the Congregation in this Index, including a copy of *Sollicita ac provida* as well as several *decreta* that would continue to appear in all subsequent Roman editions – the first major papal contributions to censorship principles since the days of Clement VIII. These clarified, for example, that certain categories of books (such as writings in support of Protestant heresy, debates over the authenticity of pseudo-Arabic lead plates discovered in the Sacromonte caves of Granada, or texts dealing with the *De auxiliis* controversy) were to be considered collectively prohibited and need not henceforth appear explicitly by either author or title on the Index.

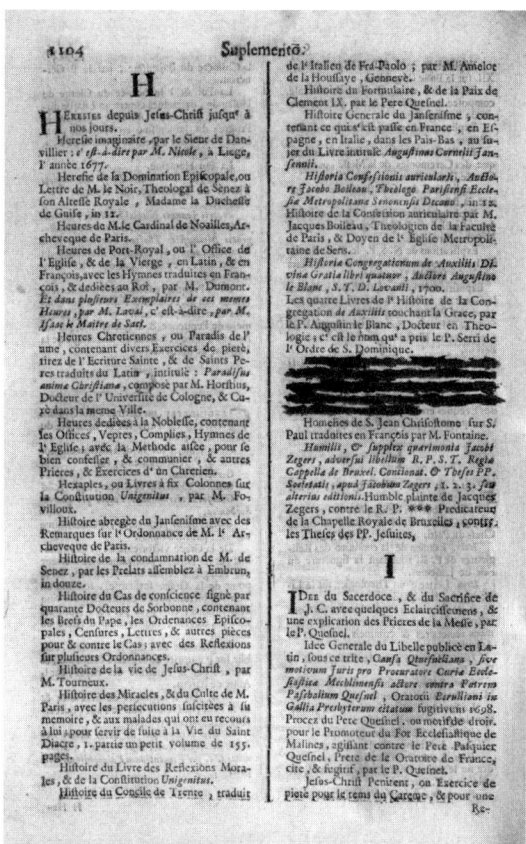

Sample page showing expurgation of a previous ban on works by Cardinal Enrico Noris, Spanish Index, 1747, vol. II, p. 1104.

Benedict's Index also reversed his predecessors' policy of perpetual growth. With only a single alphabetical list and fewer complications or ancillary documents than previous versions, the Index of 1758 was reduced to a mere 357 pages in length.[7] If some contentious new names had recently been added (including the great philosophers Baruch Spinoza and Gottfried Wilhelm Leibniz, along with the pious French archbishop François Fénelon), the pope now signalled that further additions to the Index of Prohibited Books would henceforth be subject to greater care and scrutiny.[8] A corner had been turned, at least for now; the Church, it seemed, was becoming more careful when choosing its battles, and moderate spiritual dissenters (as well as scientists who challenged accepted views on non-theological subjects) were no longer to be such clear targets as they once had been.

Science was in fact one of Benedict's passions, and he understood that the future of the Church depended on its ability to adapt to at least some aspects of modern thought rather than constantly railing against it. He granted licences to read forbidden books to several Catholic researchers and supported their work with greater enthusiasm than many of his predecessors, renewing Italy's reputation as a hub for experimentation in fields such as anatomy and medicine in the process. But there were always limits, and papal approval could be revoked when necessary, as was made evident in the case of Benedict's vacillating support for the Neapolitan aristocrat Raimondo di Sangro, prince of Sansevero (d. 1771). This colourful Enlightenment character was fascinated by a broad range of topics, from chemistry and biology to art and military strategy. He also dabbled in arcane knowledge, including alchemy and the secret teachings of the Freemasons. Benedict XIV was happy to support the prince's research at first, and to waive certain rules that might hamper the investigations of such an elite scientific mind; the spectacular family chapel of Sansevero (which remains a popular tourist attraction in Naples) provides striking evidence of his daring innovations. The prince also wrote extensively, with his 1750 *Lettera apologetica* (a learned if esoteric reflection on the possible meaning of Peruvian *quipus*) drawing particular interest from contemporaries. Ultimately suspicions about Sansevero's dabbling in the occult and in dubious masonic ideologies resulted in his fall from grace, but his fate was very different from what it could have been a century or two earlier. Raimondo di

Sangro was neither executed nor placed on the Index. Instead, after his writings were investigated by the Congregation of the Index, he was provided with pastoral advice on how to limit his behaviour in future – advice that he only partially accepted. He toned down the enthusiasm of his later writings but continued his research without papal support. The age of papal absolutism in terms of controlling Catholic scholarship had clearly waned, even in Italy – at least for elite members of the nobility.

Of course, as we will continue to see in later chapters, the prince of Sansevero was far from the only Catholic to dabble with alchemy, Freemasonry and other new forms of potentially 'heretical' thought in the eighteenth century. Notorious iconoclasts of the Enlightenment, such as Voltaire, Diderot and Rousseau, were all eventually placed on the Index (though in Spain, where inquisitors had apparently never actually seen any of his writings, a mis-transcription of the former as 'Bolter' in at least one condemnatory decree likely prevented some from ever realizing that Voltaire was in fact a prohibited author).[9] Thanks to the Index of Prohibited Books, classic texts of the French Enlightenment did become relatively hard to come by in many parts of Italy, Spain, Portugal and their colonies; in France too these books faced censorship as a result of their anticlericalism and atheism. However, the Church did not bear sole responsibility for such censorship. In France it was instead secular authorities that raided Diderot's office and threatened to destroy copies of the famous *Encyclopédie*.[10] More shockingly, it was a French secular tribunal that in 1766 sentenced the freethinking young nobleman François-Jean de la Barre to be publicly burned to death along with a copy of Voltaire's *Philosophical Dictionary* (which was brutally nailed to his chest as part of the execution).[11]

⸺✝⸺

AFTER TWO HUNDRED YEARS, then, the Index of Prohibited Books had grown from a set of small, localized handbooks listing a few dozen Protestant and otherwise objectionable writers, into massive (and in Spain, multi-volume) compendia in which nearly every conceivable type of book and author might be categorized, condemned or amended. By the mid-eighteenth century, however, that evolution took a new turn as the Index once again became a more coherent and manageable guide. Throughout, its overall purpose remained the same: warning devout Catholics to stay away from a wide range of suspect literature, or at least to apply for a licence from their bishops if total avoidance was not possible. But over time learned scholars such as Francesco Pegna and Prospero Lambertini became increasingly central to the Church's censorship apparatus, and their work became far more complex and nuanced than when it had simply been a matter of identifying Protestant theological ideas. Some of these experts agonized for years over whether, and how, to cut or rewrite passages from dubious books in hopes of preserving the bulk of their contents for future generations of readers. Others wrestled with the contested orthodoxy of Catholic Molinists, Jansenists and enlightened *philosophes*. Throughout, paperwork piled up, engorging not only fat leather-clad tomes of the Index itself but the edict-covered notice boards of local churches, and the archives of the various Inquisitions and Roman Congregations.

Contradictions and complications also piled up, at times threatening to undermine the whole Index project and expose it to the very sorts of ridicule and attacks that censorship was supposed to forestall. And human nature being what it is, sharp differences of opinion led to internal conflicts within the Congregation of the Index

Four stages of the Roman Index's physical evolution: (L–R) Tridentine (1564), Clementine (1596), Alexandrine (1664) and Benedictine (1764).

itself, as well as among the various popes, inquisitors and consultants who felt entitled to have their censorial voices heard. Pegna's fierce rivalry with Cardinal Bellarmine would be repeated by different protagonists, in difference circumstances, throughout the entire long history of the Index of Prohibited Books. The parallel and sometimes competing Indexes of the Spanish and Roman branches of the Church exposed further flaws in the Catholic hierarchy's claim to hold a monopoly on truth; even popes sometimes found themselves having to revisit the decisions of predecessors whose earlier condemnations began to seem ill-considered with passage of time and the benefit of hindsight.

Yet these struggles were not for nothing. They reflected, for the most part, the sincere efforts of exceptionally educated minds that had been tasked with a nearly impossible objective: the classification and correction of all human knowledge. And while their work might have been ultimately doomed to failure, these same minds left indelible stamps on intellectual history right alongside those of the authors they censored. In passing their judgements, they prevented some works from circulating in some times and places; they altered the contents of others and so impacted the way in which even classic texts were read; and they permitted still other texts, including some that would likely have been summarily burned if they had come before less considerate judges, to be passed on to subsequent generations relatively unharmed. The arguments they held, and the agency they exercised, for good or for ill, made a real difference. It is therefore important that we continue to examine the fine details of their work whenever possible, to gain a better sense of exactly what sorts of censorship were enacted by whom, and when, where, how and why.

4
HOW TO BAN A BOOK

On 29 July 1662, a Belgian Dominican named Joannes Baptista Verjuys sent a small package to Friar Leonard Hansen, a German colleague then resident in Rome.[1] In it he included a copy of the title page to a recently printed book that had attracted his attention. It was neatly trimmed to fit the envelope he was using, and read:

THE TRIUMPH OF LOVE AND THE LADDER OF GLORY.
OR, THE UNIVERSAL MEDICINE OF SOULS.

By Saint Ramon Llull, Martyr & Hermit
of the Third Order of Saint Francis.

Spiritual treasure or incomparable and admirable Book, which could (after Holy Scripture) be called the Book of Books, necessary to all sorts of persons both Secular and Regular: Containing the true path of the Heavenly Kingdom, & the Touchstone for all devotions of the past, present, and future, to the end of the World.

Dedicated to Saint Ramon Llull, Martyr.

Translated from Latin into French, and newly brought to light
BY JEAN D'AUBRY of Montpellier, Priest,
Abbot of Our Lady of the Assumption,
Counsellor and regular Physician to the King.

Also included in the envelope was Joannes Baptista's one-page cover letter, laying out his concerns in tiny, scrawled handwriting. The Dominican Father had grave suspicions about the orthodoxy of this new book on the 'triumph of love' (*triomphe de l'amour*), and in particular he felt certain that its author, the medieval mystic Ramon Llull, was neither a saint nor a martyr as the enthusiastic French translator of the text seemed to make out. Furthermore, Verjuys had

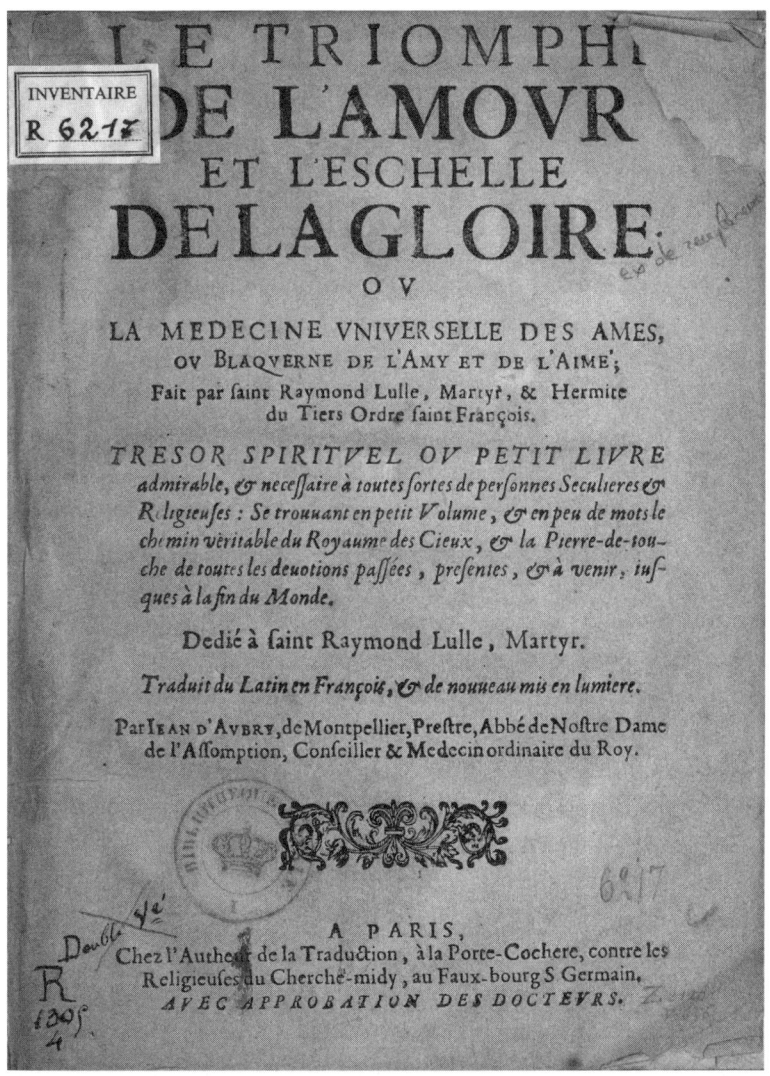

Title page for Ramon Llull, *Le Triomphe de l'amour et l'eschelle de la gloire*, trans. Jean d'Aubry (Paris, n.d.).

read in Abraham Bzovius's authoritative multi-volume Church history, the *Annales ecclesiastici*, that Llull's many errors had previously been condemned as heretical by the medieval pope Gregory XI – acting on the advice of one 'Aymeric [that is, Nicholas Eymeric], an inquisitor of our Order'.[2] Surely something should therefore be done to correct the *Triomphe de l'amour*'s misleading representation of such a dangerous author?

This letter was not just an innocent bit of gossip among friends or an exchange of arcane book trivia between academic colleagues (though it may have been that too). It was a denunciation to the Roman Inquisition. Leonard Hansen was in fact a leading figure in the great convent of Santa Maria sopra Minerva, one of the Dominicans' main headquarters and a base for the Roman Inquisition, where he served both as titular head of the exiled English Dominican Province and as *socius* (a sort of companion and lieutenant) to the Order's master-general. Hansen was also a celebrated theologian in his own right. He had the connections to pass on interesting tips about suspect writings, and to ensure that they got into the right hands for processing. Verjuys's letter was thus duly forwarded on 17 September 1662 to Petrus Franciscus de Rubeis, a respected Roman canonist and *consultor* to the Holy Office who would soon go on to be named a papal *fidei promotor* (or promoter of the faith, the so-called 'Devil's advocate' in canonization hearings). De Rubeis's dense four-page handwritten evaluation, along with the original title page, cover letter and wax-sealed envelope from Brussels, are all still held today at the Archive of the Congregation for the Doctrine of the Faith in the heart of Vatican City. It is the last of 41 case files contained in a huge bundle of documents from the C. L. section (*Censurae librorum*) for 1661–2, all wrapped up in brittle yellowing parchment and secured by two thick brown leather thongs.[3]

The surviving records of the *Triomphe de l'amour* investigation present us with a small but fascinating window into the actual practice of inquisitorial book censorship, at a time when the Index of Prohibited Books had reached the height of its comprehensiveness and power. Here we have a newly printed edition of a very old text, by a medieval author (Llull) whose name did *not* appear on current versions of the Index, but whose works were reputed to have been condemned centuries before (by Nicholas Eymeric, whose verdicts had more recently been recycled thanks to Francesco Pegna and those quoting from him, such as Bzovius). Having been translated into French and privately published in Paris, apparently with the approval of two members of the university theology faculty, this small 101-page book of spiritual poetry likely would never have come to the attention of either Spanish or Roman inquisitors if it had not been for the efforts of a watchful French-speaking informant like Verjuys. Exactly how (and why) the book came into his hands remains unclear, and unfortunately the informant's motives are not fully spelled out in his terse denunciation. Was he genuinely offended or threatened by the idea that someone had mis-identified a long-dead Catholic mystic as a saint? Had he actually read the book, and become concerned about its potential to mislead others in important matters of faith? Or was he simply trying to score points against rivals from other Catholic religious Orders, such as the Franciscans or Jesuits, who tended to take a more positive view of Llull's writings than did the Dominicans? His casual mention to Hansen (a fellow Dominican) that Llull had been condemned by an 'inquisitor of *our* Order' might suggest something of the latter, but of course mixed motivations are also possible.

Either way, the first step in bringing this case forward was to send evidence to Rome. Presumably, that was a calculated choice; as a subject of King Philip IV, ruler of the Spanish Netherlands, Friar Joannes Baptista could have sent his complaint directly to the Spanish *Suprema*. But perhaps he felt this would be ill-advised, for although Philip IV showed few signs of any particular theological interest or religious zeal, Spanish monarchs had traditionally supported Llull's writings whenever these were threatened with condemnation. Spanish inquisitors were generally reluctant to re-open the file on Llull as a result, and probably would not welcome this particular denunciation. Bypassing the Spanish Inquisition, and going straight to a trusted senior Dominican in Rome, was therefore an understandable decision for Verjuys to make.

As with many other cases preserved in the Roman *Censurae librorum* archive, there is no longer any sign that an entire copy of the work in question was ever provided by the original informant. Rather, Friar Joannes Baptista chose to send only a cut-out title page, presumably in hopes that Roman censors would be able to obtain their own copy if necessary for further scrutiny. The trouble and expense (not to mention potential criminality) of shipping bulky volumes of suspect literature from one end of Europe to the other likely made this a common practice, though actual copies of other books do seem to have been sent to the censors on occasion – books that have since for the most part simply been lost, destroyed or absorbed into other Vatican collections. In this case, however, consultation of the book in question does not seem to have been deemed necessary at all.

In his final evaluation, there are no indications that Petrus Franciscus de Rubeis ever bothered to examine the contents of the *Triomphe*, which turn out to be a fairly straightforward translation of Llull's short collection of mystical love poetry, originally written in Catalan under the title *Llibre d'amic i amat* (Book of the Lover and the Beloved). Nor did the *consultor* bother to ask the Parisian professors Jean le Comte and Robert Bertelot why they had provided an *imprimatur* permit for Jean d'Aubry's translation of this work; and he certainly didn't bother to bring this possible censorship case before the Congregation of the Index. Instead, our Inquisition consultant focused solely on the question of whether Llull was in fact a martyr and a saint, using the standard historical and legal reference sources available to him in Rome: chiefly Bzovius, and the Irish Franciscan Lucas Wadding's eight-volume *Annales minorum* (1625–54), as well as records of a previous investigation into Llull's orthodoxy that had already been conducted by the Holy Office back in 1583. De Rubeis also made a point of going straight to Nicholas Eymeric's *Directorium inquisitorum*, where he carefully checked what this authoritative 'inquisitor ordinis nostri' (and his editor Francesco Pegna) had to say about the matter. In the end de Rubeis' judgement was mixed, but not likely to please the Dominicans: Llull was indeed a martyr (having been allegedly stoned to death by Muslims during a missionary trip to Tunisia), but he had not yet been catalogued among the recognized saints of the Church. Calling him a saint was therefore indeed an error, but this was evidently not enough to place Llull, his translator or the *Triomphe de l'amour* on either the forthcoming Roman (Alexandrine) edition of the Index, or on any subsequent Spanish ones. Both Joannes Baptista Verjuys and Leonard Hansen went on to pursue other interests, and as far as we can tell nothing further was said or done about the matter.

Roman Rules

This single example by no means reflects 'standard practice' for Roman Catholic book censorship, since such a thing cannot really be said to have existed – certainly not in the sixteenth or seventeenth centuries, at any rate. More high-profile, controversial or sensitive cases might well have involved formal evaluations by many more consultants like de Rubeis, who as we have seen were known as *consultores* (*consultori* in Italian) or *qualificatores*. Such expert theologians, whether in their formal capacity as members of the Church hierarchy or merely on account of their scholarly reputations, had been assigned to read books and pass on their opinions to inquisitors since the Middle Ages on an ad hoc basis. In the sixteenth century it became common for Roman cardinal-inquisitors to have recourse to at least the judgement of the master of the sacred palace, and perhaps two or three other *consultori* – such as Francesco Pegna – before engaging in their own debates over a work's orthodoxy. Such debates, often held in the presence of the pope during the weekly Thursday gatherings of the Roman Inquisition, could sometimes stretch over many sessions and drag out for months if not years. Many (though by no means all) skeletal records of these debates can still be found in the Congregation for the Doctrine of the Faith archives (ACDF) – at least for the period after the near-total destruction of the Holy Office's records at Paul IV's death in 1559, and above all after more or less regular minutes began to be kept after the turn of the seventeenth century.

After 1571 potential cases for censorship might also be heard by the Congregation of the Index, though this organization often remained subordinate to the Inquisition and was not infrequently obliged to simply accept the inquisitors' decisions without further ado. And if a book did make its way to the Congregation of the Index its examination might have to wait, sometimes for months or even years, before finding its way onto the agenda for what were often infrequent and poorly attended meetings. Minutes taken by the secretary of the Congregation were filed in what are today the *Protocols* section of the ACDF archive. While these records rarely reveal very detailed accounts of the arguments for or against the censorship of a given work, early studies have suggested that they can provide rare insight into the divisions and complications that arose from time to time among members of the Congregation. More research into such newly accessible files will undoubtedly continue to provide further insights into the behind-the-scenes functioning of early modern Roman censorship in the near future.

The relatively swift evaluation and benign treatment of Jean d'Aubry's otherwise obscure translation of Llullian poetry in the *Triomphe de l'amour* certainly contrasts with the harshly intolerant suppression of Protestant writings over the previous century-and-a-half, as well as more recent agonizing treatments of Cornelius Jansen's *Augustinus* – or that of many others which could easily be listed. Neither the Inquisitions nor the Congregation of the Index were always consistent in the rigour of their analyses. But in many ways this case does align with the Rules that had been set down in the first Index of the Council of Trent, and which were copied into all subsequent editions of the Roman Index.

The ten Tridentine Rules (*Regulae*) of 1564 were quite broad, even vague, but they did provide at least some general guidance for those who wished to participate in the Church's ongoing censorial labours. Though expressed in sometimes florid Latin, essentially they called for the following:

> 1. All books condemned by popes or Church Councils before the year 1515 should *ipso facto* be considered banned, even if not included on the Index.
> 2. All books by heresiarchs or other leaders of heresies that had arisen *after* 1515 should also be considered banned (a list of such heresiarchs, all Protestants, was included).[4] The same applied to the writings of lesser heretics and lapsed Catholics, but only if they touched on religious topics, or lacked specific approval from appropriate Catholic authorities.
> 3–5. Certain versions of biblical texts, in various languages, were also to be banned, along with interpretive texts including prefatory materials and concordances, while others were deemed acceptable (these complicated regulations will be more fully explained later, in Chapter Five).
> 6. Accounts of theological debates between Catholics and Protestants were not to be translated or circulated in vernacular languages.
> 7. A general ban on lascivious and obscene books.
> 8. A note on the expurgation of books, which could make certain particularly valuable texts available to Catholics once objectionable sections were removed or re-written.
> 9. A general ban on books of magic and divination.
> 10. A reminder of Pope Leo x's 1515 bull *Inter sollicitudines*, requiring prior censorship and licensing for any books to be printed with the approval of the Church.

Running quickly through these, it soon becomes apparent that Ramon Llull's writings (along with those of many others who *did* in fact eventually end up on the Index) were not really among those anticipated by the Tridentine Fathers as key targets for Church censorship – unless, of course, one could prove that they had been condemned by a pope prior to 1515. That was precisely what Verjuys's letter sought to do, though his invocation of Eymeric and Bzovius was undermined by the fact that others had already examined the alleged condemnations of the medieval Pope Gregory XI and found them to be invalid. A more tenacious censor might also have looked more closely to see whether there was any heretical, obscene or magical content in the *Triomphe de l'amour*, or checked with Parisian authorities to see whether its local printing licence was in fact legitimate (the work does claim a licence, but it is undated and does not give a printer's name). But such detailed investigatory work was unlikely to be undertaken by busy Roman consultants, especially when they involved relatively minor publications that were being circulated far away, in foreign vernaculars like French.

After Sixtus V's failure to implement more substantive changes (including his proposed new set of 22 Rules), the Tridentine Rules were supplemented in 1593 by further observations, instructions and guidelines drawn up under Pope Clement VIII.[5] These 'Clementine' additions involved clarification of Rules 4 and 9 above all, as well as specific notes on the censorship of certain Jewish books. They also went into further detail on the duties and procedures appropriate to censors, expurgators and printers. Additional minor alterations and additions can be found in the later seventeenth-century Alexandrine Index, and a lengthy new constitution was drafted by Benedict XIV for inclusion in his 'enlightened' 1758 version as previously discussed in Chapter Three.[6] But for the most part all these later documents merely reinforced the basic priorities established at Trent: to ensure that appropriate official Church oversight should be given to half-a-dozen categories of writings on topics that were of particular sensitivity in the context of the Protestant crisis. Responsibility for weeding out and controlling circulation of medieval heresies, Protestant theological ideas, misreadings of Scripture (especially by Protestants, but also by Jews and others) and immoral or diabolical books, was to be shared by all Catholics. But ultimate authority was clearly to reside in the hands of papal officials, local bishops and inquisitors.

Rules in Action

Making rules was one thing, but practical means also had to be found to ensure their enforcement. As previously noted, the authority to censor any problematic books that might come to their attention was originally exercised on an ad hoc basis by local bishops and inquisitors (as well as secular authorities) across medieval Christendom; to the extent that Rome took any generalized responsibility for supervising the censorship and banning of books, this was understood to fall within the purview of the master of the sacred palace. And at first, simply responding to denunciations and scrutinizing new works prior to publication seemed to be effective enough. In theory, all books printed after 1515 in Rome itself were supposed to undergo pre-publication licensing at the hands of the master of the sacred palace, while similar *censura praevia* was supposed to be enforced by local Church (and secular) officials in other cities – as apparently was done by Parisian university professors in the case of the *Triomphe de l'amour*. The requirement of a licence to print any new text remained a fundamental check on all book publication throughout the early modern period, and continues today with the practice of granting formal statements of approval to many Roman Catholic religious texts. The Latin words *imprimatur* (let it be printed) and *nihil obstat* (nothing prevents (it)) can still be found on the first pages of theological works that have been duly approved by Church authorities, though nowadays of course Catholic writers also have the option of publishing with non-Church presses, and without Church approval, if they so wish. Members of Catholic religious Orders have an additional duty to seek permission of their superiors before publishing on religious matters.

Yet in the sixteenth century, as today, rules were not always followed. The circulation of unlicensed books, and of books suspected of bearing false licences, was never really stemmed by *Inter sollicitudines*, and the situation only worsened with the emergence of Protestant communities which actively rejected the Catholic hierarchy's censorship rights. The exponential growth of the book trade itself combined with an explosion of Protestant creativity to flood the markets of Europe with unauthorized writings from the 1520s on. The flourishing annual book fairs of Frankfurt became major sites for the diffusion of such works, as did several Protestant-controlled cities in Switzerland and the Low Countries, but subversive books were also imported quite openly into Catholic countries until the 1540s at least. In nominally Catholic centres such as Venice, Paris and Lyon, too, where many printers harboured Protestant sympathies and felt relatively protected by the growing economic power of their profession, controversial books were often produced with little or no regard for the Church in these early decades. This was, of course, part of the reason for the development of censorial indexes in the first place.

The advent of handy printed Indexes of Prohibited Books allowed local Catholic authorities to be more confident and vigorous in their efforts to prevent the importation of banned materials, and while many of their activities went undocumented there is plenty of evidence for successful book raids in Venice above all. There, after initial hesitation, a council of inquisitors and representatives of the noble elite (the *Tre Savi sopra eresia*) collaborated after 1547 to identify transgressors and bring them to justice, using their own local Index at first (as printed in 1549 and 1554) before adopting that of Trent in 1564. Index in hand, priests accompanied port officials in regular searches of cargo vessels, and they also conducted occasional sweeps of suspect private libraries as well as print-shops and booksellers. For the most part, those found guilty of producing or selling banned books were assigned monetary penalties and suffered the loss of their confiscated stock, which was periodically burned in the Piazza San Marco or near the Rialto. But in at least two separate late sixteenth-century cases, involving a bookseller named Pietro Longho and a doctor known as Girolamo Donzellini, unrepentant confessions of book smuggling led to execution in the distinctive Venetian style. Both men were taken out of the city at night, tightly bound and dropped into the sea – never to be seen again.

Venice's strict enforcement of the Index waxed and waned over the years, as did that of other regions. It is impossible to generalize about the real effectiveness of inquisitorial and other efforts to suppress the circulation of banned books, since this depended on many local factors which changed over time. Often, port officials and Church leaders grew lax in their efforts as other priorities arose to take up their attention. Smuggling flourished as a result, especially when it came to the relatively easy and lucrative shipment of illicit books (sometimes disguised with false title pages that could easily pass under the noses of all but the most careful examiners). Yet political circumstances sometimes led to strict crackdowns in which the full powers of Church and state might be combined to ensure rigourous surveillance and strict punishment. Donzellini's and Longho's experiences in 1587 and 1588 respectively, like that of Michel de Montaigne (whose books were famously confiscated and subjected to expurgation as soon as he entered Rome in 1580), occurred during a particularly fraught decade when Catholic authorities were very much on the *qui vive* for intrusions of Protestant influence. Confiscations continued from time to time thereafter, as for example occurred when the Amsterdam-registered vessel *Romana* was raided off the coast of Naples in 1643 on suspicion of transporting Hebrew books to Lisbon.[7] But such shipments continued, and by the eighteenth and nineteenth centuries it was becoming increasingly clear that anyone who wished to do so was able to obtain prohibited reading materials without too much difficulty. The task of constantly monitoring every ship's cargo and bookstore, let alone private collections, was simply too great for the limited numbers of qualified agents who could be assigned to its execution – especially using the unwieldy Index tomes they would have had to lug around by the middle of the seventeenth century.

―✠―

SHIFTING HISTORICAL REALITIES thus led to a wide variety of practices, and fluctuating degrees of strictness in enforcement, over four centuries of Index censorship. This is not surprising, and it should not lead us to be dismissive of the relative coherence and ever-increasing sophistication of institutionalized efforts, in Rome above all, to at least *theoretically* follow established rules in order to ensure that books and other cultural productions (along with their authors) received fair and principled evaluations before being definitively suppressed. With the establishment of a permanent Roman Inquisition in 1542 and then a Congregation of the Index in 1571, as we have seen, multiple sets of expert eyes were made available in a serious attempt to assist the pope and his master of the sacred palace as they struggled to fulfill their censorial duties. Weekly meetings of the Inquisition involved up to a dozen cardinal-inquisitors at a time (though quorum requirements fluctuated), along with expert assistants and often the pope himself. The Congregation of the Index's more irregular meetings, too, were in principle to be attended by as many as seven cardinals, nine councillors, a secretary and the master of the sacred palace. Additional consultants could be also brought in from time to time; Sixtus v's 1587 bull *Immensa* specifically directed the Congregation to consult with university professors from Paris, Leuven, Bologna and Salamanca whenever necessary. These were not insignificant resources, and when fully engaged the degree of spiritual and intellectual weight they could apply to a problem was considerable.

Nor, as we have seen in the case of the *De auxiliis* and Jansenist controversies, were all decisions either rubber-stamped or dealt with as summarily as was the *Triumph of Love* investigation. High profile texts in particular, such as Giordano Bruno's various books, King James of England's *Apologia* or Galileo's *Starry Messenger*, required multiple sessions of consideration and sometimes heated debate before verdicts could be rendered.[8] In particularly contentious cases, opposing factions might clash fiercely. These were exceptional, however, since for the most part the various Roman censorship authorities seem to have been able to achieve a working consensus on just where and when censorship was most needed – especially when dominated by a strong pope. Since the cardinals of the Inquisition tended to be closely advised by Dominican theologians of the Santa Maria sopra Minerva convent (from whose ranks the master of the sacred palace was also selected), and held many of their meetings there, they tended to be more or less on the same page regarding most issues; the recording secretary of the Congregation of the Index was also normally a Dominican. Personal rivalries aside, collaboration between inquisitors and the Index Congregation was similarly facilitated by the fact that all involved were members of the relatively tight-knit Roman Church hierarchy. They vied for the same sorts of patronage and related offices, and the most successful therefore soon learned how and when to compromise with their fellows. The political costs, or opportunities, of taking a stand against other hierarchs was always a factor to be considered in every verdict taken on a given work, right alongside any objective doctrinal merits or flaws which might be found in its content.

It is thus difficult to generalize about the sorts of procedures that actually resulted in the placement of books on the various Indexes throughout the centuries, and it is unhelpful to assume that all cases were handled either mindlessly, ruthlessly or expeditiously. We can only point to illustrative examples, slowly building a series of composite pictures in hopes of capturing at least some of the different ways in which Index censorship worked in a given context. New research will undoubtedly soon enrich this series, but the Roman Inquisition's *Censurae librorum* dossier for the years 1661 and 1662 alone (where the *Triomphe de l'amour* documents reside) may serve as a convenient starting point. This massive folder opens, for example, with a simple manuscript note and printed edict of Pope Alexander VII, unilaterally condemning a new French translation of the *Missale Romanum*. A little later, there is a rather longer series of documents (numbered as folios 38–54) from the inquisitors' review of a multi-volume Dominican treatise on the *Summa theologiae* of St Thomas Aquinas. This case had been dragging on since 1658, twenty years after the book's initial publication at Venice (presumably with all the usual licences). The work in question, imperial theologian Xantes Mariales's *Biblioteca interpretum ad universam summam theologiae D. Thom. Aquinatis Ecclesiae Doctoris*, allegedly contained passages dealing with the *De auxiliis* controversy; its assessment may also have been complicated by the fact that personnel from both the Roman and the Venetian Inquisitions were involved.[9]

Eventually this Dominican-authored book was only subjected to mild censorship, with the first volume alone prohibited to Catholic readers on the understanding that even this ban could be lifted if its problematic prefatory sections were removed (*nisi expuncta controversia prologomena*). The inquisitors' terse recommendation was passed on to the Congregation of the Index, which issued a formal decree publicizing this decision along with another dozen book condemnations on 20 June 1662. Signed by Congregation prefect Cardinal Marzio Ginetti and master of the sacred palace Raymond Capisuccus at the Quirinal Palace, their decree was also added to the 1664 Roman Index and Mariales's text was duly listed in its appendix.[10] But even that is not the end of the story, as Spanish inquisitors were still working on their own independent 164-page review of the *Biblioteca* in 1669.[11]

Other files tell other stories. But in general what is perhaps most striking to modern eyes is the relative informality and almost casual nature of many Roman censorship files. The carefully considered professional opinions of the papacy's hand-picked theological experts here tend to take the form of handwritten paper scraps of varying size, and they often extend to no more than a few pages. What also soon becomes evident is that these learned men were essentially tasked with providing the equivalent of a modern academic reader's report or book review – complete with a certain number of learned citations to demonstrate that the censor had done his due diligence in checking all relevant sources and precedents. Unless the book in question was particularly important or controversial, this report might be all that was required, with a verdict to censor (or not) subject to ratification at a subsequent meeting of the Congregations of either the Index or the Inquisition, or both. On the other hand, as we have seen, lengthy further consultations with the Congregations, other consultants or the papacy itself might ensue whenever something more was (perhaps quite literally) at stake.

Spanish Rules

If the *Triomphe de l'amour* had been sent to Madrid instead of Rome, somewhat different regulations and practices would have applied. Ever since 1559, the Spanish Index of Prohibited Books had contained its own general Rules – some but not all similar to the ten Rules of Trent, and at first somewhat easily overlooked since these instructions were scattered among the Index's more specific condemnations. One thus had to read through the entire 1559 Index (which, mercifully, was quite short) in order to learn them all. For the longer 1583 Spanish Index, Inquisitor-General Quiroga decided it would be better to imitate Trent by prefacing its lists of banned books with a more clearly delineated set of fourteen *Reglas generales*. These were originally (and, again, greatly simplified from the original convoluted Spanish text):

> 1. A ban on previously condemned heretical writings, up to 1515 (as per Trent Rule no. 1).
> 2. A ban on writings by more recent Protestant heresiarchs (similar to the initial section of Trent Rule no. 2 but without giving a list of heresiarchs' names).
> 3. Further reiteration of the ban on other Protestant theological writings (as found in later sections of Trent Rule no. 2).
> 4. A ban on various writings of Jews and Muslims, and in particular on the Talmud (see Chapter Five for more on this, as well as the following bans on biblical texts).

5. A ban on unauthorized Bible editions (slightly different from Trent Rule no. 3).

6. A ban on unauthorized translations of biblical texts (slightly different from Trent Rule no. 4).

7. A ban on popular religious manuals, such as Books of Hours, when these included biblical texts in the vernacular.

8. A ban on vernacular theological debates (similar to Trent Rule no. 6, but with an additional ban on debates concerning the Islamic Qur'an).

9. A general ban on books of magic and divination (per Trent Rule no. 9).

10. A general ban on irreverent songs and stories (an interesting variation on Trent Rule no. 7).

11. A general ban on anonymous books, or those whose name of author, printer or date and place of publication were missing (this was understood to take effect only from 1583 onwards, and did not apply to books published previously).

12. A general ban on irreverent or theologically unsound images, medallions or other visual imagery.

13. A general ban on theological errors in writings, even by Catholics.

14. A reminder that bans applied not only to books in their original language, but to any subsequent translations.

By the time of the *Triomphe* case in 1662, however, these had been slightly altered. Rule no. 4, for example, on Jewish and Muslim writings, was deleted in 1612 (so that this version of the Index had only thirteen *Reglas generales*). It was, however, then completely rewritten and re-inserted by 1632 as a new no. 13 – with much stricter and more detailed bans on Jewish texts in particular, including those associated with Kabbalah. In the 1640 Sotomayor Index, the *Reglas generales* were revised once again, such that they now numbered sixteen in total – reordering the first fourteen and adding two new Rules at the end concerning the granting of licences to read banned books for pious scholarly purposes, as well as detailed instructions on book expurgation.

None of this would have been helpful to Friar Verjuys in his efforts to correct the misleading title page of an obscure French translation of medieval mystical poetry. That very fact – that the Rules of the Indexes, both Roman and Spanish, were actually somewhat narrow in intention (although also sufficiently vague as to allow for a certain amount of leeway, especially for inquisitors and other Church officials whose authority extended to all aspects of Christian spiritual and moral discipline) – is important to recognize. The Indexes were originally meant to address very specific problems, in a specific historical context, with provision for future expansion that was intended to continue along the same lines. However, the fact that highly educated and well-connected Dominican theologians such as Joannes Baptista Verjuys and Leonard Hansen saw fit to pursue the denunciation and investigation of a book that would presumably have been of so little concern to the drafters of those Rules is also telling. As we have seen, censors associated with the Index cast an increasingly wide net over the course of the seventeenth century. The *Triomphe de l'amour* affair shows that sometimes they might later be obliged to toss out part of their catch. But many others did not escape so easily after becoming entangled.

Iberian Censorship Practices

The Spanish Inquisition's independence with regard to drafting and applying its own rules also extended to other areas of practice, and its decisions regarding book censorship could differ significantly from those of Rome. For while respect for papal authority was just as strong in the Iberian peninsula as it was elsewhere in the Catholic world, and Spanish theologians (including many inquisitors) were just as instrumental as Italians in the genesis of the Tridentine Index itself as well as in subsequent staffing of the Roman Congregations, the fact remained that a fully independent and centralized Spanish Inquisition had been established, with papal blessing, long before anything similar could be organized in Rome. Similarly, procedures for both Spanish indexing and expurgation of prohibited books were fully in place long before anything comparable had been developed by the papacy. After Trent, Spanish Indexes would continue to be influenced by those published under papal auspices, but they would not always be in perfect agreement. The Portuguese Inquisition for its part, after an early phase of autonomy (and extreme rigour), followed the Tridentine example and Rules very closely and after 1624 dispensed with its own Indexes altogether. Portuguese book censorship tended to be more or less in lock step with Rome thereafter, and so need no longer concern us here.

Like Portugal, book censorship in Spain was at first marked by a greater ferocity and intolerance than that practised in Italy. Though expurgation soon permitted some leniency with regard to borderline or 'mostly' permissible works, rigour continued to predominate among Spanish inquisitors in both the denunciation and the judgement of books whenever possible. Their scope for action was also generally broader. As we have seen, for example, Iberian concerns about Muslim and Jewish writings emerged earlier and more urgently than elsewhere in Christendom – for obvious reasons.[12] Furthermore, while the Spanish Inquisition was highly centralized and closely monitored by royal authority, it was also a very diverse and geographically dispersed organization. Variations in approach – and even internal contradictions when it came to censorship decisions, however limited in temporal or regional scope – were therefore also inevitable.

The 'normal' practices of Spanish inquisitorial censorship, and deviations from it, are well illustrated by yet another case involving the controversial writings of Ramon Llull. In 1663, just one year after the *Triomphe de l'amour* came to the attention of Friar Joannes Baptista Verjuys, another of Llull's medieval treatises was published – this time in Brussels itself, in a Spanish translation by the soldier-scholar Alonso de Zepeda y Adrada. As far as we know, this *Arbol de la ciencia* (Tree of Knowledge) did not inspire any action by Verjuys or any other local Dominicans. It did lead to enquiries in Spain, however, where a panel was eventually convened to discuss the matter at some length.[13] And publication of the *Arbol* would also soon send shock waves nearly halfway across the planet, to the Spanish colonies of the New World.[14]

The appearance in Mexico City of a Belgian-printed Spanish text by a medieval Catalan writer, just months after its first publication, is itself remarkable as an indication of how quickly books of all sorts could travel in the early modern Republic of Letters, and of how eager the reading public was for even quite arcane tomes promising special access to new ideas or hidden wisdom (unlike the *Triomphe de l'amour*, the *Arbol de la ciencia* was hardly light reading, at over six hundred pages in length). But still more interesting is the way in which Zepeda's *Arbol* was subsequently treated by local

Mexican inquisitors when it came to their attention. Though they could not find any such work, or its author, on the current Index of Prohibited Books, four separate *calificadores* – three Dominicans and one Augustinian friar – were immediately moved to subject the *Arbol* to a close investigation for possible heresies.[15] Soon enough, and once again guided by consultation of Eymeric's *Directorium*, they found what they were looking for and formally declared the book to be prohibited to all readers. We can perhaps assume that locally available copies later made their way onto a pyre for public burning. But the next step was to have this decision ratified by the *Suprema* and ultimately included in the next edition of the Spanish Index.

This was where over-zealous local censorship was liable to correction. As it happened, the Mexican *calificadores*' evaluations of the *Arbol de la ciencia* took quite some time to arrive in Madrid, and when they did, they did not receive an enthusiastic hearing. Whether politics intervened, with pro-Llullian pressure being applied from the court or sympathetic religious factions, or whether members of the *Suprema* simply disagreed with their New World colleagues' theological views (if they ever took the time to actually read their arguments, let alone the contents of the *Arbol* itself) we can never know since full records of the Consejo's meetings have not come down to us. But the ultimate outcome is clear: Ramon Llull's name remained absent from the Spanish Index of 1667 and thereafter, and there is no sign that the *Arbol de la ciencia* was ever subjected to any Old World censorship at all (though excessively enthusiastic panegyrics singing Llull's praises sometimes were: Pedro Bennazar's 1688 *Breve ac compendiosum rescriptum, nativitatem, vitam, martyrium, cultum immemorabilem pii haeremitae, ac venerabilis martyris Raymundi Lulli complectens* (Brief and Comprehensive Reply Including the Birth, Life, Martyrdom, and Immemorial Cult of the Pious Hermit and Venerable Martyr Ramon Llull), for example, was banned by inquisitorial decree in 1690 and placed on the Roman Index of Clement XI in 1716).

Records that have survived to the present day, both for the *Arbol* case and for many others dealt with by the Spanish Inquisition over the centuries, likely only comprise a small portion of the thousands of *expedientes* or case files originally generated by both regional and metropolitan inquisitors all across the Spanish Empire. As we have seen, denunciations of books could be created on local initiative and subjected to preliminary scrutiny by local *calificadores*. If these survived treacherous sea voyages and other vagaries of early modern travel to finally arrive at the *Suprema*, they were in theory then subject to further examination and judgement. The theological experts of Madrid were busy, however, and it is not surprising that they left evaluation of certain books (such as the latest translations of a Llullian text that had upset a few friars in Mexico) off their agendas from time to time.

When the Supreme Council of the Spanish Inquisition *did* decide to ban a book, whether on its own initiative or by endorsing a denunciation from some regional tribunal, its next steps generally mirrored those of Rome. Edicts were prepared for printing as broadsheets, which were to be posted on church doors; signed and dated, these were very similar to contemporary Roman models except for their decoration (omitting images of Sts Peter and Paul for example) and their use of the Spanish rather than Latin language. Many such posters survive today in both private and institutional collections.[16] From Madrid, instructions could also be sent out in the form of *cartas acordadas* to inform local Inquisition tribunals or episcopal authorities to have their own versions printed if necessary. And of course copies of all censorship edicts were retained in a central archive at the *Suprema* as well, so that whenever a new Index was being prepared, their prohibitions could be included.

The Index of the Spanish Inquisition was widely distributed and effectively used to inspect libraries, printers' shops and book shipments around the world. But the most zealous of Spanish clergy might even go beyond its admonitions, as was the case with the Mexican censors of the *Arbol*. Another example of such censorial enthusiasm involves the library of the exiled English Jesuits' seminary college in Valladolid, Spain. Here we have abundant physical evidence of inquisitorial inspections, with the word *visus* ('it has been seen') inscribed in ink on the title pages of many books that were checked and expurgated from 1633 on. But the Jesuits of St Alban's actually went beyond what was required by the Index, taking it upon themselves to expurgate works of English history that had previously escaped the attention of the inquisitors (and which, like the *Arbol*, were evidently deemed of too little concern to be later added by the *Suprema* to the Index itself). Nor was such 'extraordinary' censorship undertaken lightly; care was taken to obtain formal Inquisition

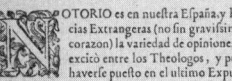

Censorship edict removing prohibitions against Cardinal Enrico Noris's *Historia Pelagiana* and banning all polemics against it. Manuel Quintano Bonifaz, Spanish inquisitor-general, 1758.

approval in advance. Thus, for example, Father T. Molyneaux of St Alban's was granted permission by the inquisitors of Valladolid to expurgate William Camden's *Britannia* in 1671. John Speed's *History of Great Britain* and Francis Godwin's *Rerum Anglicarum Henrico VIII, Edwardo VI et Maria regnantibus Annales* were next, with sections on such sore points as the Spanish Armada or the Gunpowder Plot being entirely removed.[17]

─✠─

CHURCH CENSORS thus worked in a variety of ways, across the Catholic world, from the sixteenth to the nineteenth centuries and beyond – always within contexts of ongoing book censorship, and sometimes book patronage, as conducted by secular officials. Agents of the various Inquisitions, as well as the Congregation of the Index, could be tireless in their pursuit of suspicious writings. Whether notorious or obscure (or even non-existent), texts of all sorts might in some cases be judged either worthy of prohibition or approved, on the peremptory advice of only one or two reviewers. In other cases, evaluation could drag on indefinitely and engage whole cohorts of the Church's theological intelligentsia in lengthy debates. Nor were all works equally liable to investigation. If a book were not either locally published in Latin, or at least in a vernacular that available local inquisitors happened to understand, then its chances of escaping the censorial dragnet could actually be rather good. In many cases, fortuitous denunciations by zealous informants like Friar Verjuys were necessary to trigger the review of any but the best-known of books (or artworks) – whether or not they had indeed been submitted for *censura praevia* by law-abiding authors.

The Rules for both the Roman and the Spanish Index of Prohibited Books evolved over time as censorship objectives and expectations shifted. The Church's attitude towards censorship was thus neither unthinkingly intolerant nor monolithically unchangeable. On the contrary, it was carefully developed with the participation of hundreds, or more likely thousands, of professional theologians and canon lawyers over the centuries. These intellectuals, themselves often deeply devoted to book culture, tried their best to apply rational and professionally justified standards to their task. They soon found, however, just how difficult such work could be. *Calificatores, consultores* and *qualificatores*, inquisitors and bishops, cardinals and popes all sought to fairly evaluate the books that came to their attention, but the impossibility of that undertaking was evident to all even before the end of the sixteenth century. There were simply too many books, too few qualified censors and too little time to devote to the project. The result, all too often, could be shoddy, tardy or inconsistent reviews, arbitrary decisions and laughable errors or omissions. Books like Llull's sometimes passed unscathed through the process, whatever reservations might be raised about their orthodoxy, whether because they were politically protected or simply because there were bigger fish to fry. The changing realities of Index production, and the severe limitations facing those tasked with its constant maintenance, need to be taken into account as we turn to examine the actual treatment of various types of books and images that took place over the four hundred years of this institution's inconsistent, haphazard and sometimes ridiculous – if often also horrific – existence.

PART II

5

CENSORED SCRIPTURES

The Spanish Armada's crushing defeat off the coast of Britain in 1588 was a low point in William Allen's career. A respected cardinal of the Catholic Church, Allen had long worked to bring about the invasion of his native England – and its 'liberation' from the Protestant regime of Queen Elizabeth I. Had it succeeded, he would undoubtedly have become a leading figure of the Catholic restoration, likely serving as archbishop of Canterbury and lord chancellor of the realm. Instead he retreated in disappointment to more bookish pursuits in defence of the faith. While Protestants celebrated their victory and loudly claimed it as proof that their religion was favoured by God himself, Allen went on to serve as co-founder of St Alban's English College at Valladolid (1589), prefect of the Vatican Library (1590) and a member of the Congregation of the Index, before dying in genteel poverty at the age of 62 (1594).

Nautical disappointments aside, the cardinal did much to advance Catholic interests throughout his life. And perhaps his crowning glory was patronage of the first complete English Bible ever to be authorized for Catholic use. The so-called 'Douay-Rheims Bible' marked a reversal of sorts for the Church, coming as it did in the midst of long and arduous campaigns to censor and control the production of Bibles – especially those that had been translated into vernacular languages such as English. Work on this particular Bible was essentially completed by its main translator, Gregory Martin, in 1582, when the New Testament section went to press. Funding and other issues delayed publication of its accompanying Old Testament volume until 1610, but the project was a success much appreciated by English-speaking Catholics. Soon words and phrases from this Catholic translation would even find their way into what would become the new English Protestant Bible *par excellence*, the famous 'King James Version' of 1611. Yet ecumenical peace was hardly on the horizon. Men and women continued to be persecuted and even killed by Catholic authorities for spreading the Word of God in English (and German and French, among many other languages). The suppression of illicit Bible editions, as well as theological commentaries on those editions, would remain a major goal of the Index of Prohibited Books throughout the rest of its history.

The Church hierarchy's attitude towards the Bible, and indeed towards many other ancient (and more recent) writings purporting to serve as receptacles of divine wisdom, was complex in the medieval and early modern periods. On the one hand, Scripture was considered a glorious gift from God, offering precious guidance as well as the very keys to human salvation. On the other, the Bible was recognized to be a tremendously difficult and easily misunderstood book – untutored reading of which was liable to result in confusion, heretical errors and the eternal damnation of precious souls. Access to biblical texts was therefore carefully guarded by many of the same clergy whose life's work was to preach biblical messages, and any increase to that access, by means of translation and print in particular, was a mixed blessing at best. At worst, exponential scattering of easily readable Scripture among priests and layfolk alike was seen as

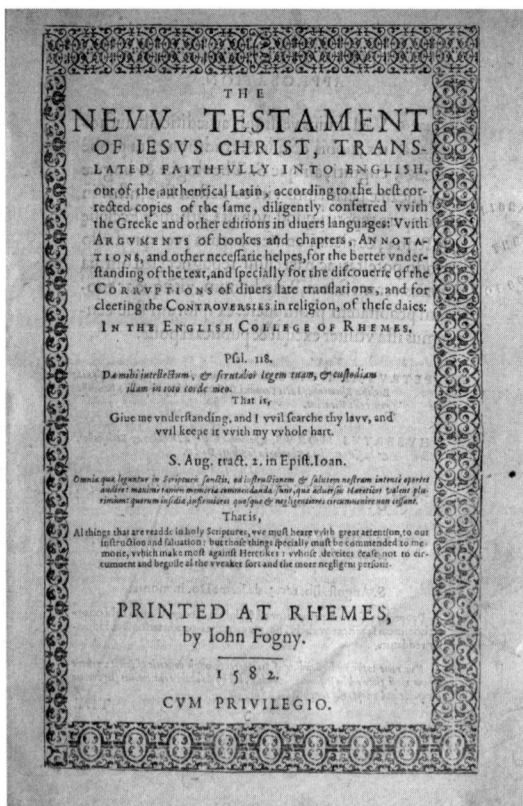

Title page for the Douay-Rheims New Testament (Rheims, 1582).

Joseph John Jenkins (after Thomas Lawrence), *Cardinal William Allen*, 19th century, stipple engraving.

one of the most serious threats the Church had ever known – and it was treated accordingly. Toleration for Allen's English Bible was thus in many ways exceptional, but as we will see such exceptions were not entirely rare. How censorship was actually applied to various scriptural writings over time and in different contexts, like so much of the history of the Index of Prohibited Books, is complicated and may at times seem almost absurd. Yet in general there *was* an underlying logic: given the extreme power of words relating to the Divine, the positive value of Scripture was always to be evaluated against potential for its harmful misuse in any given situation. Biblical and related texts *should* be made broadly available, in other words, but only if this could be done in a controlled fashion and without unduly harming the faith of true Catholic believers.

Unto All Nations

Mark 13:10, along with several related passages in the New Testament, makes it clear that Christians were expected from the first to spread the 'good news' of their Gospel to all peoples of the world (and thus presumably in all languages), and in the early days of the Church this was done, insofar as it was possible given the technological, political and geographical limitations of the age. Jewish biblical texts, which had already been translated into more commonly used tongues such as Greek (the *Septuagint* version) and Aramaic (the *Targum*) from the increasingly arcane Hebrew original, were now joined by Christian writings that circulated in a wide variety of dialects. These included not just Greek, and the Syriac form of Aramaic (languages in which Jesus and the disciples likely conversed), but soon Coptic, Geʽez, Armenian, Persian and Arabic. Spurred by the conversion of Emperor Constantine, portions of the Christian Bible were translated into Latin by the early fourth century at least (the *Vetus Latina*). By the turn of the fifth century, St Jerome was able to improve on these by completing his own Latin translation of the entire Bible, which would henceforth be known as the *Vulgate* version (in recognition of its relatively rough, 'common' form of Latin diction).

Christianity's spread, and its adoption by the Roman Empire as a state religion, facilitated further translations in the early Middle Ages. A Gothic version had been produced by the (heretical) Arian priest Ulfila even before Jerome's project was finished, and in the ninth century Sts Cyril and Methodius created both a Slavonic text for the peoples of eastern Europe, and a new 'Cyrillic' alphabet with which to read it. Early Saxon scholars and kings also seem to have converted at least portions of the Bible into Old and Middle English as well.[1] Latin, then, was only one of many languages in which the Bible had circulated by the later medieval period, and even in Latin it was well understood that manuscript versions could vary from one copy to the next. The Dominicans of Paris made it their task to try and standardize the Vulgate Bible text in the thirteenth century, as had Charlemagne's court scholars in the ninth, but even they had to admit that perfect copying was an impossible objective in the age of manuscript transmission.

The fact that some Christians began to circulate new translations of biblical texts in the twelfth and thirteenth centuries (often still merely fragments of the Psalms, or portions of the Gospels, sometimes in the form of little prayer manuals or Books of Hours) was not therefore alarming in and of itself. What *was* concerning was the fact that many of these translations were now thought to be the work of heretical preachers, seeking to subvert the normative teachings of the Church. Waldensians in particular were known for their unlicensed preaching and teaching of Scripture to the uneducated masses; Waldensian French or Occitan Scriptures were therefore examined and seized by inquisitors on a number of occasions. The Lollard followers of John Wyclif, and later the Hussites of Bohemia, similarly worked to render biblical materials into the languages of their own communities – in these cases English and Czech (and perhaps Hungarian), respectively. All were subject to inquisitorial scrutiny and punishment not so much because of the fact of translation, but because they were seeking to use Bible passages as weapons with which to combat what they took to be the corruption and errors of the institutional Church.

Martin Luther's decision to print a German translation of the New Testament in 1522, and the whole Bible in 1534, was therefore hardly unprecedented. Printed Latin Bibles had been among the first texts produced by Gutenberg's presses, and vernacular translations into German were circulated by respected printers such as Johannes Mentelin from at least 1466. But Luther's Bible definitely set off alarm bells, since it came in a context of outright religious rebellion. It also involved significant alterations to the traditional canon, with texts Luther personally deemed apocryphal either omitted or moved to a special 'inter-testamental' section placed between the Old and New Testaments. Luther wasn't alone in wanting to improve and facilitate popular reception of what he took to be the 'true' biblical text, however. Long before he began his reforms, humanist scholars such as Jacques Lefèvre d'Étaples and Desiderius Erasmus had been using their Hebrew and Greek linguistic training, as well as access to previously unknown manuscript versions, to clarify the meaning of the Latin Bible. A team of Spanish experts simultaneously worked to produce a multi-language printed Bible (in Hebrew, Latin, Greek and Aramaic) at the Complutensian University in Alcalá de Henares, from 1508 to 1522 – known to history as the 'Complutensian Polyglot'. Inspired by Erasmus and Luther, English translators such as William Tyndale and Myles Coverdale began their own new translation projects as early as 1525, but here again these were of great concern to Church officials, since they were produced by members of the incipient 'Protestant' movement, and so threatened to subvert the authority of the Catholic clergy. Error, confusion and the damnation of souls were all sure to follow.

Banned Bibles

It was in this context that the first formal prohibitions against specific editions of the Bible emerged, but it was still a slow and uncoordinated process. Luther's German translations of Scripture, representing as they did the theological interpretations of an arch-heretic (in the eyes of the Roman Catholic hierarchy), were at least potentially subject to the same prohibitions as all the rest of his writings after his 1521 excommunication. But they were not specifically singled out at first, and in the early decades of the Reformation many Church leaders were still reluctant to inflame religious tensions unnecessarily. The biblical editing and translation efforts of non-excommunicate humanist scholars such as Erasmus, though controversial to some, were therefore broadly tolerated throughout much of the first half of the sixteenth century. Bible censorship was a hit-and-miss affair in this period, with local authorities lashing out at troublesome individual editors, translators and printers when they saw fit to do so, but without any concerted policy directives from the ecclesiastical hierarchy.

Punishment, when it did come, could be severe. William Tyndale's English New Testament was condemned and publicly destroyed by Henry VIII's designated censor, Bishop Cuthbert Tunstall of London, in 1526, and Tyndale himself was burned at the stake near Brussels in 1536 on charges of heresy (though it is unclear whether this was specifically a result of his Bible translations; he had been on the run for years from both Church and state authorities, including Henry, whose divorce he publicly opposed). The printer Étienne Dolet, similarly, was strangled and burned for heresy at Paris in 1546 at least in part as a result of his publication of French versions of the New Testament. Other Bible translators such as Lefèvre d'Étaples and Robert Estienne, seeing this sign of the times, fled to safer regions soon after. Further signs were also hard to miss, as Emperor Charles V began posting notices or placards condemning heretical texts in all the major cities of his realms. These included mention of at least two partial Bible translations, a Flemish New Testament condemned in 1529 (perhaps in three separate versions, attributed to the printers Adriaen van Berghen, Christoffel van Ruremund and Joannes Zel), and an annotated Hebrew version of the Gospel of Matthew produced by Sebastian Münster in 1540.[2] Blanket imperial condemnations of heretical figures such as Luther (1526) and Helius

Eobanus Hessus (known for his versified 1540 Latin edition of the Psalms), could also be counted as examples of censorship against Bible translators and publishers.

Early proscriptions did not really target biblical texts per se, however. Most of the authors, translators and printers listed in Charles's placards were Protestant theologians, who naturally spent much of their time writing about the Bible; their publications tended to include commentaries on or excerpts from Scripture as a result, and *these* sorts of writing were most certainly liable to censorship. But there was as yet no campaign to entirely eliminate all unauthorized Bibles from circulation, whether in Latin or any other language. Devout Catholics, Protestants and ambivalent humanists alike were unanimous in their eagerness to read the Bible in whatever format they could find, and most would likewise have agreed that the comprehensibility and accuracy of available biblical texts could do with improvement. Some biblical revision and translation projects, including those of Erasmus (long a favourite of the devout Catholic Emperor Charles v) and Robert Estienne (protected and funded as royal printer to the French Catholic Francis i, until that king's death in 1547), were therefore widely appreciated international best-sellers. Even the most conservative Catholic defenders of the old Vulgate Bible saw value in efforts by orthodox theologians and linguists to explicate some of its more dubious passages through examination of earlier Hebrew, Greek and other versions. The 1527 *Veteris et Novi Testamenti nova translatio* by Italian Dominican Xantes Pagnino is just one example of Catholic interest in revision, as is the above-mentioned Complutensian Polyglot. Such interest could be wide-ranging, and by the late 1530s members of the Roman clergy were eagerly consulting even with schismatic foreign experts such as the Ethiopian scholar Täsfa Seyon – whose Ge'ez text of the New Testament went to press in Rome without any censorship in 1548.

Explicit mention of suspicious Bible editions was thus somewhat rare in the earliest French catalogues of banned books. A tentative censorship list drawn up at the University of Paris in 1542, for example, includes only three condemnations of biblical texts, amid dozens of Bible commentaries. These three were the popular (and arguably blasphemous) French *Psalms* of Clément Marot; a French New Testament printed by (the soon-to-be executed) Étienne Dolet; and an anonymous translation of the *Cinq livres de Moyse* – which may refer to Lefèvre d'Étaples' 1528 French version of the Pentateuch.³ The first Indexes printed in Paris (in 1544, 1545, 1547 and 1549) appear at first glance to show a similar lack of specific interest in biblical censorship, and none of these make a point of singling out any of the famous Protestant vernacular Bibles of Luther, Tyndale or Coverdale.⁴

Yet concern was clearly growing as Protestantism became more and more entrenched, and as volumes of Protestant Bible literature increasingly filled book markets. Thus the 1544 and subsequent Paris Indexes did include a short general notice to the effect that 'while sacred Scripture is by its very nature holy and good, in any language', there are nevertheless dangers in making it available in 'vulgar' tongues for the sake of illiterate and simple people (*idiotis & simplicibus*) – lest they fail to read it with the proper degree of piety and humility. Invoking still-raw memories of medieval heretics such as the Waldensians and Albigensians, and all the danger and malice they had unleashed with their errors, the Sorbonne theologians therefore declared that such translations were to be censored.⁵ This was a somewhat vague addendum, which could be easily overlooked by those skimming through long lists of banned titles, but it was a first hint of what was to come.

Nothing similar to the above Paris statement can be found in the first Leuven Indexes of Prohibited Books, but this is perhaps because a decision had already been taken at the Council of Trent, which would henceforth concentrate more attention on Bible publications and translations throughout the Church. On 8 April 1546, two formal Tridentine decrees were issued on the canonical Scriptures and their proper use. The first clarified the Bible's actual contents (pointedly rejecting Protestant assignations of some books to a section of *apocrypha*), 'as they have been accustomed to be read in the Catholic Church and as they are contained in the old Latin Vulgate'. The second made several further observations: that *only* the Vulgate should be used in 'public lectures, disputations, sermons and expositions'; that 'unbridled spirits' should not presume to distort the meaning of Scripture, under pain of correction by their bishops; and that editors, translators and printers should ensure that new Bible editions were always published under their own names (and with the proper licences). Further details mention additional rules for members of Catholic religious Orders who wished to publish their own versions of biblical texts. Finally, the decree concludes as follows:

In addition, the council wishes to check the lack of discretion by which the words and sentiments of sacred scripture are turned and twisted to scurrilous use, to wild and empty fancies, to flattery, detraction, superstitions, godless and devilish magical formulae, fortune telling, lotteries, and also slanderous pamphlets. So as to banish this kind of irreverence and contempt, and so that no one may in future dare in any way to make use of the words of sacred scriptures for these or similar purposes, the council orders and prescribes that all persons in that category, violators and profaners of the word of God, should be checked by the bishops by legal and imposed penalties.[6]

Evidently, the Council's decree did not actually impose a complete ban on Bible texts other than the Vulgate. Alternate Latin versions (alongside Greek, Hebrew and others) such as those found in the Polyglot, Erasmian, Pagnino or Estienne Latin Bibles were still permitted for private study, as would the soon-to-be published Ethiopian Seyon New Testament. Even vernacular translations could be countenanced by Church authorities so long as they were not deemed to be 'distorted', used for improper purposes or produced illicitly. These were fairly broad caveats, however, inviting a great deal of subjectivity from one case to the next. And the tenor of the decree itself also made it clear that the circulation of Bibles, like that of heretical writings, *was* (and should be) a matter of serious concern to the faithful. From now on, scrutiny and censorship of Scripture would become increasingly central aspects of Catholic discipline.

The first Leuven Index of Prohibited Books, issued precisely in 1546, thus actually begins with an entire section devoted to banned New Testaments, Psalters and Bibles – 48 titles in all. These include many local editions such as the Flemish New Testaments of Jan Batman and Simon Cock, as well as Latin Bibles printed in the Swiss Protestant stronghold of Basel, and several versions printed at Paris by Robert Estienne.[7] In 1550 and 1558 the same list was placed in the middle of the Index.[8] Again, it is interesting to note that no German or English Bibles appeared on either the French or the Belgian lists; as so often with inquisitorial censorship on the ground, these were focused almost exclusively on immediate threats to their local flocks, rather than seeking to be universal or exhaustive. The same can be said of the earliest Italian Indexes, such as those appearing at Milan and Venice. A handful of Bible editions can be found in each of these, but clearly they were not top of mind. The Venice Index of 1554, for example, mentions only three banned Bible versions, along with a few texts containing scriptural excerpts (such as the *Phrases scripturae sanctae*).[9]

The Tridentine decree, and associated fears of Protestant contamination, had a more noticeable impact in the Iberian Peninsula; indeed, as in France, vernacular Bible censorship in this region soon went beyond the Council's cautious approach. The earliest extant Portuguese list of banned books (1547) only makes specific mention of two Lutheran treatments of scriptural texts, both already flagged in imperial placards of 1540: the Psalms of Helius Eobanus Hessus, and Münster's annotated Bible. But the Portuguese inquisitors, like their professorial colleagues in Paris, also warned against *all* New Testaments or Bibles in the vernacular (*em lymgoajem*).[10] Further titles were added to the printed Portuguese Index of 1551, along with a more fulsome ban on 'all books of Holy Scripture in any vulgar language whatsoever' (*sacrae scripturae omnes libri in quacumque lingua vulgari*).[11]

For their part, Spanish inquisitors decided to append a short section dedicated to the 'Biblia Latina' at the end of their own 1551 Index, along with a handful of other entries scattered throughout the main body of the list. Their lack of detailed knowledge regarding heretical or otherwise objectionable Bible editions is evident from the fact that they seem to have merely copied these entries from the Leuven Index of 1550. Still, like the French and Portuguese, they also applied a terse general ban on vernacular Bible translations (*Biblia en romance castellano en otra qualquier vulgar lengua*), as well as a vague but still more comprehensive prohibition against any book at all that might 'smack of heresy' (*omnes libri sapientes haeresim*).[12] But the Spaniards paid more than just lip service to the issue: in 1552 a series of raids and confiscations netted at least four hundred Bibles in the major port city of Seville, and a further two hundred in the comparatively sleepy Aragonese town of Zaragoza.[13] From these it soon became evident that Protestant Bibles had indeed become widely available in Spain, and that the vast majority (over 90 per cent) were imported from France. A separate list entirely devoted to banned Bibles was published by the Spanish Inquisition in 1554 as a result, under the title *Censura generalis contra errores quibus recentes haeretici sacram scripturam asperserunt* (General Censorship against Errors that Recent Heretics Spread within Holy Scripture).[14]

Roman censorship Indexes, like their earlier Milanese and Venetian counterparts, show comparatively little concern for any imminent threat posed by Protestant Bibles, whether locally produced or imported. Paul IV's 1557 and 1559 Indexes do contain lists of banned Bibles, but these merely copy from the Leuven Index for the most part, augmented by a few high-profile local additions (such as the Venetian Bible of Isidore Chiari, which had also just been placed on the Spanish Inquisition's list of 1554). Nevertheless a general condemnation of 'all Bibles in the vulgar German, French, Spanish, Italian, English, Flemish and other tongues', unless specifically licensed by the Roman Inquisition, was also added for good measure.[15] In the more moderate Tridentine Index of 1564 this statement was dropped and there is no list of banned Bibles at all. Instead, previous approaches to Bible censorship were replaced by Trent Rules no. 3 and 4, which lay out general principles to be followed in such cases.[16] According to Rule 3, even Latin Bibles that have been produced by 'damned' (heretical) authors may be permitted so long as they 'contain nothing against healthy doctrine'. Alternative versions of the Old Testament in particular were acknowledged to be of great usefulness to 'educated and pious' men, as judged by their bishops, for the purpose of better understanding the Vulgate text and the intended meaning of Scripture. New Testaments edited by the Index's Class One heretics, however, were deemed to be more dangerous than useful. Problematic annotations to the Vulgate Bible should be evaluated and removed whenever necessary by university-based theologians or inquisitors. Furthermore, in a rather striking reversal of policy, both the non-Vulgate Latin editions of François Vatable (as printed by Robert Estienne), and the Vulgate as edited by Isidore Chiari (with its objectionable prologue duly removed), were now singled out as acceptable alternatives for qualified readers.

In Rule 4, earlier total bans on vernacular Bibles are also seemingly overturned, or at least mitigated. Noting that 'experience has shown that indiscriminate permission to [read] Bibles in the vulgar tongue causes more harm than utility thanks to the temerity of man,' the Trent Fathers nevertheless concede that it should be possible for local bishops or inquisitors to consult and exercise discretion when deciding whether or not a parishioner might be allowed to read such translations. So long as the reading is to be done for pious motives, and books are not hidden from the authorities, it is to be condoned. Further authorization for reading is also required for members of Catholic religious Orders, and rules for permitting the sale or lending of books are briefly addressed.

Thus, after more than twenty years of steadily rising fears that humanist or Protestant biblical literature might be corrupting the souls of the faithful, and some moves towards the possibility of a broad ban on at least some types of Bibles (especially when printed in any language but Latin, or perhaps Greek and Hebrew), the Council of Trent struck something of a pastoral compromise in its closing sessions. The dangers of mis-reading the Bible remained all too evident, as Protestants demonstrated on a daily basis with their assertions that Catholic interpretations of Scripture were fundamentally wrong. But there was no getting away from the fact that Catholic Christianity remained a biblical faith, and that its pious members could not be denied reasonable access to their holiest of books. Just what 'reasonable' might mean, of course, varied from one pope, bishop or inquisitor to the next, and the very idea that believers should be subjected to monitoring and judgement in order to gain such access was offensive to many. With Protestant Bibles continually multiplying, and so offering the constant temptation of easy access to Scripture even for those inhabiting Catholic-dominated regions, Bible censorship by Catholic authorities was seen simultaneously as both a necessity and a potential embarrassment. The vague Tridentine compromise could only be a temporary solution to these serious concerns.

Resolving the Bible Problem

Sure enough, it was not long before leading figures in the Church sought to gain still tighter control over which versions of Scripture should be made available to Catholics. Recognizing the need for an officially approved standard text to compete with the many attractive options being offered by Protestants, and concerned by the relative leniency of Tridentine rules on the matter, the inquisitor-pope Pius V quicky moved to commission a number of new publications. First among these was the Roman *Missal* of 1570, which established once and for all (until its revision in the 1960s) the precise Latin words to be used by all Catholic priests when saying Mass. Standardization of theological doctrine was also a concern, and Thomism became an officially mandated interpretive frame for all Catholic scholars (as previously agreed at the Council). This development was accompanied by publication of Thomas Aquinas's many works in the so-called *editio Piana* (also 1570). Authorized new standard editions of the Church Fathers, compilations of canon law and other fundamental Catholic doctrinal texts were all soon to be forthcoming.

Such efforts were continued by Pius' successor Gregory XIII (r. 1572–85), who reformed not only the universal calendar but the Bible itself. It was under Gregory's papacy that the Douay-Rheims New Testament was published in 1582, and plans for a full revision of the traditional Latin Vulgate were finally laid out. Pressing calls for a new and improved Vulgate had already been registered at Trent, and a papal commission to oversee the project was established as early as 1561, but work progressed slowly at first. As it happened, it would be Gregory's successor Sixtus V who claimed the first fruits of the venture when he authorized a new 'Sistine' Septuagint (Old Testament) text, soon after coming to the papal throne in 1586. Led by Cardinal Antonio Carafa (a nephew of Paul IV's), who took over following the death of Guglielmo Sirleto in 1585, work on the rest of the Vulgate continued throughout the remainder of this ambitious pontificate. Sixtus himself took a personal interest and became directly involved in editing work once he grew impatient with his experts' progress, sending a full draft of the revised Bible directly to the Congregation of the Index for review by the end of November 1589. However, members of that Congregation (including William Allen) identified numerous flaws and recommended withholding publication for several months. The Sistine Vulgate Bible was in fact published in the spring of 1590, but Sixtus continued to suggest emendations and other members of the Curia maintained serious reservations until the pope's death later that summer. Before a successor could be chosen, the cardinals had revoked permission to publish, and took steps to have all copies of the late pope's cherished new Bible destroyed.

After Sixtus' death three short-lived popes followed in succession, preventing any further definitive action, before Clement VIII rose to power in 1592 and finally brought the Vulgate project to its conclusion. Editing work had of course continued in the meantime, so it was with some confidence that the so-called Clementine (or

Sixto-Clementine) Vulgate was finally published, along with a preface by Index censor Robert Bellarmine, mere months after the pope's coronation. On 9 November 1592, it was definitively pronounced in the bull *Cum sacrorum* that this edition would henceforth be the only tolerated Bible of the Catholic Church, and that not a single word could be altered in subsequent printings, even in marginal notes. The scriptural canon was also definitively fixed, with slight adjustments to the Tridentine decrees regarding apocryphal works. This would remain true until the twentieth century, and the (lightly amended) Clementine Vulgate remains largely the basis for all Catholic Bibles in official use today.

Such a hardline stance on the unicity of the Bible text also required some adjustment of the Tridentine Rules as they applied to the Index of Prohibited Books. Sixtus v had already rewritten and renumbered Rules no. 3 and 4 as part of his complete revision of the Index in 1590, completely banning all access to Bibles produced by heretics (no matter how orthodox their content) and reserving authority to grant permits for reading translated vernacular Bibles to the pope alone.[17] And while Clement VIII reverted for the most part to the Tridentine version of the Rules, he maintained this last adjustment in his set of *Observationes* that were added to the Roman Index of 1596. From now on, Catholics were essentially barred from accessing any Latin Bible aside from the approved Vulgate, or from accessing any vernacular translations of Scripture at all, unless they could prove to the pope himself that they needed these sorts of books for exceptional bona fide scholarly studies.[18] Yet despite such totalitarian intentions, problems – and loopholes – remained.

The prior existence of the 1582 English Douay-Rheims Bible, for example, was an obvious exception to Clement's directives. Its continued use could be (and was) justified on the grounds that English-speaking 'recusant' Catholics living under Protestant rule needed special resources in order to maintain their faith. A similar exception was made for Polish Catholics, and so a new Polish translation of the entire Bible by the Jesuit Jakub Wujek was finally printed in 1599 (the project having previously receiving approval from Gregory XIII, with preliminary publication of the New Testament alone in 1593). By 1614 the archbishop of Cologne had also authorized a new German translation, to be made by a convert from Lutheranism named Kaspar Ulenberg, again justifying this move with reference to local Protestant threats. Another Jesuit, György Káldi, produced a similarly 'exceptional' translated Bible for Hungarian Catholics in 1626. A printed Arabic version of the Catholic Bible (previously suggested by Gregory XIII) was in the works by 1645, and no one ever seems to have taken steps against the Ge'ez New Testament of Täsfa Seyon or indeed any other Eastern interpretation of Scripture, including the 1613 Ge'ez translation of a Latin commentary on the Gospels by a converted Ethiopian Catholic prince named Se'ela Krestos (copies of which remained in active use among Portuguese missionaries for decades). Evidently such exotic vernacular works were perceived as posing no immediate threat to the faithful Catholics of Europe, while perhaps being useful as weapons in debates against the Monophysite Christians of Africa and the Middle East.

In regions where neither schismatic nor Protestant authority (nor a concomitant profusion of heterodox Bibles) was an issue, such as Italy and the Iberian territories, vernacular Bibles were generally not permitted at all throughout the seventeenth century. Illicit Protestant translations such as the Spanish Reina-Valera Bible, printed at Basel in 1569, continued to circulate from time to time, but otherwise no authorized Catholic Bible in Spanish was made available to believers until 1825. French Catholics, for their part, could only read the Scriptures in their own language if they were willing to defy their Church leaders, at least until the publication of a controversial 1665 *Psautier* and 1667 *Nouveau Testament* by Jansenist scholars Antoine and Louis-Isaac Le Maistre de Sacy. This was followed by an entire French Bible in 32 volumes by 1696, again published by Louis-Isaac Le Maistre de Sacy in collaboration with other Port Royal Jansensists (including Blaise Pascal), and so collectively known as the 'Port Royal Bible'. Though immediately condemned by Rome, heavily criticized by many Jesuits and other Catholics for their (allegedly) Calvinist-leaning commentaries and ultimately placed on the Index, these publications continued to circulate locally thanks to the French clergy's claims of gallican independence.[19] A similar Dutch translation of the New Testament, printed secretly by the Jansenist scholar Aegidius de Witte in 1696, was likewise condemned (first pre-emptively by a local archbishop, then definitively by the pope in 1712) but continued to circulate among Catholics nonetheless. A lengthy pamphlet war ensued, as part of the larger Jansenist controversy, which was only partially resolved with the publication of Pope Clement XI's

1713 anti-Jansenist bull *Unigenitus*. This also condemned, among other things, French biblical translations embedded in the writings of another leading Jansenist, Pasquier Quesnel, along with Quesnel's assertion that the Bible should be fully accessible to all. Mentions of both the Port Royal Bible and all but one of Quesnel's works no longer appeared in the 1758 Roman Index of Prohibited Books, but they remained on the Index of the Spanish Inquisition until its final suppression in the nineteenth century.

It was actually during the papacy of Clement XI (r. 1700–1721), and even more that of his protégé Benedict XIV (r. 1740–58), that the Catholic hierarchy began once again to slowly shift its attitudes regarding popular access to Bible translations. As Enlightenment culture took hold among the elites of Europe, including noble families who populated the Roman Curia, earlier strict efforts to keep Scripture out of the hands of the laity began to seem more and more potentially misguided as well as impractical. In the two centuries since Luther and the Council of Trent, literacy had become much more common and cheap printed books more widely available than ever before. Protestantism itself had become a more or less accepted part of global Christianity; religious toleration was still far from being official policy in most countries, but earlier Catholic hopes of reversing the Reformation altogether by coercive means were increasingly seen to be unrealistic. Therefore, while Benedict XIV remained adamant on the question of keeping vernacular Bibles out of Italy (and in 1748 refused even the publication of Cardinal Albani's proposed Italian translation of the Pauline Epistles), he did eventually soften his position. In 1757 he agreed to a new Italian translation of the entire Bible, to be undertaken by Antonio Martini, which was eventually published in 23 volumes from 1769 to 1781 (with parallel columns giving the Vulgate Latin text). Benedict even went beyond the original intent of Tridentine Rule no. 4 in his new Index of 1758, so that only local episcopal permission would be required to authorize any future vernacular Bibles. It was a small step, and censorship of unauthorized Bibles continued to be practised by Catholic authorities from time to time well into the modern era. But by the nineteenth century it was simply no longer possible to keep Bibles out of the hands of most book consumers who wanted them, and so censorship took on an increasingly symbolic quality – primarily as an expression of the Church's preferences and directives, to be heeded by the faithful whenever possible.

Censoring Non-Christian Scriptures

The clear focus of the Index of Prohibited Books in all its iterations, and of Catholic book censorship generally, was always on maintaining and protecting what censors took to be the 'true' doctrines of the faith. Christian Scriptures, as preserved in the Old and New Testaments of the Christian Bible, were therefore at the centre of their work (along with theological commentaries on these). However, even as the main battle lines were still being established in the Catholic Church's war against Protestantism, it was evident to some authorities that non-Christian writings might require increased scrutiny and prohibition as well. For the most part this concern was still limited to texts that were perceived as substantive threats against the spiritual well-being of Catholic believers; the Church had neither the capacity nor the inclination to catalogue and condemn every single piece of non-Catholic writing that had ever been produced. However, as overseas colonialism and pretensions of universal (often coerced) missionizing became more marked aspects of European Christianity in the early modern period, notions about just who should be considered members of the 'community of the faithful' were expanded in important ways – as was the Church's perception of what sorts of writings might actually constitute a 'threat' to more vulnerable members of that community. This would have the unfortunate consequence of leading to serious episodes of cultural intolerance in some cases, and acts of what is now understood to be downright cultural genocide in others.

Confiscation, destruction and expurgation of Jewish texts was already practised by medieval Christians, beginning with the thirteenth-century Talmud trials and related censorship of works by Rabbi Moses ben Maimon (also known as Maimonides, or abbreviated as RaMbaM) as previously noted in Chapter One. Claims that the Talmud contained derogatory passages insulting Jesus and the Virgin Mary were explained away in some cases, while in others it was agreed that these sentences could simply be removed from Talmud manuscripts. Episodes of Talmud-burning were generally sporadic and short-lived, albeit traumatic and costly, since Jewish leaders were for the most part able to convince Church authorities that access to the Talmud was necessary for the continuation of Jewish religious life (which was itself guaranteed, at least in principle, by long-standing papal pronouncements such as the ancient bull *Sicut judaeis*). Furthermore, some Christian scholars positively cherished Hebrew (and Aramaic) Jewish books because of their value for the study of theology.

Since medieval times, small groups of Christian Hebraists had sought out Jewish Bibles, Talmuds and other religious writings in hopes of using them to gain a better comprehension of the Old Testament's original historical and literal meaning: the *hebraica veritas*, as it came to be known. Some early modern humanists continued this tradition, and also looked to Jewish rabbis and sages for knowledge both of the 'literal' Hebrew interpretation of Scripture and of allegorical interpretations that had accumulated in Jewish oral tradition. Sometimes this consultation was done in person, but exegetical texts written by Jewish masters such as Maimonides, Rabbi Solomon ben Isaac of Troyes (Shlomo Yitzhaki, or RaSHI) and Rabbi David Kimchi (RaDaK) were also much sought-after. Even mystical texts of Kabbalah were explored by some Christians. After all, who better to serve as a guide to Holy Writ than the very people who were first given it by God, and who still spoke (or at least understood) the language in which it was originally composed?

The potential for Jewish wisdom to offer alternatives to established Christian doctrine was always both intriguing and worrisome to Church authorities. Old suspicions were periodically revived about the alleged dangers and blasphemies embedded within Jewish writings (and Talmudic literature in particular), leading for example to a series of ferocious debates in the early decades of the sixteenth century between the Christian Hebraist Johann Reuchlin and a converted rabbi-turned Catholic theologian named Johannes Pfefferkorn. Matters were further complicated by the fact that many Spanish Jews were forced to accept baptism after a series of violent pogroms in 1391; still more became more or less unwilling converts after mass expulsions of all Jews from Spain in 1492, and from Portugal in 1497. This meant that tens of thousands of formerly devout Jews were now technically considered to be members of the Christian faith, even if they did not particularly believe in (or understand) any of their new religion's doctrines. The Spanish Inquisition, as we have seen, was established in the final decades of the fifteenth century with a primary goal of determining which of these 'New Christians', or *conversos*, remained secretly loyal to Judaism (and the

Portuguese Inquisition would follow suit in 1536). Henceforth, possession of Hebrew books, or of 'Jewish' texts translated into any other language (including the biblical *Targum*), would be one of the strongest indicators of crypto-Judaic practice that inquisitors were trained to watch for. The Iberian Index's hardline stance against 'all Hebrew books, or books written in any language, that contain ceremonies of the Jews' thus tended to go far beyond that of its Italian colleagues.[20]

The same would also soon become true for censorship of Muslim books. Christian theologians, for the most part, had tended to ignore the holy Qur'an of the Islamic faith, as well as a vast corpus of (mostly Arabic) interpretive literature that had been built up over the generations to study it, simply because they did not recognize it as a 'true' Scripture. Unlike the Jewish Bible, which could not be so easily ignored since it pre-dated and formed the very basis of many Christian scriptural teachings, the Qur'an was widely dismissed as a relatively late collection of 'errors' that had little currency among European readers and so posed little threat even as a heretical text. There were exceptions of course – some Christians did read the Qur'an, especially in border regions of the Mediterranean – but in general Latin Christianity maintained a stance of deliberate ignorance towards all things Islamic throughout the medieval and early modern periods (a habit, of course, that remains common today).

Potential threats posed by Qur'ans, and by other Arabic books (which might or might not contain religious teachings), were taken more seriously in the Iberian Peninsula over the course of the sixteenth century. In part this was an echo of increased inquisitorial attention being paid to Jewish texts, and an example of the well-established Iberian tradition of treating the two religions analogously whenever it was convenient to do so. It also reflected the growing power, and indeed attractiveness to some Christians, of the Muslim Ottoman Empire (and to a lesser degree the small but wealthy independent principalities of North Africa). The phenomenon of *renegados* who sought better fortunes in Islamic lands, also known as 'Christians turn'd Turk', was familiar to everyone from Spanish prelates and Italian popes to English playwrights by the sixteenth and seventeenth centuries.[21] But most of all, there was the problem of the so-called *moriscos*. These were entire Islamic communities that had been subjected to Christian rule in Spain – some since the thirteenth century, as in Valencia, but many others as a consequence of the more recent 1492 conquest of Granada. Though initially promised freedom of religion under negotiated terms of surrender, and clearly with little inclination to accept Christianity, these hundreds of thousands of mostly Arabic-speaking Muslims were forced to accept baptism after a series of failed rebellions from 1499 to 1526. Like the converted Jews before them, the resulting unwilling converts now became subject to all the attentions of the Church and its Inquisitions. Suddenly, any piece of Arabic writing was a potential sign of disloyalty to the Church, and a possible weapon to be used by alleged 'crypto-Muslims' in their presumed efforts to contaminate the Christian faith from within. Thousands of Arabic books were summarily destroyed by the hardline archbishop of Toledo, Francisco Jiménez de Cisneros, as early as 1499 – and things did not improve in the years that followed.

From the very beginning, then, the first Spanish and Portuguese Indexes of Prohibited Books included a sweeping ban on the *Alcoranus* (Qur'an) – without specifying any particular editions or other details.[22] Since most Christians, including inquisitors, could read no Arabic and wouldn't be able to identify a Qur'anic text in any case, the same Indexes also prohibited any writings at all that might possibly contain Islamic wisdom ('any other book in Arabic, or in any language, wherein are the errors of the Mahometan sect'), just as they did with 'Jewish' books. Possession of a single scrap of writing in either Hebrew or Arabic could now unleash the full power of the Inquisition and potentially lead to a heretic's death. Entire populations were thus violently deprived not only of their religious traditions and cultural identities, but of beloved linguistic and literary traditions. Heroic efforts were made to preserve Qur'ans and other remnants of Islamic writing, even if this meant walling them up into secret compartments of houses, as was also done with Hebrew and rabbinic texts.[23] But the destruction of Spain's rich Muslim and Jewish heritage was largely achieved through the zeal of its inquisitors, stimulated by the promptings and authorization of their Indexes, by the dawn of the seventeenth century.

Ironically, of course, some members of the Church elite still recognized the value of non-Christian religious texts even as they watched them being confiscated and destroyed. The Complutensian Polyglot Bible had relied heavily on Hebrew and Aramaic sources, as did the later Antwerp or Plantin Polyglot of 1568–73, and Hebraist scholars such as Alfonso de Zamora (d. 1544), Xantes Pagnino (d. 1541) and Benito Arias Montano (d. 1598), not to mention the censor and Vatican librarian Guglielmo Sirleto, were all highly praised at both papal and royal courts for their wisdom. Chairs in Hebrew were maintained in several leading universities throughout the early modern period, and Hebrew scholarship remained essential for all revisions of the Vulgate and other scriptural editions carried out by both Catholics and Protestants. Hebrew Bibles, along with Talmuds, rabbinic commentaries and Kabbalistic works, were sometimes printed for both Christian and Jewish use by Christian printers, and many of these benefited directly from the expertise of Jews fleeing the Inquisitions of Spain and Portugal.

A backlash against the Talmud and related Jewish writings was revived at mid-century during the pontificate of Julius III (r. 1550–55). Public burnings took place in Rome and other Italian cities, with the result that 'Talmuth' appears on the Venetian index of 1554 as well as Paul IV's Roman Indexes of 1557 and 1559. This ban would be softened by the Tridentine Index of 1564, which noted that it 'may be tolerated if it appears without the name Thalmud, and without insults or calumnies against the Christian religion'.[24] In other words, key Jewish religious texts could henceforth be published in Catholic Europe only if expurgated by Church censors; uncensored versions of the Talmud were for the most part now restricted to the Islamic Ottoman Empire. Pope Clement VIII reiterated the Tridentine position on expurgation of the Talmud in 1592, adding a further ban on any vernacular translations of Jewish prayerbooks (*Mahzorim*) since these might lead good Christians (and converted Jews) into error.[25] Medieval

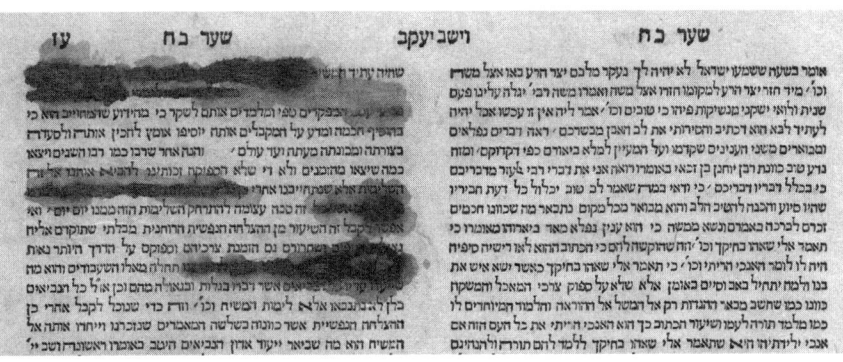

Page from Rabbi Isaac ben Arama, *Akedat Yitzak* (Venice, 1546), as expurgated by Domenico Yerushalmi.

biblical commentaries by Rashi and David Kimchi, as translated by the Protestant Paul Fagius, were also placed on the Indexes of Portugal in 1581 and Rome in 1596.[26] Hebrew books continued to be produced for both Jewish and Christian readers throughout the seventeenth and eighteenth centuries, but evidence of their censorship (often at the hands of converted Jewish scholars such as the infamous Domenico Yerushalmi, who died in 1621) remains all too apparent in many copies that are extant today. Christian censorship had a real impact on Jewish intellectual life in Europe, and it ensured that readers of Hebrew or Jewish books were subject to investigation at any time.

The Qur'an, for its part, was never taken as seriously by Roman censors as it was in Spain. Thus while the *Alchoranus Mahometis* was placed on the Index of 1559, this ban seems only to have applied to a Protestant re-edition of a medieval Latin translation, printed at Basel in 1543 with a foreword by none other than Martin Luther.[27] The 1596 Roman Index added a further note banning 'similar' works, as well as any Qur'ans 'in vernacular tongues', except with special inquisitorial permission.[28] Meanwhile, however, Catholic and Protestant scholars alike were taking a new interest in the usefulness of so-called 'Oriental' languages such as Arabic, as well as Hebrew, Greek, Aramaic (also known as Chaldean), Coptic, Armenian, Persian and the Ethiopian languages of Amharic and Ge'ez. These, it was hoped, could potentially unlock the theological and philological mysteries of the Bible and other wisdom texts. They could also prove useful in communications with foreign courts and with potential allies, including eastern Christians, residing near or within the Ottoman Empire. Furthermore, study of such exotic tongues was seen as fitting for a papacy with pretensions to universal power and responsibility for the souls of all humans. A Roman college for Arabic-speaking Maronite clergy was thus established by Pope Gregory XIII in 1584, and the Vatican's collection of Oriental books was greatly expanded under Clement XI in the early eighteenth century. And despite strong, united opposition from popes and inquisitors, the Congregation of the Index was finally prevailed upon to permit publication of a full two-volume Qur'anic edition, translation and (extremely hostile) commentary by the respected theologian and papal confessor Lodovico Marracci in 1698. Thus even while Catholic inquisitors were ruthlessly persecuting owners of Arabic and Hebrew books in

Spain, and censors deliberated over which of these books should be placed on the Index, some of those same texts were being gleefully catalogued, consulted and cautiously published – for the benefit of select experts only – in Rome itself.

Colonial Censorship

The tragic destruction of Muslim and Jewish communities through both forced religious conversion and cultural assimilation (as well as outright homicidal violence) in Spain and Portugal would also provide a training ground of sorts for agents of European colonialism who later enacted similarly genocidal practices in the Americas, as well as parts of Africa and Asia. Once again, as had been done with the Talmud and Qur'an, texts that were vital to the spiritual and cultural integrity of non-Christian colonized peoples were in some cases proscribed and violently torn from the communities that had produced them. Relatively little evidence of this process was actually inscribed in the Indexes of Forbidden Books, however, because texts associated with so-called 'pagan' peoples could not be conceived of as 'scriptural' in minds formed by a near-exclusive biblical curriculum; nor could many non-European cultural productions be fully recognized as 'books' in the sense understood by Church censors, even when taking written form. Only in a few exceptional cases, as when an Indigenous text was actually translated into a European language and printed in the physical form of a modern European codex, might it end up being placed on an Index – as was done with the so-called *Apocalypse de Chiokoyhikoy, chef des Iroquois sauvage du nord de l'Amérique* (Apocalypse of Chiokoyhikoy, Chief of the Savage Iroquois of North America), published in 1777 in Philadelphia and banned by the Spanish Inquisition's Index of 1790.[29] But either way, immeasurable damage was done; and both the model and the logic of Index censorship was used to justify that damage.

In the Americas, missionaries such as Diego de Landa and Juan Pérez Bocanegra advocated the destruction of Mayan codices and Inca *quipus* (along with idols and temples) in their zeal to eliminate all remnants of pre-Christian practice. This was sometimes done with explicit reference to the danger of potential apostasy by recent converts, as had already been witnessed among *conversos* and *moriscos* in Spain. Such campaigns of extirpation could be carried out as a matter of course, without bothering to record the banned communications of Indigenous Americans on the Index, since those doing the burning rarely took the time to learn the authorship or titles that could be associated with their victims. Cultural genocide, having been practised and perfected in the Old World, could here be conducted in an ad hoc and at times almost casual fashion. The destruction was not always total, however, even in settings where resistance proved ineffective. As was the case with Jewish and Muslim books, whenever questions arose among Church authorities over the potential interest of Indigenous texts to Christian scholars, exceptions could always be made. Having 'protected' the spiritual well-being of local converts by disrupting traditional processes of cultural transmission, it was simple enough to preserve isolated exemplars of New World literature for cataloguing in the libraries of metropolitan Europe. The rich holdings of papal libraries, among others that still house rare surviving texts of the Maya, Aztec, Inca and other Indigenous American civilizations, bear testimony to this.

Removal of non-Christian texts from organic community circulation was only a first step in ensuring that converted colonial 'New Christians' would not be harmed by their allegedly dangerous contents. The challenge of replacing such texts with orthodox teachings remained, as did the danger of permitting proselytes (many of whom were hardly enthusiastic about their adopted faith) to access those teachings on their own terms. Just as had occurred with Iberian converts from Judaism and Islam, as well as with 'Old Christian' lay populations of Europe amid the threat of Protestantism, Church authorities were now faced with a dilemma over how best to manage and police the spiritual lives of their newly baptized Indigenous charges. How could the biblical message be effectively taught without resorting to problematic translations of Scripture? With Spanish Jews the matter had been relatively simple: most had long since learned the Romance dialects of the majority population, and even the Vulgate Bible was as comprehensible to them as it was to 'Old' Christians. Assimilation was slower in the more rural Arabic-speaking *morisco* communities, and by the late sixteenth century experiments were being conducted with the use of special Arabic-language catechisms that allowed preachers to phonetically read out simplified Christian teachings to their captive audiences. The Indexes' general ban on Bible translation ruled out most further efforts to communicate more sophisticated messages based on the Gospels themselves. The frustrations of trying to convey complex religious truth through the half-measures of rudimentary catechisms, in a language the preachers themselves didn't fully understand, were soon evident. Even mission enthusiasts such as Archbishop Juan de Ribera of Valencia ultimately had to admit that catechetical instruction was a failure, further concluding that their *morisco* flocks were either too stupid or too stubborn to ever become good Christians. Those forcibly baptized Muslims who had not already fallen victim to the inquisitors were therefore deported from Spain to Islamic ports of North Africa over the course of several years, beginning in 1609.

This too would prove a tragic model for the Americas. Despite early examples of fruitful intellectual exchange between Aztec and Spanish scholars associated with the College of Santa Cruz de Tlatelolco, the possibility of translating Christian Scriptures into Indigenous languages was for the most part precluded by later Index bans on vernacular Bibles.[30] Instead, conversion efforts by the later sixteenth century centered on using simplified catechisms (themselves subject to rigourous censorship) as a means of conveying basic principles of the faith to an audience whose language remained largely incomprehensible to all but a handful of missionaries. When attempts *were* later made to provide Indigenous communities with Bibles in their own language this was generally done by Protestants, in the belief that the power of Scripture itself would somehow work miracles of conversion even if not backed up with equitable treatment and cordial relations between Indigenous and settler communities. Spanish inquisitors who came across such Protestant missionary Bibles, or related spiritual works in Indigenous languages, took steps to ban them as well.[31] The failures of this treatment were as spectacular as they were predictable, laying the groundwork for centuries of misunderstanding and contempt as European colonists became convinced that Indigenous peoples were somehow intellectually inferior because they did not always fully embrace a religion that was presented to them in incomprehensible, piecemeal fashion, by representatives who all too often did not know how to speak their language and instead communicated through violence, theft and the spread of epidemic disease.

The horrors of 'New World' colonialism could not be as thoroughly inflicted on many regions of Africa or Asia due to a wide variety of factors, including geography, demography, biological disease and political competition. But again similar attitudes can be discerned wherever European Catholics managed to establish themselves as colonizers in the early modern period, and wherever they sought to impose their religious regime. In Muslim regions of North Africa such as Oran (in modern Algeria), where Spanish forces burned Arabic books in 1509, well-established patterns of crusading violence and segregation remained the norm. In the Portuguese colonies of Angola, Cape Verde and Mozambique, for their part, local peoples were either ignored or assimilated in small numbers throughout the sixteenth century; a few Africans in Congo and Angola even learned enough Portuguese and Latin to become priests. However, the Church's insistence on maintaining absolute control over every detail of scriptural text and theological doctrine soon led to suspicions that imperfectly assimilated Africans might somehow 'corrupt' the faith. As a result, like the Indigenous peoples of the Americas, African access to the priesthood (and therefore the Scriptures) became more and more restricted after the end of the sixteenth century. Similar dynamics can be seen in Christian Ethiopia, where hopes were at first entertained that an alliance might be made against the Muslim Ottomans, especially after Emperor Susenyos I converted to Catholicism in 1622. After some ill-advised confiscations and burnings of Monophysite religious texts by Susenyos's Portuguese Jesuit advisors, however, it soon became clear that the local clergy and populace had no intention of submitting to papal standards of orthodoxy; rebellions and counter-burnings of missionary books ensued. Communications between the Roman and Ethiopian Churches subsequently reverted to what they had been for centuries: a matter of occasional envoys and scholarly exchanges, experienced on the Catholic side for the most part as exotic additions to papal libraries.

Meanwhile in Asia, small outposts of Catholic missionaries working to convert native communities in parts of the Philippines, Japan, China and India once again faced the problem of how to translate their religion into new cultural and linguistic contexts. The so-called 'Malabar Rites', 'Madurai Rites' and 'Chinese Rites' controversies resulted, in which some Church elites, primarily Jesuits, argued that it was necessary to adapt superficial or cultural aspects of Christianity (including dress, ceremony and religious terminology) to align with local expectations. Others considered this to be a gateway to heresy. The presence of Muslims in the Philippines made things easier – there so-called *moros* could simply be treated as had the *moriscos* back in Spain. In India, too, Muslim texts written in the Tamil Arwi language (using a modified Arabic script) were simply confiscated and burned. The Indian situation was complicated, however, by the discovery of local native 'St Thomas' Christian populations using age-old versions of the Syriac (Malabar) Bible, as well as by the long-standing coexistence of local Buddhists, Hindus and Jews. Portuguese inquisitors ultimately reacted by summarily burning many Indigenous Christian texts on the grounds of their Nestorian heresy, after the 1599 Synod of Diamper, without bothering to have them placed on an Index. Yet Jesuits such as Roberto Nobili simultaneously insisted on the value (and perhaps even the Christian spiritual overtones) of Hindu sacred writings such as the *Vedas*. Nobili's more tolerant approach was approved by Pope Paul v in 1616 and again by Gregory xv in 1623, despite strong opposition, and so Hindu books didn't become targets for formal Church censorship (which would likely have been impossible to enforce in any case, given the political and demographic realities of the subcontinent), despite lingering disapproval and debate.

In China and Japan Jesuits such as Matteo Ricci similarly argued that certain Buddhist, Taoist and above all Confucian practices could be fruitfully merged with Christian norms. Some went still further, translating and adapting Confucian texts such as the *Lunyu* (or 'Analects') in ways that emphasized their similarities with Christian spiritual and philosophical traditions. Once again, 'Chinese Rite' debates around the question of cultural adaptation for the most part took place in the form of theological arguments between members of the Catholic religious Orders (chiefly Jesuits, Dominicans and Franciscans) as well as at the papal Curia, rather than in the pages of the Index. But ultimately it was there that the matter was concluded: when first Clement xi (1704) and then Benedict xiv (1742) pronounced their opposition to tolerance of the 'Eastern Rites' and banned further discussion of the matter, this verdict was enshrined in the general *Decreta* of the 1758 Roman Index.[32] Polemics concerning the Jesuits' acceptance of such Rites were also censored.[33] Thus in this case censorship was aimed not at Chinese (or other 'Oriental') spiritual texts themselves, but rather at European Catholics who wanted to talk about them. Given its lack of political power in most of Asia, there was no way the Church could prevent such texts from continuing to circulate among non-Christians in places like China in any case. And, thanks to the Jesuit translators' skill at shaping, purging and revising, those versions that finally did end up circulating among European readers generally posed no offence to Christian sensibilities, making regular Index censorship unnecessary. As usual, then, Church censorship in East Asia was in principle for the most part an internal affair, directed by Catholic authorities against other Catholic authorities and for the benefit of Catholic audiences. But it would have long-term consequences for non-Christian communities as well.

⸺✠⸺

AS WE HAVE SEEN, the Indexes of Prohibited Books began as tools for those tasked with stemming the tide of printed 'heretical' challenges to Catholic doctrine that was sweeping Europe by the mid-sixteenth century, and this necessarily soon extended into censorship of Protestant editions, translations and studies of the Bible itself. The appeal of scriptural texts to pious Christians of all sorts could not be denied, however, and so even the Council of Trent's seemingly firm insistence on exclusive Catholic use of the traditional Latin Vulgate was immediately subject to numerous caveats. William Allen's efforts to promote a new Catholic Bible in English, like those of many other colleagues working in Protestant-dominated regions, were fully embraced by the Church even while inquisitors insisted that such vernacular translations – and indeed papally approved revisions to the Latin Vulgate text itself – needed to be carefully monitored and restricted in their circulation. The struggle to control text was perhaps at its most vital, and problematic, when it came to the dizzyingly complex world of early modern Bible scholarship.

Translations of the Bible into non-European languages, though hardly a novel phenomenon, inspired still more concern as colonial regimes began to spread both Christianity and gradually evolving notions of European cultural superiority into new lands in this same period. In some cases Catholic theologians were happy to discover new depths of meaning by studying alternative versions of the Bible and ancillary Scriptures, and some embraced the possibility of working with local African, Asian and Indigenous American intellectuals (and even with Muslims and Jews) to share religious insights. Yet crackdowns and prohibitions against such sharing were also all too common. Hebrew and Arabic books were feared as possible instigators of doubt, especially among recent converts from Judaism or Islam, leading to sweeping Index bans on Talmudic or Qur'anic literature even as these same texts were simultaneously being appropriated for Christian use. Other non-Christian or schismatic religious writings were similarly destroyed or seized in vast quantities, even though records of such censorship rarely made their way onto the pages of the Index itself. Colonial colleges and seminaries, at first intended to train newly converted populations and potential clergymen in the mysteries of Christianity, were ultimately closed down in a further manifestation of Church-led 'censorship' – and sophisticated translations of spiritual treatises and Bibles produced for their students' use were also suppressed. Superficial missionary catechisms and low-quality (often abusive) mission schools ultimately emerged to take their place, with predictable results.

Poorly documented (or entirely unrecorded) summary confiscations and burnings of non-Christian Scriptures, or of writings sacred to the allegedly heretical Christians of Ethiopia or India, were obviously a far cry from the more methodical, normative practices of Index censorship. Unlike Bibles and scriptural commentaries printed by European Protestants such as Martin Luther or William Tyndale (along with spiritual writings by controversial Catholics such as Ramon Llull or Desiderius Erasmus), all of which were carefully checked and duly written up by designated experts as formal targets of Church discipline, non-European texts were often dealt with on the ground by poorly trained local priests who saw any text they didn't fully understand or control as an inherent threat. All too often, precious manuscripts and inscriptions disappeared more or less completely as a result, along with transmission of oral teachings – permanently cutting colonized peoples off from vital aspects of their age-old spiritual traditions, without so much as leaving any clear trace of their elimination in the records of an official Index.

Such wanton, unsystematic and thoughtless destruction did not occur everywhere. In regions where colonial domination proved impossible (or developed more slowly), increased levels of 'Orientalist' scholarship continued to result from Catholic missionaries' contacts with non-European religious texts – above all, when it came to Confucianism, Hinduism and the other religious traditions of India and Japan from the seventeenth century on. The key difference always related to perceived levels of threat that such works might pose to Catholic Christianity itself, primarily in Europe, but also among the many catechumens of the Church's increasingly global flocks. Thus circulation of complex Latin digests of Chinese scholarship among learned European elites never concerned Church censors in the same way that Qur'anic survivals did among the *moriscos* of Spain, while continued circulation of Confucian writings within China was both inevitable and fully acceptable to defenders of the 'Chinese Rites'. Similarly, English (and other European) translations of the Bible were acceptable and even desirable to a strict Catholic censor like William Allen, so long as they were approved by Church officials, because it was understood that in their absence local Christians might instead resort to readily-available Protestant versions.

Such courtesy was not extended to Spanish or Italian Christians until modern times, since it was hoped that they could be more effectively kept away from Protestant books and forced to accept the Vulgate Latin alone. Worst of all, it was withheld altogether from colonial populations in the Americas and elsewhere, as authorities increasingly gravitated towards policies aimed at destroying Indigenous languages and cultures rather than adapting Christianity to its new milieux. Despite its lack of formal appearance in the Indexes, censorship of both Indigenous spiritual texts and translations into Indigenous languages would be one of the most long-lasting harms ever inflicted by the Catholic Church upon the New World. Combined with the distorting effects of much appropriative Orientalist scholarship, and the direct impact of Index censorship on all forms of 'heterodox' Christian religious thought, such intolerant attitudes inevitably foreclosed on many possibilities for intellectual sharing in the so-called Age of Exploration, greatly impoverishing the history of human spirituality in the process.

6 CENSORED MAGIC AND SCIENCE

On 8 February 1600, a Dominican friar was formally degraded. This meant that he was stripped of all signs relating to his religious authority, which included not only vestments and tonsure but scraping away the skin of his fingers and palms that had once been anointed with holy oil. Furthermore, this ex-friar was informed by inquisitorial decree that his many writings (bearing such provocative titles as *Theses on Magic*, *The Incantation of Circe* and *The Expulsion of the Triumphant Beast*) were henceforth to be prohibited. Nine days later, on Ash Wednesday, the same man was bound, gagged and burned alive at a wooden stake that had been constructed in the normally cheerful Campo de' Fiori marketplace in the centre of Rome. Giordano Bruno of Nola's death is today commemorated by an ominous bronze statue that looms over the flower-vendors and tourists who continue to flock to this site – many unaware of the awesome events that took place here more than four hundred years ago.

Prohibition of Bruno's writings did not come swiftly, or easily, however. It took years of effort and debate, as various parties within the Catholic Church hierarchy struggled over how best to deal with a man widely purported to be both deeply spiritual and a brilliant scientist, if also an unapologetic freethinker steeped in the dark arts of magic and demon-summoning. Bruno had first aroused suspicions by removing all the holy images from his cell while still a teenage novice in 1566, and by quarrelling with others over religious matters. The young friar was subsequently accused of secretly reading banned books (including a copy of Erasmus' *Commentaries*, which he hid in the convent latrine), and he was forced to flee first to Genoa, then to Venice and finally to Protestant Geneva by 1579. Making himself equally unwelcome among Swiss Calvinists, the runaway Dominican next travelled widely in France, England and Germany where he continued to promote his scientific theories. Finally in 1592 he returned to Venice, in the hopes of making money teaching what he marketed as Ramon Llull's secret memory-enhancing techniques, only to be denounced and arrested by local inquisitors after falling out with a wealthy patron. Bruno was handed over to the Roman Inquisition a

Ettore Ferrari, statue of Giordano Bruno, 1889, Rome.

few months later, and his trial would last for seven more years before the guilty verdict was finally pronounced by Pope Clement VIII and his cardinal-inquisitors.

Even after his shocking execution, it took still more time for Bruno's name to actually find its way onto the Index of Prohibited Books due to bureaucratic inefficiencies. Though a lengthy edict was published by the current master of the sacred palace (Bruno's Dominican colleague Giovanni Maria Guanzelli) against his *opera omnia* and the works of many other authors in 1603, this came too late to be included in either later re-printings of the Clementine Index or the Spanish Index of 1612. It was only in 1664 that Alexander VII's revised Roman Index finally included an entry for '*Iordani Bruni nolani libri, & scripta omnia*'. Meanwhile word of the ban had reached Spain, but in hopelessly garbled form: on the Spanish Index of 1632 we thus find condemnation of works by one 'Iordanus Bruerus Holanus, *phil*.'. This mistake was repeated by generation after generation of copyists who evidently had no idea who they were censoring, until by 1790 it had evolved into a first-class condemnation of a non-existent Dutch philologist now known as 'Bruerus (Jordanus), Holland. Philol. 1 *cl*.'[1]

The precise cause of brother Jordan's extraordinarily harsh treatment is also not entirely clear. His disobedience, intellectual pride and stubbornness of character probably didn't help, nor did his extensive and very public dealings with Protestants. But some of the key documents for Bruno's trial are unfortunately among the many records of the Roman inquisitorial tribunal that were later seized by Napoleon and sent to Paris, only to be pulped for cardboard or used to wrap fish after Waterloo.[2] One must instead rely on a summary of charges and other ancillary files to understand Bruno's case, as well as the severity of its outcome. From these, scholars have long debated whether the death sentence was primarily a result of his religious heresy, his sorcery or his scientific innovations. Lines between the three categories were far more blurry for Roman inquisitors than they may appear to modern eyes, however. To fully understand the ways in which works relating not only to 'magical' (and even potentially 'demonic') practices were banned right alongside books and ideas that are now considered to be invaluable milestones in the history of 'science', we need to take a closer look at just what such words meant to late medieval and early modern minds. Whether mathematical, physical, medical or social in nature, all of what we now consider to be the 'sciences' were in fact inextricably tied to religious beliefs in the eyes of premodern Church authorities – and potentially linked with more sinister arcane powers as well.

Indexes of Prohibited Books did censor many authors and texts for their 'scientific' (as opposed to more religious or imaginative) content, ranging from the famous cases of Bruno and Galileo Galilei to those of more obscure fellow-travellers such as Girolamo Cardano and Giovan Battista Della Porta. Church authorities also definitely frowned on some (but by no means all) forms of knowledge and practice that we would today call 'magic'. At the same time, the nature and extent of this censorship should not be exaggerated, as it has often been in the past. The Catholic Church as a whole was never bluntly 'anti-science', and indeed it was much more lenient towards many magicians and witches than Protestant and modern secularist polemics would suggest. On the contrary, Catholic Rome was an acknowledged centre of cutting-edge scientific thought throughout most of the early modern period, and several popes and other high-ranking Church figures could be counted among the most generously enthusiastic patrons of knowledge and research in their day. Likewise, while sorcerers were by no means safe from prosecution in Catholic lands, some of the most deadly 'witch-hunts' (including those conducted in Salem, Massachusetts, around 1692) were in fact led by Protestant or state officials. The Catholic Church's attitudes towards science and magic, in all their forms, were rather nuanced, complex and shifting, and as with so many aspects of Catholic censorship, they tended to have as much (if not more) to do with concerns about maintaining Church authority and protecting what was thought to be the spiritual wellbeing of Christian souls than with a rigid desire to stamp out all forms of intellectual deviation per se. It is therefore interesting to pay close attention not only to what was actually placed on the Indexes, but on what was left out, and why.

Censored Magic

The word *magus* in Latin originally referred to a Persian wise man, generally a priest of the Zoroastrian faith in what is today called Iran. In the Bible, Matthew 2:1–12 tells a story of how some 'magi' came from the east to worship the baby Jesus, because they had read signs in the stars. The idea that these sorts of wise scholars from an alien religious tradition might have magical powers was quite common in premodern Europe, and it was not necessarily seen as a bad thing. People from all walks of life believed in supernatural forces, and that such forces could be influenced by those who possessed secret knowledge. Exotic foreigners were exactly the kinds of people who might hold such knowledge, and they were often sought out for that reason. Persians were reputed to be great magicians from biblical times through Roman antiquity; and by the Middle Ages the same was often said of Jews and Muslims. In colonial times too, this phenomenon would be maintained as early modern African, American and Asian sages were regularly presumed to be keepers of valuable esoteric wisdom.

The *magia* that these sorts of people could wield varied, and it was evaluated accordingly. There was no overall ban on 'magic' as we understand it in the Middle Ages, because pretty much everyone agreed that certain supernatural practices were entirely legitimate and even praiseworthy. Expert interpretation of the stars or other natural phenomena (whether earth, fire, water or the lines on a human palm), for example, could help predict future events and solve problems, while love potions might help to overcome romantic hurdles.[3] Similarly, it was widely believed that special words, herbs, stones and other substances had healing powers – often compounded when used in combination, in specific arrangements (sometimes in the form of images and talismans), and under the correct alignments of the stars. Today this may sound an awful lot like magic, but for most medieval people it was simply wisdom, being used for good purposes such as healing and the betterment of human society; that is to say, more or less exactly what we now tend to think of as proper science. More problematic were instances of bad magic, or *maleficium* – literally, 'evildoing'. If a wise person used words, herbs, stones or other ingredients to curse, poison or deceive people (or to manipulate them in unwanted ways by means of love magic) then they could be considered criminals and subjected to harsh punishment. But magic itself was not illegal. It was simply illegal to harm people by misusing magic. Magic was a tool that could be used for good or ill, but few questioned whether or not it was acceptable, let alone 'real'.

Scientia, for its part, was a rather broad Latin term for 'knowledge', and specifically for the sort of disciplined expert knowledge that a scholar might learn at university or in a monastic school (though it could also involve more technical skills acquired through apprenticeship). Long before the advent of modern experimental methods, the most learned of scholars were expected to gain their wisdom above all from the teachings of the ancients, as laid down in books. 'The older the better' was often a rule of thumb, and sometimes 'the more obscure the better' too – the thought of accessing lost or hidden secret knowledge was exciting for many perfectly orthodox scholars in this period. Examples would include the English Franciscan Roger Bacon (d. 1292), later known as *Doctor mirabilis*, famous for his explorations of ancient learning and sometimes exotic, even occult, experimentation; as was the teacher of St Thomas Aquinas himself, Albert the Great. Albert (d. 1280, also canonized and named a Doctor of the Church in 1931) was a German Dominican, famed far and wide for his learning in not only theology but astrology, alchemy and divination. His reputation was indeed such that many magical works would later circulate under his name, including some that ended up on the Index.[4]

Concerns about more sinister forms of magic, and above all those that might involve the assistance of demons, started to grow by the end of the thirteenth century. Theologians now argued more forcefully that even some seemingly innocent types of magic actually depended on the aid of demonic forces, and a series of divinatory methods were therefore condemned by bishops and inquisitors in Paris in 1290, along with mysterious books on topics such as the *Decem annulorum veneris* (Ten Rings of Venus), or containing 'horrible incantations and detestable rites'.[5] Such wicked practices were among the many charges levelled against the Knights Templar in 1307, and Pope John XXII conducted a number of trials against alleged sorcerers (including several high-ranking Church officials) who were accused of poisonings and other mischief throughout his reign (1316–34). In 1326, John issued a bull imposing excommunication on all who summon demons, and henceforth this type of necromancy – and all forms of magic associated with it – could be considered a form of heretical apostasy.[6] The idea was that a good Christian should rely on the Church itself and its sacramental role in channelling divine favour. To look elsewhere by seeking the aid of demons (even in hopes of achieving good ends) was to give up on God in an inherently sinful way.

Nicholas Eymeric's 1376 *Directorium inquisitorum* reflects this trend in its important chapters on the need for inquisitors to prosecute demon summoners.[7] Eymeric also targeted several magical texts in his sections on book censorship, and (directly citing the Paris declaration of 1290), advised inquisitors to implement a total ban on any books dealing with necromancy, geomancy, pyromancy, hydromancy or chiromancy, among other practices he considered to be demonic.[8] Similar views were widely shared at the Council of Basel after 1431, and by means of writings such as Johannes Nider's *Formicarius* or the anonymous *Errores gazariorum*. These warned of a rising tendency among many magicians, and especially among female witches, to make explicit pacts with the Devil and to renounce their Christianity entirely. A demonic war against the Church was predicted, and several witch trials were held in hopes of stamping out the problem. By the end of the fifteenth century, witch-hunting had become still more common in many parts of Europe and texts such as the 1486 *Malleus maleficarum* were circulated to assist in such efforts. Similar trials, and manuals, would continue to appear throughout the early modern period.[9]

Yet at the same time, elite fascination with magical powers remained strong and indeed likely deepened. Eymeric's own secular overlord King Peter IV of Aragon (r. 1336–87), and Peter's heir, Joan I (r. 1387–96), continued to consult sorcerers on a regular basis, especially if they were Jewish or Muslim, while expelling their outspoken inquisitor for being such a nuisance. Magicians who could heal were widely admired and highly paid, as were court astrologers who could predict the future – in secular courts but also (perhaps especially) among learned churchmen and even popes. A bifurcation of magical knowledge that had always existed, between elite scholarly practice and the folk-wisdom of village healers, now intensified with the discovery (and creation) of new texts purporting to transmit ancient secrets allegedly connected to such figures as Plato, Aristotle, King Solomon and a semi-mythical ancient Egyptian sorcerer known as Hermes Trismegistus.

To the resulting Renaissance craze for scholarly Neoplatonic and Hermetic knowledge was added a fascination with Jewish Kabbalah. As noted in Chapter Five, some late medieval and early modern Christians believed that Kabbalistic literature could be used to deepen their understanding of the Bible; it was also argued that such works might hold great potential as resources for arcane knowledge as well. Chief among the proponents of such enhanced varieties of elite bookish magic were the Florentine Marsilio Ficino (d. 1499), who first translated the *Pimander* of Hermes into Latin in 1471; his colleague Giovanni Pico Della Mirandola (d. 1494); and the Germans Johannes Trithemius (d. 1516) and his student Henricus Cornelius Agrippa von Nettesheim (d. 1535).

Yet only one of these four prominent magical pioneers, Agrippa, would actually be placed on the Index of Forbidden Books during the sixteenth century. From 1544 his name appears in the earliest Parisian Indexes, with explicit mention of three books including his *De vanitate scientiarum* (On the Vanity of the Sciences) – ironically, a text in which he claimed to reject illicit magical practices, as well as some more acceptable ones. The posture was not uncommon, and it was soon recognized for what it was: a defensive ruse. By 1546 compilers of the first Leuven Index had also banned his three-part *De occulta philosophia*, a sorcerer's handbook that would remain notorious throughout the early modern period. A commentary by Agrippa on Ramon Llull was prohibited by the Leuven Index of 1558, and Agrippa's complete works (*opera omnia*) were placed on the Roman Index from 1559. Such attention was no doubt warranted, but the paucity of Index entries for other Hermetic authors throughout the sixteenth century suggests a strong ambivalence on the part of Church authorities. Certainly a handful of more obscure titles can be found on various Indexes, such as the otherwise unknown *Les commandements & doctrine du philosophe Aristote, a son disciple Roy alexandre*, which may or may not have contained arcane knowledge. The astrologer, physician and mathematician Girolamo Cardano's *De subtilitate rerum* (On the Subtlety of Things) appeared on the 1551 Paris Index, as did several of his other works over the decades (with general exceptions made for most of his 'valuable' medical treatises), but otherwise censorship of patently magical materials was remarkably rare for several decades after the Council of Trent. Isolated further examples can always be found, such as scattered prohibitions against Paracelsus (d. 1541) after 1580, or the Spanish Inquisition's 1583 ban on Giovan Battista Della Porta's *Magia naturalis* (this work was also briefly added to the Roman Index in 1590 and 1593, though Della Porta continued to enjoy great prestige until his death in 1615). But it remains telling that Trithemius' *Steganographia* was only prohibited

Anon., *Henricus Cornelius Agrippa*, 16th century, engraving. Note that the death date given here is incorrect.

by a Roman edict of 1609, and placed on the Spanish Index from 1612 – nearly a century after his death.[10]

The fact that well-known Hermetic scholars such as Ficino and Pico, not to mention later figures such as the infamous John Dee (d. 1608) never seem to have appeared at all on the Indexes of Prohibited Books need come as no real surprise. Despite occasional broad pronouncements of condemnation – including Rule no. 9 in the Trent Index, which banned books of geomancy, hydromancy, aeromancy, pyromancy, onomancy (name-magic), chiromancy, necromancy and astrology along with 'sorcery, poisons (*veneficia*), auguries, predictions and magical incantations' (and made exceptions only for certain types of 'judgements and natural observations to aid in the navigational, agricultural and medical arts') – many powerful figures continued to trust in diviners and astrologers who consulted magical texts. Furthermore, both Church and state authorities showed little interest in condemning any but the most objectionable (and generally demon-assisted) forms of alchemy. Giordano Bruno himself was at first welcomed at the courts of Henry III of France (whose mother, Catherine de' Medici, was a well-known Hermetic enthusiast) and Elizabeth I of England, among others. Elizabeth also relied heavily on the skills and predictions of magi such as John Dee, as did Emperor Rudolph II at his trend-setting court in Prague (r. 1576–1612). The Platonist philosopher Francesco Patrizi (Patricius, d. 1597) was similarly welcomed and admired in papal courts from the reign of Gregory XIII to that of Clement VIII, in spite (or perhaps rather because) of his strong interests in Hermetic wisdom. Patrizi fell only partially from grace after his *Nova de universis philosophia* was placed on the Roman Index of 1596, with politics and then fatal illness preventing his planned defence of their validity. Most of his writings continued to circulate, and they were only lightly expurgated in Spanish Indexes after 1612. Thus while the Church hierarchy maintained a strong suspicion of many magical practices, while witch-hunts raged and while fears of demonic connections even to long-established forms of divination were revived after 1578 by the re-publication of Eymeric's *Directorium* (with enhanced notes from Francisco Peña as noted in Chapter Three),[11] exceptions continued to be made and treatises inspired by 'magical' Hermetic ideas, including some far more suspicious than Patrizi's, continued to circulate above all in the highest levels of Christian society.

Censored Science

Hermetic influences notwithstanding, the chief motives for censoring texts like Patrizi's *Nova de universis philosophia* were in fact closely linked to later sixteenth- and early seventeenth-century debates that we would now tend to recognize as scientific rather than magical. For one thing, Patrizi suggested that the earth moved, rotating on its axis, a thesis rejected as contrary to biblical teachings by both the Dominican Pedro Juan Zaragoza and the Jesuit Benedetto Giustiniani in their reports to Clement VIII's master of the sacred palace Bartolomeo de Miranda. Patrizi was also condemned for levelling Platonist attacks against traditional Aristotelian physics, along with Ptolemaic astronomical knowledge, thus impugning the prestige and authority of the entire (mostly Church-led) scientific community. Patrizi was neither the first nor the last to make such arguments, of course, and the movement of which he was a part was beginning to be seen as a serious threat by some ecclesiastical authorities. The censorship he faced was thus very much a sign of the times. Writings and theories associated with what would eventually be called the 'Scientific Revolution' were gradually becoming almost as important a battleground for Church authorities by the early seventeenth century as the suppression of Protestant and otherwise problematic 'religious' texts had been in the days of the first Indexes of Prohibited Books.

As previously noted, however, making hard distinctions between science (or magic) and religion would have been difficult for the parties most directly involved. Zaragoza, Giustiniani and their colleagues saw religious implications – indeed an irresponsible threat to the spiritual well-being of good Christians – in accepting the prospect of a less-than-solid or moveable earth at the centre of God's creation. And they were undoubtedly aware, as was Patrizi, that such theories derived as much from the ancient writings of Hermetic and Pythagorean magi as they did from more recent physical observations. Like Copernicus, who had proposed the revolutionary thesis of a heliocentric universe with orbiting, rotating planets in his 1543 *De revolutionibus orbium coelestium* (On the Revolutions of the Heavenly Spheres), Patrizi (and Cardano, and other would-be astronomers including Giordano Bruno) was not yet able to access the telescopic technology that would permit advancement of new astronomical concepts with ever-greater degrees of certainty after

1609. Yet philosopher-mages like Patrizi and Bruno, as well as more celebrated pioneers of modern observational and experimental science such as Copernicus, Brahe, Kepler, Galileo and later Newton, were all part of a growing intellectual tendency that would challenge some of the Church's most basic accepted beliefs about the natural world. All of these men found themselves named in the pages of the Index of Prohibited Books as a result.

Reactions were not always total, or swift. Copernicus was finally added to the Roman Index thanks to an edict of 1616, 73 years after his death, and then only 'pending correction' of the *De revolutionibus*. Johannes Kepler's discussion of Copernicus, titled *Epitome astronomicae copernicanae*, followed suit in 1619 (even before the appearance of its final volume), but his more influential writings such as the 1609 *Astronomia nova* were never specifically banned. Many works by Kepler's predecessor Tycho Brahe were also permitted to continue in circulation, though subject to expurgation in Spain.[12] Such censorship reflected a gradual hardening of attitudes that would culminate in the case of Galileo Galilei, whose sensational observations and powerful endorsements of previous Copernican theories caused serious factional disputes within the Roman Curia after publication of his *Sidereus nuncius* (Starry Messenger) in 1610. It was no coincidence that he found himself before a tribunal of the Inquisition six years later, precisely as papal censors were finally moving (despite some lingering hesitations) to place the ideas of Copernicus on the Index.

Galileo's dealings with the Inquisition and the Index are well documented, if still often poorly understood by many readers of history, as are the opinions of various Church leaders both for and against him. Simplified versions of the story have served critics of the Church well as an integral pillar of so-called 'Black Legend' allegations that Catholicism is inherently opposed to science, but the truth is that every stage of Galileo's career – from his early studies in Pisa, to his well-endowed research career at the Medici court in Florence, to his membership in the Accademia dei Lincei and elite contacts with popes, culminating in his two high-level inquisitorial hearings in 1616 and 1632 – was part of a much more complex historical tragedy in which scientific ideas, religious beliefs, legal arguments, political rivalries and economic interests, as well as clashing personalities, all played a role.

To fully recount and dissect the matter would go well beyond the limits of this chapter. Suffice it to say that Galileo was simultaneously praised as a groundbreaking genius by his sympathetic allies in the Church hierarchy, and mistrusted by others as an egotistical and dangerous self-promoter who put the marketing of his dubious theories (even in Protestant lands) ahead of papal authority and collegial consensus – an authority and consensus that they saw as more or less equivalent to the good of the Church community as a whole. Whatever the intricacies and merits of either characterization, the outcome remains: Galileo was cautioned to retract his most daring claims regarding Copernican heliocentrism in 1616, and (much like the theologians previously instructed to keep their silence on the divisive question of *De auxiliis*) he was ordered not to write about them anymore. However, after several years of continued research, and the 1623 elevation of his erstwhile friend Urban VIII to the papacy, Galileo decided to publish the *Dialogo sopra i due massimi sistemi del mondo* (Dialogue Concerning the Two Chief World Systems), which was widely seen as a violation of his previous discipline and a personal insult to the pope. Published in 1632 and condemned in 1634, this was in fact the only one of Galileo's astronomical and other writings to be placed on the Roman Index (and like Copernicus and Kepler, Galileo never appeared in the Spanish Indexes). The astronomer spent the rest of his days under house arrest, but he continued to write until his death in 1642. A final major final study entitled *Discorsi e demostrazioni matematiche intorno a due nuove scienze* (Discourses and Mathematical Demonstrations Relating to Two New Sciences) was secretly dispatched to a publisher in the Protestant Netherlands in 1638, where it could be circulated beyond the reach of Catholic censorial interference.

The placement of Copernican theories on the Index, and the inquisitorial prosecution of Galileo, was immediately condemned by many scholars all over the emerging international Republic of Letters, and would eventually become a symbol of Catholic error once heliocentrism had been accepted as scientific orthodoxy. Giordano Bruno's magical and spiritual experiments, along with his more extravagant musings about topics such as the existence of multiple solar systems, life on other planets and the possible colonization of the moon, were less sympathetically received until very recently. The fact is that once bold new theories and experiments successfully lead to modern scientific conclusions, they can easily be hailed with the benefit of hindsight; yet when they do not, they are readily dismissed as the work of quacks and dreamers. Censors working in the seventeenth century followed what they believed to be the best scientific consensus of their day, and sought to suppress what they considered junk science that could be harmful to society. We may well disagree with their decisions today, and lament the damage they caused, especially when it is evident that political influence or incompetence led to particularly unfair outcomes. But it is still worth keeping in mind the realities of the historical context in which they necessarily operated, in order to fully appreciate the causes, effects and meanings of their actions.

This holds true for other disciplines aside from astronomy as well, though Galileo's relatively minor place on the Index has unfortunately eclipsed many other equally or more important instances of Church censorship. Girolamo Cardano may have been charged as a heretic primarily because of his astronomical and divinatory astrological writings, but prohibition of his *opera omnia* also prevented his legitimate mathematical discoveries (primarily concerning probability and algebra) from achieving wide circulation. Disputes over the acceptability of Bonaventura Cavalieri's controversial mathematical research too, which would later prove essential to the development of Newtonian calculus, also led to a 1632 prohibition against the teaching of his theories on infinitesimals throughout the Jesuit Order and its many schools.[13] This ban was secured by the same scholars who engineered Galileo's condemnation a few months later, and for very similar reasons, though with a rather less dramatic result. For while the Jesuit ban in this case resulted in no formal entry on the Index, a point was still clearly being underlined for the benefit of Cavalieri and others: innovations in mathematics, like astronomy, which might challenge accepted Catholic notions about the structure of the universe, would not be tolerated. Curricular suppression, threats and self-censorship, especially in the wake of Bruno's death and Galileo's imprisonment, would sometimes prove just as powerful as the Index itself in terms of temporarily stifling new ideas.

In the somewhat less politicized field of medicine, we find that Johannes Dryander's *Anatomia capitis humani* (Anatomy of the Human Head), the first illustrated treatise to describe the physical structures of the brain, was nevertheless placed on the Index as early as 1546; it was soon joined by the many medical writings of Leonhart Fuchs (d. 1566), including his summaries of Vesalius in *De humani corporis fabrica ex Galeno et Vesalio epitome*. The first volume of Vesalius' important *De humani corporis fabrica* (1543) may also have been banned at one point, though the cryptic nature of entries for '*Vesseli to. primo*' in the Venetian and Milanese Indexes of 1554 make it impossible to be sure. Certainly Vesalius' book 5, chapter 15 (on the female reproductive system) was subjected to some relatively minor expurgation in the Spanish Index of 1747. The reasons for such censorship remain unclear in some cases: Dryander and Fuchs may have been banned as much for the fact that they were Protestants as for their medical contributions. Medical science was normally highly valued, and the Church generally had no problem with anatomical dissection in its service; hence even if Vesalius was briefly placed on the Index in 1554 and again in 1747, he and his readers were for the most part left alone by Index censors. Official toleration notwithstanding, however, recent studies have shown that anatomical illustrations in physical copies of *De humani corporis fabrica* were often subjected to ad hoc censorship by local inquisitors, owners and over-zealous librarians.[14]

There are other examples of censored medical texts scattered about the Indexes, but apparently no sustained campaigns similar to the early seventeenth-century attack on heliocentrism (and mathematics). Published medical anecdotes that reflected poorly on the dignity of the Church were taken very seriously, leading for example to expurgation of Amatus Lusitanus' *Curationum medicinalium centuriae* ('Hundreds of Medical Cures', published in seven volumes from 1551–61) for its mention of a pregnant nun.[15] Of course some censored medical practices were indeed of dubious value, and their suppression may not always have been a bad thing (as with 'junk science' today); regular Index warnings against 'superstitious' rites were undoubtedly aimed at least in part at quacks preying on the vulnerable. But the full extent of Index censorship on medical texts is just beginning to be explored, and while wholesale elimination of medical scholarship never seems to have been a goal for any inquisitors, the insidious effect of micro-managing and expurgating potentially valuable knowledge, not to mention the impact of self-censorship when subjected to authoritarian surveillance, is always hard to assess.

The continuation of interest in, and measured censorship of, studies on demonology and magic (both of which continued to be taken seriously as potential academic disciplines) must also be kept in mind as we survey these instances of more 'scientific' censorship, since individuals targeted in either case were often one and the same; neither the Scientific Revolution nor the Enlightenment really ever put a damper on arcane pursuits. Spanish and Roman censors decided to place the *Clavis Salomonis* (Key of Solomon), a book of spells and instructions for calling upon spirits, on their earliest Indexes in the 1550s, but a century later this text remained popular enough to inspire a still more frankly demonological 'Lesser Key of Solomon', complete with passages drawn from Trithemius and Paracelsus, among others. The Spanish Index also prohibited the astrological writings of Abu Mashar Jafar ibn Muhammad ibn Umar al-Balkhi (d. 886, there listed as 'Albumasar Arabs, alias Japhar'), from 1632 to 1790, while making an exception for what censors took to be the meteorological and medical value of his treatise *De mutatione aeris* (On Changes of the Air).[16]

Early modern defenders of demonological studies continued to insist on the harmless and potentially valuable nature of their own work, too, so long as it was conducted by trained experts. Agrippa's Dutch student Johann Weyer (or Wier, d. 1588), a medical doctor whose *De praestigiis daemonum* (On the Tricks of Demons) argued against the persecution of witches and claimed that most beliefs concerning them (such as those contained in the *Malleus maleficarum*) were simply delusional, still did not hesitate to include an appendix entitled *Pseudomonarchia daemonum* (False Monarchy of Demons) – in which he provided extensive 'scientific' descriptions of demonic forces, along with detailed instructions on how to summon and control them. Inquisitors disapproved, and *De praestigiis* was placed on the Antwerp Index of 1569 soon after its publication (a ban that was subsequently taken up by the Spanish Inquisition in 1583, and at Rome by 1596). Weyer was also opposed by the French historian, statesman and amateur demonologist Jean Bodin (d. 1596), whose competing *Demonomania* was placed on the Roman Index in 1590.[17] Yet censorship and disapproval did not prevent an English parliamentarian named Reginald Scot (d. 1599) from fully endorsing and reproducing Weyer's ideas in his 1584 *Discoverie of Witchcraft*, which would also be read with great interest (and distaste) by the future King James I of England.[18]

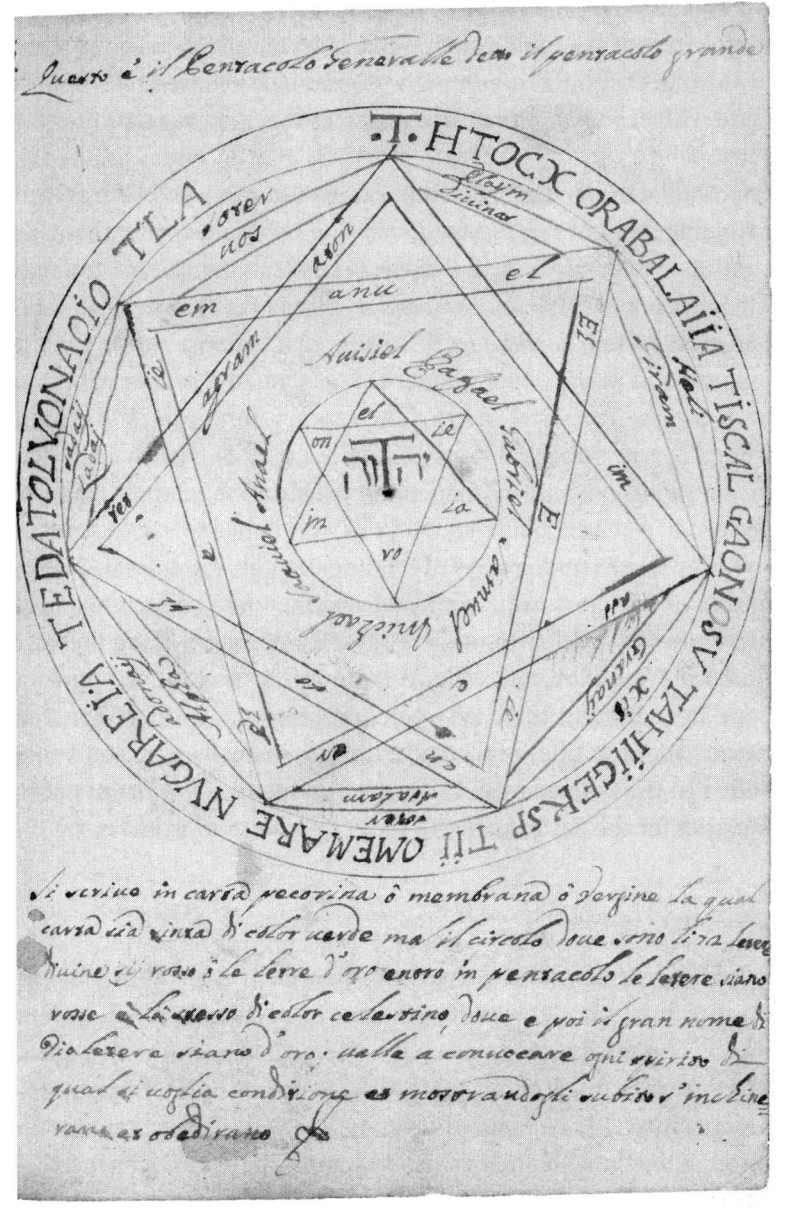

Magical diagram and text, from an Italian translation of the Key of Solomon, *Clavicolo di Salomone Re d'Israel figlio de David*, 18th century.

Debates over the status of magical science and the dangers (or usefulness) of demonic contact, like all scientific debates, evolved over time. Demon-summoning was gradually eclipsed by a fascination with exorcism, which also gradually emerged as a new field for censorship by the eighteenth century. Despite an initial attempt by Pope Paul V to standardize Catholic demon-taming procedures with his publication of the *Rituale Romanum* in 1614, existing manuals continued to be used, including the Franciscan inquisitor Girolamo Menghi's popular Italian *Compendio dell'arte essorcistica* (1576) and Latin *Flagellum daemonum* (Scourge of Demons, 1576). Expert opinion and professional standards regarding the proper handling of demons shifted over the ensuing century, however, to the point where overly elaborate Renaissance-era rituals (which included incantations, talismanic images and even potion recipes) came to be seen as not only outdated but positively dangerous, and open to abuse by those seeking ways of binding demons for more nefarious purposes. Menghi's exorcism texts were therefore banned by papal decree in 1704 and 1707, as were several others including the 1582 *Practica exorcistarum* of Valerio Polidoro. In 1725 the Dominican pope Benedict XIII imposed a total prohibition on all unapproved rituals, and new titles of banned exorcism manuals were still being added to the 1790 Spanish Index – all in the name of maintaining integrity for the performance of properly 'scientific' exorcisms.[19]

Censored Humanities

Scientific entries of all sorts thus abound in the Indexes of the seventeenth and eighteenth centuries in particular, to the extent that it is impossible to list or analyse them all here. But even a quick survey reveals much about some of the ways in which European (for the most part) knowledge evolved from the Scientific Revolution through the Enlightenment period, along with the Church's increasingly futile efforts to control it. Scientific publications by the prolific French (and Francophile) *philosophes*, often iconoclastic and anticlerical if not downright atheistic in perspective, were an especially serious challenge for Index censors. And, in addition to the theoretical and physical sciences, such 'enlightened' freethinkers began to push the boundaries of traditional human and social sciences, in some cases by bringing entirely new disciplines to light. Horrified by their 'materialism' as much as by their lack of deference to traditional Catholic authorities, Index censors were quick to add prominent authors such as Voltaire, Rousseau, Hume and Kant, as well as the entire *Encyclopédie* of Diderot and D'Alembert, to their ever-growing lists, as previously discussed in Chapter Three. They also catalogued many lesser luminaries, including several whose contributions to human knowledge would ironically be all-but-unknown today were it not for the Index's record of their prohibition.

History was perhaps the most dangerous of the so-called 'humanities' disciplines from a religious point of view, and so it is not surprising that unorthodox historical books were already among the first targets for censorship to appear on the Indexes of Paris and Leuven in the 1540s. The political and religious implications of getting history 'wrong', from a Catholic perspective, were obvious: historical narratives permitted criticisms of papal leadership, for example, and endorsements for various figures and movements the Church considered to be heretical. Some prohibitions may now strike us as absurd and petty, such as those against Andrea Althameri's obscure commentary on the Roman historian Tacitus, Achilles Gasser's *Historiarum et chronicorum totius mundi epitome* (Epitome of the Histories and Chronicles of the Whole World), or Johannes Rhellicanus' annotations on the *De bello gallico* (On the Gallic War) of Julius Caesar. All three authors were Protestants (and Gasser a prominent Copernican to boot), which likely explains their presence on the 1544 and 1549 Parisian Indexes, and that of Leuven from 1550, respectively.[20] More serious were Matthias Flacius (Illyricus) and other Lutheran scholars' *Magdeburg Centuries*, a popular and influential Protestant version of Church history that pulled no punches in denouncing the papacy as a diabolical office. *Centuries* was placed on the Index in Antwerp, Portugal, Spain and Rome soon after its first volumes began to appear in 1559, and Flacius' *opera omnia* had already been listed as early as 1554 in Venice. Of course, critical histories of the Inquisitions themselves, such as those written by Charles Dellon (d. 1709), Philippe Limborch (d. 1712) and Jacques Marsollier (d. 1724), also deserved special places on the Index.[21] Such censorship of historians, whether Protestant or not, obscure or famous, would continue throughout the history of the Index, including bans on important Enlightenment works such as Oliver Goldsmith's and David Hume's *Histories* of England or Gibbon's *Decline and Fall of the*

Roman Empire, all produced in the 1770s (though each only came to the inquisitors' notice once they were translated into Italian, which in Hume's case took until 1827).

Books on political theory also posed potential threats, both on a spiritual level and as challenges to the Church's claims to secular power. Medieval authors who had taken the imperial side in John XXII's fourteenth-century struggles against Emperor Louis IV, such as Dante, Marsilius of Padua and William of Ockham, were all therefore placed on the Index in the mid-1550s; Marsilius was already to be found on the Leuven Index of 1550 (though he was later removed from the Roman Index in 1596). Machiavelli's *Prince* (printed in 1532) also became something of a *cause célèbre*, as various inquisitors and Index censors struggled over what to do with this acknowledged masterpiece of Renaissance statecraft. On the one hand it clearly had to be proscribed, both for the apparent immorality of its teachings and for its insulting portrayal of prominent Church figures. Yet Machiavelli had many admirers, including the powerful Jesuit censor Robert Bellarmine, who felt that this book was too valuable to consign entirely to the flames. Various unsuccessful attempts at expurgation and emendation were tried over the years by members of the Machiavelli family as well as writers such as Justus Lipsius (d. 1606) and Kaspar Schoppe (d. 1649), both of whose (unrelated) works were also banned by Roman decrees in the seventeenth century.[22] Machiavelli's books continued to circulate widely in spite of the Index, however, and his critics sometimes fared no better than he did: the Huguenot Innocent Gentillet's 1576 *Discours sur les moyens de bien gouverner . . . Contre Nicolas Machiavel* (also known as *Anti-Machiavel*), for example, was itself placed on the Roman Index, first by means of a 1605 decree aimed at its 1577 Latin version, and then again in 1695 when the Congregation of the Index finally became aware of the original French text.[23]

Later editions of the Index of Prohibited Books would provide a veritable who's who of European political theorists, all guilty of placing some element in their writings that struck Roman or Spanish inquisitors as inappropriate reading for a Catholic audience: Jean Bodin (whose historical and political writings were banned right along with his demonological ones), Grotius (d. 1645), Hobbes (d. 1679), Pufendorf (d. 1694), Locke (d. 1704), Montesquieu (d. 1755), John Stuart Mill (d. 1873) and many others thus joined company with figures now mostly forgotten beyond specialist circles, such as the Polish republican Andrzej Frycz Modrzewski (d. 1572), German courtier Caspar Facius (d. 1646), English parliamentarian Algernon Sydney (d. 1683) and Spanish reformer Gaspar Melchior de Jovanellos (d. 1811). Fields ancillary to political science also found their way onto the Indexes. Works by important legal thinkers such as Johannes Calvin (not to be confused with the earlier Reform theologian), Hugo Grotius, John Selden, Jean Barbeyrac and Jeremy Bentham were all prohibited. The founding father of modern criminology, Cesare Beccaria, was also banned by papal decree in 1766 and later placed on the Roman Index for his groundbreaking *Dei delitti e delle pene*.

Economic theory aroused censorial interest as well. Most entries falling into this category related to authors writing in Italian, French or Spanish, for the simple reason that Catholic inquisitors of the Enlightenment period generally could not be bothered to search out what Protestant heretics were publishing in other lands. Thus we find names such as Antonio Genovesi (d. 1769), Pompeo Neri (d. 1776), the Abbé Raynal (d. 1796) and Count Pedro Rodríguez de Campomanes (d. 1803) in later Roman censorship decrees – above all for their proposals to limit Church property rights.[24] The famous Scottish economist Adam Smith, too, managed to find his way onto later editions of the Spanish (but never the Roman) Index, if only through a rather complex series of events. First published in 1776, his *Wealth of Nations* remained unknown to the inquisitors of Catholic Europe until 1791, when a French translation was noticed in a bookshop in Pamplona, Spain. Three inquisitorial *calificadores* were quickly assigned to evaluate its contents, which they decided were overly materialistic and lacked sufficient attention to the ethical and metaphysical aspects of economic wealth. A condemnatory edict was therefore issued in 1792, banning 'M. de Smith, Recherches sur la nature et les causes de la richesse des nations, traduit de l'anglois: impr. en Lóndres, año de 1788'. After a long delay, this somewhat confusing passage would finally be printed in the post-inquisitorial Spanish Index of 1873 (on which see Chapter Eight). Censorship did not prevent a Spanish translation of Smith's work from appearing in 1794, however, and several readers argued that since the Inquisition's ban only applied to a specific French translation, they should be free to read the work in Spanish (or in English) if they wished. By this time the Spanish Inquisition had clearly ceased to hold much power over elite readers anyway, and despite the Church's evident disapproval, Adam Smith's thoughts on capitalism seem to have been fairly well received by Spanish economists throughout the turbulent decades of the nineteenth century.

=✠=

THIS BY NO MEANS exhausts the list of scientific disciplines, let alone books and authors, that managed to make their way onto the various Indexes one way or another over the centuries. Geographers such as Philipp Clüver (d. 1622) were banned, as was the famous Mercator *Atlas* of 1595 (indeed, Mercator's *Atlas* was named in the same 1603 edict that prohibited the writings of Giordano Bruno), though means were often found to ensure that the valuable information they contained was able to circulate among elite Catholic experts nevertheless.[25] Travel literature, and related descriptions of various parts of the globe, were also frequently censored if they contained material deemed unacceptable to Church authorities. The reasons behind such bans on 'scientific' texts are sometimes unclear, and only in some cases do documents survive in the archives of the Roman Congregation for the Doctrine of the Faith that might one day provide further information. Preliminary studies by Ugo Baldini and Leen Spruit have already begun to show this potential, but there is still much more work to be done.[26]

Certainly the case of Giordano Bruno was exceptional, and most authors of scientific (and even frankly magical) texts were not so violently treated. Practising witches might be burned at the stake, especially if they were women who lacked powerful protectors or other resources. But most scholarly elites (almost all of whom were male in this period) could expect no more than the sort of house arrest imposed on Galileo, or a strict warning even if they chose to write or read books containing heterodox ideas about the universe. Galileo's case too was exceptional, revolving as it did around accusations of relapse after a first offence, and coming at precisely a time when the stakes had never been higher for struggles over Copernican cosmology. Of course, suspicion of Protestantism (or crypto-Judaism) as well as open defiance of the Church were two other ways of upping the ante and ensuring more severe treatment. But for the most part proscribed Catholic authors were simply ordered to stop writing, and in many cases their censorship came long after they had already died. Many books that would have made excellent candidates for inclusion on the Index were ignored, or accidentally left out for long periods due to institutional limitations. Protestants for their part naturally ignored the Index's prohibitions, and many Catholic readers were also granted licences to read banned books if they could convince their local bishops or inquisitors that they needed them to pursue legitimate scientific studies.

Bruno's case was also to some extent accidental. His execution was the culmination of a series of unfortunate events, all of which were unforeseeable even (apparently) for a trained astrologer. If he had expected an arrest, he certainly would not have returned to Venice. Like Galileo, he assumed that his status as an elite intellectual made him valuable to powerful protectors and allies within the Church. And for a long time, he (like Galileo) was right. But historical circumstances ultimately worsened for both men, as generalized Counter-Reformation fears of losing control over the academic as well as the religious world deepened among many in the Church hierarchy. As Wars of Religion continued to rage and fears of demonic conspiracy grew, above all in the half-century leading up to the Peace of Westphalia (1648), Catholic leaders became less and less tolerant of any challenge to their dignity and authority. Deviant academics would now be censored with nearly as much severity as were heretics. A century later, the focus had shifted somewhat towards threats posed by newly materialistic and frankly atheistic interpretations of the world, so that Enlightenment authors would become primary targets for Index censors even while 'enlightened' popes such as Benedict XIV sought to preserve what they deemed to be the best of this new learning. The French Revolution, and subsequent major losses by the Catholic Church throughout the nineteenth and twentieth centuries, fully justified such fears in the eyes of many traditionalists.

Deceptive words written about the divinely created natural world and its workings posed nearly as great a challenge to Christian souls as did misleading words about God himself, according to the censors' logic. So too did words that threatened to undermine the authority of the Church in any way, since that authority and the institutions it upheld were seen (using the same logic) as the most important bulwarks standing between true religion and the damnation awaiting those who fell prey to deception. The political implications of books thus joined with religious and scientific reasons for justifying their suppression, much as we might disagree with those justifications now.

The Catholic Church and its censors were clearly hostile neither to 'scientific' nor to 'magical' books as an undifferentiated mass. Fundamental issues were considered, sometimes at great length, before texts were finally condemned to confiscation, incineration or expurgation. And interpretation of those issues changed over time. Censors disagreed with one another, and the resulting discrepancies between Indexes (as well as eventual reversals, such as the 1822 removal of Galileo's *Dialogue* from the Roman Index) could lead to both confusion and embarrassment. Changes were made, and a greater place for modern (as well as traditionally Aristotelian) science was eventually found within most Catholic institutions. But this took more time, and more struggle, as will be further explored in Chapter Eight. In the meantime, serious damage was done to the history of human thought. Galileo's books may have survived, as did Bruno's, to inspire new generations of thinkers. But we will never know what more they might have written in a censorship-free parallel universe. Ironically, Thomas More's *Utopia* and Tommaso Campanella's utopian *Città del sole* (City of the Sun), as well as Bruno's own thoughts on the existence of other worlds, were all censored by the Index – but it is tempting to imagine that Friar Giordano had some such vision of a better place before his eyes as he paid the ultimate price for remaining true to his beliefs.

7

CENSORED SEX, FAITH AND THE ARTS

The year is 2440 CE. There are no priests or monks; there is no Church. Slavery has been abolished and war is a thing of the past. Beggary is no longer a problem, men and women are free to love whomever they wish and the injustices of political corruption have vanished. Instead, a benevolent philosopher-king rules mildly for the good of all, with the assistance of a parliament. The arts, too, have been purified and freed from servile dependence on wealthy patrons. The only problem is that there is no coffee (or tea, or tobacco).

This is not a realization of John Lennon's 'Imagine' – the part about no tea or tobacco immediately gives that away. In fact it is the utopian vision of Louis-Sébastien Mercier's 1771 novel *L'an 2440: rêve s'il en fut jamais* (The Year 2440: A Dream if Ever There Was One). In 1772 it was translated into English by one William Hooper, who inexplicably decided to alter its title to *Memoirs of the Year Two Thousand Five Hundred*. Mercier's tale involves a philosophical time traveller who suddenly wakes up in a Paris of the future, where he proceeds to wander about marvelling at all the changes that have taken place for the betterment (mostly) of society. Not surprisingly, given the book's less-than-subtle critique of organized religion, traditional marriage and the existing monarchy, it was very swiftly subjected to international censorship. King Louis XV of France, Pope Clement XIV and Charles III of Spain all had it banned, the latter allegedly burning copies with his own hands. Clement's papal edict ensured that this offending work of science fiction *avant la lettre* would be firmly placed on the Roman Index from 1773, though the Spanish Inquisition took somewhat longer to process its disapproval. Seven years after publication, on 7 March 1778, an inquisitorial edict was finally ready for distribution in Spain and the offending work was duly inscribed on the Spanish Index of 1790 – though with a thoughtful caveat, allowing for preservation of consultation copies in the royal library at Madrid.[1]

The disruptive potential of art – whether novels and other forms of creative literature, paintings and sculpture or musical performance – was not an immediate concern to most of the early Index compilers. As we have seen, these censors tended to focus much more on Protestant theology, on regulating access to religious Scriptures and on scientific writings with theological implications than on suppressing more imaginative flights of the human mind. Yet here too, over time as the Index of Prohibited Books became fully established as a normative aspect of life in Catholic Europe and its colonies, authorities would in some cases come to fear artistic licence almost as much as they did spiritual and intellectual freedom. The faith, after all, could be harmed just as easily by corruption of good morals as it was by the dissemination of erroneous beliefs. Furthermore, artistic works could provoke error, doubt and rebellion against authority just as easily as could scholarly texts, especially among the masses. If the censors' job was to protect Christian society from falling prey to the temptations and falsehoods of heretical writings, then they might also be expected to do all they could to keep their flocks' eyes, ears and imaginations free from the scandalous influence of artists as well.

Mercier's utopian vision of the future was just one in a long series of artistic renderings placed on the Index because of the perceived threat they posed to Christian faith and morals. By offering imaginary alternatives to the status quo, such writings and related images threatened to open people's minds to possible worlds far removed from the normative ones they inhabited. The religious establishment, by definition, was naturally concerned with any discussion of 'alternatives' and sought whenever possible to prohibit the production and distribution of creative works that were deemed liable to provoke scandal, undermine traditional morality or in any way cause affront to the dignity of the Catholic Church and its authoritative hierarchy. Mercier's fantasy thus joined others such as Thomas More's *Utopia* (1516) and François Rabelais' harshly satirical *Gargantua and Pantagruel* series (1532–52) on early lists of banned books – the former appearing on the Portuguese and Spanish Indexes from the 1580s, largely as a result of its permissive approaches to religious tolerance, while the latter was much more promptly placed on the Indexes of Paris (1544) and Rome (1559) as well as that of Spain (1583). Tommaso Campanella's utopian *Città del sole* was also banned by Roman authorities, along with all his other works (*opera omnia*), in the same 1603 decree that condemned writings by his fellow Dominican Giordano Bruno. There was clearly no licit place for such dangerously alternative utopias in a Christian society that already claimed to be as perfect as possible in a fallen world – and which intended to stay that way, in defiance of all criticism.²

The Evolution of Prudery

Precisely what sorts of artistic texts, images and even sounds might require correction or prohibition changed over time, of course, as attitudes and conceptions of 'traditional' morality, politics and spirituality changed. Overly permissive or deviant sexual mores, for example, were definitely a topic of concern for censors in early modern times, as they remain today. Yet what were considered to be 'normal', or at least unremarkable (and therefore accepted) artistic depictions of sexual behaviour varied considerably over the ages. In ancient Greece, homosexual relations between males were entirely accepted and indeed lauded; the nude body, both male and female, was also frequently celebrated in sculpted and other forms. Classical Roman attitudes towards sexuality were somewhat different, with adultery and some aspects of homosexuality seemingly frowned upon, yet licit heterosexual sex was portrayed with remarkable frankness in both literature and the visual arts. Medieval people too tended to take a fairly casual attitude towards various types of sexual activity, despite the fact that Catholic Christianity promoted ascetic renunciation of sex as a spiritual virtue (above all for members of the clergy, monks and nuns). Indulging in immoderate sexual pleasure (characterized by lust, or *luxuria*) was increasingly regarded as sinful in the later Middle Ages, but for a society where privacy was rare and even the smallest children were regularly exposed to copulating barnyard animals if not humans, the strict prudery of later times was simply unthinkable. Sex, and sexual pleasure, might be a topic to be avoided in certain sorts of polite company, but reproduction was essential to community survival and couples tended to be encouraged to mate early and often so long as they could do so within the bounds of marriage (or more informal arrangements, especially but not exclusively for members of the lower classes). Desire, and the pleasurable joining of lover to beloved (literally, *coitus*), were also subjects frankly discussed and allegorically evoked in all sorts of literature, ranging from theological writings such as Ramon Llull's *Book of the Lover and the Beloved* to courtly romances like the *Roman de la rose*, while medical treatises did not shy away from discussing the human body and its sexual functions in great detail.

Far from the 'Victorian' attitudes towards sex and sexuality that continue to haunt much of modern society, ancient and medieval cultures bequeathed a wide range of sensual and often bawdy artistic traditions to the worlds of Renaissance and Counter-Reformation Catholicism. Revivals of classicism ensured that nudity was widely accepted as a tasteful style of presentation for the human body throughout much of the early modern period, even in religious settings. Humanist scholars revelled in the beautiful literary stylings of Latin and Greek texts that were often overtly lascivious and/or homoerotic. And courtly love epics and pastoral ballads, replete with thinly veiled allusions to the pleasures of sexual trysts (often adulterous), remained popular favourites well into the seventeenth century – only to be refashioned in the new idioms of Cervantes and Shakespeare.[3] Meanwhile Baroque artists continued to refine their depictions of ecstatic moments both physical and spiritual, as exemplified by such celebrated works as Peter Paul Rubens's *Venus and Adonis* and Artemisia Gentileschi's *Sleeping Venus* (both c. 1630), not to mention Gian Lorenzo Bernini's *Ecstasy of Saint Teresa* (c. 1650).

Neither sexuality nor nudity were thus necessarily antithetical to social expectations in premodern European cultures. Nevertheless, sex (then as now) remained a formidable aspect of human life, with great power to both inspire and unsettle. Many audiences appreciated and enjoyed representations of sexually attractive themes and figures. But others worried about the potential for excessive, unbridled or disorderly sexual thoughts and activities to disrupt the established social, political and religious order. Artistic depictions of sexuality – even if veiled or allegorical, and especially when accompanied by nude or partially nude imagery – were therefore increasingly liable to be censored in some (but by no means all) contexts under postmedieval inquisitorial regimes. Sexual immorality and licentiousness were part of the Paris theologians' rationale for censoring Rabelais in 1544, and they would remain matters of serious concern for Catholic censors some four centuries later.

This is not to say that sex was the only, or even the main, reason for Index and related censorship of artistic productions. Index censors' primary objective as always was to protect what they saw as the integrity of Catholic Christianity itself, and while sexual immorality might indeed lead Christians into sin and perhaps erode such institutions as clerical celibacy or the patriarchal family, there were also many other ways in which authors, painters, sculptors and performers could undermine the authority and stability of the Church. Mockery of clerical failings and hypocrisies (including sexual failings), satiric or utopian critiques of the clerical regime and distortions of orthodox religious teachings in artistic works (whether intentional or not) were all seen as serious threats. Fears of scandal, disruption, dogmatic error and subversion of religious authority were therefore causes for the prohibition, expurgation and even destruction of countless great works of art at the hands of Catholic censors – as well as many inferior ones, which might (perhaps justifiably) be all but forgotten today if it were not for their presence on the Index of Prohibited Books.

Scandalous Words

As previously noted, Rule no. 7 of the Tridentine Index mandated the following:

> All books are to be entirely prohibited which deal with, recount, or teach lascivious or obscene things, since reading of such books tends to easily corrupt not only faith but also morals; and those who already own [such books] are to be severely punished by [their] bishops. Ancient works by pagan authors are permitted on account of their elegance of phrasing and propriety; however this does not justify reading [such materials] before young boys.[4]

Such vague instructions would inevitably cause confusion and varied interpretations in the decades to follow, as authors, printers, booksellers and censors struggled to determine just what constituted actionably 'lascivious or obscene things'.[5] Moreover, the exemption for 'ancient works by pagan authors' raised still more questions. Which ancient works qualified as sufficiently 'elegant' to excuse their otherwise troubling contents? If such works were not in fact to be censored, what steps needed to be taken to keep them away from 'young boys'? And just how old (or wise) did one need to be to read these elegant books?

Classical Latin texts such as Ovid's *Metamorphoses* and *Ars amatoria* (Art of Love) were obvious candidates for exemption from Rule no. 7, as were various writings by Catullus and Juvenal. Greek erotic poetry and the sometimes racy plot lines of much Greek mythology, not to mention Homer's *Iliad* and *Odyssey*, were also widely appreciated, above all by humanist scholars of the later Middle Ages and Renaissance due to their venerable pedigrees and stylistic qualities. If they also provided sensual delight, this was a price many readers were willing to pay. Attempts were made to gloss over or allegorize some of their more overt references to sexual passion, in much the same way that biblical exegetes such as St Bernard of Clairvaux had long dealt with the undeniably erotic passages in King Solomon's *Song of Songs*. But nothing could really prevent generations of readers, including schoolboys ostensibly in quest of 'elegant' style, from being titillated and inspired by what they read about the love affairs (and more troubling sexual transgressions) of the Ancients. Thus while Ovid's Latin *Metamorphoses* were placed on Portuguese and Spanish Indexes in the 1580s, Inquisitor-General Quiroga specified that the same author's notorious *Ars amatoria* should only be prohibited in its vernacular translations. By 1612, Spanish censors further clarified that recent Latin editions of Ovid's *opera* could be permitted – but only so long as they were purged of any marginal references to Erasmus or Melanchthon. Meanwhile Iberian students could always find copies of these works in Italy, where specific references to Ovid were generally omitted from the Index. A single prohibition, against Gaetano Vernice's late Italian translation of the *Ars amatoria*, is the exception that proves the rule. This edition (illicitly published circa 1705 in Frankfurt) was only banned under Clement XI in 1708.

The medieval author Giovanni Boccaccio was nearly as popular as Ovid among Renaissance scholars, and his *Decameron* (first written in 1353) provided plenty of sexy anecdotes for interested readers. The book was duly placed on Iberian and Roman Indexes in the 1550s, though later Spanish Indexes would specify that their bans applied only to unexpurgated versions, or to translations into Spanish (which were confusingly listed under 'N' for 'Nouelas de Iuan Bocaccio' (Novels by John Bocaccio)). Popular demand for the *Decameron* in Italy also forced a reconsideration of total censorship, and by 1573 a team of Florentine scholars led by Vincenzo Borghini had prepared a 'corrected and emended' version for the press that enjoyed inquisitorial approval. Corrections (allegedly restoring Boccaccio's presumed pious authorial intent) included revision of Day 4, Tale 1, in which some lecherous monks smuggle women into their cells. In Borghini's version, the escapade is retained but the monks are transformed into lecherous university students instead, smuggling women into their dorm rooms. Evidently the sexual aspect of this story was less troubling than its anticlerical implications. Yet even Borghini's relatively light-handed expurgation could easily be undone: on more than one surviving copy of the 1573 *Decameron*, later readers have made a point of writing the original story out by hand, and placing it in the margins of the censored text.[6]

The earliest Index censors' lack of serious concern with sexual peccadillos is also evident in their treatment of writings by Enea Silvio Piccolomini, who would later go on to become Pope Pius II (r. 1458–64). The potential scandal of censoring a former pope was certainly at issue when his case was considered during the Council of Trent. But hesitations were overcome and Piccolomini's politically embarrassing *Commentarii de Concilio Basileae celebrato* ('Commentaries on the Council of Basel', a council which had been notorious for its clashes with papal authority) was indeed placed on the Indexes of Venice (1554) and Rome (1559 and 1564). By 1584, the work was once more at issue since one of Pius' relatives (himself an archbishop) sought to have it republished, and Francesco Pegna was assigned the task of applying necessary expurgations. Shocked by the gossipy details of Pius' writing, which involved quarrels among cardinals, papal nepotism and undignified expressions, Pegna cut or rewrote whole passages before grudgingly permitting its release. Yet in contrast, the same papal author's unabashedly erotic and semiautobiographical novel entitled *Historia de duobus amantibus* (The Tale of the Two Lovers) was never placed on the Index at all, and it continued to circulate widely both in Latin and in multiple translations, long after Pegna had finished with his commission.

This is not to say that erotic literature was ignored; graphic passages in Rabelais (along with his anticlerical cynicism) certainly added to the censors' reasons for banning him. They also led to the placement of Ludovico Ariosto's *Satire* on the Index of Parma in 1580 (though that ban would not spread to the Roman Index until a full century later, when it was finally placed on the Index of Innocent XI in 1681). The Spaniard Fernando de Rojas's famously bawdy

La Celestina, first published in 1499, was also an obvious target for inquisitorial attention thanks to its witty portrayal of a procuress who uses magic and deceit to help an unmarried couple in their pursuit of lustful embraces. Yet Spanish inquisitors were generally even less interested in immoral literature than were Italians in the later sixteenth century, so even mild expurgation of *Celestina* was remarkably late to emerge (just in time to appear on the 1632 Spanish Index). The same could not be said for Feliciano de Silva's continuation of the same story in his 1536 *Resurrection* [sic] *de Celestina*, which was promptly added to the Spanish Index of 1559, or for the rather audaciously pornographic works of the Italian Pietro Aretino. Revelling in classical allusions that left no doubt regarding his enthusiasm for sexual pleasure, including homosexual and pederastic entanglements, Aretino's *opera omnia* were placed on the Roman Index in 1559 and that condemnation was subsequently confirmed by the Tridentine Index of 1564, the Clementine Index of 1593 and all Spanish Indexes from 1583 to 1790.

Sexual transgressions were definitely among the main reasons for Aretino's condemnation, but he had also drawn concern for the religious and political implications of his satires and *sonneti lussuriosi*. Pure smut, in fact, might well have escaped the censors' notice or even attracted appreciative smiles from some of them in the sixteenth century. But transgressive, utopian and satirical depictions of realities that differed from what Church authorities wanted to preserve or aspire to in Christian society repeatedly led to the prohibition of many works even by truly great artists throughout this period. Discussion of alternative sexual mores generally struck only a minor note within works whose main intent was to reflect critically on the hypocritical or corrupt realities of contemporary life: works as varied as Petrarch's fourteenth-century Babylonian sonnets, Baldassare Castiglione's *Cortegiano* (The Book of the Courtier, 1528), the anonymous *Lazarillo de Tormes* (1554), Michel de Montaigne's *Essais* (1580), Ferrante Pallavicino's *La retorica delle puttane* (The Rhetoric of Whores, 1642), Lafontaine's *Contes et nouvelles en vers* (Tales and Novellas in Verse, 1666) and Montesquieu's *Lettres persanes* (Persian Letters, 1721), for example, among many lesser works that can be found on the various Indexes from the sixteenth to the eighteenth centuries.

Some authors, too, were denounced for their imaginative treatments of politico-religious themes when these were determined to

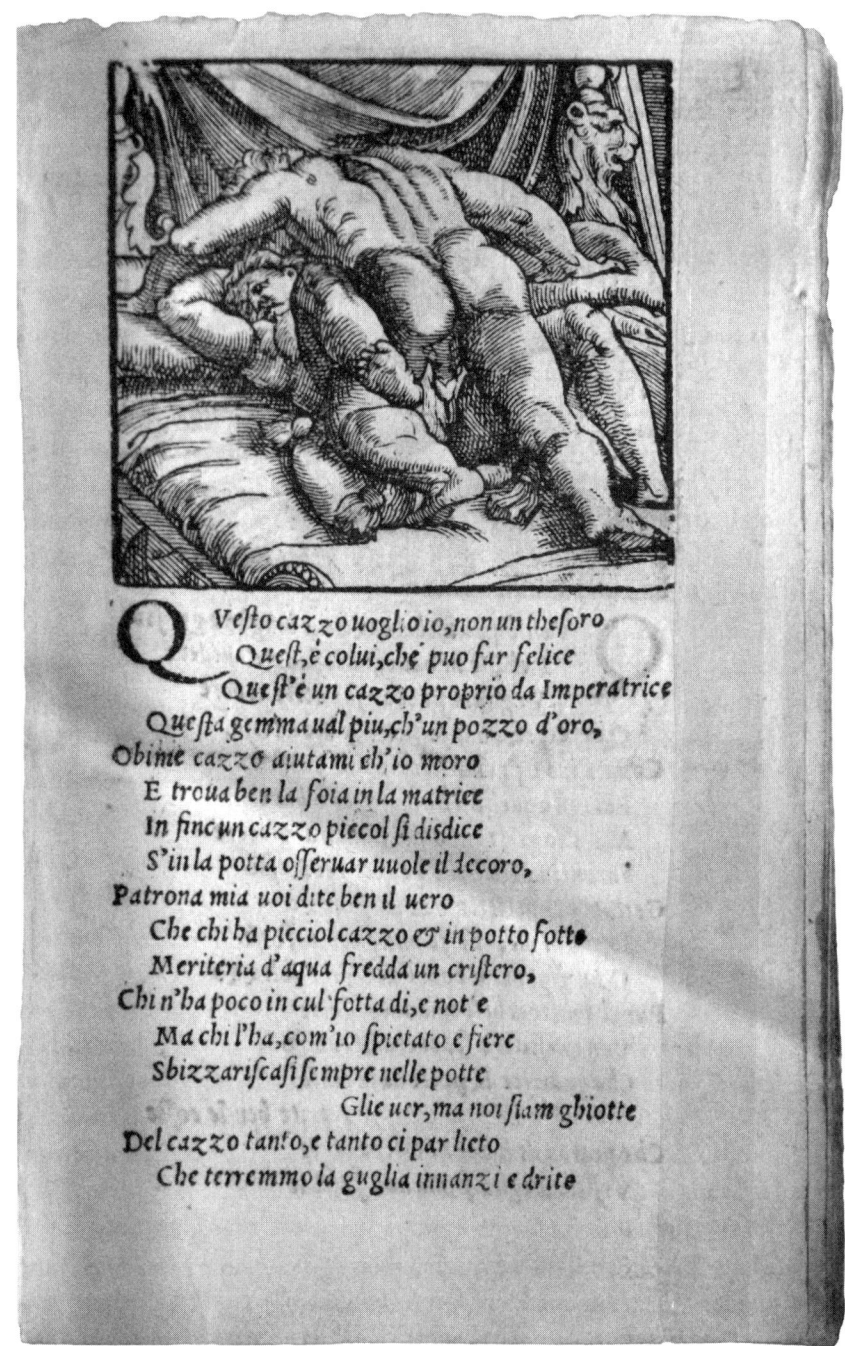

Questo cazzo uoglio io, non un thesoro
Quest'è colui, che può far felice
Quest'è un cazzo proprio da Imperatrice
Questa gemma ual piu, ch'un pozzo d'oro,
Obime cazzo aiutami ch'io moro
E troua ben la foia in la matrice
In fin c'un cazzo piecol si disdice
S'in la potta osseruar uuole il decoro,
Patrona mia uoi dite ben il uero
Che chi ha picciol cazzo & in potto fotte
Meriteria d'aqua fredda un cristero,
Chi n'ha poco in cul fotta di, e not'e
Ma chi l'ha, com'io spietato e fiere
Sbizzariscasi sempre nelle potte
          Glie uer, ma noi siam ghiotte
Del cazzo tanto, e tanto ci par lieto
Che terremmo la guglia innanzi e drite

Erotic illustration from the 'Toscanini volume' of Pietro Aretino's *Sonneti lussuriosi*. Original engraving by Marcantonio Raimondi after Giulio Romano; here copied by an anonymous artist, 16th century.

have contradicted Catholic dogma. By the seventeenth century efforts to list all Protestant authors had largely been abandoned (since they were all automatically prohibited by virtue of their authors' heresies in any case), but Catholic authors of fiction came under strict scrutiny, and every now and then a non-Catholic too might be noticed and added to the Index. Miguel de Cervantes's *Don Quixote* was thus lightly expurgated in the Spanish Index of 1632, which required only the excision of a single theologically dubious phrase: 'Works of charity that are done poorly have no merit, and are worth nothing.'[7] Alexander Pope (d. 1744), an English convert to Catholicism, was also selectively censored in both Spain and Mexico, though his name didn't appear on any Index as such until 1804.[8] His countryman, the Calvinist John Milton (d. 1674), similarly found his way onto the Index once his political and religious ideas began to arouse interest in the Catholic world. Milton's posthumous 1676 Latin collection of *Literae pseudo-Senatus Anglicani, Cromwelli, reliquorumque perduellium nomine ac iussu conscriptae* was banned at Rome in 1694 and placed on the Spanish Index from 1707 (under the name 'Milthonius'). But his more important *Paradise Lost*, though completed a decade earlier than the *Literae*, was not censored in Rome until 1732 – and then only because the text had finally appeared in an Italian translation which papal censors were able to read (*Il paradiso perduto*, 1730). Similar treatment was applied to Jonathon Swift's *Tale of a Tub* (1704), and to Daniel Defoe – whose 1726 *Political History of the Devil* (which responded in part to Milton) was banned in 1743 by the Roman Inquisition as a result of its having been translated into French as the *Histoire du diable* in 1729. Tellingly, as evidence of the fortuitous and inconsistent nature of such bans, it should be noted that neither Milton's polemic against censorship and intolerance (*Areopagitica*, 1644), nor Defoe's novel about a 'fallen' woman of dubious morals (*Moll Flanders*, 1722), were ever placed on any versions of the Index.[9]

By the mid-eighteenth century, however, the political and religious stakes of embedding sexual themes in literature were becoming higher. When Samuel Richardson's *Pamela, or Virtue Rewarded* (1740) was published in French (1742), its portrayal of sexual misbehaviours quickly led to prohibition by Roman decree (1744). *Pamela*'s success also attracted rebuttals and imitators, including an anonymous *Anti-Pamela* which was itself placed on the Index a year later (though

Henry Fielding's pseudonymous 1741 spin-off, *Shamela*, was completely ignored). John Cleland's much more salacious *Memoirs of a Woman for Pleasure* (also known as *Fanny Hill*) appeared soon after, in 1748, but never seems to have been noticed by Catholic censors at all – perhaps because it was immediately banned by secular authorities in Britain, and only circulated in pirate editions until the twentieth century.

Then, as *philosophes* of the French Enlightenment turned more and more to explorations of materialist thought, they too began to produce books that deliberately questioned (and often violently rejected) all the spiritual and moral teachings of the Church, including those intended to regulate human sexuality. Notorious figures such as Jean-Jacques Rousseau and Voltaire were among these, banned for their attitudes towards traditional marriage as well as the Church in works such as *Julie ou la nouvelle Héloïse, lettres de deux amans* (1761) and *Candide, ou l'optimisme* (1759). Still more overtly pornographic were later works such as the *Erotika Biblion* of Honoré Gabriel Riqueti, Count of Mirabeau (d. 1791). A politician and erstwhile leader of the French Revolution, Mirabeau published his treatise on absolute sexual licence in 1783, provocatively using a title with grandiose religious connotations, and listing 'L'Imprimerie du Vatican' as its place of publication. The book was duly prohibited by papal order in 1804, once the now-deceased Mirabeau's memory had fallen from favour under the Napoleonic régime, though his other works (including both tedious policy papers and other erotic texts) were never placed on the Index.[10]

While imprisoned for sedition and abduction in the Château de Vincennes, where he wrote the *Biblion* as well as several pornographic letters to his married mistress, Mirabeau also met Donatien Alphonse François, Marquis de Sade, whose *Justine* (1794) would later cement his reputation as the inventor of 'sadism'. *Justine* was banned by the Spanish Inquisition in 1805 but does not seem to have come to the notice of the papal Curia (which was busy dealing with occupation by French forces and the exile of its pope by 1809). The *Anti-Justine*, written in response to Sade by Nicolas Edme Restif de la Bretonne in 1798, was also banned by Spanish inquisitors along with many of the same author's other erotic works such as the Rousseau-inspired *Nouvel Abailard ou lettres de deux amans qui ne se sont jamais vus* and *Le paysan perverti* (though not, strangely enough, his *Pornographe* or

Le pied de Fanchette, the latter a celebration of foot-fetishism). Spanish disapproval of sexual liberty had evidently grown significantly since the days when *Celestina* could be blithely ignored by censors. Even a humble traveller's guide to London brothels, entitled *The Woman's* [*sic*] *of Pleasure Pocket Companion*, could be found on the Spanish Index supplement of 1805 – but never on the Index of Rome.

Scandalous Images

The ten Rules of the Tridentine Index were silent on the topic of banned images. But this did not mean that Church censors had no opinions on the matter. The Spanish Index of 1559 had already included a general statement (hidden away under 'O', for *omnis*) condemning 'all (*omnis*) pictures and figures or effigies that are impugning or insulting to our lady the most holy Virgin Mary; or to saints'.[11] Furthermore, in the final session of Trent, held on 3 and 4 December 1563, a decree was issued 'On the invocation, veneration and relics of saints, and on holy images'. The main point of both the Spanish and the Tridentine statements was to counteract Protestant disrespect for Catholic images, rooted as they were in a literal reading of the First Commandment. Such disrespect was a serious issue, having grown into violent iconoclastic attacks in some cases that left churches despoiled of all their holy images. Many Protestant theological texts addressing the issue of 'idolatry' were also placed on various Indexes over the years, due to the challenge they posed to traditional Catholic veneration of those images.

In the Clementine Roman Index of 1596, however, additional prefatory instructions began to explicitly warn censors that 'obscene or disgraceful images' should also not be permitted to adorn large capital letters in printed books.[12] This took scrutiny of the visual arts a step further, beyond a simple interest in defending religious images from heretical attack. In parallel with hardening clerical attitudes towards sexual content in literature, inquisitorial censors would gradually pay more and more attention to what they saw as 'obscenity' in the visual arts over the decades and centuries that followed. But the task was not easy. Even more than books, images tended to be hard to keep track of, and to clearly identify for censorship purposes – especially when produced anonymously, as they often were. Opinions also varied widely about just what actually constituted a 'disgraceful' drawing, painting or sculpture. As a result, Index censorship of scandalous images tended to rely upon generalized statements and the discretion of individual examiners, rather than on creating a detailed list of banned works.

Lewd images, like erotic literature, had in fact concerned Churchmen long before specific mention of the issue made its way into an actual Index of Prohibited Books. Nude figures and other potentially lascivious woodcut drawings were already being printed as illustrations to accompany several books in the late fifteenth century, most notoriously in already suspect editions of Boccaccio's *Decameron* and the anonymous courtly romance allegory *Hypnerotomachia Poliphili*.[13] The nudity of Michelangelo's *David* (c. 1504), and of many figures in his *Last Judgement* on the ceiling of the Sistine Chapel, famously aroused the ire of some clerics in the early sixteenth century as well. Yet the Farnese pope Paul III protected Michelangelo from his critics, even permitting the artist to paint a nude caricature of one outspoken Vatican official as a donkey-eared denizen of Hell in the very midst of this solemn fresco.

Like his predecessors Clement VII and Leo X, Paul was an avid patron of the arts and he appreciated the classical stylings of Renaissance masters – nudity and all. The Vatican palace itself was indeed filled with suggestive imagery during this period, with erotic wall decorations in Cardinal Bibbiena's *stufetta* (a bathroom, painted by Raphael in 1516) standing out for being particularly racy; a series of pornographic images was also briefly painted on the walls of the *sala di Constantino* before Clement had them painted over in 1524 (only to see them reprinted in book form that same year, and then again in a collaboration with the ever-provocative Pietro Aretino by 1527). It was a licentious time in some ways, but change was already in the air. Cardinal Carafa began pressing to have Michelangelo's *Last Judgement* altered before it was even finished in 1541. And when he was finally elevated to the papacy in 1555 as Paul IV, Carafa quickly began censoring nude images and castrating statues wherever he found them – a state of affairs noted with sorrow by Michel de Montaigne in his *Essais*. This would mark the beginning of what later came to be known as the original 'Fig-Leaf Campaign'.

In the 1563 Tridentine decree on holy images, one passage mentions the need for 'all lasciviousness to be avoided; in such wise that figures shall not be painted or adorned with a beauty exciting to lust'.

While this referred primarily to images of saints, the increasingly puritanical mood of the times was clear. The ceiling of the Sistine Chapel came up explicitly in discussions at Trent, and in 1565, just a few months after Michelangelo's death, an artist named Daniele da Volterra (nicknamed *Il Braghettone*, 'the loincloth-maker') was assigned to cover up its nude figures – often using painted draperies or foliage to do so. In the years that followed, many more Roman images were clothed with the addition of fig leaves or other devices, and Clement VIII toured the city in 1592 to ensure that all sculptures and images on public display were now suited to contemporary standards of 'decency'. Similar papal efforts would continue sporadically thereafter, well into the nineteenth century.

It was not until 1640, though, that the Spanish Index added a brief paragraph on 'lascivious' images to what was now its Rule no. 11 (*Regla* XI, formerly Rule no. 12, which was otherwise mostly concerned with the prohibition of insulting or mocking illustrations of holy personages). 'In order to avoid in part the grave scandal and no little harm' occasioned by inappropriate artworks, this ruling strictly forbade all creation or importation of 'lascivious paintings, plates, statues, or other sculptures'. Punishment was set at a fine of 500 ducats, and a year of exile for transgressors. Yet circulation of pornographic images continued in Spain, and in its overseas colonies, despite such (often toothless) admonitions. Scores of cases involving the illicit production and sale of erotic images and objects have been identified in the surviving late eighteenth- and early nineteenth-century files of the Mexican Inquisition alone. And as François Soyer has suggested, the Spanish Inquisition actually sought to make suppression of pornography into one of its defining features by the turn of the nineteenth century, as a means of finding political and social legitimacy in its dying days. The high-profile 1814 seizure of Francisco Goya's erotic masterpiece, *La Maja Desnuda* (Naked Maja), from the home of Spanish Prime Minister Manuel Godoy, clearly demonstrates the extent to which intolerance for pornographic images had become more central to inquisitorial concerns in the late Enlightenment period.

⸺✠⸺

THE THREAT of erotic art to public morality was never as important to Index censors as was that of irreligious art, however. The

1559 Spanish Index's brief condemnation against images found to be 'disrespectful to religion' was further elaborated and clarified in successive Spanish Index editions, to the point where censorship of impious (as opposed to erotic) images was addressed no less than four times in the 1790 version of the *Reglas*. At the end of Rule no. 8, attention was drawn to '*laminae* [inscribed plates], seals, medallions, rings, beads, crosses, images, and portraits' that might be used for superstitious or magical purposes. Magical images (*figuras*) were also mentioned in Rule no. 9, which condemned books of sorcery. Rule no. 11 further prohibited 'portraits, figurines, coins, imprints, illustrated capital letters, novelties, masks, and medallions of all sorts' that might be in 'derision or mockery' of any aspect of Catholic practice or authority. Rule no. 16, for its part, advised censors to confiscate or correct 'painted images and portraits of persons who have not been beatified or canonized by authority of the Apostolic See, if these contain rays, halos, or other insignia which are permitted only to saints duly recognized by the Church'.

Skimming through the pages of the 1790 Index, one can also find scattered entries banning unauthorized religious woodcut prints (under 'E', for *estampas*); an otherwise obscure 'Insignia of the Holy Sacrament, and Image of Our Lady' printed on a single sheet (under 'I'); and multiple references to a 1767 prohibition against 'sacred images, paintings, and insignia' being added to jewels, presumably in the production of amulets. Even razors and knives (listed under 'N' for *navajas y cuchillos*) appear in this Index, out of concern that they might contain holy images engraved on their handles or blades.

Francisco Goya, *La Maja Desnuda*, c. 1800, oil on canvas.

All this was in sharp contrast with the same Index's rather fleeting mention of *pinturas lascivas* at the end of *Regla* XI, with no specific works of that type listed elsewhere in the Index itself. Index evidence alone would thus seem to suggest a lack of concern with erotica, despite clear archival evidence for how seriously the Spanish Inquisition was actually beginning to take pornographic images at this time. Once more, it is important to recognize that the Index proper only reveals one aspect of the overall workings of actual Church censorship.

In Rome, too, irreligious, anti-religious or superstitious images seem always to have been much more of a concern than erotic ones, at least as recorded in the pages of the Index. As previously mentioned, abuse of religious art was debated at the conclusion of the Council of Trent in 1563, and details of this discussion can be gleaned not only from canon 2 of that final session but in the published memoirs of a future cardinal who was present at the time, in his capacity as a member of the papal Rota court. Gabriele Paleotti (d. 1597) in fact played a leading role in drafting this canon, and he later put his very extensive thoughts on the need for more censorship of illicit art into printed form with his *Discorso intorno alle imagine sacre et profrane* (Discourse Concerning Sacred and Profane Images). This ambitious treatise was never fully completed, but a preliminary Italian version was published in 1582, while another still-unfinished Latin version entitled *De sacris et profanis imaginibus* appeared in 1594.

In the interim, Cardinal Paleotti began to advocate for a separate Index of Prohibited Art, which certainly would have changed the course of censorship history as presented here had it succeeded. He clashed politically with Sixtus V, however, and eventually failed in his bid for the papacy itself with the elevation of Clement VIII. Nevertheless, his works make extremely interesting reading and shed much light on the state of artistic culture in Rome at the end of the sixteenth century. After Trent, and certainly by the 1590s, Catholic authorities were demanding that art (and religious art in particular) should always be sober, decorous and true to life – without any unnecessarily troubling, confusing or decorative adornments that might lead believers astray. The extravagance of much Baroque art would undo this mandate to some extent, soon after the passing of Paleotti's generation, but the general Tridentine rules of artistic propriety would remain in the minds of Church censors right up to modern times.

WE HAVE ALREADY SEEN how popes like Clement VIII, following in the footsteps of Paul IV, sought to shelter Catholic eyes from the sight of nudity in religious paintings such as Michelangelo's *Last Judgement*, as well as in classical statuary (if not necessarily from their own more refined eyes, in the privacy of their Vatican quarters). But in Italy, as in Spain, nudity was not the only artistic detail that might cause an image to fall afoul of Church censors. In the case of Paolo Veronese's *Last Supper*, for example, Venetian inquisitors insisted that this seemingly pious depiction of a biblical event was in fact wholly inappropriate as a decoration for the refectory of the Dominican Basilica di Santi Giovanni e Paolo (for which it had been commissioned). At his interrogation in 1573, questions were specifically asked about why Veronese had chosen to surround his depiction of the dining Christ and disciples with a number of figures who were not specifically described in the Gospels – such as a servant with a nosebleed, an armed soldier (in the dress of a sixteenth-century German), a jester and (worst of all) a dog. The detailed, not to say pedantic, level of critical analysis the inquisitors felt justified in applying to such a masterpiece of Renaissance art is quite remarkable, though political factors may also explain why these particular inquisitors decided to interrogate this particular artist at this particular time.

In the end, a compromise was reached that illustrates both the power of Counter-Reformation Church censorship and its limits. Veronese refused to accept the inquisitors' original recommendation (that he overpaint at least the dog, with an image of Mary Magdalene). Instead, he kept the painting exactly as it was but renamed it

Paolo Veronese, *Last Supper* (*The Feast in the House of Levi*), 1573, oil on canvas.

The Feast in the House of Levi. By lowering the religious significance of his composition ever so slightly (Christ and the apostles are clearly still present, but the meal in question is no longer the biblical Last Supper), the painter evidently satisfied his persecutors that the work's level of propriety and decency was now adequately suited to its theme. Like Veronese's very similar companion piece, *The Feast in the House of Simon the Pharisee* (now adorning a massive ceiling at the palace of Versailles, and also prominently featuring a dog), the painting survived essentially untouched and remains a highly valued example of Venetian art. The inquisitors were apparently more interested in simply making a point, than in single-mindedly pursuing the destruction of any and all artworks they found to be problematic.

New Roman regulations on the depiction of both heretics and saints appeared in 1633 and 1642 respectively, and in 1656 specific attention was paid to images of Franciscan saints; all three of these decrees subsequently appeared in the 1664 Index of Alexander VII. Then, in Benedict XIV's revised Index of 1758, previous statements on art censorship were once more repeated along with an entirely new set of warnings, coming under part 3 of his *Decreta de libris prohibitis, nec in indice nominatim expressis* (Decree on Prohibited Books Not Explicitly Named in the Index). As had already been highlighted in Spanish Indexes since 1640, and as would again be repeated in that of 1790, Benedict here drew attention to the problem of 'images with halos, or rays' that might inappropriately imply the sanctity of a person who had not yet been canonized.[14] He also gave specific instructions on the suppression of several other categories of religious images and decorative objects that had evidently been causing problems at the time but which have since fallen into oblivion: images, engraved coins and small chains (*catenulae*) associated with confraternities such as the 'Slaves of the Mother of God'; images of Jesus as a child surrounded by Doctors of the Church; images depicting Joannes Cala (an obscure thirteenth-century hermit who was apparently being advanced for possible canonization at the time); and a pro-Jesuit image depicting Christ and the Virgin between two Jesuit saints, holding a book and rosary.

Ephemeral religious images such as these (and the written inscriptions that frequently accompanied them), especially when cheaply printed on slips of paper or inscribed onto ordinary household items for devotional use, might seem innocuous to modern eyes. But they always had the potential to convey messages that the Church hierarchy of the eighteenth century identified as either irreverent, disobedient or superstitious. They were also more easily accessible to many people (including the illiterate majority) than were books, especially books written in Latin, and they were extremely widespread throughout early modern Catholic Europe as a result. The trick for censors was to distinguish between 'good' images of the Virgin, Christ or the saints, such as might piously be worn around the neck or adorn the hut of a simple peasant, and 'bad' ones that could misdirect the spiritual energies of pious folk into heretical territory. Benedict's list was intended to help Catholic believers, through their priests, to identify and avoid the latter category. Popular veneration of unauthorized holy figures, as well as incorrect veneration of genuinely divine or saintly ones, posed particular threats to the Church and the monopoly it claimed on religious authority, and were therefore taken quite seriously.

It was difficult to distinguish between 'pious' and downright 'superstitious' use of images in many cases. As discussed in Chapter Six, lines were often blurred between religious appeals for divine aid in times of trouble, and beliefs or practices that we would now call 'magical' (as well as some we might recognize as more or less 'scientific', such as the use of healing herbs). Images, whether taking the form of pictures, figurines, inscribed talismanic objects or patterns traced on floors or walls, were often part of the repertoire of 'magical' performance in this period. Nicholas Eymeric's oft-repeated medieval ban on magical texts such as 'Books of the Image of Tobias Bantricat' and 'Books of the Image of Ptolemy' (and the magical drawings to be found or described within these texts), reflects this enduring concern. But for the most part such images circulated under the radar, without discernible author or title. They might be confiscated and destroyed from time to time, often in connection with witch trials, but aside from vague statements such as those to be found in Eymeric, or *Reglas* nos 8 and 9 of the Spanish Indexes from 1640 on, superstitious images generally did not find their way onto more specific lists of prohibited materials.[15]

It should be noted, though it would go beyond the scope of this book to explore in the detail it deserves, that Christian censors also destroyed many of the artistic images produced by Jews, Muslims and colonized 'pagan' peoples all around the world – again, on suspicion of impious, lascivious or superstitious intent, which might undermine the 'true' faith. This was similar to those same censors' treatment of non-Christian texts, as discussed in Chapter Five. Thus, while never specifically mentioned in any Index, it is well-known from other Inquisition, Church and state documents that (ex-)Jewish *conversos* and (ex-)Muslim *moriscos* were regularly scrutinized for artistic practices such as using henna to draw talismanic good-luck images on the hands, feet and forehead of brides, mothers and newborn infants. The loss of artworks caused by looting and destruction of mosques, synagogues and private buildings seized from non-Christians are also incalculable, though one can imagine how beautiful some of these must have been by contemplating the glories of surviving structures such as the old mosque (now cathedral) of Cordoba, or the synagogue of Santa María la Blanca (formerly a church, now a museum) in Toledo. In Africa, Asia and the Americas, too, countless Indigenous ceremonial objects, idols and decorated temples were destroyed over the centuries, along with other expressions of local creativity, by censors who feared the potential power such objects and graven images might retain. This destruction was never specifically mandated by a formal Index, nor were its targets given the same sort of cataloguing attention that the Index of Prohibited Books provided to European materials. It derived from the same sort of disciplinary logic, however, and its effects were deeply felt nonetheless.

Scandalous Music

Non-Christian incantations, songs, music and dances were also subjected to Church censorship in Spain and a number of colonial settings – another understudied, complex and tragic subject that would take us well beyond the bounds of this book.[16] If we return our gaze to early modern Europe, however, we see that musical composition and performance also became issues for censors, above all in the wake of the Council of Trent. Though never as prominent as the other arts on the Index itself, this aspect of Catholic censorship did leave a few minor traces which deserve at least some brief attention, along with evidence from other sources, even if not always connected with the Index proper. The following, therefore, is intended only as a summary introduction to a complex subject that – while thematically related to the Index of Prohibited Books – deserves more research, in a different sort of book.

Church music, like religious painting and sculpture, was a significant though not crucial topic at Trent. In its 22nd session, on 17 September 1562, canon 8 asserted that any music to be performed in conjunction with the Catholic Mass should conform to certain general principles: it should serve to spiritually uplift the faithful, it should only use intelligible (and spiritually beneficial) words, and secular themes or modes of expression should be avoided. This was neither very strict, nor very clear, and that was indeed the point. A year later, in November 1563, the Council agreed that further details could be worked out locally by Provincial Synods since Rome lacked either the will or the ability to impose uniformity of musical practice throughout the entire global Church. Synods had indeed already drawn attention to existing problems: musicians who took performance opportunities to show off with overly long and intricate instrumental solos, parishioners who demanded bawdy country dance songs for decidedly non-spiritual purposes, and even vulgar parodies of the mass itself, complete with impromptu theatrical displays. Such disruptions of eucharistic solemnity may have been only episodic, perhaps at carnival or harvest time, or in protest against localized clerical abuses, but mitigating details were generally not recorded in the formal complaints lodged before Church authorities. There were less dramatic aesthetic and technical issues at stake as well, ranging from concerns that excessive polyphony was beginning to distort the comprehensibility of important liturgical passages, to Bishop Cirillo Franco's 1549 suggestion that all Church music should be restricted to the Phrygian, Lydian, Dorian and Mixolydian modes.[17]

Such critiques, along with the somewhat vague decisions taken at Trent, would eventually have a real impact on the competitive (and occasionally lucrative) world of liturgical composition. Early modern musicians, like most other artists, could not afford to ignore the tastes and wishes of their patrons; their work generally had little to do with personal expression, and much more with following instructions. Once local patrons had decided on a new direction for sacred music, therefore, composers soon complied without any need for actual censorship. The polyphonies and secular, vernacular elements of pieces such as Josquin des Prez's *Missa l'homme armé super voces musicales* (a popular liturgical rendition of a late medieval theme, printed in 1502) were therefore gradually abandoned for more solemn and simple pieces. Plainsong styles such as those commonly associated with 'Gregorian' chant, for example, received a boost from the publication in 1582 of an instructive *Directorium chori ad usum omni ecclesiarum, cathedralium, & collegiatarum* (Guide for Choirs, for Use in All Churches, Cathedrals and Collegiate Churches) by the papal master of ceremonies Giovanni Domenico Guidetti (d. 1592). This was followed by the equally influential Medici *Graduale* of 1614, which sought to align newly simplified liturgical music to the now-standardized text of the 1570 *Missale Romanum*. No further official encouragement was necessary to effect the desired changes, and no thought seems to have been paid by Index censors to the possibility of intervening to clean up ribald songs outside the confines of a religious setting. The extent to which polyphonic masters such as Giovanni Pierluigi da Palestrina (d. 1597) altered their style to conform to new the Tridentine directives remains controversial, but generally speaking there was never any question of direct censorship or coercion; rather there was a subtle and gradual shifting of tastes, akin to the slow hardening of opinions regarding erotic images and literature at the same time.

Examples of musical entries in the Index itself are therefore quite few and far between. Mathieu Malingre, an early Protestant preacher (d. 1572), did have his *Chansons Chrestiennes* (Christian Songs) and *Chansons spirituelles* (Spiritual Songs) placed on the first Paris Index of 1544, a condemnation that was later repeated in the Antwerp (1570) and Spanish Indexes (1583). Marco Antonio Pagani suffered a similar fate when his collected sonnets and a songbook (*carminum liber*) entitled *Triunfo angelico* were all placed on the 1559 Roman Index. A few isolated references to printed songs and hymns (*carmina* or *hymni*) appear from time to time after that, but rarely with an identifiable author's name attached. One exception, the prohibition of a German composer already burdened with the unfortunate name of Andreas Krapp (or Crappius, d. 1623), appears only in the Spanish Indexes of 1632 and later; apparently Rome either didn't know or didn't care about him or his music. The Spanish Index specifically mentions Crappius' 1582 *Cantiones ecclesiae* (Church Songs) as being worthy of censure, but it seems likely that his Protestant sympathies were as much or more of a factor in his drawing inquisitorial attention as was the quality of his compositions. Krapp, it turns out, was a nephew of Philip Melanchthon's.

Of all the arts, then, music was perhaps the least impacted by the emergence and evolution of Indexes of Prohibited books from the sixteenth to the eighteenth centuries. Yet at the same time, Church authorities cared very much for the preservation of orderly services, and they often saw appropriate musical accompaniment as a key aspect of this. Encouraging and rewarding certain types of artistic performance, while choosing not to patronize others, is certainly a far cry from outright censorship; but in some ways the end result could be quite similar. The very fact that few named musicians ever found themselves on the Index may also be an indication that self-censorship was effective in their milieu. As has been repeatedly noted in previous chapters, the impacts of self-censorship (and unrecorded censorship) are unfortunately all but impossible to calculate.

⸺✠⸺

THE MOST EFFECTIVE CENSORSHIP of thought, and creativity, is likely always that which we never even see. When artists never receive the necessary support or resources to pursue their work, their creations simply do not get made. When they are discouraged or threatened, even implicitly, they often find other pursuits. And the more successfully their works are prohibited, the more likely it becomes that audiences will never know that those works ever existed in the first place.

For this reason, it is all the more important to seriously reflect on the various Indexes both as records of suppression targeting creative works – even though this was generally not their main focus – and as records of those lost works of art themselves. Some authors and creators actually may have benefited from inquisitorial scrutiny and censorship, which helped publicize the tantalizingly transgressive nature of their oeuvre. Naughty reputations certainly do not seem to have hurt sales of books by Boccaccio, Rabelais or Samuel Richardson. Others, like Montaigne, Cervantes, Lafontaine and Swift remained essentially unscathed by their brushes with Church censorship; Paolo Veronese merely shrugged it off as an annoyance. But for many other, perhaps lesser, lights who were condemned to a place on the Index, that condemnation itself has ironically preserved at least some record of their existence.

One could write an alternative history of early modern European literature simply by delving into the lists of the Index; dredging up obscure names now generally known only to specialists, such as the poets Adam Siberi (German, d. 1584), Guillaume de Salluste (French, d. 1590) and Giambattista Marini (Italian, d. 1625), to name just a few who appear on the 1640 Spanish Index. Women writers too, so rarely present among banned theological or scientific writers in the early modern period, were banned as they began to write fictional, confessional and satirical works such as Anne-Marguerite Dunoyer's *Lettres historiques et galantes de deux dames de condition, dont l'une était à Paris et l'autre en Provence* (Anglicized as 'Letters from a Lady at Paris to a Lady at Avignon'); Anne de la Roche-Guilhem's *Jacqueline de Bavière*; or Françoise Grafigny's *Lettres d'une Péruvienne* (all banned at Rome, in 1722, 1725 and 1765 respectively).[18] These and many others are authors and poets who will be unknown to most modern readers, especially in the English-speaking world, and their banned books have left few traces in canons of literary history. But the Index at least proves that they did once seek to express themselves, and in some cases it is to be hoped that this proof may provide interested modern students and scholars with just enough of a starting point to initiate new research into previously unknown chapters of literary history. Knowing that he was on the Index is certainly one of the few motivations some of us will ever really have to justify trudging through the often turgid prose of Mercier's *An 2440*, for example.

The inconsistent treatment of artistic works throughout the history of the Index of Prohibited Books reveals a number of paradoxes. Art was identified early on as a potential threat to the Catholic faith; never to the extent of specifically theological writings, but a threat worth addressing nonetheless. Yet educated elites, including the clerical elite, appreciated artistic productions and saw value in preserving even the most risqué books and images for their own consumption. This helps to explain the generally quite vague terms in which artistic works tended to be listed in the Index, with passing mentions in the Spanish and Tridentine Rules that merely gesture at categories of works to be banned, rather than setting down exhaustive lists of actual compositions. The censorial and broader clerical elite wished to be trusted to arrive at its own ad hoc judgements regarding which works were acceptable and which were not: essentially to 'know it when they saw it'. This naturally led to variations over time, and by region, determined by the evolution of contemporary tastes and norms.

Art censorship, especially in cases that did not involve printed books, also once again reveals the limitations and the often fortuitous nature of the whole Index project. Condemnations were often delayed for years or even centuries, or omitted altogether, as censors struggled to keep up with the constant flow of publication and creative works. Lacking sufficient resources to consult copies of each and every book, image or musical composition, they instead targeted individuals on a selective (and often somewhat random) basis, according to what came to their attention, what fell into their possession, and what they were actually able to comprehend. This is not to say that they did not invest tremendous levels of intellectual energy into their task; in many cases the censors' expertise and attention to detail is remarkable. Montaigne was quite dismayed by the close expert scrutiny his *Essais* received on his arrival in Rome, and it must have been a hawk-eyed reader indeed who managed to pick out a single offending passage in the hundreds of pages of Cervantes's *Don Quixote*. But even the best experts are products of their own time, culture and political context. Inconsistency (sometimes to an absurd degree) was thus to be expected in a censorship campaign that spanned multiple centuries and encompassed much of the globe.

The artistic losses instigated by Index censors and their colleagues were perhaps much less serious in many cases than Black Legend propaganda and modernist stereotypes presume. Human ingenuity continued, even under close inquisitorial scrutiny, and it adapted many aspects of its creative production as a result. But one can still only imagine what was in fact lost due to such censorship, whether in terms of works destroyed or never essayed, or in terms of works distorted by expurgation to a greater or lesser degree. Generations of readers, viewers and listeners never knew what they were missing due to simple lack of availability, or as they consumed censored artworks that no longer truly reflected the original intent of their creators – for better or for worse. This is indeed tragic, but perhaps not so far removed from the reality that artists have always faced, and continue to face in much of the contemporary world as well.

8 CENSORSHIP AND MODERNITY

On 8 December 1864, Pope Pius IX dropped two bombshells onto a weary, divided and sometimes disheartened Church. One was the encyclical letter *Quanta cura*, in which he railed against what he perceived to be the many pernicious errors of the modern age. The other was a *Syllabus of Errors*, an addendum to the encyclical, in which eighty of those errors were duly listed. The *Syllabus* ended with a final sentence sure to send chills down the spines of many progressively minded Catholics (and Protestants, Eastern Orthodox and non-Christians too): Error no. 80, Pius solemnly stated, consists of any suggestion whatsoever that 'The Roman Pontiff can, and ought to, reconcile himself and come to terms with progress, liberalism and modern civilization.' In other words, no such reconciliation was possible; the pope had no intention of ever making any concessions to the contrary, and anyone who disagreed should be considered a potential heretic. It was, essentially, a declaration of war against the changing modern world and all the challenges it posed to the power of the Roman Catholic Church hierarchy.

This anti-modern stance was by no means new in the Church. For more than seventy years, Catholics had struggled to resist distressing changes that had been forced upon them (often violently) by the French Revolution and its aftermath. The Industrial Revolution too had brought many technological, social and political innovations which deeply unsettled Church traditionalists. Hardliners such as Cardinal Luigi Lambruschini (d. 1854) had long made their distaste for modern culture absolutely clear, and Pius himself (who only narrowly succeeded against Lambruschini in the papal conclave vote of 1846) had pronounced very similar thoughts to those contained in the *Syllabus* in a whole series of other documents, published periodically for over a decade. *Quanta cura*, and the *Syllabus*, were to some extent simply clarifications of established Roman policy.

But they were also much more than that. They marked a totalizing consolidation of a conservative position that many had hoped would soon lose its grip on papal leadership. When Pius was first elected, it was on the understanding and expectation that he would

Adolphe Braun, *Pope Pius IX (Giovanni Maria Mastai-Ferretti)*, 1875.

in fact be a 'liberal' pope: a relatively young man who had grown up in the post-Revolutionary world and was well equipped to come to terms with it in a sensible and even sympathetic way. Born Giovanni Maria Mastai-Ferretti in 1792, the same year in which French radicals declared their first Republic, he had already set new precedents before embarking upon what would become the longest verifiable pontificate in history from 1846 to 1878 (only legends attributing a 38-year reign to St Peter would challenge this record). He was the first pope to have visited the Americas, on a diplomatic mission to Chile in 1824; he freed political prisoners after an uprising swept his diocese in 1831; and he fully embraced train travel, funding the installation of over 300 kilometres (185 mi.) of railway lines across the Papal States during the course of his papacy. His election was greeted with enthusiasm by Catholic liberals such as the outspoken French priest Félicité de Lamennais (d. 1854), a humanist and democrat who helped found the influential periodical *L'Avenir* but who had already been censored for his critical views on Church politics. Hopes were even entertained by some that Pius might fundamentally reform the Church and cleanse it of past excesses, including what they saw as the unjust activities of the Roman Inquisition and the Congregation of the Index. When the pope ended forcible preaching to Jews, and allowed them to leave their centuries-old Roman ghetto, such great expectations did not seem ill-founded.

Pius IX's about-face came in large part as a result of his experiences during the Revolution of 1848–9. Having survived the challenges of Napoleonic rule and failed republican uprisings in 1830–31, this latest attempt to overthrow the old order and install an anticlerical democratic regime struck home with the pope and impelled him to completely revise many of his assumptions about the possibility of adapting Catholicism to contemporary cultural developments. After narrowly escaping angry mobs and suffering several months of forced exile in southern Italy, in 1849 he therefore began gradually developing the policies and theological positions that culminated in *Quanta cura*, the *Syllabus* and soon afterwards the canons of the first Vatican Council (Vatican I, 1869–70).

Far from permitting a slow erosion or softening of inquisitorial and censorship powers in the modern era, then, conservative Church leaders such as Pius (and his equally long-lived successor Leo XIII,

Karl Bryullov, *Political Manifestation in Rome (Speech of Pope Pius IX from the Balcony of the Papal Palace)*, 1850, oil on canvas.

r. 1878–1903) would in fact double down on papal claims to absolute power when it came to determining what was truth, what was error and how the latter should be eliminated by means of strict censorship practices. Unapproved approaches to religion, to scientific knowledge and to art would all continue to be placed on the Index for nearly a full century after the end of Pius' reign, with ideas and practices stemming from atheism, materialism and rationalism as primary targets for suppression. This anti-modernist turn would ultimately be reversed with the advent of a new Vatican Council (Vatican II, 1962–5), followed closely by a final suppression of the Index of Prohibited Books in 1966. But much more controversy, struggle and trauma would unfold in the meantime.

Plus ça change . . .

The events of the French Revolution, and subsequent Napoleonic occupations of Spain, the Papal States and most of Italy in the first decade of the nineteenth century, provided near-fatal blows to Church regimes already weakened by declining elite and popular support throughout the Enlightenment period. The Spanish Inquisition, already in disfavour with the Bourbon monarchy, was disbanded by Joseph Bonaparte in 1808 – along with the Index of Prohibited books that it normally compiled. Inquisitors would once more be allowed to perform their duties after the restoration of King Ferdinand VII in 1814, but this would only be a temporary reprieve. The Spanish Inquisition was permanently closed by a new liberal government in 1834, and its American tribunals in Mexico, Peru and Colombia had already ceased to function by then thanks to the Wars of Independence that were sweeping those countries. Meanwhile Venetian inquisitors ceased their functions in 1797, and after decades of minimal activity the Portuguese Inquisition too closed its doors in 1821. Though Spanish publishers continued to issue updated lists of banned books in later years (including an important Index of 1873, compiled by journalist León Carbonero y Sol and authorized by a panel of bishops), Spanish clergy of the nineteenth century were more and more inclined to look to the latest Roman Indexes for definitive guidance in matters relating to book censorship. Closure of the Iberian and other Inquisitions thus left the papally directed Congregations of the Inquisition and of the Index as the sole remaining official Catholic censors of prohibited and expurgated works by the reign of Gregory XVI (1831–46), Pius IX's immediate predecessor.

The concerns and priorities of Roman censors naturally shifted over the course of the nineteenth and twentieth centuries, but in many ways old patterns continued to be followed. The only recognized authentic version of the Bible remained the Clementine Vulgate, and though a proliferation of new editions and translations was increasingly difficult to ignore or completely avoid, Church authorities continued to denounce those Bibles that lacked papal approval as heretical innovations. Theological writers too, or those writing about the beliefs and practices of the Church, continued to face careful scrutiny – especially if they were themselves Catholic, and above all if they wrote in languages current in the Roman Curia such as Italian, French or Spanish (and perhaps German or Portuguese). Books circulating only in English, Polish or other less-familiar languages remained unlikely to be read by Roman censors, and generally escaped Index censorship on that basis alone.

Internal criticism of the Church, its practices and its beliefs remained the surest way to get placed on the Index. Lamennais, for example, was censored in 1836 for his publication of works such as *Affaires de Rome* (audaciously subtitled 'Memoires Addressed to the Pope on the Ills of the Church and Society, and How To Remedy Them'). Debates, sometimes heated, over the controversial Catholic doctrine of the Immaculate Conception of Mary also resulted in authors such as Thomas Braun (d. 1864) finding themselves proscribed.[1] Re-interpretations of Scripture using new historical-critical methods could easily lead to censorship, as could related studies of the 'historical Jesus' such as Ernest Renan's *Vie de Jésus* (banned 1863) or Prosper Alfaric's *Le problème de Jésus et les origines du christianisme* (banned 1933). The proper relationship between religion and science too was a dangerous subject to discuss, as the New York University professor John William Draper discovered when his 1874 *History of the Conflicts Between Religion and Science* was placed on the Index (as soon as it was translated into Spanish, in 1876). Scholarly books on relations between Church and state were even more likely to lead to possible censorship if they did not closely toe the official policy of Papal supremacy, as will be seen below.

Scientific texts, as always, continued to be banned whenever they seemed to pose a threat to the Church. Galileo's writings were formally removed from the Index in 1822, but antimodernist clergy still strongly objected to any new challenges to their traditional worldviews. Works by influential historians including Jules Michelet (d. 1874) and Leopold von Ranke (d. 1886), as well as less prominent figures such as Michele Amari (d. 1889) were banned as a result, as were those of Auguste Comte, the father of positivism – for being overly materialistic in their analyses, and insufficiently sympathetic to traditional Catholic viewpoints. François Vincent Raspail's groundbreaking work in organic chemistry was proscribed in 1834, while Giuseppe Barilli's popular guide to astronomy was banned in 1875. Charles Darwin himself was never placed on the Index, but his grandfather Erasmus Darwin was, as were many Catholic scholars silenced for their own studies on evolution: Émile Ferrière's *Le darwinisme*, for example, landed on the Index in 1872, as did Pietro Siciliani's *Socialismo, darwinismo e socologia moderna* in 1882. Pierre Teilhard de Chardin, a Jesuit paleontologist who died in 1955, was simply ordered never to publish any of his writings that were suspected of being tainted by unorthodox theories of evolution and an expanding universe.[2]

In medical science, controversial work by François-Joseph-Victor Broussais, whose concepts of 'physiological' medicine and inflammation theories would be influential in the development of homeopathy, was placed in the Index in 1830. The new field of psychology also struck many Roman censors as deeply problematic for its focus on the material and experiential causes of mental disorders, rather than their spiritual aspects. Pioneering works, above all in Italian, were thus prohibited – including Francesco Bonucci's *Fisiologia e patologia dell'anima umana* ('Physiology and Pathology of the Human Soul', banned 1855), Giuseppe Bianco's *Le psicopatie contagiose* ('Contagious Psycopathies', banned 1869) and Roberto Ardigò's *La psicologia come scienza positiva* ('Psychology as Positive Science', banned 1872), along with various other works by the above-mentioned Pietro Siciliani, between 1878 and 1882.

Of course, modern experts might also agree that some of these nineteenth-century scholars were in fact objectively wrong in many of their conclusions, and perhaps therefore worthy of being kept out of scientific curricula. Some contemporaries certainly thought so during the nineteenth century, not all of whom were following the dictates of the Catholic Church; materialist psychology was excluded

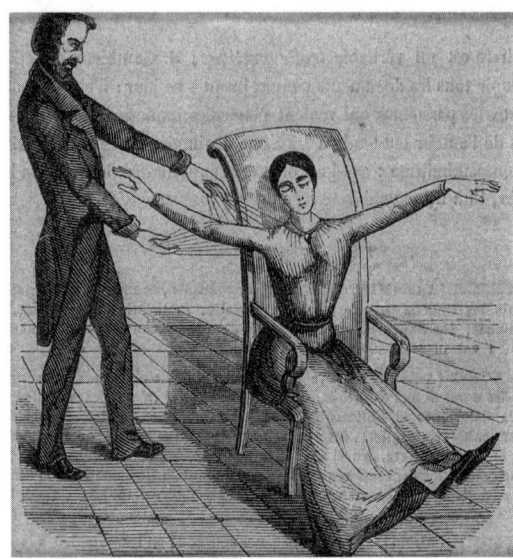

Anon., 'A mesmerist using animal magnetism on a woman who responds with convulsions', 1845, engraving.

from most secular and Protestant universities too, a state of affairs that long delayed the establishment of professional psychology programmes even at places such as Oxford, Cambridge and Harvard. And indeed, the Index targeted not only writers who ended up being part of the mainstream history of academic thought, but outliers such as purveyors of 'animal magnetism' theories who would today certainly be dismissed (and prevented from publishing in respectable journals) as nothing but quacks and charlatans.[3] Jules Bois' earnest research into satanism and magic (condemned in 1896) might also fall into this category.

But it was perhaps the arts that suffered most seriously, or at least most visibly in the eyes of the general public, from Index censorship in the nineteenth and early twentieth centuries. The Industrial Revolution's impetus towards urbanization and public schooling (not to mention exponential multiplication of inexpensive publishing houses and serialized newspapers) resulted in a tremendous expansion of the literate middle class at this time, with novelists and poets becoming celebrated figures well beyond the usual confines of a small intellectual elite. It was therefore shocking to contemporaries, as it remains today, to see prohibitions against beloved literary figures piling up over and over as the decades progressed: Gabriele Rossetti (d. 1854), George Sand (born Amantine Lucile Aurore Dupin, d. 1876), Heinrich Heine (d. 1856), Alexandre

Dumas (both *père*, d. 1870 and *fils*, d. 1895) and Émile Zola (d. 1902) to name just a few who were condemned before 1900. The year 1864 in particular – which, not coincidentally, also gave rise to Pius IX's *Quanta cura* – saw the placement of numerous modern 'naturalist' and 'realist' works by the likes of Stendhal (born Henri Beyle, d. 1842), Honoré de Balzac (d. 1850), Gustave Flaubert (d. 1880) and Victor Hugo (d. 1885) on the Index. French authors may have predominated among additions to the Index at this time over Italians (whose leading *verismo* figures do not seem to have been targeted in the same way) in part due to the acrimonious nature of contemporary French journalism, and the influence that Louis Veuillot's ultraconservative *L'Univers* in particular wielded over the formation of clerical literary opinions.[4] Nor did the pace slacken much in the twentieth century, with condemnations even of Nobel Prize winners and nominees such as Maurice Maeterlinck (awarded 1911, banned 1914), André Gide (awarded 1947, banned 1952) and Jean-Paul Sartre (banned 1948, Nobel award declined 1964).

Anatole France was placed on the Roman Index in 1924, Simone de Beauvoir in 1956, Miguel de Unamuno in 1957; the list goes on and on, a veritable who's who of modern authors – mostly, but not all, European and Catholic (as had been the case since Trent, Protestant authors were not generally listed since they were already banned *ipso facto*). Of course one could also turn the tables and wonder why so many other modern authors do *not* appear on the Index, especially those (like D. H. Lawrence, Henry Miller or the lapsed

Henry de Malvost, 'Le banquet de Satan et de ses fidèles', illustration in Jules Bois, *Le Satanisme et la magie* (1895).

Catholic James Joyce) who were indeed heavily censored by secular authorities. This was sometimes due to Roman censors' ignorance of contemporary literature, especially in languages they did not read well, while in other cases there was perhaps simply no perceived need to prohibit works that had already been dealt with by other jurisdictions. Due to the secrecy of many processes, it is impossible to be sure which books or authors were in fact examined, if they did not result in any formal condemnation. Each case has its own important details and fascinating back story, some of which have only recently come to light; for example, it is now known that acclaimed novelist Graham Greene (whose name is *not* on the Index) was investigated and considered for inclusion on the Roman Index in 1953 for his irreverent portrayal of an alcoholic priest in *The Power and the Glory* (1940). He escaped censure only because Holy Office officials worried that a ban on such a high-profile English convert to Catholicism might harm the political interests of the Church, and so they arranged for a private meeting of admonition instead (at which Greene humbly promised not to repeat his offence). Neither author nor book was thus formally 'Indexed', but de facto censorship was accomplished nonetheless.[5]

Censorship of the theatre, opera and music in the modern era was equally complicated. The later Indexes reveal only a handful of bans on musical compositions such as Pierre-Jean de Béranger's highly popular collected *Chansons* (1820, banned 1834). Many more works were censored by state authorities for various moral, political or even religious reasons during the turbulent nineteenth century, and this may again explain why it was deemed unnecessary to also have them placed on the Index. Plays such as Voltaire's blasphemous *Saül et David* (performed only once before its censure in 1765) were certainly to be found on the Index, but it was state censorship that prevented even a single performance of Rameau's *Samson* (published in 1734, with libretto by Voltaire). Camille Saint-Saëns' later opera on the same theme (*Samson et Dalila*, 1877) was similarly prohibited for its controversial depiction of biblical events, but not by the Catholic Church. Instead, it was the British government that prevented it from being staged in the UK, right up until 1909.

Censorship and Politics

While much post-Napoleonic Church censorship remained largely as it had been conducted in previous generations, existential threats posed to the Church by anticlerical, republican, nationalist and socialist-inspired uprisings throughout the nineteenth century did fundamentally alter some priorities. Protestant challenges of the sixteenth century had been largely rooted in theological differences, even though they often took political forms as well, once warfare and competition over economic resources were added to the stakes of religious conflict. Since then, as discussed in Chapters Six and Seven, the seventeenth and eighteenth centuries saw shifts towards new censorship concerns such as control over scientific knowledge, artistic production and morality. But now, as the fourth century of Index censorship began to dawn, direct political threats to the Church's claims of power and authority, even from fellow Catholics, became more central than ever before. In some cases priests, bishops and even popes themselves felt that they were literally fighting for their lives, and those of their colleagues, as well as for the continued survival of the age-old religious establishment to which those lives had been dedicated.

Organized political (as opposed to religiously motivated) anticlericalism had manifested in many forms long before the archbishop of Paris lost his head to the guillotine in 1794. Given the power of the Church, its inquisitorial tribunals and allied state regimes, however, such movements tended to operate only with great secrecy within Catholic-dominated polities. Freemasonry became one type of private association in which anticlerical sceptics joined with likeminded fellows, as did later groups such as the Italian *Carbonari*, and Catholic officials soon identified these as serious sources of subversion that needed to be suppressed using all the tools at their disposal. Censorship was of course chief among these tools (along with secret police investigations and occasional arrests), and the writings of many known or suspected Masons were placed on the Index as a result. Membership in Masonic and other secret societies was formally condemned by the 1738 papal bull *In eminenti apostolatus*, and this (in addition to various problematic aspects of their actual writing) helps to explain the presence of authors who were known Freemasons (like Gabriele Rossetti) on later editions of the Index.

In the wake of the French Revolution's mass executions, defrockings and dispossessions of clerical personnel and property, and above all its declaration of a new secular state regime in which the Church no longer had power to discipline its enemies, areligious and anti-religious political movements began to operate more openly. These included republicans, nationalists and democrats, for many of whom religion was a matter of personal belief that should be kept separate from affairs of state, including government itself, the economy, public education and justice. Censorship, they argued, if it was to be retained at all, should also be imposed only for reasons of state or public morality – not as a means of imposing religious dogmas. Teachings associated with socialism, anarchism and communism tended to go still further, sometimes insisting that organized religion played a downright negative role in society and should be eliminated once and for all.

It is not surprising, then, that socialist writers such as Claude-Henri de Saint-Simon (d. 1825), Charles Fourier (d. 1837) and his Brazilian disciple José Ignácio de Abreu y Lima (d. 1869), as well as the anarchist Pierre-Joseph Proudhon (d. 1865), were all placed on the Index. It may be surprising that others like Marx, Engels, Bakunin and Kropotkin were not – but again, these were not Catholics and so their writings could already be considered beyond the pale, without any need for further Church censorship. Advocates of secular public education, as opposed to traditional Church-run schools, were also heavily censored; this was the fate of Paul Bert (d. 1886) and Gustavo Bonelli (d. 1926), among many others. Given the popes' particular vulnerability to localized republican and nationalist uprisings associated with the Italian *Risorgimento* (resurgence), it was also all but inevitable that Index censors would prohibit works by seditious Italian authors such as Niccolò Tommaseo – whose 1835 *Libri Cinque dell'Italia* were anonymously published in Paris under a false title which implied that they were actually medieval writings by Girolamo Savonarola, in an unsuccessful bid to avoid such censorship. Vincenzo Gioberti (a priest and university professor who opposed the Jesuit education system) and Girolamo Mascagni (author of a 'Manual of Civic Instruction, in which are Laid Out the Formation, Powers and Government of Political Society') were banned in 1849 and 1860 respectively. Philosophical as well as literary writings by prominent

Risorgimento figures such as Ugo Foscolo (d. 1827) and Giacomo Leopardi (d. 1837) were similarly prohibited.

Defining Truth and Error

External threats to clerical authority, however, whether from non-Catholics or subversive members of the Catholic laity, were never as fully represented in nineteenth-century censorship decrees and Index updates as were internal debates among Catholic priests and their elite intellectual colleagues regarding the present governance and future prospects of the Church. Debates between ultramontanists (those who supported more or less total papal supremacy in Church governance, and uniformity of practice) and gallicans (those, mostly but not exclusively in France, who favoured a greater measure of independence and diversity for local bishops and their flocks) raged bitterly throughout this period. So did conflicts over the extent to which the Church should continue to claim a leadership (and therefore controlling) role in all aspects of civil society. Liberal Catholics, looking back on the traumas of Enlightenment criticism and Revolutionary violence directed against what was perceived as a moribund and abusive clerical tradition, argued for acceptance of the increasingly normative modern concepts of religious freedom, and the need for division between Church and state. In practical terms, they also argued for such innovations as democratic government (even in the Papal States of the Italian peninsula), secular public schools, taxation (or even confiscation) of Church properties, the reform of restrictive marriage laws and an end to the state-sponsored enforcement of religious orthodoxy (including Inquisitions, and Indexes of banned books). These sorts of proposals, often lumped under the term 'progressive' as well as 'liberal', were naturally opposed by those who felt that the Church should continue to maintain (or even expand) its monopoly over the governance of every aspect of human life, from cradle to grave – with few if any concessions made for those who did not wish to enjoy its attentions.

These were precisely the sorts of conflicts that lay behind the errors denounced in the *Syllabus of Errors*. And leading Church conservatives placed the blame for pernicious 'modern' thinking squarely on what they took as the primary underlying heresy of the times: *materialism*. Human society, they argued, had drifted away from a healthy respect for God, and for the superiority of spiritual life (as defined by the Church) over worldly concerns. People were deluded by this inversion into thinking that they would be well-served by more rights and freedoms, better technology and higher wages, when in fact their eternal happiness depended on nothing but obedience to their priests and to the Word of God (again, as defined by the Catholic Church). Pius IX's encyclicals had made it clear after 1849 which side he was on, but of course to liberal and gallican Catholics that didn't necessarily matter; they could still hope for a future papal reversal of policy, or insist that papal opinion needed to be balanced against the contrary voices of other Church leaders around the world. For ultramontanes, the response to such objections was simple: in order to eliminate all division, Catholics must accept the contentious principle of papal infallibility. The idea that the pope could not err, at least in certain types of solemn decision-making, would become the defining issue of the first Vatican Council, which finally ended all debate and defined papal infallibility as an official Church dogma in 1870.

The arguments and divisions leading up to Vatican I, and their echoes which continued to resonate long after, left many traces in the pages of the Index. Radical voices on both sides were silenced, including the ultramontane Louis Chaillot (d. 1891), director of *L'Avenir Catholique*, as well as gallican authors such as Pierre-Louis Blanchard (d. *c.* 1826), Henri Bernier (d. 1859) and Jean de Bonnefon (d. 1928). In addition to Lamennais, prominent liberal priests such as Antonio Bernabeu (d. 1825) and Ernesto Buonaiuti (d. 1946) were also placed on the Index; but then so too were arch-conservatives including Emmanuel Barbier (d. 1925), as well as Charles Maurras' far-right journal *L'Action Française*. Louis-Auguste Bosseboeuf sought for balance in his *Le Syllabus sans parti pris* (The Syllabus, Without Taking Sides) but this did not prevent his name from being added to the Index in 1886; his fellow archivist and (canon-law expert) Paul-Marie Viollet, an avowed liberal, was also denounced in 1906 for his publication 'On the Infallibility of the Pope and the Syllabus'. Opposition to papal infallibility similarly resulted in bans on books by Andrea d'Altagena (in 1865), Rocco Bombelli (in 1887) and Attilio Begey (in 1913), along with many others. A disillusioned ex-priest named William Laurence Sullivan, writing on this theme, gained the distinction of being the very last American author to appear on the Index for his *Letters to His Holiness, Pope Pius X, by a Modernist* (banned in 1912).

Vatican I was an overwhelming victory for ultramontane conservatives, cementing the Church's anti-modern stance and guaranteeing a continued future for the Index of Prohibited Books in the process. Some of those who disagreed with its decisions left the Church (as did Sullivan), or were excommunicated (as was the Munich theologian Johann Joseph Ignaz von Döllinger, who died in 1890). Others, like the English Catholic Lord Acton, stayed in the Church but still made their disapproval known and were listed on the Index as a consequence (even though Acton ceased to publish after the Council). A splinter group known as the 'Old Catholics', which had already formed before the Council met, insisting that papal infallibility and absolutism were neither biblical nor traditional in the Church; several of its members were also soon to be found on the Index, including Joseph Berchtold (d. 1895) and that pioneering historian of the Index of Prohibited Books, ex-priest Franz Heinrich Reusch (d. 1900).

Though direct control over the Papal States, and therefore most of the papacy's remaining secular power, was lost in 1871 to Italian unification under the regime of King Victor Emmanuel, Pius IX's successor Leo XIII struggled to minimize the resulting damage as best he could. Going on the offensive, Pope Leo maintained a steady stream of censorship edicts while also publishing his own pronouncements against various problems in the modern world. As a remedy to the errors of materialism, he proposed a return to study of the medieval St Thomas Aquinas with his 1879 encyclical letter *Aeterni patris*, arguing that Thomas's moderate realism offered a better and more spiritual explanation for human beings' place within the natural world than did voguish new trends in modern science. Leo also lamented the attractions of secular labour politics, socialism and communism to members of the Catholic working classes. A better solution to social injustices in an age of capitalist abuse, he argued in the 1891 encyclical *Rerum novarum*, was for workers to unite in Catholic unions that were organized along the lines of medieval guilds. These should be focused on mutual aid and the promotion of good morals (maintained under the benevolent guidance of local clergy), through which workers and employers might find common ground. New studies in medieval history and Neo-Thomist thought flourished as a result of these and other documents, and new Catholic universities sprang up all over the world to teach appropriately Thomistic curricula in order to prevent students' falling into the traps of modernist secularism. This did not, however, prevent even some Neo-Thomist scholars from coming to the 'wrong' conclusions, and therefore having their own works placed on the Index – as happened to Luis Alonso Getino (d. 1946), the Dominican editor of *Ciencia Tomistica*, whose book on salvation was banned in 1936 despite his intense devotion and absolute submission to Church authority.[6] As will be seen in the following pages, Getino was far from being the only Dominican student of St Thomas to fall afoul of Index censors in the twentieth century.

Censorship in the Twentieth Century

Despite the ultramontanes' and conservatives' insistence on preventing any changes at all from taking root in the Catholic Church, unfolding events naturally continued to require responses and adjustments, as Leo XIII's foray into the politics of labour and social justice made clear. Responding to recommendations from Vatican I, Leo also made changes to the function of the Index of Prohibited Books with his important 1897 apostolic constitution *Officium ac munerum*. New editions and updates of the Index had already been promulgated throughout Leo's reign, but this document (after musing on the importance of the censorial task and giving a brief history of Church censorship dating back to the New Testament) now imposed a complete rewriting of Index regulations, expanding them from ten to a total of fifteen *capitula*, divided into two sections. These *Decreta generalia de prohitione et censura librorum* (General Decrees on the Prohibition and Censorship of Books) formally abrogated the old Tridentine Rules, along with all the *Observationes*, *Instructiones*, *Decreta* and *Monitus* that had been added by subsequent popes, with the sole exception of Benedict XIV's *Sollicita ac provida* (which remained in full force). Leo acknowledged that Rule no. 10 (on pre-publication censorship) had already largely ceased to be operative under Pius IX; his new version also moderated, streamlined and clarified restrictions on various categories of books and art, including translated Bibles and magical texts, while adding new details on the censorship of newspapers. Penalties were generally limited to warnings, chastisement and excommunication – a de facto recognition that the papacy generally no longer enjoyed the power to impose more serious punishments on its enemies. When the next edition of the Index was published, in 1900, it was also noticeably shorter, with nearly 3,000 outdated or revoked condemnations quietly removed from its pages.

The next major change to the Index came about in 1917, with Pope Benedict XV's complete overhaul not only of inquisitorial procedures but of canon law itself. New rules regarding Catholic believers' access to books were codified in the updated *Codex iuris canonici*, the Church's most important legal code. In a seemingly dramatic organizational shift, the Congregation of the Index was now altogether dissolved by means of a papal decision entitled *Alloquentes proxime*. Responsibility for evaluation and censorship of books and art would henceforth be placed squarely in the hands of the Roman Inquisition (which had been renamed the 'Supreme Sacred Congregation of the Holy Office' in 1908, under Pius X). No real change in policy or severity was discernible in the end, but certainly these new measures were meant to improve the efficiency of procedures which had always been subject to bureaucratic delays and internal conflicts.

As Europe descended into the chaos of the First World War, followed soon after by a near-global Great Depression, new challenges were in the air. Moving pictures presented an unprecedented challenge to censors, and some local bishops and other Catholic authorities reacted enthusiastically – usually, though not always, with dire warnings – to the advent of this extremely popular technology. Pope Pius XI (r. 1922–39) himself issued a brief if pointed warning about the 'dangers of moral and religious shipwreck' that might assail 'inexperienced youth' if that youth were overly exposed to unregulated cinemas, as well as to impious books, radio and theatrical performances. This message was somewhat buried within *Divini illius magistri*, a lengthy 1929 encyclical on Christian education, but a subsequent encyclical entitled *Vigilanti cura* (1936) was specifically devoted to the dangers of the motion picture industry. Here Pius effusively praised an American organization known as the Catholic Legion of Decency, and gave his blessing to its strenuous lobbying efforts (which had already helped to ban numerous productions and bring about the notorious 1934 Hayes Code for Hollywood). The Curia thus made its opinion clear in general terms; yet the Roman Holy Office did not explicitly make film censorship a formal part of its overall mandate. Individual films were not placed on the Index. Instead, it was left to local Catholic activist groups to lobby governments and other supervisory bodies whenever they felt a film needed to be cut or prohibited.

Radio (and later television), too, was seen to present both opportunities for more effectively spreading the Catholic message, and grave dangers, since dissident and anti-Catholic voices alike all obtained access to the same airwaves. A Vatican radio station was set up by the inventor Guglielmo Marconi himself in 1931, at the command of Pius XI, and broadcasts by the Canadian-American 'radio priest' Charles Edward Coughlin were enormously popular with some audiences. Based in Michigan during the 1920s and '30s, Coughlin at first limited his more political messages to denunciation of Ku Klux Clan cross-burnings and other anti-Catholic provocations; but soon he broadened his messages to include antisemitic and pro-fascist propaganda in support of figures such as Benito Mussolini, Francisco Franco and Adolf Hitler. Coughlin was finally censored and forced off the air by the Roosevelt administration in 1939, but he continued to publish his views in the press. Finally, in 1942 (following an FBI investigation and arrests of Catholic agitators who had threatened anti-Jewish violence), he was silenced by order of his own Church hierarchy – though his name was never placed on the Index.

Fascist sympathies evidently ran deep in many Church circles at the time, though some particularly noxious books by far-right authors were in fact placed on the Index right alongside those of their leftist enemies – above all if they advocated forms of state totalitarianism that left insufficient space for authority to be wielded by the papacy, or if they otherwise violated Church teachings in spiritual or moral matters. Poetry by Guido da Verona (d. 1939), a signatory to the 1925 *Manifesto of Fascist Intellectuals* who was later marginalized for his Jewish ancestry, was subject to Index prohibition in 1920 due to its erotic nature. Da Verona's fellow poet Gabriele D'Annunzio, a rival to as well as an important influence on Mussolini, was similarly censored as early as 1911. Prominent Nazis such as Alfred Rosenberg and Ernst Bergmann were placed on the Index in the 1930s due to their extremist views on religion, which included rejection of traditional Catholicism in favour of a more pointedly racist and antisemitic German National Church (*Die deutsche Nationalkirche*).

The Second World War was a traumatic time for many Catholics, as it was of course for nearly everyone involved (and most especially for Jewish and other victims of Nazi genocide). Led by Pope Pius XII (r. 1939–58), who has since been lauded for his efforts to minimize the harm caused by fascist movements and his protection of some Roman Jews, but also vilified for his failure to take a clear stand against Hitler or the Holocaust, the Church entered upon a period of reflection and adjustment in the aftermath of the conflict. This did not at first include any change to the Index of Prohibited Books, which was yet again printed in 1948 with new titles and authors listed for censure – just as it had been periodically since the sixteenth century. The Holy Office continued its investigations of suspected heterodoxy among the clergy, the faithful and occasionally further afield, whenever an objectionable work was brought to its attention (such as the Greek Orthodox Nikos Kazantzakis's *Last Temptation of Christ*, the feminist Jacqueline Martin's *Plenitude*, subtitled 'Testimony of a Woman on Love', or the communist-leaning Catholic journal *La Quinzaine*, which were all banned in the mid-1950s). Furthermore, Pius continued to express concerns about the dangers of modern mass media communications, above all film and radio but now also adding television, in his encyclical *Miranda prorsus* (1957). In spite of all that had happened, including new threats of nuclear apocalypse that loomed large as the Cold War began to heat up, ultramontane conservatives' grip on Catholic leadership seemed unbreakable. Change was not to be expected any time soon, and the Index was as authoritative as ever.

The End of the Index

Yet seeds of change had long been sown, and in the end it was only a matter of time and fortuitous circumstance before they began to sprout. Like any organization dependent on popular support, the Catholic Church had always been sensitive to public opinion. Indeed, that sensitivity at least partly explains one of the very *raisons d'être* of the Index itself: to prevent scandal, and to silence hurtful criticism. Some Catholics had been uncomfortable with the Church's censorship practices at every stage of the history that has been summarized in this book; but denunciations, scorn and mockery from Protestants had naturally been even more forceful and vocal than any internal mutterings. Such criticisms were generally brushed off or ignored (if not censored outright) by the Church hierarchy for centuries, but their insistence and conviction inevitably took a toll. By the middle of the twentieth century, the perceived disconnect between modern values of religious, intellectual and artistic freedom on the one hand, and Church traditions of Index censorship on the other, had become so widely recognized that they could no longer be easily or safely dismissed.

Protestants had naturally decried and mocked the pretensions of the Catholic Church to command total control over the publication of 'heretical' literature ever since the inception of the Index of Prohibited Books, and as noted earlier they even distributed false imprints of the Index as a means of drawing attention to its excesses and 'errors'. By the nineteenth century, however, such criticism, subversion and mockery had reached entirely new heights. Respected intellectuals such as Joseph Mendham, William Knapp, Franz Heinrich Reusch and George Haven Putnam published learned studies on Index history that were at least implicitly critical, and sometimes crossed over into open polemic. More strident texts such as the ex-monk Joseph McCabe's *History and Meaning of the Catholic Index of Forbidden Books* (1931) were even clearer in their intention of exposing the inconsistencies and absurdities of Index censorship to public scrutiny and ridicule. These were in addition to more general scholarly treatments of inquisition history, pioneered by the likes of Henry Charles Lea, which also drew increased attention to the troubled history of Catholic religious discipline around the turn of the twentieth century. Publication of unapproved editions of the Index continued as well, with Mendham releasing a new annotated edition of Sixtus v's suppressed Index of 1590 in 1835, and Reusch following suit with his 1889 edition of the little-known Parma Index of 1580. Special collector's editions of some Indexes were published by the De Vinne company of New York in the 1890s, further feeding elite American distrust and contempt for the tradition of Catholic book censorship.

And then there were the pornographers. Index censorship lists, now available to anyone who wanted to consult them, were further subverted and mocked by some of the more licentious *fin de siècle* authors and printers, who turned to them for lurid inspiration. Henry Spencer Ashbee, writing under the pseudonym Pisanus Fraxi, thus produced a collection of erotic tales entitled *Index Librorum*

Prohibitorum: Being Notes Bio- Biblio- Icono- graphical and Critical, on Curious and Uncommon Books (1878). Meanwhile, inspired in part by the Index prohibition of Mirabeau's eighteenth-century *Erotika Biblion*, Harry Sidney Nichols and Leonard Smithers founded the Erotika Biblion Society – a London-based venture that published a whole series of pornographic works between 1888 and 1907. Erotic images were commissioned to adorn numerous specialized editions of other banned works, including Boccaccio's *Decameron*.[7] Together with a well-established tradition of inquisition-bashing 'gothic' literature, which had flourished in the English- and French-speaking worlds above all for over a century, these sorts of books helped to ensure that the Index of Prohibited Books was truly an embarrassment for many Catholics by the early decades of the twentieth century if not before. Apologetic works such Alphonse de Pavillez' pamphlet *L'Index, un éteignoir ou un phare?* (The Index, Candle-Snuffer or Beacon?, 1943) could only do so much to stem the tide.

In such a context, blunt conservatism and a refusal to compromise became increasingly impossible to maintain. In the aftermath of the Second World War, and certainly by the end of Pius XII's pontificate, a clear majority of Catholic prelates around the world were coming to a consensus that fundamental changes were needed if the Church was to remain healthy and relevant in the modern world. This became evident soon after the election of Pius' successor John XXIII (r. 1958–63), who announced the convening of a second Vatican Council in January of 1959. Though the Index itself was never on the agenda at Vatican II, clashes between conservatives and liberals were evident throughout the three years of its sitting (1963–5). Cardinal Alfredo Ottaviani, head of the Holy Office and a leader of the minority conservative faction, was regularly infuriated as his colleagues voted overwhelmingly, again and again, to reverse long-standing Church policies on issues such as the exclusive primacy of the Latin Vulgate Bible, (in)tolerance for religious freedom and recognition of the need in some cases for a separation of Church and state. Both Pope John and his successor Paul VI (r. 1963–78), who took over the reins of the Council soon after it got underway, realized that changes in censorship policy would likely be required as a consequence.

Paul's new decree on communications media, *Inter mirifica* (1963), struck an unaccustomed tone in its praise for 'the wonderful technological discoveries which men of talent, especially in the present era, have made with God's help'. Anti-modernism was evidently no longer the Church's non-negotiable watchword, and compromise was finally on the table. Then, just months after the Council's closure, the pope announced a major overhaul of the Holy Office – which would henceforth be known as the Sacred Congregation for the Doctrine of the Faith. Ottaviani remained in charge until his resignation in 1968, but he had been publicly humiliated by his losses at the Council and his wings had clearly been clipped. No new editions of the Index had been issued since 1948, and on 14 June 1966 it was announced that no further editions would be forthcoming. Instead, Catholics were advised that while its general intent remained in force as a moral admonition to avoid pernicious literature (ideally with guidance from appropriate clerical leaders), the Church would no longer compile or enforce any lists of banned books. The Index was no more.

But its ghosts lingered on. In the leadup to Vatican II, Ottaviani and the Holy Office had been busy investigating and in some cases censoring a number of prominent Catholic intellectuals, including several who ended up being welcomed and giving presentations at the Council itself. These included the French medievalist Marie-Dominique Chenu and the theologian Yves Congar, both Dominicans associated with the 'Worker Priest' movement, and the Jesuit theologians Karl Rahner, Henri de Lubac and John Courtney Murray (an American expert on Church–State relations). While only Chenu had actually been named on the Index (since 1942), the others faced varying degrees of official condemnation and suppression. Rahner and Murray, for example, were ordered not to publish, while Chenu, Congar and de Lubac were all removed from their teaching duties in Catholic universities.

This sort of 'internal' censorship of Catholic teachers and priests, which could certainly be considered relatively benign in comparison with the fate that Chenu and Congar's Dominican colleague Giordano Bruno had received three and a half centuries previously, was nevertheless a serious matter. And it did not end with either the reform of the Holy Office, or the abolition of the Index. Professor Hans Küng was investigated in the late 1960s and finally stripped of his licence to teach Catholic theology in 1979, for publicly opposing the doctrine of papal infallibility. The Belgian Dominican Edward Schillebeeckx was similarly interrogated by the Congregation for the Doctrine of the Faith in the 1970s and '80s, although he was never

Pope Paul VI
(Giovanni Battista
Enrico Antonio
Maria Montini),
1969, photograph.

formally condemned for his theological writings. The American nun Jeannine Gramick has been repeatedly reprimanded since the late 1980s for her work supporting lesbian, gay and transgender rights. Lacking the power to physically punish, imprison or silence transgressors, the Church nevertheless retains a great deal of control over its own personnel, and it can complicate or end careers. Censorship of writings by devout Catholics, especially when it comes to theological or pastoral topics, therefore remains firmly in place despite the abolition of the Index of Prohibited Books.

THE FINAL CENTURY of the Index thus encompassed a remarkable period which saw the Index of Prohibited Books go from absolutism to abolition. Clawing its way back from the brink of annihilation at the hands of revolutionary anticlerical zealots, the increasingly conservative and centralized papal Church of the nineteenth century was in some ways much more dedicated to censorship and control of all forms of human expression than had ever been the case in the medieval or early modern periods. The Index reached its highest point of sophistication at this time, and its prominence in the minds of many Catholics led it to become a key bastion in their struggle against both the threats and the siren calls of modernity. Its mission had grown to become all-encompassing, in ways that would have surprised many of the original Index compilers of the sixteenth century. Like papal infallibility, an Index that censored not only religious texts but scientific, literary and political ones (not to mention newspapers), thumbing its nose at modern culture in defiance of all public opinion, would have been unthinkable to even the most ambitious Church hierarchs just three centuries earlier – though Paul iv and Francisco Peña would probably have been delighted with the result.

Ultimately popular opinion did matter, though, and even the Supreme Sacred Congregation of the Holy Office could not stop the march of time and progress. The end, when it came, was swift and unsettling for Curial insiders who had taken ultramontane conservatism for granted throughout their entire careers. For many others, of course, the changes brought about in the wake of Vatican ii were too little, too late. Damage to reputations, careers, human knowledge and creativity, and in some cases to human lives, was already done and to a certain extent continued even after the Index ceased to function. Still, Paul vi's difficult decision to discontinue four whole centuries of institutionalized Church censorship, ironically first instigated and shepherded by his direct namesakes Paul iii (founder of the Roman Inquisition), Paul iv (founder of the first Roman Index) and Paul v (the first pope to judge Galileo), was a momentous one. And though much more could be said about every aspect of that fascinating history, it also brings our story to a close.

CONCLUSION

Today it is easy for many of us to joke about the 'Inquisition', and about the Index of Prohibited Books. Monty Python's 'Spanish Inquisition' sketch is by now over fifty years old, but it continues to resonate by poking good fun at the absurdities of self-righteous religious intolerance (without ever mentioning the role Cardinal Jiménez de Cisneros, one of its main characters, really played in the sixteenth-century destruction of Spanish Muslim books). The Index itself has become an obscure historical phenomenon for the most part, at best evoking vague notions of evil monks maliciously hoarding away or burning ancient tomes at some point in the distant past. It can also become an essentially meaningless cipher. If you are an aficionado of Japanese anime, perhaps you know 'Index Librorum Prohibitorum' (or *Kinsho Mokuroku Indekkusu*) as the name of a female protagonist with silver hair who somehow serves as a magical vessel for the preservation of thousands of volumes of secret lore in the manga *Toaru Majutsu no Indekkusu*. This recycling of the historical Index into postmodern fantasy plots demonstrates both how remote and exotic the actual history of the Index has become, and how intriguing it can be even in the most oblique of distorted glimpses. If nothing else, I hope that this book has shed a bit more light on the subject, and clarified what the Index truly *was* – at least sufficiently to inspire others to learn more about the history of censorship, about the nature of religious conflict and about some of the many fascinating works that were prohibited for one reason or another over the centuries.

The Index was not just a strange feature of ancient times, a curiosity far distant from modern concerns. Indeed 'book censorship' as exercised by the Index and its compilers didn't really exist, couldn't really exist, in ancient or medieval times at all – the pioneering efforts of Akhenaten and Nicholas Eymeric notwithstanding. It must instead be understood as a comparatively recent phenomenon, unique to the modern world. The Index was born from the emergence of modern print technology, the enduring sixteenth-century division of European Christianity into Catholic and Protestant confessional camps and the professionalized, bureaucratized mechanisms of intolerance that were developed by the early modern Inquisitions. But it remained active, and arguably more effective than ever, well into the second half of the last century.

The director of libraries at Chicago's DePaul University, Redmond Burke, wrote in 1952 about how to effectively implement Index rules for American university students and professors: all good Catholic university collections should be provided with a special locked compartment for housing banned books, which were only to be consulted with special permission from the appropriate bishop or his delegate.[1] Far from being a barrier to scholarship, Burke argued, this was the best possible solution since it would keep worthless and deceptive materials from wasting researchers' time or leading them astray. And he was not entirely wrong; most librarians today would agree that it *is* their job to keep collections stocked only with carefully selected materials (whose relevance and usefulness may evolve over time, as determined by leading experts in a field). Decisions need to be made, if only due to lack of shelving space, and sometimes books need to be moved to special units or weeded out altogether. Setting aside 'prohibited' compartments, sometimes taking the form of cages, is a rather extreme version of this practice, but it was a historical compromise that continued to be used into the 1960s at leading research schools such as the University of Notre Dame in the United States, and the Laval University Seminary in Canada, where it was known as 'the Grill', or *l'enfer* (hell), respectively. Special stickers were also sometimes affixed to 'Indexed' books, in order to warn library patrons of special measures in place to prevent their regular circulation. Implementation of the Index's prohibitions thus extended well into the living memory of many Catholics today, and indeed in the course of researching this book I met and spoke with several who lamented its loss as what was for them a valuable moral compass.

The issue of censorship is not by any means absent from twenty-first-century life either. Recent developments in surveillance technology and cultural politics have ensured that our reading and viewing habits are now in many ways *more* subject to scrutiny, manipulation and potential discipline than ever before. From Internet browser histories to purchase records and library borrowing patterns, nearly everything we view, read or listen to today is digitally recorded and therefore at least potentially available to agencies which might be interested in their contents. Whether for political repression, to maximize corporate profits or for policing purposes (anti-terrorist, or anti-pornographic for example), not to mention journalistic and more or less academic research, this information can be and often is actively used to keep tabs on who consumes what information. In some countries, religious censorship rules also remain entirely enforceable. The results can, in exceptional cases, be as deadly as they once were for Giordano Bruno.

Precisely *what* gets censored (or at least critically scrutinized), and *why*, has of course changed over time – just as it did over the *longue durée* of the Index of Prohibited Books. When several volumes from the popular *Tintin* cartoon series were recently removed from Catholic school collections in Canada over concerns about racist content, for example, it caused a predictable outcry – but it should not be overlooked that the same series was also subjected to heavy censorship of a rather different type when it was originally created. From the 1930s to the mid-1970s, state censorship boards in France ordered the removal of several allegedly violent, anti-social or politically sensitive elements from *Tintin* as well as many other *bandes dessinées*. Church

Library sticker requiring special permission to consult a book listed on the Index of Prohibited Books, 20th century.

authorities also quietly imposed demands of their own (including the prominent addition of pious Christmas scenes in certain seasonal issues).[2] Since then, the Internet has both exponentially increased the quantity of potentially offensive material available to consumers *and* increased the likelihood of censure, since even casual inflammatory remarks made online can now instantly result in serious personal consequences, up to and including loss of employment, criminal charges and death threats. Clearly we live in a very different world from the one in which Index censors and their informants had to physically track down rare copies of individual texts, perhaps waiting until they came out in translation, in order to evaluate whether or not they might pose a threat to Church interests, before finally adding them to a printed list that might only be published several decades later. This is not to say that readers, and authors, are any better or worse off today than they were five hundred years ago. But the purposes, nature and processes of censorship have evolved.

Controlling the Word

The original purpose of the Index of Prohibited Books was to list those texts, mostly written (or, in the case of Bibles, translated or edited) by Protestants, that undermined or corrupted the revealed Word of God. This encompassed not only the literal words of the Bible, but their true 'meaning': deep, even mysteriously coded divine messages that could only partially be conveyed through human language, and therefore required ongoing recourse to authoritative interpreters. Precisely who these interpreters should be, and who was qualified to grant them their authority, was of course one of the main problems at the heart of the whole Reformation crisis. For Luther and his followers, Scripture alone was the foundational bedrock of the Christian faith and all who claimed to interpret it could be judged by how closely their teachings followed the literal words of the Bible text. From this principle, it was easy to consider dispensing with clerical elites altogether and replacing them with a more universal 'priesthood of all believers'. Given the complexities of the Bible, however, even the most scripturally minded Protestants soon realized that 'literal' reading was easier said than done.

Translations and alternative versions of the Bible further muddied the waters of comprehension, such that inevitably believers *had* to resort to accepting authority of one sort or another in order simply to decide precisely which Bible was to be read, whether literally or not. This meant a return to trusting in specialists, and Luther himself soon moved away from the idea of allowing all Christians to personally interpret the Scriptures once it became clear that they so frequently came to different conclusions than he had. The early modern Wars of Religion not only pitted Catholics against Protestants; Protestant and Catholic factions warred among themselves, sometimes viciously, while all too often remaining violently hateful and intolerant of non-Christians as well. The Word of God, it turned out, was not always a source of peace and goodwill to all. Something more might be required, some sort of authoritative oversight, without which the power of holy words could be dangerously misused.

This argument, for sixteenth-century Catholics, justified the retention of traditional Church structures, authorities and interpretive texts compiled over centuries of theological study and writing. It also justified strict policing of those structures, authorities and texts in order to weed out anything which might be conducive to error, whether inadvertently or (in the case of outright heresy) through stubborn refusal to accept 'the truth'. Since apostolic times, the Church had struggled and experimented with ways of doing this – from Paul's admonition in Titus 3:10 that heretics should simply be twice warned and then avoided, to later medieval notions that, like weeds at harvest time, they should be gathered up and burned in order to prevent contamination of the faithful (based on the parable of the wheat and the tares, in Matthew 13:24–30). Temporary heresy inquisition tribunals to determine precisely who was deserving of such treatment eventually led to the institutionalization of permanent Inquisitions, as we have seen, and their duties almost immediately extended to judging not only persons but their words, teachings and writings. Protestant leaders too soon found themselves having to act very similarly, developing their own techniques for disciplining followers and preventing the spread of noxious books within their various denominations; a much more complex story, in many ways, than that which has been the subject of this book, but important nonetheless and worthy of further study.

In the preceding chapters we saw how the Catholic Church made control over the divine Word its fundamental objective in book censorship across more than four full centuries of Index history. This often meant prohibiting the interpretive writings of Protestant theologians, who read the words of Scripture differently than did Catholic exegetes, and above all rejected the authority of a papally led Church hierarchy to determine which meaning should be accepted. It also sometimes meant prohibiting editions of the biblical Scriptures themselves, in whole or in part, when these were deemed to have been erroneously or maliciously distorted. Writings by Catholic theologians could be similarly forbidden whenever they threatened to contradict accepted Church dogmas, as could Jewish interpretations of the Hebrew Bible. Other non-Christian spiritual writings were generally less of a concern, though the temptations they might pose for new converts to apostatize did lead to formal bans (as well as many undocumented seizures). And it must also be understood that in the holistic religious worldview that was current at the time, 'control over the divine Word' dealt with much more than biblical or theological texts. Scientific concepts about God's created world might also lead to spiritual errors, just as artistic creations could provoke moral as well as spiritual transgression. Even political beliefs were inherently religious in this context, since no clear division had yet been established between Church and state. Hence the inherent logic of the Index of Prohibited Books: those appointed to look out for the well-being of Catholic Christian souls had a positive duty to weed out pernicious doctrines or ideas wherever they were to be found (even in visual or musical form), for the good of the community, and ultimately the greater glory of God.

Though the Index ceased to be produced after 1948, and after 1966 papal authority no longer directed its maintenance under the auspices of the newly renamed Congregation for the Doctrine of the Faith, neither its underlying purpose nor its theoretical moral authority over Catholic consciences have ever changed. The Church remains committed to ensuring that only what it considers to be 'authentic doctrine' is taught in its name. To this end, in Paul VI's dogmatic constitution on divine revelation, *Dei verbum*, promulgated on 18 November 1965, even while making important concessions to encourage the broader dissemination of biblical teachings throughout the world, it was clearly stated that such dissemination was *only* to be done 'with maternal concern', using 'suitable and correct' texts, and 'under the watchful care of the sacred teaching office of the Church' – by which the pope meant episcopal and ultimately papal authority, as informed by the Congregation for the Doctrine of the Faith.³ The importance of maintaining such vigilance in the modern age was further repeated at the end of the document, which insists that 'shepherds of the Church' must ensure that only 'suitable instruction' is given, along 'with the necessary and really adequate explanations so that the children of the Church may safely and profitably become conversant with the Sacred scriptures and be penetrated with their spirit'.

The spirit of this doctrine has since been applied, at least in principle, to guide and restrict the teaching of theology in Catholic universities by means of Pope John Paul II's 1990 apostolic constitution *Ex corde Ecclesiae* (From the Heart of the Church). The Index no longer exists, but the general principle remains that true Catholic believers should refrain from reading the books it condemned (as well as any books like them, which *could* have been condemned), unless they have good reason for doing so. When in doubt, they should seek advice from the appropriate clerical authorities. And Catholic writers, especially when dealing with matters of religion or morality, are still expected to submit to Church authority in some circumstances, for example seeking formal permission (the *imprimatur*) before publishing theological texts with a Catholic press. Catholic university professors are even, at least theoretically, now required to seek a special licence to teach theological subjects (known as the *mandatum*) under the terms of *Ex corde Ecclesiae*. This latter requirement has proven difficult to enforce in practice, due to concerns over the widely accepted principle of academic freedom in higher education (and older traditions of professorial religious authority, as exercised in early modern times by theology faculties at universities such as Paris and Leuven even over members of the clergy). But it remains official Church policy nonetheless.⁴

Impossible Tasks

If the experience of more than four hundred years of religious censorship by the Roman Catholic Church has in some ways not really changed the hierarchy's fundamental views on the importance of preventing the harmful effects of pernicious books (and images), some lessons were certainly learned along the way. In particular, the sheer magnitude of the work involved in actively policing the entirety of human cultural production had already become painfully evident by the end of the sixteenth century at least. Although prideful stubbornness, combined with institutional inertia and hardening cultural attitudes, continued to propel increasingly futile efforts for well over a century thereafter, it was clear that some sort of narrowing of focus would be required if the Index was to even partially fulfill its objective of prohibiting the most dangerous books in an age of ongoing global Protestant Reformation and Scientific Revolution.

Unless the Church was to entirely dedicate its personnel and financial resources to the performance of nothing but censorship duties, it could simply never keep up with the pace of book publication once printing presses had become operational all over the world. Furthermore, as the swollen Indexes of the late seventeenth century amply demonstrate, at a certain point massive lists of names and titles actually become useless for the officials who are tasked with recognizing suspect materials on the ground. If compiling the Index was itself an onerous task, so was looking up every single author and title in a bookstore, a library or a ship's manifest using a 1,400-page tome (which was likely to be at least ten years out of date in any case), perhaps accompanied by a sheaf of separate edicts. Compounding this challenge, as we have seen, were inaccuracies, omissions and inconsistencies of spelling – not to mention complicated instructions for the expurgation of some works, which might take days to properly accomplish for each volume.

Inconsistency was perhaps the greatest failure of the Index project, and the one which exposed it to the most criticism over time. Why was one work banned *in toto*, while another of clearly more pressing concern was passed over or subjected to only minor alterations? Banning Bibles was bad enough, especially when these seemed to have been produced by pious and well-intentioned Catholics (such as the Port-Royal Jansenists). But why was a fifty-year-old minor English novel like Laurence Sterne's *Sentimental Journey Through France and Italy* banned by a special decree of the Roman Inquisition in 1819? The author was by now long dead, and his work of sentimental fiction largely forgotten by most of his own countrymen. Was it because he was a Protestant (indeed, a low-ranking Anglican clergyman)? If so, why wasn't the still-living (and much more prolific) Presbyterian Freemason Sir Walter Scott banned at the same time? It is hard to see just what in the rather meandering narrative of the *Sentimental Journey* could possibly have so offended the censors, since even its depiction of the Catholic clergy is quite respectful for the most part, and its oblique references to sex are tame compared to many other works of the day (including Sterne's own better-known, but never indexed, *Tristram Shandy*). Ironically, Sterne was in fact subjected to rather harsher censorship by his own superior, the Anglican archbishop of York, who had most copies of his *Political Romance* burned in 1759 because he didn't appreciate the satirical fun it poked at a local lawyer.[5] But the likely cause of Sterne's posthumous inquisitorial condemnation was much more prosaic: it simply happened to be translated into Italian in 1813, someone complained, and a ban was issued. If there are further justifications for this censorship buried somewhere in the files of the Congregation for the Doctrine of the Faith, it is to be hoped they will someday be found and published. Until then, the case stands more as an example of inquisitorial inefficiency and misplaced priorities, rather than diabolical thoroughness.

Of course there were more serious cases too, such as the banning of Galileo, or the much more violent silencing of Giordano Bruno. These are rightly held up as examples of how the Index of Prohibited Books, and the inquisitorial mechanisms behind it, harmed legitimate scholars and stood in the way of science. But as we have seen, each of these cases must be understood in its wider context – not to exonerate the Church of wrongdoing, but on the contrary to show the episodic, incoherent, accidental and sometimes contradictory nature of much contemporary censorship even when it involved high-profile authors. Bruno may have conjured demons, disobeyed Church orders, speculated wildly about the universe and fraternized with Protestants, but he was far from alone in any of these activities, most of which were aided and abetted by other clergymen and even by some of the crowned heads of Catholic Europe. Bruno was likely as surprised as anyone when his twenty years of lucrative adventurism suddenly caught up with him. Galileo was similarly treated very well, until suddenly he wasn't, and that change in attitude was neither objectively nor exclusively related to the content of his writings. Politics underlay many of the prohibitions on the Index, as did coincidence, timing and simple bad luck. The details of each case are worth exploring to find out more about exactly how and why a work came to be censored, and often those back-stories reveal more about the circumstances of the censors' time and place than they do about the religious, intellectual or artistic qualities of the banned publication itself.

Attempts in the mid-eighteenth century, and then again at the turn of the twentieth, to rationalize and simplify the Index could only partially address the core problem: books continued to be published too fast, and in too great numbers, for censors to keep up with them in even a cursory way. Fully subjecting a text to critical scrutiny takes time, as does writing up a report and then defending it, if necessary, in committee debates. This was, ideally, the treatment books were supposed to receive before being subjected to condemnation or expurgation. But all too often beleaguered censors instead simply cribbed titles from previous lists, or from the sales catalogues of the Frankfurt Book Fair (even if they had no idea what the book was about, and sometimes when it didn't actually exist).

This problem was further compounded by the Church's pretensions to universality. It was one thing to try and keep up with local publications, as was attempted by officials in many regions. But efforts to centralize book censorship under the auspices of the Roman Curia via the Congregation of the Index were ultimately doomed to abject failure. Lacking the basic ability to read works published in all the languages of the world, not to mention the ability to comprehend sophisticated cultural works derived from non-European traditions such as Hinduism, Confucianism or the diverse belief systems of Africa and the Americas, it was all but inevitable that masses of 'pagan' texts and images would almost never be seriously considered for inclusion on the Index. Poorly documented (or completely undocumented) seizures and destruction of such materials in colonial contexts remain among the greatest tragedies perpetrated by Catholic authorities throughout the history of Index censorship, even though they rarely involved the Index as such.

The Will to Censor

Despite these obvious failings, Church censorship remained a going concern throughout the early modern period. Prominent Catholic theologians continued to volunteer their services from one generation to the next, and many ecclesiastical careers were advanced by means of successful work on the evaluation of suspicious books and artworks. A multitude of extremely well-educated and intelligent scholars (along with many less talented ones, of course) worked over the centuries on various Indexes of Prohibited Books, and most of them likely took their work quite seriously. Certainly absurd errors and oversights were committed, but it also remains true that impressive figures such as Guglielmo Sirleto, Robert Bellarmine and Francesco Pegna, not to mention the long succession of Dominican masters of the sacred palace (often established authors themselves), contributed greatly to the development of the Index over time. In more recent times, Cardinal Ottaviani was clearly no fool, while Joseph Ratzinger – who directed the Congregation for the Doctrine of the Faith from 1981 to 2005, helped draft *Ex corde Ecclesiae*, and dealt with many evaluations of controversial books – remains widely respected for his well-informed theological writings and views. Ratzinger's elevation to the papacy in 2005 as Benedict XVI, while contentious, further demonstrates that participation in censorship and Church discipline continues to be a prestigious and valued activity within the Roman Curia.

But it is also important to realize that the Index of Prohibited Books was never by any means the exclusive preserve of scholarly friars and clerical careerists, let alone haunted religious fanatics as portrayed in the myths of Black Legend polemic. It was at its inception a product of university-based academia, and in some ways it never strayed very far from those roots. The first lists of banned books were drawn up at the universities of Paris and Leuven as we have seen, part of a time-honoured tradition whereby professors had been entrusted with evaluations of religious orthodoxy ever since the medieval origins of the university system itself (including the first judgements against the Talmud, as well as the trial of Joan of Arc). Theology professors at other prominent universities such as Cologne, Salamanca and Bologna, not to mention the various institutions of higher learning in Rome, continued to pass judgement on books and their authors throughout the history of the Index, as did professors at the universities of Oxford and Cambridge for as long as these remained Catholic institutions (and even after they converted to Protestantism, Anglican university faculty largely retained their authority to pass judgement on the orthodoxy of British recusants).

Professors jealously guarded their academic privilege of determining what texts could and could not be retained on the curriculum for proper student learning, and of course in many ways they retain that power today as part of their right to academic freedom. But their expertise in discerning good from bad knowledge was also generalized more broadly in the early modern period, leading to an influence that stretched in some instances far beyond the halls of academe. As a result, some university professors became part of the overall censorship infrastructure that has been the subject of this book – serving as inquisition *qualificatores*, for example, or contributing reports to the Congregation of the Index. University professors sometimes became victims of Church censorship and had their own writings placed on the Index; but more often, *they* were in fact the censors. And this was especially true when it came to silencing the unpopular opinions of their own peers.

Censorship was at first mostly the domain of theology professors, but as Mario Biagioli has pointed out, censorship powers began to be exercised more and more by scientists as well (whether university-based or not) after the emergence of the seventeenth-century Republic of Letters.[6] This resulted in part from the advent of organized learned societies in major intellectual centres, which allowed scientists to gather and compare notes long before the creation of formal university departments in many scientific fields. It also, however, encouraged the formation of factions and professional quarrels. Galileo's own Accademia dei Lincei was certainly an exclusive club, and he fought hard both to obtain a place there and to keep rivals out. The same was true of the Académie Française (founded in 1635) and the British Royal Society (founded in 1660 as the 'Royal Society of London for Improving Natural Knowledge'), both prestigious gatherings of scholars who carefully guarded access to their ranks. The stakes involved in this sort of academic membership could be high, since approval from recognized scientific organizations held the promise of opening doors to lucrative patronage and publishing opportunities. Famous intellectual feuds developed as pioneering scientists such as Robert Hooke, Isaac Newton and Gottfried Leibniz disputed each others' claims to new discoveries in physics and mathematics, undermining and even setting up obstacles to each other's research in the process. From such controversies arose the first systems of scientific peer review, as a means of breaking the sometimes self-serving stranglehold that jealous editors and Society presidents such as Newton used to keep their enemies out of the pages of prestigious journals. The Royal Society of Edinburgh thus introduced peer review for medical articles in 1731, and it gradually became an accepted academic norm by the nineteenth and twentieth centuries.

The principle of peer review was also embraced, in part, because it served to replace the sorts of inquisitorial and state scrutiny that had formerly been applied to academic publications. With the retreat of much Roman and Spanish censorship in the later decades of the eighteenth century, some Catholic scholars felt that they needed to take up the slack lest wrong-headed religious, scientific or cultural ideas begin to seep into their learned milieux – or worse, into the public sphere – under the guise of legitimate academic research. The same was true of Protestant or irreligious academics throughout the rest of Europe and beyond: dismayed that 'enlightened' monarchs such as Frederick II of Prussia, Holy Roman Emperor Joseph II and Catherine the Great of Russia were backing away from most forms of non-political censorship (as were the liberal ministerial regimes predominating in England, Spain, Portugal and elsewhere), many intellectuals felt that it was up to them to find ways of establishing and maintaining standards within their particular fields of expertise.[7] Keeping inferior scholarship from establishing a place in universities or academic publishing houses therefore remained an important aspect of professorial work throughout the Enlightenment and beyond, and indeed this prerogative took on a new urgency as university-based scientific knowledge began to replace Church-based religious knowledge as a pre-eminent form of European cultural capital. Systems of formal peer review seemed like one effective means of achieving this end without resorting to external authority, and experience has since confirmed this to be true.

As any professional academic (or artist) knows, however, peer review – much like Index censorship – is far from a perfectly fair means of determining the objective quality of a project, or its suitability for publication. Intellectual and personal rivalries continue to plague modern-day university campuses and arts boards almost as much as they did the Congregation of the Index in Pegna's day, or the Royal Society under Newton (as do conservatism and genuine lack of comprehension); unwarranted censorship and favouritism can result. Such abuses aside, moreover, the function and effect of peer review processes may still remain uncomfortably similar to those of other forms of censorship, including the Index. Modern academic and cultural gatekeepers are empowered to make decisions about what gets published or funded, and what is not permitted to go forward. With 'maternal concern' and 'watchful care' (reminiscent of Pope Paul's words in *Dei verbum*), they pass judgement on the merits of colleagues' arguments, interpretations of evidence and style, as well as whether or not their contributions are 'suitable and correct' for a given discipline. And while there may be opportunities to allow for publication in alternative venues these days, including vanity presses and self-publication on the Internet, in highly competitive situations being blocked from publishing in a particularly prestigious journal or denied a major grant can have a severe impact on the careers of those who deviate too far from accepted norms. Modern scholars, authors and artists do not, in other words, generally need to fear (or expect) actual interference from some sort of Pythonesque 'Spanish Inquisition' nowadays; instead they interfere with, and sometimes censor, one another.

Lessons Learned

This may seem like a rather cynical and unhelpful way of ending a book on the Index of Prohibited Books. In many ways, it does seem like there are few real lessons to be drawn from this four-hundred-year span of history, interesting though it is in its own right. It is a complicated, messy history, as history generally is when one looks at it closely and honestly enough, which makes drawing simple conclusions all but impossible. So where do we go from here?

Evidently, for all its horrors, flaws and absurdities, 'censorship' remains very much a feature of the modern world even if for most of us it no longer takes the form of comprehensive Indexes and religious book-burnings (or cages). The Roman Catholic Church ultimately realized that it was in fact too much work, and indeed rather pointless, to try and keep track of every publication it didn't approve of in real time, using only the technologies available before the advent of computers. But it remains committed to the *principle* of suppressing what it takes to be faulty or dangerous knowledge, especially in its own highly specialized realm of Catholic theology, even though it must now rely only on the goodwill and obedience of its own members rather than the coercive power of a state to enforce its decisions. University professors, publishers, granting agencies and gallerists often operate in a not dissimilar way, providing their (generally good faith) opinions on the merits of work in their fields of expertise in order to promote good contributions while suppressing problematic ones – though they too must generally rely on the soft-power of suggestion, reputation and neglect, rather than force, to achieve their desired results. Such contemporary processes of discernment are in some ways direct legacies of the Index of Prohibited Books that remain with us today. The only differences are that their personnel and criteria for judgement have evolved, while their potential to actually harm those who fall subject to their evaluations has largely evaporated – except, of course, for individuals whose careers rely upon gaining institutional approval. Membership always comes with obligations, as well as privileges.

The bigger problem, I think, is that much more powerful government and corporate forces are today able to exercise far more wide-ranging forms of censorship and manipulation than ever before, with the potential to someday control the communications and self-expression of nearly all the citizens of the globe. Thanks to digital surveillance technologies, Cardinal Carafa's dream (or Orwell's nightmare) of total censorship is now close to becoming a reality. Nor is this situation likely to get any better before it gets worse. But we need to be clear about the differences between worst-case scenarios of irresponsibly harmful authoritarian censorship on the one hand, and more moderate forms of discernment on the other. At its 'best' (if there is such a thing), there are probably types of censorship which are not all that bad, and perhaps even desirable. Without making distinctions of *any* kind, all knowledge, information and expression must be treated as entirely equal – and this can also have unfortunate consequences. It may be arbitrary in some cases to judge between right and wrong, fact and fiction or quality and trash, but in others we ignore such distinctions at our peril. When we lack any means of discernment, genuine life-saving scientific advances can be rejected while bogus claims are marketed by hucksters; classrooms and galleries can become incoherent sites for nothing more than purposeless sharing of randomized, meaningless and unverifiable trivia; and even electoral ballot-counts can be reduced to a matter of opinion, subject to argument and violent confrontations promoted by fake newsmongers, rather than the hard facts of maths. We need to think long and hard about where, and how, we as a society want to draw useful lines between competing values and truth claims, without falling into the grip of either didactic totalitarianism or unmitigated know-nothing-ism.

I don't think there is any real way to eliminate, or to 'perfect' censorship. I do, however, believe that the history of the Index of Prohibited Books demonstrates just how much the parameters of censorship are in fact always subject to change, and this leaves the door open to positive activism. Index censorship was, at the end of the day, both driven and limited by the decisions of individuals and groups – such as Paul IV, Francesco Pegna and the theology faculties of Paris and Leuven, who acted according to the dictates of their consciences and their understanding of the needs and values of the societies in which they lived. Their success was never guaranteed, nor was it unopposed. Paul struggled his whole life to bring in the Roman Index of 1559, only to die before it could be fully implemented. Pegna was thwarted on a regular basis by Bellarmine, and sometimes (regarding Llull, for example) by Philip II. Both would have been horrified by the concessions later made by Benedict XIV or Leo XIII, not to mention Paul VI – who by 1966 theoretically wielded 'infallible' power, but used it to instead begin a process of further limiting Church censorship practices – with widespread support from much of the clergy, laity and secular society alike. Institutional challenges, pressure from internal and external voices and other historical circumstances, clearly influenced and dictated the parameters of whatever decisions these individuals were able to make, for better or for worse.

Those who care about ongoing struggles to limit censorship and minimize its abuse should take some heart from this reminder that *everything* is subject to change in history, and that abusive regimes or practices need not go unchallenged for centuries, let alone indefinitely. Individuals and groups can make their voices heard to ensure that judicious discernment (or 'censorship', if you will) is only used minimally, fairly and transparently, for purposes that align as closely as possible with the genuine needs and interests of the day. It should therefore also be responsive to both expert and public feedback, and subject to adjustment over time. Peer review (including ethics boards) in the sciences and academia more broadly, media reviews and reportage, and adjudicating councils in the arts all seem to be fairly good ways of achieving this, though they too are far from perfect and should never be immune from scrutiny and reform. We need to ensure that funding shortfalls, too, are not used as a de facto means of censorship. Research and creative work requires material support, and this should similarly be made available fairly, transparently and without imposing undue pressure in order to distort outcomes. This is why academic freedom and tenure are so essential, in order to protect university-based creators at least from falling prey to political, religious or corporate demands that they change or suppress inconvenient findings. If we fail to preserve vital, professional, honest works from being developed in relatively free spaces such as universities, and the minds of independent artists, then society can only suffer from the resulting intellectual and creative deficits – just as, or even worse than, it did when such works were stifled by the Index.

Our evaluation of Index history, in other words, need not be reduced to a smug accounting of whether it was entirely worthy of modern condemnation, or praise; we can instead look critically at the multiple and constantly shifting roles it played in surveying, organizing, evaluating and ordering a particularly large and important swath of human knowledge over a very long period of time. Censorship and the suppression of knowledge and creativity was a major part of its legacy, often tragically so, and ultimately to an incalculable extent. But even as it worked against some forms of knowledge, it was doing so in the service and promotion of others. Like all censorship, it stemmed from decisions taken, by those with power to do so, to defend and spread those forms of knowledge which *they* most valued at the time. Just whose words, whose images and whose values prevailed from one period to the next was a matter of constant struggle and negotiation – and that struggle continues today. I find this endlessly fascinating to examine, and even empowering at times. Informed by our understanding of what has happened in the past, and how censorship continues to evolve in the present, we must now work towards better outcomes for the types of knowledge and creativity *we* wish to preserve and promote in the future.

In the end, the history of the Index of Prohibited Books does have interesting things to tell us about how censorship works (or doesn't) in various circumstances, and why. It also contributes to our understanding of parallel histories of persecution and intolerance, first on a European and later to some extent on a global level. And it intersects with many aspects of intellectual and cultural history as well. The Index was after all an intellectual project, designed and executed by intellectuals to evaluate and control the work of other intellectuals and artists. Its lists thus tell us what a certain group of educated men took to be the most dangerous cultural productions of their day. Thomas James recognized the subversive value of this sort of listing in 1627. Though intended to facilitate destruction, the Indexes also inadvertently recorded much that might otherwise have gone unnoticed, as well as much that has since been entirely lost. They therefore remain largely untapped but invaluable resources for the study of religious, scientific, literary, artistic and cultural history. Their changing forms and styles of organization shed light on the history of books and reading. They naturally obscure as much as they reveal – histories of women in particular, who are almost entirely left out of the Index until at least the eighteenth century, as well as histories of non-European cultures. But this is true of all historical sources. Nothing tells the *whole* story. We must approach the Indexes of Prohibited Books for what they are, and what they have to tell us, even while searching for other pieces of the wider historical puzzles of which they were only ever a small part.

If this book helps to facilitate such further research, by clarifying what the Index of Prohibited Books was, what it wasn't and what sorts of information can be gleaned from its pages, then it will have served its purpose. There are many more stories to be told, many more observations to be made and many more conclusions to be drawn – some undoubtedly refining, contradicting and correcting aspects of the findings presented here. Such a wide-ranging and lengthy history naturally leaves a great deal of room for new explorations and analyses. And in many ways new research on the Index is now more accessible than it has ever been: not only have the archives of the Congregation for the Doctrine of the Faith been open to academic researchers for over two decades, but electronic copies of nearly all the Indexes of Prohibited Books have been uploaded to free Internet sites, where they can be consulted by anyone in the world who has the technology (and linguistic ability) to do so. A very promising wave of fresh scholarship has therefore begun to emerge in the last few years. Old assumptions are constantly being revised, long-held errors corrected and entirely unexpected discoveries unveiled on a regular basis. I have tried to incorporate many of these within the pages of this book, but many have undoubtedly escaped my notice, and many more will emerge in the near future.

The subtitle of this book makes reference to a motto of the Jesuit Order, attributed to its founder St Ignatius Loyola in 1541: *ad maiorem Dei gloriam inque hominum salutem* ('for the greater glory of God and the salvation of man'). This could well apply to the work of the Index censors as well, some of whom were in fact Jesuits. But it may also be fitting to conclude with another Latin phrase, used both in Leo x's bull condemning Martin Luther and as a motto for the Inquisition itself: *Exurge Domine et judica causam tuam* ('Arise, O Lord, and judge thy own cause'). This is from Psalm 73:22 (Psalm 74 in the Protestant King James Version, and deviating slightly from the way it would later be phrased in the Clementine Vulgate). Perhaps at the end of the day, if one is a believer in such things, it is up to God to judge how well the Index and those who served it truly worked in His cause, for His greater glory and for the salvation of humanity. But we are all also entitled to our own opinions on the legacy of the Index, as well as on broader histories of censorship and persecution, based on the best available documentary evidence. Or at least we are for now. Here's hoping we can keep that power, by ensuring that no barriers to research – whether religious, political or corporate – are ever allowed to stand in the way of our constant unfettered efforts to better understand this fascinating chapter in human history.

ABBREVIATIONS AND BIBLIOGRAPHICAL NOTES

References to individual volumes of Jesús Martínez de Bujanda, ed., *Index des Livres Interdits*, 12 vols (Sherbrooke, Geneva, Montreal and Madrid, 1985–2016), are cited in abbreviated fashion, as follows:

Bujanda vol. I: Jesús Martínez de Bujanda, Francis M. Higman and James K. Farge, eds, *Index de l'Université de Paris 1544, 1545, 1547, 1549, 1551, 1556* (Sherbrooke and Geneva, 1985)
Bujanda vol. II: Jesús Martínez de Bujanda, ed., *Index de l'Université de Louvain 1546, 1550, 1558* (Sherbrooke and Geneva, 1986)
Bujanda vol. III: Jesús Martínez de Bujanda, ed., *Index de Venise 1549. Venise et Milan 1554* (Sherbrooke and Geneva, 1987)
Bujanda vol. IV: Jesús Martínez de Bujanda, ed., *Index de l'Inquisition Portugaise 1547, 1551, 1561, 1564, 1581* (Sherbrooke and Geneva, 1995)
Bujanda vol. V: Jesús Martínez de Bujanda, ed., *Index de l'Inquisition Espagnole 1551, 1554, 1559* (Sherbrooke and Geneva, 1984)
Bujanda vol. VI: Jesús Martínez de Bujanda, ed., *Index de l'Inquisition Espagnole 1583, 1584* (Sherbrooke and Geneva, 1993)
Bujanda vol. VII: Jesús Martínez de Bujanda, ed., *Index d'Anvers 1569, 1570, 1571* (Sherbrooke and Geneva, 1988)
Bujanda vol. VIII: Jesús Martínez de Bujanda, ed., *Index de Rome 1557, 1559, 1564. Les Premiers Index Romains et l'Index du Concile de Trente* (Sherbrooke and Geneva, 1990)
Bujanda vol. IX: Jesús Martínez de Bujanda, Ugo Rozzo, Peter G. Bietenholz and Paul F. Grendler, eds, *Index de Rome 1590, 1593, 1596. Avec Étude des Index de Parme 1580 et Munich 1582* (Sherbrooke and Geneva, 1994)
Bujanda vol. X: Jesús Martínez de Bujanda, ed., *Thesaurus de la Littérature Interdite au XVIe Siècle. Auteurs, Ouvrages, Éditions avec Addenda et Corrigenda* (Sherbrooke and Geneva, 1996)
Bujanda vol. XI: Jesús Martínez de Bujanda, ed., *Index Librorum Prohibitorum, 1600-1966* (Montreal and Geneva, 2002)
Bujanda vol. XII: Jesús Martínez de Bujanda, ed., *El Índice de Libros Prohibidos y Expurgados de la Inquisición Española (1551-1819)* (Madrid, 2016)

References to individual editions of the various Indexes are generally to their facsilime editions as published in volumes of Bujanda. When these are not available (that is, for the seventeenth to twentieth centuries), reference is made instead to issuing authority (Roman, Spanish) and date of publication. Scans of most, if not all, of the printed Indexes are currently accessible via online repositories such as Google Books, HathiTrust and Internet Archive, as well as library collections around the world.

ACDF: Archivio della Congregazione per la Dottrina della Fede, Vatican City
AGN INQ: Archivo General de la Nación, *sección Inquisición*, Mexico City
BNF: Bibliothèque nationale de France, Paris
ND INQ: University of Notre Dame, Harley L. McDevitt Inquisition Collection, Notre Dame, Indiana

Note that all translations are my own unless otherwise indicated. Bible citations follow either the Latin Clementine Vulgate, *Biblia Sacra Vulgatae Editionis Sixti v Pontificis Maximi Jussu Recognita et Clementis VIII Auctoritate Edita. Nova Editio Accuratissimae Emendata* (Paris, 1882) or the English Douay-Rheims version (London, 1955), unless otherwise indicated. For Hebrew texts, I consult the *Jewish Publication Society Hebrew-English Tanakh*, 2nd edn (Philadelphia, PA, 1999).

REFERENCES

INTRODUCTION

1 *Index* is a Latin word that can mean either a list, or a guide that points to something (hence *index finger*, or the related *indicator*). Its Latin plural is *indices*, but for the purpose of this book the more colloquial English *indexes* will be preferred. Though many different types of censorship lists were produced by various early modern and modern Catholic authorities, as will be further explored below, and not all received the formal title of 'Index', for the sake of simplicity I will often refer to 'the Index' as shorthand for a generalized Church censorship project of which individual lists, catalogues and 'indexes' formed integral parts.

2 Haig Bosmajian, *Burning Books* (Jefferson, NC, 2006), p. 108. On Spinoza, see Steven M. Nadler, *A Book Forged in Hell: Spinoza's Scandalous Treatise and the Birth of the Secular Age* (Princeton, NJ, 2011).

3 Bosmajian, *Burning Books*, pp. 128–30. Chinese imperial censorship of the early modern period has indeed been compared to an 'inquisition', complete with indexes of prohibited books; see Luther Carrington Goodrich, *The Literary Inquisition of Ch'ien-Lung* [1935] (New York, 1966).

4 The current *Code of Canon Law* for the Catholic Church includes sections on 'Instruments of Social Communication and Books in Particular' (cann. 822–32). Since publication of the 1963 papal bull *Inter mirifica* on social communications, the Vatican has regularly updated its positions on proper use of modern media by the faithful – including the Internet. See for example John Paul II's 2002 address entitled 'Internet: A New Forum for Proclaiming the Gospel', *The Holy See*, www.vatican.va/content/vatican/en.html, 12 May 2002.

5 In general, I rely throughout this study on the twelve-volume survey of Index censorship recently completed under the direction of Jesús Martínez de Bujanda (hereafter Bujanda). While his decisions regarding which texts should be considered 'Indexes' could be challenged in some cases, this monumental contribution to scholarship remains a convenient, reliable and standard work of reference in the field.

6 John 1:1–5, in both the Clementine Vulgate Latin version (in italics) and my literalizing adaptation based on the Douay-Rheims and King James English versions. *Bible* derives from the Greek word for book (*biblos*). It normally refers to a set of writings considered by religious believers to be particularly holy and therefore 'scriptural'. However, religious groups differ among themselves about just which books are truly 'holy', and just

what that holiness really means. For Jews, the Bible consists of the five books of Moses (Hebrew *Torah*), certain books of prophecy (*Nevi'im*) and assorted historical and other writings (*Ketuvim*). Christians generally consider this Jewish Bible to be their 'Old Testament', to which they add a 'New Testament' made up of anecdotes and teachings from the lives of Jesus Christ and his immediate followers or apostles. The Jewish Bible was originally written in Hebrew, whereas the New Testament was for the most part composed in Greek; its subsequent complicated history of editing and translation (including the emergence of a Latin 'Vulgate' text) will be further explored in chapters one and five below.

7 *Ipsum* and *ipso* in lines 3 and 4 are ambiguous, as they could be either masculine or neuter pronouns, but the neuter *hoc* in line 2 can only grammatically apply to *verbum* – not a masculine Christ. Bibles following the Douay-Rheims or King James versions fudge the issue at first by translating John 1:2 as 'The same was in the beginning with God [my emphasis]', before reverting to 'he/him'.

8 This is the evocative if imprecise translation of D. W. Robertson Jr, from Augustine's *On Christian Doctrine* [1958], repr. in *The Norton Anthology of Theory and Criticism*, ed. Vincent B. Leitch (New York, 2001), p. 190, for a passage in book 2, chapter 4 of Augustine's *De doctrina Christiana* which originally reads 'verberato aere statim transeunt nec diutius manent quam sonant'. For the Latin text, reproduced from a *Patrologia Latina* edition of 1861, see www.augustinus.it/latino/index.htm, accessed 28 October 2021.

9 Thomas Aquinas, *Super evangelium S. ioannis lectura*, in *Corpus Thomisticum*, ed. Enrique Alarcón, www.corpusthomisticum.org, 2019 (based on the 'Textum Taurini' edition of 1952), chapter 1, *lectio* 1. See also the discussion in Augustine, *De doctrina Christiana*, part 2, chapter 6, at www.augustinus.it/latino/index.htm, accessed 28 October 2021.

10 Walter J. Ong, *Orality and Literacy. The Technologizing of the Word* [1982] (London and New York, 2002), p. 32. Philosophers of language such as J. L. Austin and Ludwig Wittgenstein have also long discussed the broader implications of such 'speech acts'.

11 Hebrew, like other Semitic languages, uses a system of consonant clusters to express many variations of the same concept. Hence the consonants d-b-r (or d-v-r since the Hebrew letter *bet* can be pronounced as either B or V) appear in the verbal form 'to speak' (*ledaber*) and nouns such as 'speech' or 'speaker' (*dibur/dover*) as well as 'mouth' (*midbar*) or 'commentaries' (*divrei*). The relation of language to material reality is also reflected in the fact that Hebrew *devarim* can refer to both 'words' and 'things'.

12 Note that Psalm 18 in the Jewish, Protestant and some Catholic Bibles is numbered as Psalm 17 in the Vulgate and Douay-Rheims editions.

13 Exodus 20:4, Douay-Rheims translation. Jewish, Catholic and Protestant versions of the biblical texts for the Ten Commandments vary slightly in their division and numbering of the commandments.

14 George Orwell, *Nineteen Eighty-Four* (London, 1949).

15 Disney's aggressive lobbying to protect its control of intellectual property rights has led, for example, to greater limits via the Copyright Term Extension Act of 1998 (also known as the 'Mickey Mouse Protection Act'); see Louis Krasniewicz, *Walt Disney: A Biography* (Santa Barbara, CA, 2010), p. 43.
16 Peer review is a set of customary practices by which university professors criticize, rank and discipline one another. It normally involves the formal evaluation of a colleague's academic writings, and is often conducted for the purpose of hiring, tenure and promotion, as well as for the distribution of funding, awards and publishing opportunities. In extreme cases it can be used to impose punishment for professional misconduct. This system, which is intended to replace the intrusion of outside authorities (whether religious, state or corporate), is considered by many to be fundamental to the maintenance of autonomy and academic freedom in modern universities; see the Conclusion of this book for further discussion.

1 CENSORSHIP BEFORE THE INDEX

1 Barak Blum, 'Banned from the Libraries? Ovid's Books and Their Fate in the Exile Poetry', *American Journal of Philology*, CXXXIII/3 (2017), pp. 489–526.
2 Note that many modern English versions misleadingly translate *libros* as 'books of magic', on the assumption that these are what *eis qui fuerant curiosa sectati* would be reading.
3 Richard I. Pervo, *The Acts of Paul: A New Translation with Introduction and Commentary* (Cambridge, 2014), p. 54.
4 Full Latin text and study of the Decree is in Ernst von Dobschutz, *Das Decretum Gelasianum de libris recipiendis et non recipiendis* (Leipzig, 1912), esp. pp. 3–13 (the passage here quoted is from p. 10). Gelasius' selection of canonical readings is mostly the same as can be found in modern Catholic Bibles today; however, some texts, such as 'The Letter of the Apostle Judas the Zealot', are no longer considered to be scriptural.
5 Edgar Hennecke, *New Testament Apocrypha* [1904], ed. Wilhelm Schneemelcher, ed. and trans. R. McL. Wilson, revd edn (Cambridge, 1991), vol. I, pp. 38–40, provides an English version of this final prohibitory list. Another important early text included in Gratian's twelfth-century canon law compilation was the bull *Fraternitatis* of Pope Gregory I, dated 599 CE, in which he calls for the censorship of certain chapters in 'a heretical manuscript sent over to me from the royal city' due to their containing teachings of the heretics Coelestius and Pelagius. This bull became a canon law precedent for book censorship and was therefore pointedly included in the first section of part two in Eymeric's *Directorium inquisitorum*.
6 Most of the surviving evidence for early heretical texts, apart from accidental discoveries of hidden documentary troves such as at Nag Hammadi, is actually found embedded in the anti-heretical and related

theological literature of orthodox writers – fragments for the most part, copied as illustrative examples for purposes of refutation. Some 'heretical' groups such as the Arians, Monophysites and Nestorians continued to thrive beyond the borders of Rome after the fifth century, for example under the patronage of Gothic, African, Persian or Arab rulers. The advent of Islam in the early seventh century, moreover, could in some ways be considered one of the last major instances of a Christian splinter-group expanding and ultimately succeeding in propagating its own canonical Scripture and belief system. The Church's censorship of Islamic writings will be discussed further in this chapter.

7 Edward Watts, 'Justinian, Malalas, and the End of Athenian Philosophical Teaching', *Journal of Roman Studies*, XCIV (2004), pp. 168–82.
8 The manuscript tradition is described in David Luscombe, ed. and trans., *The Letter Collection of Peter Abelard and Heloise* (Oxford, 2013), pp. xxxviii–civ.
9 The formal charge was that his arguments revived the Sabellian heresy, one of the many condemned in pseudo-Gelasius' decree. Constant Mews, 'The Council of Sens (1141): Abelard, Bernard, and the Fear of Social Upheaval', *Speculum*, LXXVII/2 (2002), pp. 342–82.
10 The comment occurs in his *Historia calamitatum*, trans. Betty Radice, *The Letters of Abelard and Heloise* [1974], revd edn (London, 2003), p. 33.
11 The 1290 Parisian condemnation of divinatory and magical books (one of many) is discussed in Henry Charles Lea, *A History of the Inquisition of the Middle Ages* (London, 1888), vol. III, p. 438; also Jean-Patrice Boudet, *Entre Science et Nigromance* (Paris, 2007), pp. 251–7.
12 This is a point made repeatedly in his *Practica*, as highlighted in Karen Sullivan, *The Inner Lives of Medieval Inquisitors* (Chicago, IL, 2011), pp. 142–4.
13 Richard Kieckhefer, 'The Office of Inquisition and Medieval Heresy: The Transaction from Personal to Institutional Jurisdiction', *Journal of Ecclesiastical History*, XLVI/1 (1995), pp. 36–61.
14 Edward Peters, *Inquisition* (New York, 1988), pp. 11–39.
15 This text, as recorded by Gui, is given in Walter L. Wakefield and Austin P. Evans, *Heresies of the High Middle Ages* (New York, 1969), pp. 438–9.
16 The full text, which first appears in the bull as issued by Gregory XIII in 1583, is: 'ac eorumdem libros haeresim continentes vel de religione tractantes, sine auctoritate nostra et Sedis Apostolicae, scienter legentes aut tenentes, imprimentes seu quomodolibet defendentes' (Alfonso Gutiérrez-Maturana y Camañes, 'El delito de herejía: "Iter" jurídico', PhD thesis, Universidad de Navarra, 1991, p. 229). Paul III's earlier 1536 version also mentioned books, but with specific reference to the writings of Martin Luther alone.
17 Robin Vose, 'Books, Damned Books, and Heretics: Censorship and Dominican Inquisitors in Nicholas Eymeric's *Directorium inquisitorum*', in *Virtuosos of Faith: Monks, Nuns, Canons, and Friars as Elites of Medieval Culture*, ed. Gert Melville and James D. Mixson (Berlin, 2020), pp. 151–69.
18 Sean L. Field, *The Beguine, the Angel, and the Inquisitor* (Notre Dame, IN, 2012). There were others as well, some of whom we will meet in

subsequent chapters as their medieval 'heresies' were rediscovered by much later Index compilers.
19 These are the subject of *Directorium* part 2, *quaestio* 4: *De erroribus philosophorum priscorum* (On the Errors of the Early Philosophers).
20 See in particular part 2, *quaestiones* 21–2 of his *Directorium*: *De erroribus Sarracenorum* (On the Errors of the Saracens) and *De Judaeorum erroribus* (On the Errors of the Jews), respectively.
21 Dante's *De monarchia* was condemned posthumously and burned at Bologna in 1328 for its political arguments against papal supremacy; see Anthony Cassell, *The Monarchia Controversy* (Washington, DC, 2004). Wyclif was formally condemned by Pope Gregory XI in a series of bulls released in May 1377, a few months after Eymeric's list was completed, but the inquisitor must have been aware of this case since he had been present at the papal court in Avignon for several years by that point and he was particularly close to Gregory (whose support for Eymeric is mentioned several times throughout the *Directorium*).
22 Vose, 'Books', pp. 163–5. There are only about 30 MSS of the *Directorium* in existence today, two of which are autographs by Eymeric himself and seem to have remained unused in his home convent of Girona after his death. The rest seem to have circulated in the fifteenth century, especially in the German lands and northern Italy (but not in Spain or France), and most are missing significant portions of *quaestio* 26 (among other alterations). I hope to provide full details on this manuscript tradition in a forthcoming study.

2 INVENTING THE INDEX

1 In Rome, these censoring authorities were to be the pope's vicar and 'master of the sacred palace' (*magister sacri palatii*), a Dominican friar who served as his official theologian. In other cities episcopal officials or inquisitors were expected to take on censorship duties resulting from this bull, which obviously did not foresee the print industry ever expanding beyond the production of a handful of new books per year from one city to the next.
2 Many Bible translations had been executed before Luther, including several in German, and the legacy of manuscript transmission had ensured that no absolute 'standard' text of the Bible had been established anywhere in the Catholic Church. Variations remained minor for the most part, but this lack of standardization was a major concern to later inquisitors and Index compilers.
3 On the link between medieval universities, censorship and inquisitorial judgements see Chapter One.
4 Bujanda vol. I, pp. 433–5. Though he died in disfavour in 1537, Beda's role as an influential leader of Paris university 'conservatives' (against both Protestantism and the humanism of Erasmus) is examined in James K. Farge, 'Noël Beda and the Defense of the Tradition', in *A Companion to Biblical Humanism and Scholasticism in the Age of Erasmus*, ed. Erika Rummel (Leiden, 2008), pp. 143–64.

5 Erasmus' *Liber de sarcienda Ecclesiae concordia* was placed on the Leuven Index of 1558, where it joined a previously banned Lutheran polemic written against it: Antonius Corvinus' *Contra libellum Erasmi de sarcienda Ecclesiae concordia*, which had been on the Leuven Index since 1550. Bujanda vol. II, pp. 35–6.
6 Manuscript copies of the *Directorium* were certainly present in Bologna and at Rome by this time, and a 1503 Barcelona printed edition had also begun to reach interested Italian readers. It is likely that Francisco Peña first encountered the *Directorium* in Italy, not in his (and Eymeric's) native Aragon.
7 The 'medieval' type of local heresy inquisitor continued to operate in many parts of Italy and elsewhere in the Catholic world, right up to modern times. Their functions tended to become increasingly bureaucratic and pastoral over time, with important cases being sent on to Rome.
8 Pole's votes in the conclave seem to have come close to the required two-thirds majority before Carafa intervened. If the moderate Pole had become pope in 1549, it is likely that Church history would have been very different thereafter.
9 Kenneth R. Stow, 'The Burning of the Talmud in 1553, in the Light of Sixteenth Century Catholic Attitudes Toward the Talmud', *Bibliothèque d'Humanisme et Renaissance*, XXIV/3 (1972), pp. 435–59.
10 Carranza had previously been close to Paul III as well. He censored books for both the Spanish Inquisition and the English crown (at Oxford), and represented Spain at the Council of Trent. See John Edwards and Ronald Truman, eds, *Reforming Catholicism in the England of Mary Tudor: The Achievement of Friar Bartolomé Carranza* (Aldershot, 2005).
11 Bujanda vol. III, pp. 380–81.
12 Bujanda vol. VIII, pp. 28–9.
13 Paul was likely aware of this but perhaps content to thumb his nose at the king in 1557 since Spain and the papacy were then at war. Philip's opinion on the matter would be much harder to oppose later on.
14 Typographical layout, font and page size vary considerably among the different print runs of the Tridentine Index; as a result dimensions and page numbers also differ from one exemplar to the next. Title page illustrations vary widely, and some versions are paginated while others are not.

3 EXPANDING THE INDEX

1 A manuscript copy of Pegna's unpublished *diario* or notes on the *De auxiliis* proceedings remains at the Archive of the Congregation for the Doctrine of the Faith (ACDF O5i): *Acta Congregationum habitarum Romae, in causa de Auxiliis, ab initio anni 1601 usque ad annum 1604.* This large volume of over five hundred pages is only part of a fuller set of notes, which apparently continued until 1607. Similar records produced by the Spanish Dominican de Lemos (d. 1629) were later printed as *Acta omnia congregationum ac disputationum quae coram ss. Clemente VIII et Paulo V summis pontificibus sunt celebratae in causa et controversia illa*

magna de auxiliis divinae gratiae (Leuven, 1702). Despite prohibitions against publishing materials on the *De auxiliis* controversy by this time, de Lemos's *Acta* seems never to have been placed on the Index.

2 Francisco Bethencourt, *The Inquisition: A Global History, 1478–1834* [1995], trans. Jean Birrell (Cambridge, 2009), pp. 174–210. Several Mexican edicts are held in the Notre Dame McDevitt Collection, dating from 1621 (ND INQ 219) to 1810 (ND INQ 403–5). Mexican inquisitors also issued edicts of their own, such as AGN INQ vol. XC, *expediente* 33, folios 99–100 (a 1577 ban on biblical texts translated into Indigenous languages; on which, see Chapter Five).

3 Georges Bonnant, 'Les Index prohibitifs et expurgatoires contrefaits par des protestants au XVIe et au XVIIe siècle', *Bibliothèque d'Humanisme et Renaissance*, XXXI/4 (1969), pp. 611–40.

4 Thus James includes 'Iordanus Brunus Nolanus' (under 'Br'), despite the fact that Giordano Bruno's 1600 condemnation would not be fully adopted by a Roman Index until 1664.

5 Carranza was placed on the Spanish Index of 1559 by Inquisitor-General Valdes (who, not coincidentally, was the one who arrested Carranza that same year), and maintained in 1583 by Inquisitor-General Quiroga (who also took Carranza's place as archbishop). Sixtus V tried to have Carranza's name posthumously added to the Roman Index in 1590, and it was briefly included on the Clementine Index of 1596, but quietly omitted from subsequent Roman Indexes.

6 Emile de Heeckeren, ed., *Correspondence de Benoît XIV* (Paris, 1912), vol. II, pp. 294–5 (letter of 3 October 1753).

7 The 1716 Roman Index, by comparison, had reached well over 550 pages.

8 Leibniz, interestingly enough, was banned not for his philosophical work but for having edited a centuries-old biography of the Borgia Pope Alexander VI by Johannes Burchard (d. 1506), entitled *Historia arcana* (Hannover, 1697), which included scandalous accounts of papal indecencies. See Irena Backus, *Leibniz: Protestant Theologian* (Oxford, 2016), p. 197. Leibniz's name appears under 'G' (for *Godef. Guilielm. Leibnizio*) in the Roman Index of 1716, on p. 196.

9 Spanish edict of 1824, printed 1826 (ND INQ 147). Clearly someone was not paying attention, since 'Voltayre' had in fact previously been registered in the 1790 Spanish Index.

10 Robert Darnton, *Censors at Work: How States Shaped Literature* (New York and London, 2014), pp. 58–9. The 1759 raid was essentially political theatre, since the official in charge (C. G. de Lamoignon de Malesherbes) tipped Diderot off and even helped him to move most of his papers in advance.

11 These events are described in a letter of Voltaire's to the prison reformer Cesare Beccaria, sent that same year; see *Oeuvres Complètes de Voltaire* (Paris, 1860), vol. XIX, pp. 434–45.

4 HOW TO BAN A BOOK

1 The Belgian friar's last name appears as 'Veriuis' in the manuscript text; he is alternatively called Verjus or Verjuys in later biographies.

A Leuven-trained theologian (who also spent time in Spain and Portugal), he was lecturing at the Brussels convent in 1662 and completed his own text on missionary work in 1664.

2 The *Annales* had originally been the project of Vatican librarian Caesar Baronius (in twelve volumes published from 1588 until 1607). Work continued after his death by several others, including Bzovius: a Polish Dominican who completed new volumes covering the period from 1198 to 1571 (published 1625–30).

3 The *Triumph of Love* file comprises only eight folios (441r–449v) of the larger bundle.

4 Luther, Zwingli, Calvin, the Anabaptist Balthasar Pacimontanus Hubmaier) and Caspar Schwenckfeld are explicitly named in this *regulum*.

5 Both the 1590 Sistine Rules and the 1593 Clementine additions are discussed in Bujanda vol. IX, pp. 342–52. Full text of the 22 Sistine Rules can be found in Bujanda's reproduction of the 1590 Index (pp. 795–800 of vol. IX), or in Joseph Mendham's edition: *Index librorum prohibitorum a Sixto V, papa, confectus et publicatus: at verò a successoribus ejus in sede romana suppressus* (London, 1835).

6 Alexander's brief *observationes* on Rule 10 were added to the Index of 1758 (p. viii). The more extensive constitution *Sollicita ac provida*, originally promulgated in 1753, takes up more than a dozen printed pages at the beginning of Benedict's 1758 Index (pp. xvii–xxx) and is followed by a handful of further *decreta* by the same pope (pp. xxxi–xxxvi).

7 ACDF St. st. CC 1-b: *Censura dei libri ebrei*, file no. 1. By the 1680s, however, Venetian bookstore raids seem to have become much less of a concern; see Federico Barbierato, *The Inquisitor in the Hat Shop: Inquisition, Forbidden Books and Unbelief in Early Modern Venice* (Farnham and Burlington, VT, 2012), pp. 47–50.

8 Peter Godman, *The Saint as Censor: Robert Bellarmine Between Inquisition and Index* (Leiden, 2000), pp. 187–206, examines the agonized debates and behind-the-scenes manoeuvring involved in the censorship of King James, whose return to Catholicism was fervently hoped for in the early years of his reign. Bruno and Galileo's cases will be discussed in Chapter Six.

9 Xantes Mariales was theologian to Emperor Ferdinand III (r. 1637–57); see Jacques Quétif and Jacques Echard, *Scriptores ordinis praedicatorum* (Paris, 1721), vol. II, pp. 600–601. Correspondence between the Roman and Venetian Inquisitions in this instance seems to have been for the most part quite polite, but evidently it caused delays.

10 Its title appears on p. 218 of the 1664 Roman Index, under 'B'; the 1662 decree is no. 76 of the series copied into this Index.

11 A. Paz y Mélia, *Papeles de Inquisición. Catalogo y Extractos*, 2nd edn (Madrid, 1947), p. 41, n. 122. The Spanish inquisitors' verdict was 'to prohibit or correct it, in order to avoid disputes among Franciscans, Jesuits and Dominicans', but the work does not appear to have been placed on the next published Spanish Index in 1707. It did finally appear, with instructions for expurgation, on the Spanish Index of 1747 (vol. II, p. 1089).

12 Spain and Portugal, unlike most European regions at the end of the Middle Ages, housed large and fairly prominent Jewish and Muslim populations. Even after the expulsions of Jews in the 1490s and subsequent forced conversions of remaining Muslims, survivals of Jewish and Islamic culture remained much more evident in Iberia than elsewhere in Europe.
13 Paz y Mélia, *Papeles de Inquisición*, p. 47, n. 140. The surviving file is 55 folios in length. Arguments in favour of censorship were duly advanced, but the book never appeared on the Index.
14 Rafael Ramis Barceló, 'La inquisición de México y la calificación del *Árbol de la ciencia* de Ramon Llull (1665-1669)', *Estudios de Historia Novohispana*, XLVIII (2013), pp. 189–214.
15 *Calificadores* were the Spanish equivalent of Roman *consultores* or *qualificatores*. The complete evaluations of the friars Diego de Reina, Jacinto de Guevara y Mota, Fernando de Monroy and Alonso de la Barrera (the last three of whom were Dominicans) can be found printed ibid., pp. 204–13.
16 A large number, for example, were collected by Anastasio Páramo (in Spain) and José Porrúa (mostly in Spain and Mexico) before their eventual purchase for the McDevitt Collection at the University of Notre Dame.
17 Michael E. Williams, 'The Library of Saint Alban's English College Valladolid: Censorship and Acquisitions', *British Catholic History*, XXVI/1 (2002), pp. 132–42.

5 CENSORED SCRIPTURES

1 The earliest of these biblical glosses, Psalters and Gospels emerged from Northumbrian scholarly communities associated with the Venerable Bede (d. 735). Alfred the Great (d. 899) also circulated selected sections of biblical texts in English, and some more extensive late tenth-century Anglo-Saxon translations survive today in manuscript copies collectively known as the *Wessex Gospels*, among others (David Daniell, *The Bible in English: Its History and Influence* (New Haven, CT, 2003), pp. 19–65).
2 Bujanda vol. II, p. 45.
3 Bujanda vol. I, pp. 416–7 (no. 512).
4 The first mentions of 'Gulielmus Tindalus' and 'Milo Converdale Eboracensis' are in the Roman Index of 1557, where they are listed as banned heretics – but with no specific mention of their Bible translations. Bujanda vol. VIII, pp. 727 (no. 353) and 746 (no. 738).
5 Bujanda vol. I, pp. 470–71. The same statement was reprinted in the 1551 and 1556 editions of the Paris Index.
6 Norman P. Tanner, ed., *Decrees of the Ecumenical Councils*, trans. Tanner (Washington, DC, 1990), vol. II, p. 665.
7 Bujanda vol. II, pp. 408–12.
8 Bujanda vol. II, pp. 440–42 and 475–8. Very few new Bible editions were added to the Antwerp Index of 1570, revealing the essential conservatism of its list-makers (Bujanda vol. VII, pp. 670–73; cf. the comparison ibid., pp. 74–7).

9 Bartholomaeus Westhemerus, *Phrases seu modi loquendi divinae scripturae, ex sanctis et orthodoxis scriptoribus* (Antwerp, 1536); Bujanda vol. III, pp. 72 and 342.
10 Bujanda vol. IV, pp. 565–6.
11 Bujanda vol. IV, p. 585.
12 Bujanda vol. V, pp. 273–5 and 598–9.
13 William Monter, 'French Bibles and the Spanish Inquisition, 1552', *Bibliothèque d'Humanisme et Renaissance*, LI/1 (1989), pp. 147–52.
14 Bujanda vol. V, pp. 276–302.
15 Bujanda vol. VIII, pp. 784–5.
16 Text in Bujanda vol. VIII, pp. 814–16.
17 See Sixtus' *Regulae* no. 6 and no. 7 in Bujanda vol. IX, p. 796.
18 Bujanda vol. IX, p. 929.
19 See the Roman Index of 1716, pp. 358–9 (along with general bans on heretical and vernacular Bibles in any language, p. 75).
20 *Todos los libros Hebraycos, o en qualquier lengua escriptos, que contengan cerimonias Iudaicas* (Bujanda vol. V, p. 679).
21 This was the title of a play by Robert Daborne, printed at London in 1612. See also Nabil Matar, *Islam in Britain, 1558–1685* (Cambridge, 1998).
22 The 'Alcoranus' was banned in the Indexes of Portugal and Spain from 1551, and in both Venice and Milan from 1554 (Bujanda vol. IV, p. 296; vol. V, p. 218 and 307; and vol. III, p. 214, respectively). Interestingly, an 'Alcoranus of the Franciscans' is frequently cited in the Index, but this internal Church polemic had nothing to do with Islam.
23 Nuria de Castilla, 'Uses and Written Practices in Aljamiado Manuscripts', in *Creating Standards*, ed. Dmitry Bondarev, Alessandro Gori and Lameen Souag (Berlin, 2019), pp. 111–29.
24 Bujanda vol. VIII, pp. 691 and 869–70.
25 Bujanda vol. IX, pp. 930–31.
26 Bujanda vol. IV, pp. 439–41; and vol. IX, p. 494.
27 Bujanda vol. VIII, pp. 362–4 and 756.
28 Bujanda vol. IX, pp. 665–6 and 933.
29 Bujanda vol. XII, p. 291; cf. Donald A. Grinde Jr and Robert Griffin, eds, *Apocalypse de Chiokoyhikoy*, trans. Grinde and Griffin (Sainte-Foy, 1997). It is unlikely that this was in fact an authentic Indigenous text.
30 The Colegio was first opened in 1536, and Franciscans such as Bernardino de Sahagún worked there alongside Nahuatl-speaking scholars to produce translations of numerous Christian texts as well as original scientific works such as the *Libellus de medicinalibus Indorum herbis*. By the 1550s, however, funding declined and in 1555 the First Mexican Church Council barred Indigenous Christians from entering the clergy. In the 1570s Bibles in Indigenous languages were formally proscribed, though translations and compositions continued to be produced in many other literary genres.
31 The *Biblia traducida en lengua Mexicana*, for example, which was added to the Spanish Index of 1747, seems to refer to a Protestant publication (Bujanda vol. XII, p. 338).
32 Roman Index, 1758, p. xxxvi, *decretum* IV, section 6.

33 Thus Joseph (Jouvancy) Juvencius' 1710 pro-Jesuit *Historiae Societatis Jesu* was expurgated in a papal edict of 1722, while the later anti-Jesuit *Memorie storiche intorno alle missioni dell'Indie orientali* by Norbert de Bar-le-Duc (also known as Parisot) were more fully banned in 1745 and 1751 (Bujanda vol. XI, pp. 475 and 683–4 respectively; cf. Roman Index, 1758, pp. 142 and 191).

6 CENSORED MAGIC AND SCIENCE

1 See Spanish Index 1632, p. 631; and Spanish Index 1790, p. 36.
2 Some surviving documents later turned up the hands of a private collector, and now reside in Trinity College, Dublin. On Napoleon's plans to include them in a projected Parisian 'universal library', and their subsequent fate in Ireland, see John Tedeschi, 'The Dispersed Archives of the Roman Inquisition', in *The Inquisition in Early Modern Europe: Studies on Sources and Methods*, ed. Gustav Henningsen and John Tedeschi (DeKalb, IL, 1986), pp. 13–32.
3 These forms of divination are known respectively as geomancy, pyromancy, hydromancy and chiromancy. Necromancy (consultation of spirits, including those of the dead), aeromancy (reading atmospheric conditions) and scapulimancy (reading of animal bones), among other practices, were also common in many regions.
4 Albert's works allegedly included the *De secretis mulierum et virorum* (On the Secrets of Women and Men), *De magia et aggregationis* (On Magic and Combination) and *De natura animalium quadrupedum, avium, piscium, de arboribus, herbis, lapidibus pretiosis, metallis et Cosmographia* (On the Nature and Cosmography of Four-Legged Animals, Birds and Fish, and on Trees, Herbs, Precious Stones and Metals), which were all placed on the Spanish Index by 1583; they were later joined by a Book of Secrets (*Liber secretorum*), also known as the 'Grand Albert' (Bujanda vol. XII, pp. 274–5).
5 Henry Charles Lea, *A History of the Inquisition of the Middle Ages* [1888] (Cambridge, 2010), vol. III, p. 438.
6 The (abbreviated) bull *Super illius specula*, and other important documents illustrating the development of European attitudes towards magical practices, can be found in Alan C. Kors and Edward Peters, eds, *Witchcraft in Europe, 1100–1700: A Documentary History* (Philadelphia, PA, 1972), here p. 82.
7 *Directorium, pars 2, quaestiones* 42 (*De sortilegis & divinatoribus*) and 43 (*De invocantibus daemones*) are the most relevant, but magic and demon-summoning emerge as themes throughout several other sections of the text as well. Kors and Peters, *Witchcraft*, pp. 84–92.
8 The full passage (from *Directorium, pars 2, quaestio* 29) reads:
   Item in partibus Gallicanis, videlicet Parisiis, Episcopi Parisien. & Senonen., ac Inquisitor de ordine praedicatorum, de magno consilio magistrorum in Theologia, & in decretis doctorum ut erroneos & sacrilegos, & blasphemos sententialiter condemnarunt omnes libros divinationum & sortium, scilicet Libros necromantiae. Libros Geomantiae. Libros Pyromantiae. Libros Hydromantiae. Libros

Chiromantiae. Libros decem annulorum veneris. Libros tot Graeci, & Germaniae Babylonensis. Libros quatuor speculorum, eorundem. Libros imaginum Tobiae Bantricat. Libros imaginum Ptolemaei. Libros Hermetis magi ad Aristotelem, quem librum, dicunt Aros, idest, Gabrielem docuisse a Deo, in quo sunt horribiles invocationes, & fumigationes detestabiles. In omnibus enim istis libris, sunt pacta & foedera cum daemonibus, & invocationes, & sacrificia, tacite vel expresse, quae exhibere daemonibus sapit haeresim manifeste, ut dicitur infra q. 43.

9   Major examples of early modern inquisitors' studies on witchcraft include Martín Del Río, *Disquisitiones magicae* (Leuven, 1599); and Pierre de Lancre, *Tableau de l'inconstance des mauvais Anges et Demons* (Paris, 1622).

10 The *Steganographia*, a complex work on cryptology, was understood by many readers as a manual for remote communications with the aid of spirits (at least potentially including demons). See Noel L. Brann, *Trithemius and Magical Theology: A Chapter in the Controversy over Occult Studies in Early Modern Europe* (Albany, NY, 1999).

11 Eymeric had of course already begun to influence the approach to magic (as well as the censorship of heretical books) taken in the Venetian and Milanese Indexes of 1554, as noted in Chapter Two. Both of these Indexes essentially copied Eymeric's list of banned arts and texts drawn from *pars* 2, *quaestio* 29; both also follow Eymeric in adding his condemnations of books by 'Raymundus Lulius' and 'Arnoldus de Villanova' to their lists. These two medieval authors would subsequently develop reputations as great sorcerers and alchemists. Eymeric's influence (and the relative lack of Church censorship of alchemical writings) is partially explored in Neil Tarrant, 'Between Aquinas and Eymerich: The Roman Inquisition's Use of Dominican Thought in the Censorship of Alchemy', *Ambix*, LXV/3 (2018), pp. 210–31, but I would suggest that he has overlooked Eymeric's direct inspiration on such key papal pronouncements as Sixtus V's 1586 anti-magic bull *Coeli et terrae*.

12 Bujanda vol. XII, p. 359. For Spanish expurgations of Kepler, see ibid., p. 699.

13 Amir Alexander, *Infinitesimal: How a Dangerous Mathematical Theory Shaped the Modern World* (New York, 2014). Cavalieri, it should be pointed out, also published works on astrology (which were never placed on the Index).

14 Vesalius' depictions of sexual organs seem to have been most targeted, with illustrations being cut out or covered with bits of sticky paper in some cases. One creative Jesuit in Bourges even seems to have drawn a pair of shorts over an overly revealing image of male musculature: Dániel Margócsy, Mark Somos and Stephen N. Joffe, *The Fabrica of Andreas Vesalius: A Worldwide Descriptive Census, Ownership, and Annotations of the 1543 and 1555 Editions* (Leiden, 2018), pp. 121–30, here p. 127.

15 Dov Front, 'The Expurgation of Medical Books in Sixteenth-Century Spain', *Bulletin of the History of Medicine*, LXXV/2 (2001), pp. 290–96; see also Isilda Rodrigues and Carlos Fiolhais, 'The Inquisitorial Censorship

of Amatus Lusitanus *Centuriae*', *Asclepio*, LXX/2 (2018), https://doi. org/10.3989/asclepio.2018.13. Lusitanus' status as a converted Jew may have heightened scrutiny of his writing.

16 Bujanda vol. XII, p. 265; Spanish Index 1632, p. 40 (a Class Two prohibition). The same page further censors the Tunisian astrologer Abu Hasan Ali ibn Abi Rijal al-Shaybani (d. 1037), under the name 'Albohazen Haly Filius Abenragel', for a work first translated into Spanish for Alfonso X of Castile in 1254 and later printed in Latin at Venice (1485).

17 Bodin's *Demonomania* was banned in the Spanish Indexes of 1612 and 1632 as well, but only expurgated in that of 1640 (Bujanda vol. XII, p. 347). As Peter Godman notes in *The Saint as Censor: Robert Bellarmine Between Inquisition and Index* (Leiden, 2000), p. 159, Francisco Peña accepted the idea of expurgating this text but only so long as it was circulated in Latin alone (and thus among experts), not in a vernacular edition that might fall into gullible (and especially female) hands.

18 Scot's oeuvre did not appear on the Index, likely because he wrote in English and Index censors had largely given up on keeping track of Protestant authors by this point in any case. A persistent legend that Scot's book was burned by King James I (who also wrote his own 1597 book on demonology, entitled *Daemonologie*), may not be true, but it does reflect the monarch's strong disapproval of Scot's work.

19 Bujanda vol. XI, pp. 609 and 718; and vol. XII, p. 544. The early eighteenth-century bans were also partly in response to Protestant mockery, as pointed out in George Haven Putnam, *Censorship of the Church of Rome* (New York, 1906), vol. II, pp. 134–6.

20 Gasser's *opera omnia* were further banned by the Venetian Index of 1554, and then those of Rome (1559), Parma (1580) and Spain (1583); Bujanda vol. X, p. 195.

21 In later years, Juan António Llorente (former Inquisition commissary and author of a tell-all study entitled *Histoire critique de l'Inquisition en Espagne* [1817–18], trans. Alexis Pellier, 4 vols), Alexandre Herculano (author of the three-volume *História da origem e estabelecimento da Inquisição em Portugal* [1845–59]) and even Franz Heinrich Reusch (author of a foundational two-volume study on the Index of Prohibited Books, *Der Index der Verbotenen Bücher: Ein Beitrag zur Kirchen und Literaturgeschichte* [1883–5]) would also appear on the Indexes.

22 Bujanda vol. XI, pp. 551 and 818.

23 Bujanda vol. XI, p. 378.

24 Bujanda vol. XI, pp. 376, 651, 744 and 780 (respectively).

25 On the 1603 edict, which contains 55 entries in all, see Jesús Martínez de Bujanda and Eugenio Canone, 'L'editto di proibizione delle opera di Bruno e Campanella. Un' analisi bibliografica', *Bruniana & Campanelliana*, VIII/2 (2002), pp. 451–79.

26 Ugo Baldini and Leen Spruit, eds, *Catholic Church and Modern Science: Documents of the Holy Office and the Index* (Rome, 2009), vol. I in four tomes. Documents relating to the cases of Agrippa, Bodin, Cardano, Copernicus, Della Porta, Fuchs, Mercator, Paracelsus and Patrizi, among many others, are given at varying length in this collection.

7 CENSORED SEX, FAITH AND THE ARTS

1 Spanish Index 1790, p. 9.
2 This is not to say that utopian literature was prohibited across the board. Neither Francesco Patrizi's *Città felice* (1553) nor Francis Bacon's *New Atlantis* (1626) was ever placed on an Index. Books were targeted for the degree of challenge and danger they seemed to present to the forces of Catholic authority, and 'utopianism' was just one way in which an implicit critique could be manifested.
3 Some of Cervantes's works did eventually find their way onto the Spanish and Portuguese (but not Roman) Index – though only barely. Shakespeare was never subjected to explicit censorship in any of the Indexes.
4 Reprinted in Bujanda vol. VIII, p. 817:
   Libri, qui res lascivas, seu obscoenas ex professo tractant, narrant, aut docent, cum solum fidei, sed & morum, qui huiusmodi librorum lectione facile corrumpi solent, ratio habenda sit, omnino prohibentur: & qui eos habuerint, severe ab Episcopis puniantur. Antiqui vero, ab Ethnicis conscripti, propter sermonis elegantiam, & proprietatem permittuntur: nulla tamen ratione pueris praelegendi erunt.
5 The U.S. Supreme court struggled with the same problem in 1964, in a landmark obscenity trial where the presiding judge Potter Stewart famously declined to provide a clear definition for 'hard-core' pornography, instead suggesting that 'I know it when I see it.'
6 See, for example, the handwritten reader's notes, in this case attributable to Marco Dotto, in a copy of the *Decameron* held by the British Library: Olga Kerziouk, 'Il Decamerone – "Corrected" by Rome', *European Studies Blog*, https://blogs.bl.uk, 26 September 2016. A similarly 'corrected' exemplar can be found in the Rare Books Library at the University of Notre Dame.
7 'Las obras de caridad que se hacen flojamente, no tienen merito, ni valen nada'. From the second part, chapter 36; see Spanish Index 1632, p. 980. The writings of Cervantes, including his *Novellas exemplares*, were more thoroughly but still quite lightly dealt with in the Portuguese Index of 1624, pp. 905–7 (which found a total of six problematic passages in *Quixote*).
8 Pope was influential in Spain, where his writings circulated in both Spanish and French translation. However this also meant that they were carefully checked for errors in the final decades of the eighteenth century. This eventually resulted in the prohibition of a volume of his *Oeuvres diverses* for containing passages deemed irreverent in tone, as well as ideas that smacked of religious tolerance; Frieda Koeniger, 'Pope-Bashing by Papists? A Curious Censoring of Alexander Pope's Letters by the Mexican Inquisition', *Eighteenth-Century Life*, XXVI/2 (2002), pp. 45–52.
9 *Moll Flanders* was, however, censored by various state agencies until well into the twentieth century.
10 Isabel Dotan-Robinet, 'L'interdit et ses limites dans l'Erotika Biblion de Mirabeau', in *Reading and Writing the Forbidden: Essays in French*

Studies, ed. Bénédicte Facques, Helen Roberts and Hugh Roberts (Reading, 2003), pp. 19–29. Mirabeau's *Secret History of the Court of Prussia*, on the other hand, was immediately censored by French authorities for political reasons.
11 Bujanda vol. v, pp. 661–2.
12 Bujanda vol. IX, p. 928.
13 Bujanda vol. III, p. 30.
14 Supporters of the cult of Ramon Llull were accused of these sorts of excesses in the eighteenth century, and indeed Benedict may have had them at least partially in mind. See Francisco José García Pérez, *La Cruzada Antilulista* (Mallorca, 2017), esp. pp. 259–75.
15 *Regla* 8 and 9 remain the same after 1640. In 1632, the prohibition against magical books is *Regla* 8, not 9, and the section appended to *Regla* 7 (which would later become 8) lacks the paragraph specifically targeting superstitious images.
16 'Morisco' songs and dances were criminalized by Spanish authorities in the 1530s, as noted by the contemporary Francisco Núñez Muley, *A Memorandum for the President of the Royal Audiencia and Chancery Court of the City and Kingdom of Granada*, trans. Vincent Barletta (Chicago, IL, 2007), p. 61 – though he also rhetorically complained that this prohibition was especially galling when even 'black slaves of Guinea' were 'allowed to sing and dance to their instruments and songs, and in the languages in which they normally sing them' (ibid., p. 81). Nevertheless, Indigenous songs and dances would indeed be similarly (if often selectively) proscribed by later European colonial authorities around the globe.
17 K. G. Fellerer and Moses Hadas, 'Church Music and the Council of Trent', *Musical Quarterly*, XXXIX/4 (1953), p. 583, n. 27. Franco (d. 1575) was bishop of Loreto and a participant at Trent.
18 Early female writers on religious topics remained rare on the Index, due both to their comparative scarcity and the failure of male scholars to take women's contributions seriously whenever they did manage to appear. Nevertheless, exceptions can be found: the Protestant hymn composer Magdalena Heymair (or Heymarius, d. *c.* 1586) was placed on the Index of Antwerp in 1570, and later those of Spain (1583) and Rome (1596), while a 1670 edition of writings by the medieval mystic Gertrud of Helfta (d. 1302) was prohibited pending expurgation (*donec corrigatur*) in 1709.

8 CENSORSHIP AND MODERNITY

1 Braun opposed the Marian dogma, and thus also the doctrine of papal infallibility which upheld it, in works such as *Katholische Antwort auf die Päpstliche Bulle über die Empfängniss Mariae* (published 1856, banned 1857).
2 John W. O'Malley, *What Happened at Vatican II* (Cambridge, MA, 2008), p. 88. As O'Malley points out, Teilhard's books were published posthumously and condemned by the Holy Office in 1962, but not placed on the Index since it was no longer being issued by this date.

3 Franz Mesmer's theory of 'animal magnetism' was held in deep suspicion by many inquisitors, and though Mesmer (d. 1815) himself does not appear on any Index, works by his disciples were later banned; see George Haven Putnam, *Censorship of the Church of Rome* (New York, 1906), vol. II, p. 189. Louis-Alphonse Cahagnet's *Guide du Magnétiseur* and *Magnétisme*, as well as the journal *Le Magnétiseur spiritualiste, journal rédigé par les membres de la Société des Magnétiseurs Spiritualistes de Paris*, were banned in 1851, as was Martino Tommasi's *Il Magnetismo animale consideratio sotto un nuovo punto di vista; saggio scientifico*.

4 John O'Malley thus notes that: 'As Veuillot rose in the esteem of Pius IX, his influence with the Index grew accordingly, to the point that a negative review of a publication in the *Univers* almost inevitably led to an investigation of it by the Congregation of the Index.' (*Vatican I: The Council and the Making of the Ultramontane Church* (Cambridge, MA, 2018), p. 90).

5 Stephen Schloesser, '"Altogether Adverse": The Story of Graham Greene and the Holy Office', *America* (11 November 2000), pp. 8–13; Peter Godman, 'Graham Greene's Vatican Dossier', *Atlantic Monthly*, CCLXXXVIII (July–August 2001), pp. 84–8.

6 'The Pilgrim', 'Being Placed on the Index', *America* (18 July 1936), p. 347.

7 Guyda Armstrong, 'Eroticism à la Française: Text, Image, and Display in Nineteenth-Century English Translations of Boccaccio's *Decameron*', *Word and Image*, XXX/3 (2014), pp. 194–212.

CONCLUSION

1 Redmond A. Burke, *What Is the Index?* (Milwaukee, WI, 1952).

2 'Censorship in Belgian Comics', *Europe Comics*, www.europecomics.com, 26 February 2021.

3 *Dei verbum* went so far as to permit, if cautiously, the possibility of permitting Catholics to read Bibles produced jointly with Protestant theologians: 'should the opportunity arise and the Church authorities approve, if these translations are produced in cooperation with the separated brethren as well, all Christians will be able to use them.'

4 On *Ex corde Ecclesiae* and its impact on Catholic universities, see Michael W. Higgins and Douglas R. Letson, *Power and Peril: The Catholic Church at the Crossroads* (Toronto, 2002), esp. pp. 146–83. See also James L. Heft, *The Future of Catholic Higher Education* (Oxford, 2021). The actual implementation of *Ex corde*, it should be noted, remains minimal if not entirely absent on many nominally Catholic university campuses, including my own.

5 Laurence Sterne, *A Sentimental Journey and Other Writings*, ed. Ian Jack and Tim Parnell (Oxford, 2003), pp. xi–xiv.

6 Mario Biagioli, 'From Book Censorship to Academic Peer Review', *Emergences: Journal for the Study of Media and Composite Cultures*, XII/1 (2002), pp. 11–45.

7 Heather Morrison, 'Authorship in Transition: Enthusiasts and Malcontents on Press Freedoms, an Expanding Literary Market, and Vienna's Reading Public', *Central European History*, XLVI/1 (2013), pp. 1–27.

FURTHER READING

The following is a highly selective survey of published research that may be of interest to those who wish to learn more about the history of the Index of Prohibited Books, the many works it served to both censor and record, and some of the broader historical contexts which impacted them. It has been assembled with non-specialist readers in mind, and is for the most part limited to English-language resources.

GENERAL

Previous studies on the general topic of censorship abound, though many of them tend to focus on relatively recent and well-known examples of banned literature and art. Given the enormity of the topic, they also tend to restrict analysis to specific linguistic or thematic categories (that is, literature in English, or works banned for political reasons). Useful recent examples would include Matthew Fellion and Katherine Inglis, *Censored: A Literary History of Subversion and Control* (Kingston and Montreal, 2017); Nicholas J. Karolides, *Literature Suppressed on Political Grounds*, 3rd edn (New York, 2011); and Dawn B. Sova, *Literature Suppressed on Social Grounds*, 3rd edn (New York, 2011). Green and Karolides's convenient one-volume *Encyclopedia of Censorship* (New York, 2005) also includes numerous entries relevant to the subject of this book. Richard Ovenden's *Burning the Books: A History of Deliberate Destruction of Knowledge* (London and Cambridge, MA, 2020) is a welcome new addition to this literature.

The Index of Prohibited Books itself has generated a significant literature of its own, but few broad surveys of much scholarly value since Heinrich Reusch's still-standard (but sadly never translated) *Der Index der Verbotenen Bücher*, 2 vols (Bonn, 1883–5) and George Haven Putnam's *Censorship of the Church of Rome*, 2 vols (New York, 1906). The most important recent development in this field is undoubtedly the completion of Jesús Martínez de Bujanda's monumental twelve-volume *Index des Livres Interdits* (variously published, with a series of co-editors and assistants, from 1985 to 2016 as detailed in the 'Abbreviations' section of this book). Most of its contents are in French, though the last volume appeared in Spanish as *El Índice de Libros Prohibidos y Expurgados de la Inquisición Española (1551–1819)*. The first nine volumes include reproductions of the most important sixteenth-century Indexes, as well as analytic essays and charts; vol. X contains a comprehensive overview and index to the foregoing, while vols XI and XII provide higher-level overviews of the later centuries of Roman and Spanish Index censorship (respectively). Together they comprise an indispensable research aid for anyone seeking to gain an understanding of the Indexes and how they evolved over time. Specialized studies on particular aspects of Index censorship, including my own, have greatly benefited from this resource, as they have also from the decision to open up the archives of the Vatican's Congregation for the Doctrine of the Faith in 1998. The essays in Gigliola Fragnito, ed., *Church, Censorship and Culture in Early Modern Italy*, trans. Adrian Belton (Cambridge, 2001) provide just a few early examples of the sorts of new research made possible as a result.

Historians of the various medieval and early modern inquisitions are still indebted to the pioneering efforts of Henry Charles Lea, whose three-volume *History of the Inquisition of the Middle Ages* (London, 1888) and four-volume *History of the Inquisition of Spain* (New York, 1906–7), along with various other studies, set new standards of professionalization in the highly polemical field of inquisition studies. They should, however, be updated with reference to more recent surveys such as Edward Peters, *Inquisition* (New York, 1988); Jennifer Kolpacoff Deane, *History of Medieval Heresy and Inquisition* (Lanham, MD, 2011); and Francisco Bethencourt, *The Inquisition: A Global History, 1478–1834* [1995], trans. Jean Birrell (Cambridge, 2009). Further details on specific early modern Inquisitions can be found in Christopher F. Black, *The Italian Inquisition* (New Haven, CT, 2009); Thomas F. Mayer, *The Roman Inquisition* (Philadelphia, PA, 2013); and John Edwards, *The Spanish Inquisition* (Stroud, 1999), among others. Readers of Italian will benefit from the extensive articles in Adriano Prosperi, John A. Tedeschi and Vincenzo Lavenia, eds, *Dizionario Storico dell'Inquisizione*, 4 vols (Pisa, 2010).

For a general history of the popes mentioned in this book see Eamon Duffy, *Saints and Sinners: A History of the Popes* [1997], 4th edn (New Haven, CT, 2014). The older forty-volume work of Ludwig von Pastor, *The History of the Popes from the Close of the Middle Ages*, ed. Frederick Ignatius Antrobus et al. (London, 1891–1953), is also extremely useful and gives detailed individual biographies in many cases.

INTRODUCTION

The Calvinist execution of Michael Servetus for heresy is colourfully described in Roland H. Bainton, *Hunted Heretic: The Life and Death of Michael Servetus 1511–1533* [1953] (Boston, MA, 1960). On Elizabethan censorship see Cyndia Susan Clegg, *Press Censorship in Elizabethan England* (Cambridge, 1997); Phebe Jensen, 'Ballads and Brags: Free Speech and Recusant Culture in Elizabethan England', *Criticism*, XL/3 (1998), pp. 333–54; and various articles in Teresa Bela et al., eds, *Publishing Subversive Texts in Elizabethan England and the Polish-Lithuanian Commonwealth* (Leiden, 2016). The various Protestant and Catholic approaches to religious discipline are further explored in Charles H. Parker and Gretchen Starr-LeBeau, eds, *Judging Faith, Punishing Sin: Inquisitions and Consistories in the Early Modern World* (Cambridge, 2017).

On historical distinctions between legitimate icon-veneration and idolatry, see Kristine Kolrud and Marina Prusac, eds, *Iconoclasm from Antiquity to Modernity* (Farnham and Burlington, VT, 2014). For Aquinas's views on idolatry, Denys Turner, 'On Denying the Right God: Aquinas on Atheism and Idolatry', *Modern Theology*, XX/1 (2004), pp. 141–61.

Nazi-era book censorship is surveyed in Guenter Lewy, *Harmful and Undesirable: Book Censorship in Nazi Germany* (Oxford, 2016). For an 'official' American position on the need for censorship during the Second World War, see the essay by Byron Price, U.S. Director of Censorship, 'Government Censorship in Wartime', *American Political Science Review*, XXXVI/5 (1942), pp. 837-49. A more critical analysis is in Michael S. Sweeny, *Secrets of Victory: The Office of Censorship and The American Press and Radio in World War II* (Chapel Hill, NC, and London, 2001). On the issue of corporate influence and control over various forms of expression, see *inter alia* Herbert I. Schiller, 'Corporate Sponsorship: Institutionalized Censorship of the Cultural Realm', *Art Journal*, L/3 (1991), pp. 56-9, and Henry A. Giroux and Grace Pollock, *The Mouse that Roared: Disney and the End of Innocence* (Lanham, MD, 2010).

For historians of the medieval period, fruitful discussion of 'persecution' often begins with R. I. Moore, *The Formation of a Persecuting Society: Authority and Deviance in Western Europe 950-1250* [1987], 2nd edn (Oxford, 2007). This classic study has been much criticized and nuanced since its first appearance more than thirty years ago; see for example Michael Frassetto, ed., *Heresy and the Persecuting Society in the Middle Ages: Essays on the Work of R. I. Moore* (Leiden, 2006), and Moore's own new concluding chapters composed for the second edition of his (Moore's) book. The concept of persecution continues to defy clear definition even in international law, as noted by Scott Rempell, 'Defining Persecution', *Utah Law Review*, MMXIII/1 (2011), pp. 283-344.

1 CENSORSHIP BEFORE THE INDEX

Connections between ancient Egyptian and Israelite religion, as well as the potentially 'intolerant' implications of monotheism, are explored in Jan Assmann, *Of God and Gods: Egypt, Israel, and the Rise of Monotheism* (Madison, WI, 2008) and James K. Hoffmeier, *Akhenaten and the Origins of Monotheism* (Oxford, 2013).

The fabled Library of Alexandria was established during the reign of Ptolemy II Philadelphus (285-246 BCE). Its subsequent fate is discussed in Mostafa el-Abbadi, *Life and Fate of the Ancient Library of Alexandria* (Paris, 1992), as well as Mostafa el-Abbadi and Omnia Mounir Fathallah, eds, *What Happened to the Ancient Library of Alexandria?* (Leiden, 2008). See also Andrew Erskine, 'Culture and Power in Ptolemaic Egypt: The Museum and Library of Alexandria', *Greece and Rome*, XL/1 (1995), pp. 38-48.

On distinctions between Roman censors and Roman censorship, see generally Alan E. Astin, 'Regimen Morum', *Journal of Roman Studies*, LXXVIII (1988), pp. 14-34, and Vasily Rudich, 'Navigating the Uncertain: Literature and Censorship in the Early Roman Empire', *Arion: A Journal of Humanities and the Classics*, Third Series XIV/1 (2006), pp. 7-28. Roman erotic images from Pompeii, now contained in the Gabinetto Segreto of the Museo Archeologico Nazionale at Naples, are introduced as foundational to modern concepts of 'pornography' in Walter Kendrick, *The Secret Museum: Pornography in Modern Culture* (Berkeley, CA, 1996), pp. 2-18. They are more closely examined by Antonio Varone, *Eroticism in Pompeii* (Los Angeles, CA, 2001).

On apocryphal, pseudepigraphic and Gnostic writings associated with biblical literature (including the Nag Hammadi collection, discovered in 1945), see J. K. Elliott, *The Apocryphal New Testament: A Collection of Apocryphal*

Christian Literature in an English Translation (Oxford, 1993); James M. Robinson, ed., *The Nag Hammadi Library in English* [1977] (San Francisco, CA, 1981); and Elaine Pagels, *The Gnostic Gospels* (New York, 1979).

For an introduction to the work of Peter Abelard, see Babette S. Hellemans, ed., *Rethinking Abelard: A Collection of Critical Essays* (Leiden, 2014), as well Michael T. Clanchy's *Abelard: A Medieval Life* (Oxford, 1997) and John Marenbon, *The Philosophy of Peter Abelard* (Cambridge, 1997). On Abelard's experiences of censorship specifically, see also Peter Godman, *The Silent Masters: Latin Literature and its Censors in the High Middle Ages* (Princeton, NJ, 2000). The broader context of the high medieval intellectual 'renaissance', made possible by the translation of Aristotelian and other philosophical and scientific works (mostly from Arabic), is treated in Thomas E. Burman, 'The Four Seas of Medieval Mediterranean Intellectual History', in *Interfaith Relationships and Perceptions of the Other in the Medieval Mediterranean*, ed. Sarah Davis-Secord, Belen Vicens and Robin Vose (New York, 2022), pp. 15–47.

The medieval Dominican curriculum, including bans on Aristotle (and their reversal), is discussed in Robin Vose, *Dominicans, Muslims and Jews in the Medieval Crown of Aragon* (Cambridge, 2009), pp. 99–102, and Marian Michèle Mulchahey, *'First the Bow is Bent in Study –': Dominican Education before 1350* (Toronto, 1998). The Parisian ban of 1277, and subsequent university-based censorship campaigns against figures such as Nicholas of Autrecourt, are examined in J.M.M.H. Thijssen, *Censure and Heresy at the University of Paris, 1200–1400* (Philadelphia, PA, 1998).

For the influence of Hebrew learning on medieval Christian studies of the Bible, especially those of the Victorine canons and later the Dominicans at Paris, see the classic survey by Beryl Smalley, *The Study of the Bible in the Middle Ages* [1940], 2nd edn (Notre Dame, IN, 1964). The destruction of Maimonides's *Guide* remains a poorly documented and obscure episode, with motivations for the Dominican intervention left unclear as a result; see Daniel Silver, *Maimonidean Criticism and the Maimonidean Controversy, 1180–1240* (Leiden, 1965), and more recently Idit Dobbs-Weinstein, 'The Maimonidean Controversy', in *History of Jewish Philosophy*, ed. Daniel H. Frank and Oliver Leaman (London, 1997), pp. 275–91. James A. Diamond, *Maimonides and the Shaping of the Jewish Canon* (New York, 2014) sheds further light on reactions to Maimonides's controversial work. Christian censorship of the Talmud is much better known and has been described many times (and will be further examined in subsequent chapters of this book); see for example John Friedman, Jean Connell Hoff and Robert Chazan, *The Trial of the Talmud: Paris, 1240* (Toronto, 2012) and part 2 of Harry Freedman, *The Talmud – A Biography: Banned, Censored and Burned, the Book They Couldn't Suppress* (London, 2014). On medieval Christian scholars' treatment of the Muslim Qur'an and related texts, see Thomas E. Burman, *Reading the Qurʾān in Latin Christendom, 1140–1560* (Philadelphia, PA, 2007), and now Cándida Ferrero Hernández and John Tolan, eds, *The Latin Qur'an, 1143–1500* (Berlin, 2021).

The bibliography on Christian heresies of the Middle Ages is massive and continually expanding. Good places to begin for an overview are Malcolm Lambert, *Medieval Heresy: Popular Movements from the Gregorian Reform to the Reformation* [1977], 3rd edn (Oxford, 2002) and Kolpacoff Deane, *History*, as well as recent essays (with up-to-date bibliographies of their own) in Louise Nyholm Kallestrup and Raisa Maria Toivo, eds, *Contesting Orthodoxy in Medieval and Early Modern Europe: Heresy, Magic and Witchcraft* (London, 2017); Michael D. Bailey and Sean L. Field, eds, *Late Medieval Heresy: New Perspectives* (York, 2019); and Donald S. Prudlo, ed., *A Companion to Heresy Inquisitions* (Leiden, 2019). Scepticism regarding the evidence for organized heresies has been expressed by Mark Gregory Pegg, among others; see the discussions in Antonio Sennis, ed., *Cathars in Question* (York, 2016).

A good introduction to medieval magic is Richard Kieckhefer, *Magic in the Middle Ages* (Cambridge, 1989), while astrology in particular (along with Nicholas Eymeric's attitude towards it) is further examined by Michael A. Ryan, *A Kingdom of Stargazers: Astrology and Authority in the Late Medieval Crown of Aragon* (Ithaca, NY, 2011). Demonic magic and its increasing importance throughout the later Middle Ages is the subject of Michael D. Bailey's *Battling Demons: Witchcraft, Heresy, and Reform in the Late Middle Ages* (University Park, PA, 2003); see also Nancy Caciola, *Discerning Spirits: Divine and Demonic Possession in the Middle Ages* (Ithaca, NY, 2003).

Bernard Gui and Nicholas Eymeric are both described, along with some of their works, in Karen Sullivan, *The Inner Lives of Medieval Inquisitors* (Chicago, IL, 2011) and Derek Hill, *Inquisition in the Fourteenth Century: The Manuals of Bernard Gui and Nicholas Eymerich* (York, 2019). Their complete manuals are only available in Latin editions, although excerpts of varying quality have been published in a variety of languages such as Janet Shirley's partial translation of Gui's *Practica: Inquisitor's Guide: A Medieval Manual on Heretics* (Welwyn Garden City, 2006). On the importance of the bull *Coena domini* in the evolution of canonical conceptions of heresy, see G. E. Biber, *The Papal Bull, 'In Coena Domini'* (London, 1848) and Alfonso Gutiérrez-Maturana y Camañes, 'El delito de herejía: "Iter" jurídico', PhD thesis, Universidad de Navarra, 1991.

For the controversies surrounding Ramon Llull and his censorship by Nicholas Eymeric, the best introductory volume remains Jocelyn N. Hillgarth, *Ramon Lull and Lullism in Fourteenth-Century France* (Oxford, 1971), but also now Robin Vose, 'Books, Damned Books, and Heretics: Censorship and Dominican Inquisitors in Nicholas Eymeric's *Directorium inquisitorum*', in *Virtuosos of Faith: Monks, Nuns, Canons, and Friars as Elites of Medieval Culture*, ed. Gert Melville and James D. Mixson (Berlin, 2020), pp. 151–69.

On the prosecution of later medieval heresies (and books) associated with John Wyclif and his followers, sometimes known as 'Lollards', see, among others, Henry Ansgar Kelly, 'Lollard Inquisitions: Due and Undue Process', in *The Devil, Heresy and Witchcraft in the Middle Ages*, ed. Alberto Ferreiro (Leiden, 1998), pp. 279–303; Ian Forrest, *The Detection of Heresy in Late Medieval England* (Oxford, 2005); further context in Kathryn Kerby-Fulton, *Books under Suspicion: Censorship and Tolerance of Revelatory Writing in Late Medieval England* (Notre Dame, IN, 2006). The related trial of John (Jan) Hus is examined by Thomas A. Fudge in *The Trial of Jan Hus: Medieval Heresy and Criminal Procedure* (New York, 2013).

2 INVENTING THE INDEX

Early (partial and ad hoc) bans on printed books, including Pope Sixtus IV's 1479 order to confiscate a treatise on the teachings of Ramon Llull which had recently been printed at Barcelona, are described in Rudolf Hirsch, 'Pre-Reformation Censorship of Printed Books', *Library Journal*, XXI (1955), pp. 100–105; see also Nelson H. Minnich, 'The Fifth Lateran Council and Preventive Censorship of Printed Books', *Annali della Scuola Normale Superiore di Pisa*, II/1 (2010), pp. 67–104. The emergence of print technology, and subsequent development of modern 'book culture' with its many historical implications, have been surveyed in the still-influential studies of Lucien Febvre and Henri-Jean Martin, *The Coming of the Book: The Impact of Printing, 1450–1800* [1958], trans. David Gerard (New York, 1976) and Elizabeth L. Eisenstein, *The Printing Press as an Agent of Change: Communications and Cultural Transformations in Early-Modern Europe*, 2 vols (Cambridge, 1979), the latter of which was later abridged and updated as *The Printing Revolution in Early Modern Europe* [1983], 2nd edn (Cambridge, 2005). See also more recently Adrian Johns, *The Nature of the Book: Print and Knowledge in the Making* (Chicago, IL, 1998); Sabrina Alcorn Baron, Eric N. Lindquist and Eleanor F. Shevlin, eds, *Agent of Change: Print Culture Studies After Elizabeth L. Eisenstein* (Amherst and Boston, MA, 2007); and Elizabeth L. Eisenstein, *Divine Art, Infernal Machine: The Reception of Printing in the West from First Impressions to the Sense of an Ending* (Philadelphia, PA, 2011).

On the legacy of Savonarola in the early sixteenth century, see Lorenzo Polizzotto, *The Elect Nation: The Savonarolan Movement in Florence, 1494–1545* (Oxford, 1994); Lauro Martines, *Fire in the City: Savonarola and the Struggle for the Soul of Renaissance Florence* (Oxford, 2006); and Tamar Herzig, *Savonarola's Women: Visions and Reform in Renaissance Italy* (Chicago, IL, 2008).

The career of Martin Luther, and the Protestant Reformation that is inevitably linked to his name, have each generated vast quantities of literature. General introductions can be found in Heiko Oberman, *Luther: Man Between God and the Devil* (New Haven, CT, 1989); Euan Cameron, *The European Reformation* [1991], 2nd edn (Oxford, 2012); R. Po-chia Hsia, *A Companion to the Reformation World* (Oxford, 2004); and Carter Lindberg, ed., *The Reformation Theologians* (Oxford, 2002), as well as Alberto Melloni, *Martin Luther: A Christian Between Reforms and Modernity* (Berlin, 2017). Protestant use of print media is examined in Robert W. Scribner, *For the Sake of Simple Folk: Popular Propaganda for the German Reformation* [1981] (Oxford, 1994) and Mark U. Edwards, *Printing, Propaganda, and Martin Luther* (Berkeley, CA, 1994).

On Luther's chief theological opponents and prosecutors, Cajetan and Prierias (Sylvester Mazzolini, who also served as master of the sacred palace to popes Leo X, Adrian VI and Clement VII), and Thomas de Vio Cajetan (Prierias's superior as Dominican master general from 1508 to 1518, and then a cardinal as well as a papal legate), see Michael Tavuzzi, *Prierias: The Life and Works of Silvestro Mazzolini da Prierio, 1456–1527* (Durham, NC, 1997) and Charles Morerod, *Cajetan et Luther en 1518*, 2 vols (Fribourg, 1994).

The German 'Peasants' War' of 1525 is described in Peter Blickle, *The Revolution of 1525: The German Peasants' War from a New Perspective* [1981], trans. Thomas A. Brady and H. C. Erik Midelfort (Baltimore, MD, 1991). Of course all of these events took place within a wider context of political, economic and religious turmoil; see for example Euan Cameron, ed., *The Sixteenth Century* (Oxford, 2006), who provides a lucid introduction to the history of the period. For further details on the 'placards' affair confronting Francis I, see R. J. Knecht, *Francis I* (Cambridge, 1982), pp. 248–52. Henry VIII's censorship of Lutheran and other texts in the 1520s is noted in Hubert Wolf, *Index: Der Vatikan und die Verbotenen Bücher* (Munich, 2006), p. 19. On this matter, as well as Henry VIII's subsequent conflict with Rome (which resulted in the Act of Supremacy in 1534 and the beginnings of a separated 'Anglican' Church), see further Christopher Haigh, *English Reformations: Religion, Politics, and Society under the Tudors* (Oxford, 1993).

On the multiple jurisdictions claiming authority over censorship of heretical books (and other religious offenses) in early sixteenth-century France, see James Farge's 'Introduction Historique' to Bujanda vol. I, pp. 33–76; also Elizabeth Armstrong, *Before Copyright: The French Book-Privilege System, 1498–1526* (Cambridge, 2002). The genesis and contents of the first Parisian lists of banned books are described in some detail in Bujanda vol. I, and summarized in Bujanda vol. X, p. 18. For the Leuven Indexes, see Bujanda vol. II and Bujanda vol. X, p. 19. On the complicated matter of Erasmus' many writings and their mixed reception in the Catholic Church, see the classic study of Marcel Bataillon, *Érasme et l'Espagne* (Paris, 1937), as well as Karl A. E. Enenkel, ed., *The Reception of Erasmus in the Early Modern Period* (Leiden, 2013) and the incomparable, ongoing 89-volume *Collected Works of Erasmus* (Toronto, 1974–).

The first Spanish Indexes are more fully examined in Bujanda vol. V and Bujanda vol. XII, pp. 9–47. For the Portuguese Indexes, see Bujanda vol. IV. The Venetian and Milanese Indexes of 1549–54 are treated in Bujanda vol. III and Bujanda vol. X, pp. 19–20.

The Catholic 'Spirituali' of the sixteenth century who were opposed by Cardinal Carafa and his inquisitors for allegedly being too sympathetic to Protestant theology (and who did in some cases end up converting to Protestantism) have generally been studied as individuals rather than as members of a coherent movement; see for example Anne Jacobson Schutte, *Pier Paolo Vergerio: The Making of an Italian Reformer* (Geneva, 1977). Other important characters are studied in Adam Patrick Robinson, *The Career of Cardinal Giovanni Morone (1509–1580): Between Council and Inquisition* (London and New York, 2017); Torrance Kirby, Emidio Campi and Frank A. James III, eds, *A Companion to Peter Martyr Vermigli* (Leiden, 2009); Michele Camaioni, *Il Vangelo e l'Anticristo: Bernardino Ochino tra francescanesimo ed eresia (1487–1547)* (Naples, 2018); Massimo Firpo and Dario Marcatto, eds, *I Processi Inquisitoriali di Pietro Carnesecchi (1557–1567)*, 2 vols (Vatican City, 1998–2000); Marco Faini, *Pietro Bembo: A Life in Laurels and Scarlet* (Cambridge, 2017); Massimo Firpo, *Juan de Valdés and the Italian Reformation*, trans. Richard Bates (Farnham, 2015); and Carol H. Madison, *Marcantonio Flaminio: Poet, Humanist and Reformer* [1965] (Chapel Hill, NC, 2011). The English cardinal Reginald Pole has perhaps understandably attracted the most attention in recent Anglophone scholarship, including John Edwards, *Archbishop Pole* (London and New York, 2018); Thomas F. Mayer, *Reginald Pole: Prince and Prophet* [2000] (Cambridge, 2007); and Mayer, *Cardinal Pole in European Context: A 'via media' in the Reformation* (Aldershot, 2000). Camilla Russell's *Giulia Gonzaga and the Religious Controversies of Sixteenth-Century Italy* (Turnhout, 2006) brings welcome attention to the importance of women's patronage in this milieu. On Vittoria Colonna, too, see now Abigail Brundin, Tatiana Crivelli and Maria Sapegno, eds, *A Companion to Vittoria Colonna* (Leiden, 2016), as well as Ramie Targoff, *Renaissance Woman: The Life of Vittoria Colonna* (New York, 2019). M. Anne Overell, *Italian Reform and English Reformations, c.1535–c.1585* (London and New York, 2016) is only a partial exception to this biographical rule, framing the lives of important figures such as Ochino and Pole within their larger Italian and English contexts.

The best concise history of the Council of Trent is John W. O'Malley, *Trent: What Happened at the Council* (Cambridge, MA, 2013), but its powerful echoes even in distant colonial lands are further explored in Michela Catto and Adriano Prosperi, eds, *Trent and Beyond: The Council, Other Powers, Other Cultures* (Turnhout, 2018). For the foundation of the Jesuit Order see John W. O'Malley, *The First Jesuits* (Cambridge, MA, and London, 1993); their later history is surveyed in O'Malley, *The Jesuits: A History from Ignatius to the Present* (Lanham, MD, 2014). On the Roman Inquisition, see Jane K. Wickersham, *Rituals of Prosecution: The Roman Inquisition and the Prosecution of Philo-Protestants in Sixteenth-Century Italy* (Toronto, 2012), as well as Christopher F. Black, *The Italian Inquisition* (New Haven, CT, 2009), and Thomas F. Mayer, *The Roman Inquisition* (Philadelphia, PA, 2013).

The First Roman Indexes (up to the 1564 Index of Trent) are described in Bujanda vol. VIII, and again more succinctly in Bujanda vol. X, pp. 21–3. For the contested and evolving status of Ramon Llull's writings, which were widely favoured in the earlier half of the sixteenth century above all in the university centres of Barcelona and Paris, see Mark D. Johnston, 'The Reception of the Lullian Art, 1450–1530', *Sixteenth Century Journal*, XII/1 (1981), pp. 31–48; the historical context for Paul IV's condemnations is examined in Virgilio Pinto Crespo, 'La Censura Inquisitorial, Inquietud e Incertidumbre: El Caso Ramón Llull (1559–1610)', in *Miscelánea de la Universidad Autónoma de Madrid* (Madrid, 1982), pp. 293–314, and Mario Scaduto, 'Laínez e l'Indice de 1559. Lullo, Sabunde, Savonarola, Erasmo', *Archivum Historicum Societatis Iesu*, XXIV (1955), pp. 3–32. On the Antwerp (Anvers) Indexes, see Bujanda vol. VII.

3 EXPANDING THE INDEX

No full biography of Francisco Peña has yet been attempted, in part because the sources for his life are so scattered and incomplete. A composite picture may, however, be formed through consultation of Peter Godman, *The Saint as Censor: Robert Bellarmine Between Inquisition and Index* (Leiden, 2000), pp. 90–99 and passim (focusing in particular on his role in the evaluation of Pius II's *Commentaries*); Stefan Bauer, *The Invention of Papal History: Onofrio Panvinio between Renaissance and Catholic Reform* (Oxford, 2020), pp. 187–200; Jane K. Wickersham, *Rituals of Prosecution: The Roman Inquisition and the Prosecution of Philo-Protestants in Sixteenth-Century Italy* (Toronto, 2012), pp. 12–16 and passim; and occasional references in works such as Kimberly Lynn's *Between Court and Confessional: The Politics of Spanish Inquisitors* (Cambridge, 2013). Peña's editorial contributions to the revival of Eymeric's *Directorium* are traced in Edward M. Peters, 'Editing Inquisitors' Manuals in the Sixteenth Century: Francisco Peña and the *Directorium inquisitorum* of Nicholas Eymeric', *Library Chronicle*, XL (1974), pp. 95–107, and Agostino Borromeo, 'A Proposito del *Directorium inquisitorum* di Nicolás Eymerich e delle sue Edizioni Cinquecentesche', *Critica Storia*, XX (1983), pp. 499–547.

Further work still needs to be done to clarify the manuscript tradition Peña had to work with, and closer attention to his political manoeuvrings and extensive unpublished writings would undoubtedly shed important light on the significance and intent of his *Directorium* commentaries.

Agostino Valier's *Opusculum de cautione adhibenda in edendis libris* has never been translated, but receives extensive treatment in Giovanni Cipriani, *La mente di un inquisitore. Agostino Valier e l'Opusculum De cautione adhibenda in edendis libris (1589–1604)* (Florence, 2008). Robert Bellarmine, canonized in 1930, is the subject of many specialized studies including Stefania Tutino, *Empire of Souls: Robert Bellarmine and the Christian Commonwealth* (Oxford, 2010), as well as Godman, *Saint as Censor*. On the later sixteenth-century Roman Indexes of Sixtus V and Clement VIII, see Bujanda vol. IX. For the expurgatory Index, and frustrations surrounding its completion, see Gigliola Fragnito, 'The Central and Peripheral Organization of Censorship', in *Church, Censorship and Culture*, ed. Fragnito, trans. Adrian Belton (Cambridge, 2001), pp. 13–49.

The Quiroga Spanish Indexes of 1583–4 are reproduced and analyzed in Bujanda vol. VI, with further discussion in Bujanda vol. XII, pp. 47–71, while the Spanish Indexes of the seventeenth and eighteenth centuries are discussed in Bujanda vol. XII, pp. 73–200. On the Bourbon reforms of the Spanish Inquisition and its censorship practices in the eighteenth century, see John Edwards, *Torquemada and The Inquisitors* (Stroud, 2005), pp. 165–84.

Various aspects of the *De auxiliis* conflict are discussed in Jordan J. Ballor, Matthew T. Gaetano and David S. Sytsma, eds, *Beyond Dordt and 'De auxiliis': The Dynamics of Protestant and Catholic Soteriology in the Sixteenth and Seventeenth Centuries* (Leiden, 2019); a more succinct summary can be found in Part I of Richard H. Bulzacchelli, *Judged by the Law of Freedom* (Lanham, MD, 2006), esp. pp. 40–48. On Molinism specifically, see Kirk MacGregor, *Luis de Molina: The Life and Theology of the Founder of Middle Knowledge* (Grand Rapids, MI, 2015). William Doyle, *Jansenism: Catholic Resistance to Authority from the Reformation to the French Revolution* (London, 2000) provides a brief yet helpful introduction to Jansenism. Various popular as well as scholarly forms of early modern neo-Pelagianism are explored in Stuart Schwartz, *All Can be Saved* (New Haven, CT, 2008).

On Benedict XIV, in addition to the overview provided in Ludwig von Pastor, *The History of the Popes from the Close of the Middle Ages*, ed. Frederick Ignatius Antrobus et al. (London, 1891–1953), vols XXXV–XXXVI, see Rebecca Marie Messbarger et al., eds, *Benedict XIV and the Enlightenment: Art, Science, and Spirituality* (Toronto, 2016), as well as Hubert Wolf and Bernward Schmidt, eds, *Benedikt XIV und die Reform des Buchzensurverfahrens: zur Geschichte und Rezeption von 'Sollicita ac Provida'* (Paderborn, 2011). On the remarkable experiments of Raimondo di Sangro see Clorinda Donato, 'Between Myth and Archive, Alchemy and Science in Eighteenth-Century Naples: The Cabinet of Raimondo di Sangro, Prince of San Severo', in *Life Forms in the Thinking of the Long Eighteenth Century*, ed. Keith Michael Baker and Jenna M. Gibbs (Toronto, 2016), pp. 208–32; also Antonio Emanuele Piedimonte, *Raimondo di Sangro Principe di Sansevero* (Naples, 2018). Censorship of French Enlightenment works is discussed in general terms by Marcelin Defourneaux, *L'Inquisition Espagnole et les Livres Français au XVIIIe siècle* (Paris, 1963); see also the specific works cited in Chapters Six and Seven.

4 HOW TO BAN A BOOK

The various characters involved in the evaluation of *The Triumph of Love* are relatively obscure, but basic biographical facts can be gleaned from their own writings as well as early biographies such as Bernardus de Jonghe, *Belgium dominicanum* (Brussels, 1719), p. 238, and Jacques Quétif and Jacques Echard, *Scriptores ordinis praedicatorum* (Paris, 1721), vol. II, p. 621 (on Verjuys) and pp. 705–6 (on Hansen, best known for his 1664 hagiographical biography of St Rosa de Lima); also Jean-Pierre Niceron, *Mémoires pour Servir à l'Histoire des Hommes Illustres dans la République des Lettres* (Paris, 1733), vol. XXII, pp. 262–81 (on D'Aubry, a seventeenth-century mystic, alchemist and Llull enthusiast from Montpellier).

On the early modern Church historians cited in the *Triumph of Love* case, see Cyriac Pullapilly, *Caesar Baronius: Counter-Reformation Historian* (Notre Dame, IN, 1975); Eric Cochrane, *Historians and Historiography in the Italian Renaissance* (Chicago, IL, 1981); and Simon Ditchfield, *Liturgy, Sanctity and History in Tridentine Italy* (Cambridge, 1995). The background to Lucas Wadding's Franciscan historiography, which was quite favourable to Llull, is treated in Clare Lois Carroll, *Exiles in a Global City: The Irish and Early Modern Rome, 1609–1783* (Leiden, 2018), pp. 51–88.

The ongoing evaluation of Llullian works in the seventeenth and eighteenth centuries has been studied by Lorenzo Pérez Martínez, 'Lulismo e Inquisición a Principios del Siglo XVII', in *Perfiles Jurídicos de la Inquisición Española*, ed. José Antonio Escudero (Madrid, 1989), pp. 727–51, and now Francisco José García Pérez, *La Cruzada Antilulista* (Mallorca, 2017), who focuses on the Dominican-led campaign to have Llull's cult (if not his books) banned once and for all in the 1770s. Roman deliberations over Llull's orthodoxy in the later sixteenth century are described and documented in Ugo Baldini and Leen Spruit, eds, *Catholic Church and Modern Science: Documents from the Archives of the Roman Congregations of the Holy Office and the Index* (Rome, 2009), vol. I, tome 3, pp. 1983–2050. Though Llull's own work generally remained absent from both Roman and Spanish Indexes after the 1550s, many authorities remained deeply ambivalent about his orthodoxy and 'Llullian' works such as Giovanni Bracesco's 1548 *De alchemia dialogi duo* or the anonymous *Philosophia amoris* (actually *Proverbia Raemundi*, edited by Jacques Lefèvre d'Étaples at Paris in 1516) were themselves regularly prohibited by the Spanish Indexes.

The remaining archives of the Italian, Spanish and Portuguese Inquisitions are summarily described in a series of articles published in Gustav Henningsen and John Tedeschi, eds, *The Inquisition in Early Modern Europe: Studies on Sources and Methods* (DeKalb, IL, 1986). However, the opening of the Roman Archive of the Congregation for the Doctrine of the Faith (ACDF) since 1998 has permitted a re-evaluation of Tedeschi's pessimistic assumption that 'relatively few documents' survived therein (ibid., p. 13). In the still-active palace of the Holy Office, just steps away from St Peter's Basilica in the heart of Vatican City, many interesting files can now be consulted in a comfortable reading room if one takes the time to secure appropriate credentials and navigate its somewhat awkward schedules and filing systems. The Archivo Histórico Nacional (AHN) in Madrid contains still greater quantities of documents for the Spanish Inquisition, though they are also far from complete; see Joaquín Pérez

Villanueva et al., eds, *Historia de la Inquisición en España y América* (Madrid, 1984), esp. vol. I, pp. 61–78, for details on the AHN's *Sección Inquisición* and above all its *calificaciones y censuras*. These censorship files are mostly to be found in *legajos* 4416–522, which were partially catalogued long ago in A. Paz y Mélia, *Papeles de Inquisición. Catalogo y Extractos*, 2nd edn (Madrid, 1947).

On the procedures of the early modern Roman Inquisition and Congregation of the Index (with consideration of other Italian tribunals as well, such as the important Venetian Inquisition), see Christopher F. Black, *The Italian Inquisition* (New Haven, CT, 2009), esp. pp. 56–101 and 158–207; Thomas F. Mayer, *The Roman Inquisition* (Philadelphia, PA, 2013), pp. 39–40, provides more detailed information on the staffing and shifting quorum requirements of the Holy Office. Paul F. Grendler's *The Roman Inquisition and the Venetian Press, 1540–1605* (Princeton, NJ, 1977) provides further rich details regarding the evidence for Venetian arrests and books seizures. For Spain and Portugal, see Francisco Bethencourt, *The Inquisition: A Global History, 1478–1834* [1995], trans. Jean Birrell (Cambridge, 2009), pp. 221–34. Spanish edicts of banned books are also discussed in ibid., pp. 204–5. The Mexican Inquisition's book censorship practices are more fully examined in Martin Austin Nesvig, *Ideology and Inquisition: The World of the Censors in Early Mexico* (New Haven, CT, 2009), and interesting documents are provided in translation by John F. Chuchiak IV, *The Inquisition in New Spain, 1536–1820* (Baltimore, MD, 2012), pp. 318–42.

The English College of St Alban's at Valladolid is described in Michael E. Williams, *St. Alban's College Valladolid: Four Centuries of English Catholic Presence in Spain* (New York, 1986).

5 CENSORED SCRIPTURES

The story of the Douay-Rheims version, and its relation to contemporary Protestant English Bible translations, has been told many times. See for example Craig R. Thompson, *The Bible in English, 1525–1611* (Ithaca, NY, 1958), esp. pp. 12–13; also David Daniell, *The Bible in English: Its History and Influence* (New Haven, CT, 2003). On the life and legacy of William Allen, see Eamon Duffy, 'William, Cardinal Allen, 1532–1594', *British Catholic History*, XXII/3 (1995), pp. 265–90. The subsequent Polish iteration of this project is discussed in David A. Frick, 'Anglo-Polonica: The Rheims New Testament of 1582 and the Making of the Polish Catholic Bible', *Polish Review*, XXXVI/1 (1991), pp. 47–67, while early Hungarian Catholic Bibles are analysed in Edina Zvara, 'Scholarly Translators and Committed Disputants: The First Century of the Hungarian Bible', *Hungarian Studies*, XXXI/2 (2017), pp. 271–82.

The foundational work on medieval Bible studies remains Beryl Smalley, *The Study of the Bible in the Middle Ages* [1940], 2nd edn (Notre Dame, IN, 1964). For further details on medieval translations of biblical texts into vernacular languages, see Leonard Boyle, 'Innocent III and Vernacular Versions of Scripture', *Studies in Church History. Subsidia*, IV (1985), pp. 97–107; Peter Biller and Anne Hudson, eds, *Heresy and Literacy, 1000–1530* (Cambridge, 1994); and Mary Dove, *The First English Bible: The Text and Context of the Wycliffite Versions* (Cambridge, 2007). On the Hussites, see the essays in Thomas Fudge, *Heresy and Hussites in Late Medieval Europe* (Farnham, 2014). While no 'Hussite' Bible manuscripts remain, apart from possible Hungarian versions dating to the early fifteenth century, it is clear that Czech versions were also in wide circulation for several decades despite the efforts of inquisitorial censors (see Zvara, 'Scholarly Translators').

Various articles in Erika Rummel, ed., *A Companion to Biblical Humanism and Scholasticism in the Age of Erasmus* (Leiden, 2008) shed valuable light on the context in which scholars such as Erasmus, Luther, Tyndale, Lefèvre d'Étaples and the Complutensian Polyglot editors sought to make the Bible more fully understandable to modern readers. Struggles over the production of Jansenist-inspired Bibles have generated a very complex historiographical legacy over the last three centuries that is often mired in polemic and partisan bias, but modern scholarship continues to explore its many fascinating episodes. Brian E. Strayer, *Suffering Saints: Jansenists and Convulsionnaires in France, 1640–1799* (Portland, OR, 2008) provides a useful overview to supplement William Doyle, *Jansenism: Catholic Resistance to Authority from the Reformation to the French Revolution* (London, 2000). For the banned Dutch New Testament of 1696, see Els Agten, 'The Condemnation of Jansenist Vernacular Bibles in the Low Countries: The Case of Aegidius de Witte (1648–1721)', *Ephimerides theologicae lovanienses*, XCI/2 (2015), pp. 271–80.

On Christian Hebraism, see Allison Coudert and Jeffrey Shoulson, eds, *Hebraica Veritas? Christian Hebraists and the Study of Judaism in Early Modern Europe* (Philadelphia, PA, 2004) and Erika Rummel, *The Case Against Johann Reuchlin: Religious and Social Controversy in Sixteenth-Century Germany* (Toronto, 2002). Censorship of Jewish texts is discussed in Fausto Parente, 'The Index, the Holy Office, the Condemnation of the Talmud and Publication of Clement VIII's Index', in *Church, Censorship and Culture*, ed. Gigliola Fragnito, trans. Adrian Belton (Cambridge, 2001), pp. 163–93, and Amnon Raz-Krakotzkin, *The Censor, the Editor, and the Text: The Catholic Church and the Shaping of the Jewish Canon in the Sixteenth Century* [2005], trans. Jackie Feldman (Philadelphia, PA, 2007). Domenico Yerushalmi's role in Hebrew book censorship, on which he wrote a manual of his own entitled *Sepher Ha-Ziquq*, is examined in Shifra Baruchson-Arbib and Gila Prebor, '*Sepher Ha-Ziquq* (An Index of Forbidden Hebrew Books): The Book's Use and Its Influence on Hebrew Printing', *Bibliofilía*, CIX/1 (2007), pp. 3–31. Further examinations of Yerushalmi's and other censors' impacts on extant copies of both printed and manuscript early modern Hebrew books, building on early research by William A. Popper in *The Censorship of Hebrew Books* (New York, 1899), are now being conducted by Gila Prebor and others at Bar-Ilan University in Israel, as well as the collaborative online Footprints project: https://footprints.ctl.columbia.edu.

Alastair Hamilton, *The Forbidden Fruit: The Koran in Early Modern Europe* (London, 2008) briefly summarizes European Christian attitudes to the Qur'an and Arabic writing in the early modern period. The Protestant Bibliander edition of the translated Qur'an is discussed in Gregory Miller, 'Theodor Bibliander's *Machumetis Saracenorum Principis eiusque Successorum Vitae, Doctrina ac ipse Alcoran* (1543) as the Sixteenth-Century "Encyclopedia" of Islam', *Islam and Christian-Muslim Relations*, XXIV/2 (2013), pp. 241–54, and Jon Balserak, 'The Renaissance Impulses that Drove Theodor Bibliander to Publish *Machumetis Saracenorum*', *Muslim World*, CVII (2017), pp. 684–97. On the evolution of early modern scholarly Orientalism generally, see Robert Irwin, *For Lust of Knowing: The Orientalists and their Enemies* (London, 2007), and Alexander

Bevilacqua, *The Republic of Arabic Letters: Islam and the European Enlightenment* (Cambridge, MA, 2018).

The concept of 'cultural genocide', while disputed in some contexts, was first elucidated by Raphael Lemkin in the 1940s; see Leora Bilsky and Rachel Klagsbrun, 'The Return of Cultural Genocide?', *European Journal of International Law*, XXIX/2 (2018), pp. 373-96. The impact of wholesale cultural destruction as imposed by colonial regimes against Indigenous peoples in particular, even in the absence of outright mass murder, is clearly recognized in the *United Nations' Declaration on the Rights of Indigenous Peoples* (which was adopted by the General Assembly on 13 September 2007).

The topic of colonial censorship of Indigenous culture in the Americas is evidently a vast topic and cannot be fully covered here. See *inter alia* David Timmer, 'Providence and Perdition: Fray Diego de Landa Justifies His Inquisition Against the Yucatecan Maya', *Church History*, LXVI/3 (1997), pp. 477-88, and Priya Shah, 'Language, Discipline, and Power: The Extirpation of Idolatry in Colonial Peru and Indigenous Resistance', *Voces Novae*, V (2018), article 7. For the complications of translation in this context (with specific reference to the treatment of Inca *quipus*) see also Alan Durston, *Pastoral Quechua: The History of Christian Translation in Colonial Peru, 1550-1650* (Notre Dame, IN, 2007) and John Charles, 'Unreliable Confessions: Khipus in the Colonial Parish', *The Americas*, LXIV/1 (2007), pp. 11-33.

Efforts to catechize the Muslims of Spain are recounted in Ben Ehlers, *Between Christians and Moriscos: Juan de Ribera and religious reform in Valencia, 1568-1614* (Baltimore, MD, 2006), and Jason Busic, 'Order and Resistance in the Polemical and Catechetical Literature of Early Modern Spain (1515-1599): Christians, Muslims, and Moriscos', *Hispanic Review*, LXXXII/3 (2014), pp. 331-58.

On suppressed Nahuatl scholarship generated at the College of Santa Cruz de Tlatelolco, see Mark Z. Christensen, *Translated Christianities: Nahuatl and Maya Religious Texts* (University Park, PA, 2014), and Martin Austin Nesvig, *Ideology and Inquisition: The World of the Censors in Early Mexico* (New Haven, CT, 2009); also Nesvig, 'The Epistemological Politics of Vernacular Scripture in Sixteenth-Century Mexico', *The Americas*, LXX/2 (2013), pp. 165-201. David Tavárez has drawn further attention to newly discovered examples of Nahuatl translations of Christian spiritual texts: 'A Banned Sixteenth-Century Biblical Text in Nahuatl: The Proverbs of Solomon', *Ethnohistory*, LX/4 (2013), pp. 759-62, and Tavárez, 'Nahua Intellectuals, Franciscan Scholars, and the *Devotio Moderna* in Colonial Mexico', *The Americas*, LXX/2 (2013), pp. 203-35. Louise Burkhart, 'The "Little Doctrine" and Indigenous Catechesis in New Spain', *Hispanic American Historical Review*, XCIV/2 (2014), pp. 167-206, shows how simplified catechisms were later used in place of such learned works.

Similar experiences in the Portuguese colonies of southwest Africa are discussed in John K. Thornton, 'Conquest and Theology: The Jesuits in Angola, 1548-1650', *Journal of Jesuit Studies*, I (2014), pp. 245-59, while treatment of Ethiopian Christian Bibles is the subject of Kristen Windmuller-Luna, '*Guerra com a Lingoa*: Book Culture and Biblioclasm in the Ethiopian Jesuit Mission', *Journal of Jesuit Studies*, II (2015), pp. 223-47. For a broader overview see Festo Mkenda, 'Jesuits and Africa', www.oxfordhandbooks.com, August 2016.

Literature on the Oriental Rites issue is steadily expanding. See for example Ines G. Županov and Pierre Antoine Fabre, eds, *The Rites Controversies in* the Early Modern World (Leiden, 2018); George Nedungatt, ed., *The Synod of Diamper Revisited* (Rome, 2001); and David Mungello, ed., *The Chinese Rites Controversy: Its History and Meaning* (Nettetal, 1994).

On the European 'discovery' of Confucianism, see Lionel M. Jensen, *Manufacturing Confucianism: Chinese Traditions and Universal Civilization* (Durham, NC, 2003); also Trude Dijkstra and Thijs Weststeijn, 'Constructing Confucius in the Low Countries', *De Zeventiende Eeuw*, XXXII (2016), pp. 137–64. The most influential early European edition of the *Analecta*, attributed to Confucius and published in 1687 by Belgian Jesuit Philippe Couplet as *Confucius sinarum philosophus, sive, Scientia sinensis latine exposita*, was recently translated by Thierry Meynard as *The Jesuit Reading of Confucius: The First Complete Translation of the Lunyu (1687) Published in the West* (Leiden, 2015). Buddhism and Taoism were less positively depicted by most missionaries, but see Mei Tin Huang, 'The Encounter of Christianity and Daoism in Philippe Couplet's *Confucius Sinarum Philosophus*', *Frontiers of Philosophy in China*, IX/4 (2014), pp. 615–24.

6 CENSORED MAGIC AND SCIENCE

Giordano Bruno's life and works (including his *Theses de Magia, Cantus Circaeus* and *Spaccio de la Bestia Trionfante*) are well described in many studies ranging from Frances Yates's classic *Giordano Bruno and the Hermetic Tradition* [1964] (London, 2002) to the more readable recent biography of Ingrid D. Rowland, *Giordano Bruno Philosopher/Heretic* (Chicago, IL, 2008). Alberto A. Martínez, *Burned Alive: Giordano Bruno, Galileo and the Inquisition* (London, 2018), emphasizes the scientific aspects of Bruno's persecution. The extant documentation for his case is presented in Ugo Baldini and Leen Spruit, eds, *Catholic Church and Modern Science: Documents from the Archives of the Roman Congregations of the Holy Office and the Index* (Rome, 2009), vol. I, tome 1, pp. 862–972.

The importance of Rome as a hub for early modern scientific exchange is underlined by Elisa Andretta and Federica Favino, 'Scientific and Medical Knowledge in Early Modern Rome', in *A Companion to Early Modern Rome*, ed. Pamela M. Jones et al. (Leiden, 2019), pp. 515–29; see also Francisco Malta Romeiras, 'The Inquisition and the Censorship of Science in Early Modern Europe: Introduction', *Annals of Science*, LXXVII/1 (2020), pp. 1–9. Lynn Thorndike's eight-volume *History of Magic and Experimental Science* (New York, 1923–58) remains an essential guide to premodern intersections of magic and science, though for cases investigated by the sixteenth-century Roman Inquisition it should now be supplemented with the more recent discoveries of Baldini and Spruit in *Catholic Church and Modern Science*.

On African healers and fortune-tellers who seem to have practised their craft quite openly in early modern Europe and its colonies (even if themselves enslaved, and subject to inquisitorial investigation), see Kathryn Joy McKnight, '"En su Tierra lo Aprendió": An African *Curandero*'s Defense before the Cartagena Inquisition', *Colonial Latin American Review* XII/1 (2003), pp. 63–84; Javier Villa-Flores, 'Talking through the Chest: Divination and Ventriloquism among African Slave Women in Seventeenth-Century Mexico', *Colonial Latin American Review*, XIV/2 (2005), pp. 299–321; and James H. Sweet, *Domingos*

Álvares, African Healing, and the Intellectual History of the Atlantic World (Chapel Hill, NC, 2011).

Helpful guides to the complex topic of late medieval and early modern magic include Edward Peters, *The Magician, the Witch, and the Law* (Philadelphia, PA, 1978), and Owen Davies, *Magic: A Very Short Introduction* (Oxford, 2012), in addition to Richard Kieckhefer, *Magic in the Middle Ages* (Cambridge, 1989). Roger Bacon's interest in natural science, evident for example in his pioneering description of gunpowder, would later evolve into a reputation for alchemy and sorcery as discussed in Brian Clegg, *The First Scientist: A Life of Roger Bacon* (London, 2003); further context in Amanda Power, *Roger Bacon and the Defence of Christendom* (Cambridge, 2013). For Albert the Great (Albertus Magnus), including his research into both astronomy and astrology as well as magic, see David Collins, 'Albertus, *Magnus* or *Magus*? Magic, Natural Philosophy, and Religious Reform in the Late Middle Ages', *Renaissance Quarterly*, LXIII (2010), pp. 1–44, and Irven Resnick, ed., *A Companion to Albert the Great: Theology, Philosophy, and the Sciences* (Leiden, 2013). Roman Inquisition *censurae* of Pseudo-Albertan texts are discussed in Baldini and Spruit, *Catholic Church and Modern Science*, vol. I, tome 1, pp. 720–26.

On growing concerns about demonic influence in the later medieval period see Michael D. Bailey and Edward Peters, 'A Sabbat of Demonologists: Basel, 1431–1440', *The Historian*, LXV/6 (2003), pp. 1375–95, as well as Bailey, *Battling Demons: Witchcraft, Heresy, and Reform in the Late Middle Ages* (University Park, PA, 2003). Stuart Clark, *Thinking with Demons: The Idea of Witchcraft in Early Modern Europe* (Oxford, 1997) shows how fears of demonic influence became still more potent in early modern times.

Michael A. Ryan, *A Kingdom of Stargazers: Astrology and Authority in the Late Medieval Crown of Aragon* (Ithaca, NY, 2011), discusses the importance of Muslim and Jewish (as well as Christian) astrology in the late medieval kingdom of Aragon. For an overview of Hermetic thought, see both Yates, *Giordano Bruno* and Florian Ebeling, *The Secret History of Hermes Trismegistus: Hermeticism from Ancient to Modern Times*, trans. David Lorton (Ithaca, NY, 2007). Girolamo Cardano's case is examined in Jonathan Regier, 'Reading Cardano with the Roman Inquisition: Astrology, Celestial Physics, and the Force of Heresy', *Isis*, CX/4 (2019), pp. 661–79, while his original trial documents are translated in Baldini and Spruit, *Catholic Church and Modern Science*, vol. I, tome 2, pp. 1033–472.

On Della Porta, see Neil Tarrant, 'Giambattista Della Porta and the Roman Inquisition: Censorship and the Definition of Nature's Limits in Sixteenth-Century Italy', *British Journal for the History of Science*, XLVI/4 (2013), pp. 601–25. His *Physiognomonia*, a pseudo-medical treatise on predicting character traits using bodily signs which would later influence the criminologist Cesare Lombroso (d. 1909), was never banned. *Magia naturalis*, for its part, was removed from the Clementine Index (Rome 1596), only to be censored once more (in its Italian translation) by papal edict in 1668; Bujanda vol. XI, p. 275. See also Baldini and Spruit, *Catholic Church and Modern Science*, vol. I, tome 2, pp. 1507–64; sections of this documentary collection are also devoted to Agrippa and Paracelsus.

Some of the mixed views of Roman officials at this time regarding astrology are captured by Neil Tarrant, 'Reconstructing Thomist Astrology: Robert

Bellarmine and the Papal bull *Coeli et Terrae*', *Annals of Science*, LXXVII/1 (2020), pp. 26–49; Ugo Baldini, 'The Roman Inquisition's Condemnation of Astrology: Antecedents, Reasons and Consequences', in *Church, Censorship and Culture*, ed. Fragnito, pp. 79–110; and Elio Costa, '"Starry Leo," the Sun, and the Astrological Foundations of Sixtine Rome', *RACAR: Revue d'Art Canadienne/Canadian Art Review*, XVII/1 (1990), pp. 17–39.

On Patrizi's complicated mix of Hermetic, Platonic and Christian thought see Yates, *Giordano Bruno*, esp. pp. 202–5, and John Henry, 'Francesco Patrizi da Cherso's Concept of Space and its Later Influence', *Annals of Science*, XXXVI/6 (1979), pp. 549–73. See also Luigi Firpo, 'The Flowering and Withering of Speculative Philosophy – Italian Philosophy and the Counter Reformation: The Condemnation of Francesco Patrizi', in *The Late Italian Renaissance, 1525–1630*, ed. Eric Cochrane (London, 1970), pp. 266–84, and Baldini and Spruit, *Catholic Church and Modern Science*, vol. I, tome 3, pp. 2197–264.

The politics of Galileo's Accademia dei Lincei are discussed in Sabina Brevaglieri, 'Science, Books and Censorship in the Academy of the Lincei: Johannes Faber as Cultural Mediator', *Conflicting Duties*, Warburg Institute Colloquia XV (2009), pp. 133–57. Galileo himself, his writings and his trials, have of course been the subject of innumerable studies of varying quality and insight over the centuries. Helpful modern works include Mario Biagioli, *Galileo Courtier: The Practice of Science in the Culture of Absolutism* (Chicago, IL, 1993); Maurice A. Finocchiaro, *Retrying Galileo, 1633–1992* (Berkeley, CA, 2005); Ernan McMullin, ed., *The Church and Galileo* (Notre Dame, IN, 2005); Richard J. Blackwell, *Behind the Scenes at Galileo's Trial* (Notre Dame, IN, 2006); and Thomas F. Mayer, ed., *The Trial of Galileo, 1612–1633* (Toronto, 2012).

On anatomical works subject to Index censorship in this period, see William C. Hanigan, 'Dryander of Marburg and the First Textbook of Neuroanatomy', *Neurosurgery*, XXVI/3 (1990), pp. 489–98, and Dániel Margócsy, Mark Somos and Stephen N. Joffe, *The Fabrica of Andreas Vesalius: A Worldwide Descriptive Census, Ownership, and Annotations of the 1543 and 1555 Editions* (Leiden, 2018), pp. 121–30. Sachiko Kusukawa, *Picturing the Book of Nature* (Chicago, IL, 2012) examines the censorship of illustrated botanical works such as Fuchs's *Historia stirpium* as a form of copyright control. On early modern medical censorship more generally see Maria Pia Donato, ed., *Medicine and the Inquisition in the Early Modern World* (Leiden, 2019) and Hannah Marcus, *Forbidden Knowledge: Medicine, Science, and Censorship in Early Modern Italy* (Chicago, IL, 2020).

Distinctions between 'legitimate' and false science, of course, remain difficult to navigate even in modern times. On fraudulent scientific claims in the early modern period, see Tara E. Nummedal, 'The Problem of Fraud in Early Modern Alchemy', in *Shell Games: Studies in Scams, Frauds, and Deceits, 1300–1650*, ed. Mark Crane et al. (Toronto, 2004), pp. 37–58. Banned exorcism manuals are discussed in Bert Roest, 'Demonic Possession and the Practice of Exorcism: An Exploration of the Franciscan Legacy', *Franciscan Studies*, LXXVI (2018), pp. 301–40, and Guido Dall'Olio, 'The Devil of Inquisitors, Demoniacs and Exorcists in Counter-Reformation Italy', in *The Devil in Society in Premodern Europe*, ed. Richard Raiswell and Peter Dendle (Toronto, 2012), pp. 511–36.

There is an extensive literature on Church censorship of Machiavelli's writings, including the *Discorsi* on Livy and his Florentine history as well as

The Prince, in part because it was so controversial to ban such a respected author whose work had previously been approved by Pope Clement VII. See for example Carlo Ginzburg, 'Machiavelli, Galileo and the Censors', *New Left Review*, CXXIII (2020), pp. 91–109; Sydney Anglo, *Machiavelli – The First Century: Studies in Enthusiasm, Hostility, and Irrelevance* (Oxford, 2005); Peter Godman, *From Poliziano to Machiavelli: Florentine Humanism in the High Renaissance* (Princeton, NJ, 1998), esp. pp. 303–33; and Robert Bireley, *The Counter-Reformation Prince: Anti-Machiavellianism or Catholic Statecraft in Early Modern Europe* (Chapel Hill, NC, 1990).

For Adam Smith's influence in Spain, and his placement on the Spanish Index, see R. S. Smith, '*The Wealth of Nations* in Spain and Hispanic America, 1780–1830', *Journal of Political Economy*, LXV/2 (1957), pp. 104–25, reprinted in Cheng-chung Lai, ed., *Adam Smith Across the Nations: Translations and Receptions of the Wealth of Nations* (Oxford, 2000), pp. 313–41. See also Scott Meikle, 'Adam Smith and the Spanish Inquisition', *New Blackfriars*, LXXVI/890 (1995), pp. 70–80.

The troubled career of Gerardus Mercator (d. 1594), who had long been suspected of Protestant sympathies and suffered interrogation by the Inquisition in 1543, is described by Nicholas Crane, *Mercator: The Man Who Mapped the Planet* (New York, 2002). See also Daniel Stolzenberg, 'The Holy Office in the Republic of Letters: Roman Censorship, Dutch Atlases, and the European Information Order, circa 1660', *Isis*, CX/1 (2019), pp. 1–23, as well as Baldini and Spruit, *Catholic Church and Modern Science*, vol. I, tome 3, pp. 2051–67.

7 CENSORED SEX, FAITH AND THE ARTS

Interpretations of sex and sexuality in ancient Greece and Rome are complex and constantly evolving in modern scholarship. See, for example, Kirk Ormand, *Controlling Desires: Sexuality in Ancient Greece and Rome* (Westport, CT, 2009) and Marilyn B. Skinner, *Sexuality in Greek and Roman Culture* [2005], 2nd revd edn (Chichester, 2014). Nude and erotic visual images from ancient cultures are surveyed in Natalie Boymel Kampen, ed., *Sexuality in Ancient Art* (Cambridge, 1996).

Medieval attitudes to sex and sexuality, while quite different from those of the ancient world, were also complex and now generate a wide range of fascinating modern historiographical treatments. These run the gamut from Mark D. Jordan's investigation of theological attitudes in *The Invention of Sodomy in Christian Theology* (Chicago, IL, 1997) to Joan Cadden's study of scientific texts in *Nothing Natural Is Shameful: Sodomy and Science in Late Medieval Europe* (Philadelphia, PA, 2013), and Clarissa M. Harris's literary-focused research in *Obscene Pedagogies: Transgressive Talk and Sexual Education in Late Medieval Britain* (Ithaca, NY, 2018), to name just a few examples. See also the range of essays in Satu Lidman et al., eds, *Framing Premodern Desires: Sexual Ideas, Attitudes, and Practices in Europe* (Amsterdam, 2017). For an introduction to medieval discussions of sex in medical contexts in particular, see Danielle Jacquart and Claude Thomasset, *Sexuality and Medicine in the Middle Ages* [1985], trans. Matthew Adamson (Princeton, NJ, 1988) and Laura Jose, 'Monstrous Conceptions: Sex, Madness and Gender in Medieval Medical Texts', *Comparative Critical Studies*, V/2–3 (2008), pp. 153–63. On the *Roman de la Rose*, see Alistair Minnis, *Magister Amoris. The 'Roman de la Rose' and Vernacular Hermeneutics* (Oxford, 2001).

Medieval re-interpretations of Ovid are explored in Peggy McCracken, 'Metamorphosis as Supplement: Sexuality and History in the *Ovide Moralisé*', in *Ovidian Transversions: 'Iphis and Ianthe', 1300-1650*, ed. Valerie Traub, Patricia Badir and Peggy McCracken (Edinburgh, 2019), pp. 43–59. For an example of how Renaissance authors sought to reinterpret explicit sexual content in classical works, see Todd W. Reeser, *Setting Plato Straight: Translating Ancient Sexuality in the Renaissance* (Chicago, IL, 2016). On 'sensuality' in post-Tridentine art, there is Marcia B. Hall and Tracy E. Cooper, eds, *The Sensuous in the Counter-Reformation Church* (Cambridge, 2013).

Early Spanish inquisitors' lack of interest in erotic works, compared to their Italian counterparts, is noted in Jesús Martínez de Bujanda, 'Literatura e Inquisición en España en el Siglo XVI', in *La Inquisición Española. Nueva Visión, Nuevos Horizontes*, ed. Joaquín Pérez Villanueva (Madrid, 1980), pp. 579–92. Theatrical works were also for the most part only lightly censored in Spain: Antonio Márquez, 'La Censura Inquisitorial del Teatro Renacentista (1514–1551)', in Pérez Villanueva, *Inquisición Española*, pp. 593–603.

Censorship of each of the works listed in this chapter, among many others, deserves further in-depth discussions that are impossible to completely survey here; however, it is hoped that the following brief references to a few select cases will suffice to suggest some possible avenues for additional research. For example:

On Boccaccio, Christina McGrath, 'Manipulated, Misrepresented, and Maligned: The Censorship and *Rassettatura* of the *Decameron*', *Heliotropia*, XV (2018), pp. 189–203.

On Petrarch, Peter Stallybrass, 'Petrarch and Babylon: Censoring and Uncensoring the *Rime*, 1559-1651', in *For the Sake of Learning*, ed. Ann Blair and Anja-Silvia Grafton (Leiden, 2016), pp. 581–601.

On the censorship of Pius II's various writings (but *not* the erotic *Historia de Duobus Amantibus*), Peter Godman, *The Saint as Censor: Robert Bellarmine Between Inquisition and Index* (Leiden, 2000), pp. 95–9; also Chiara Sbordoni, '*Amatoria turpis in amatorial honesta*: l'*Historia de duobus amantibus* di Enea Silvio Piccolomini', *The Italianist*, XXX (2010), pp. 325–51.

On Rabelais, Bernd Renner, ed., *A Companion to François Rabelais* (Leiden, 2021) provides background on various religious and political issues, with up-to-date bibliographies covering many years of scholarship.

On *Lazarillo*, Felipe E. Ruan, 'Literary History, Censorship, and *Lazarillo de Tormes Castigado* (1573)', *Hispanic Research Journal*, XVII/4 (2016), pp. 269–87, and Rita Bueno Maia, 'Iberian Censorship and the Reading of *Lazarillo* in 19th Century Portugal', in *Translation and Censorship in Different Times and Landscapes*, ed. Teresa Seruya and Maria Lin Moniz (Newcastle, 2008), pp. 298–307.

On Aretino, Saad El-Gabalawy, 'Aretino's Pornography and Renaissance Satire', *Rocky Mountain Review of Language and Literature*, XXX/2 (1976), pp. 87–99, and Raymond B. Waddington, *Aretino's Satyr: Sexuality, Satire, and Self-Projection in Sixteenth-Century Literature and Art* (Toronto, 2004). But note also Raymond B. Waddington, 'Pietro Aretino, Religious Writer', *Renaissance Studies*, XX/3 (2006), pp. 277–92.

On Castiglione, Peter Burke, *The Fortunes of the Courtier: The European Reception of Castiglione's* Cortegiano (University Park, PA, 1995), esp. pp. 100–106.

On Montaigne, Malcolm Smith, *Montaigne and the Roman Censors* (Geneva, 1981); see also Godman, *Saint as Censor*, pp. 45–8.

On Pallavicino (and Antonio Rocco), Paolo Fasoli, 'Bodily *Figurae*: Sex and Rhetoric in Early Libertine Venice, 1642–51', *Journal for Early Modern Cultural Studies*, XII/2 (2012), pp. 97–116.

On Swift, Nicholas McDowell, 'Tales of Tub Preachers: Swift and Heresiography', *Review of English Studies*, LXI/248 (2010), pp. 72–92, examines the religious implications of this satire for contemporary Protestant and Catholic readers alike, and how it may have been received in the context of debates over the 1689 Toleration Act. See also David Bywaters, 'Anticlericalism in Swift's *Tale of a Tub*', *Studies in English Literature*, XXXVI/3 (1996), pp. 579–602.

On Milton, Edward F. Kenrick, '"Paradise Lost" and the Index of Prohibited Books, *Studies in Philology*, LIII/3 (1956), pp. 485–500, and Matteo Brera, '"Non istà bene in buona teologia": Four Italian Translations of *Paradise Lost* and the Vatican's Policies of Book Censorship (1732–1900)', *Italian Studies*, LXVIII/1 (2013), pp. 99–122. For mention of his much less studied *Literae*, see also Angelica Duran, 'John Milton: "Of the Devil's Party" per the Spanish Inquisition', *Reception: Texts, Readers, Audiences, History*, II (2010), pp. 22–47.

On Protestant iconoclasm and Catholic reactions against it, see Giuseppe Scavizzi, *The Controversy on Images from Calvin to Baronius* (New York, 1992), and Lee Palmer Wandel, *Voracious Idols and Violent Hands: Iconoclasm in Reformation Zurich, Strasbourg, and Basel* (Cambridge, 1994). Gabriele Paleotti's *Discorso intorno alle imagine sacre et profrane* has recently been rendered into English as *Discourse on Sacred and Profane Images*, trans. William McCuaig (Los Angeles, CA, 2012).

Censorship of erotic art by the Spanish and Mexican Inquisitions in the last decades of their existence is discussed by Lee M. Penyak in 'The Inquisition and Prohibited Sexual Artworks in Late Colonial Mexico', *Colonial Latin American Review*, XXIV/3 (2014), pp. 421–36, and Janis Tomlinson, 'Burn It, Hide It, Flaunt It: Goya's *Majas* and the Censorial Mind', *Art Journal*, L/4 (1991), pp. 59–64, as well as François Soyer, 'The Inquisition and the Repression of Erotic and Pornographic Imagery in Early Nineteenth-Century Madrid', *History*, CIII (2018), pp. 60–81. This belated attention to pornography also extended to literature: María José Muñoz García, 'Erotismo y Celo Inquisitorial. Expedientes de escritos obscenos censurados por la Inquisición en el siglo XVIII y principios del XIX', *Cuadernos de Historia del Derecho*, X (2003), pp. 157–207.

On Michelangelo's Sistine Chapel frescoes, see Bernadine Barnes, 'Aretino, the Public, and the Censorship of Michelangelo's Last Judgment', in *Suspended License: Censorship and the Visual Arts*, ed. Elizabeth C. Childs (Seattle, WA, 1997), pp. 59–84.

The inquisitorial investigation of Veronese's *Last Supper* is intriguingly examined in Edward Grasman, 'On Closer Inspection: The Interrogation of Paolo Veronese', *Artibus et Historiae*, XXX/59 (2009), pp. 125–34. For Spanish religious art, see François Soyer, 'Inquisition, Art, and Self-Censorship in the Early Modern Spanish Church, 1563–1834', in *The Art of Veiled Speech: Self-Censorship from Aristophanes to Hobbes*, ed. Han Baltussen and Peter J. Davis (Philadelphia, PA, 2015), pp. 269–92; also Virgilio Pinto Crespo, 'La Actitud de la Inquisición ante la Iconografía Religiosa. Tres Ejemplos de su Actuación (1571–1665)', *Hispania Sacra*, XXXI (1978), pp. 285–321.

On the issue of 'proper' Church music at Trent and after, see Craig A. Monson, 'The Council of Trent Revisited', *Journal of the American Musicological Society*, LV/1 (2002), pp. 1–37, and Marianne C. E. Gillion, 'Editorial Endeavours: Plainchant Revision in Early Modern Italian Printed Graduals', *Plainsong and Medieval Music*, XXIX/1 (2020), pp. 51–80, in addition to K. G. Fellerer and Moses Hadas, 'Church Music and the Council of Trent', *Musical Quarterly*, XXXIX/4 (1953), pp. 576–94.

8 CENSORSHIP AND MODERNITY

For a rich yet readable summary of Pius IX's complex reign, see Eamon Duffy, *Saints and Sinners: A History of the Popes* [1997], 4th edn (New Haven, CT, 2014), pp. 286–305. The best recent summaries of events at Vatican I and II are, respectively, John W. O'Malley, *Vatican I: The Council and the Making of the Ultramontane Church* (Cambridge, MA, 2018), and O'Malley, *What Happened at Vatican II* (Cambridge, MA, 2008). Documents for Vatican II are conveniently printed in both Latin and English in Norman P. Tanner, ed. and trans., *Decrees of the Ecumenical Councils* (Washington, DC, 1990), vol. II. Other papal documents cited in this chapter can for the most part be found in English at the Vatican website, www.vatican.va. Some older documents, however, have not been made available in translation; Leo XIII's 1897 *Officium ac munerum*, for example, only appears in Latin and Italian.

On Catholic approaches to Darwinism, see Mariano Artigas, Thomas F. Glick and Rafael A. Martínez, eds, *Negotiating Darwin: The Vatican Confronts Evolution, 1877–1902* (Baltimore, MD, 2006); also Miguel Ángel Puig-Samper, Armando García González and Francisco Pelayo, 'The Evolutionist Debate in Spain During the Nineteenth Century: A Re-Examination', trans. Catherine Jagoe, *História, Ciências, Saúde*, XXIV/3 (2017), pp. 1–17.

The work of Broussais is discussed in Erwin H. Ackerknecht, 'Broussais or a Forgotten Medical Revolution', *Bulletin of the History of Medicine*, XXVII/4 (1953), pp. 320–43, and more recently Jacques Chazaud, *F.-J.-V. Broussais: De l'Irritation à la Folie: Un Tournant Méthodologique de la Médecine au XIXe Siècle* (Toulouse, 1992). Broussais' influence on homeopathic thought is only mentioned in passing in Alice A. Kuzniar, *The Birth of Homeopathy out of the Spirit of Romanticism* (Toronto, 2017), whose focus is more on German literature.

For Church opposition to psychiatry, see Robert Kugelmann, '*Imprimi Potest*: Roman Catholic Censoring of Psychology and Psychoanalysis in the Early 20th Century', *History of the Human Sciences*, XXVII/5 (2014), pp. 74–90; see also Renato Foschi, Marco Innamorati and Ruggero Taradel, '"A Disease of Our Time": The Catholic Church's Condemnation and Absolution of Psychoanalysis (1924–1975)', *Journal of the History of Behavioral Sciences*, 54 (2018), pp. 85–100. I am indebted to Dr Ian Nicholson for the latter article, and other information on the reception of psychoanalytic theory. The role played by Bois (and his friend the Catholic novelist J.-K. Huysmans, who was however not placed on the Index) in fin-de-siècle French debates over Satanism is discussed in Massimo Introvigne, *Satanism: A Social History* [2010], trans. Tancredi Marrone and Massimo Introvigne (Leiden, 2016), esp. Chapter Seven.

The essays in Silvana Patriarca and Lucy Riall, eds, *The Risorgimento Revisited: Nationalism and Culture in Nineteenth-Century Italy* (New York, 2012) provide a useful introduction to the *Risorgimento* and its cultural challenges. On the *Syllabus of Errors* and the Church's struggle with modernism see Marvin R. O'Connell, *Critics on Trial: An Introduction to the Catholic Modernist Crisis* (Washington, DC, 1994), and C.J.T. Talar, '"The Synthesis of All Heresies": 100 Years On', *Theological Studies*, LXVIII (2007), pp. 491–514.

The evolution of the Roman Index from the reigns of Pius IX and Leo XIII to that of Paul VI is briefly summarized in Bujanda vol. XI, pp. 29–30 and 34–41. For an introduction to modern canon law, including sections relevant to censorship, see Charles Augustine Bachofen, *A Commentary on the New Code of the Canon Law*, 8 vols, 2nd edn (St Louis, MO, 1918), and Laurence J. Spiteri, *Canon Law Explained* (Manchester, NH, 2013). See also José Bettencourt, *The Imprimatur: Ecclesiastical Tradition, Canonical Basis, and Contemporary Function* (Rome, 1999).

Church involvement in early film censorship is examined in Frank Walsh, *Sin and Censorship: The Catholic Church and the Motion Picture Industry* (New Haven, CT, 1996), and Alexander McGregor, *The Catholic Church and Hollywood: Censorship and Morality in 1930s Cinema* (London, 2013). On contemporary Catholic attitudes towards literature and culture in general, see Stephen Schloesser, *Jazz Age Catholicism: Mystic Modernism in Postwar Paris, 1919–1933* (Toronto, 2005), and Una Cadegan, *All Good Books are Catholic Books: Print Culture, Censorship, and Modernity in Twentieth-Century America* (Ithaca, NY, 2013).

On Index censorship of fascist authors, and papal relations with fascist regimes in general, see Guido Bonsaver, *Censorship and Literature in Fascist Italy* (Toronto, 2007); David I. Kertzer, *The Pope and Mussolini: The Secret History of Pius XI and the Rise of Fascism in Europe* (New York, 2014); and Matteo Brera, 'The Holy Office Against Fascism: Book Censorship and the Political Independence of the Church (1928–1931)', *Between*, V/9 (2015), pp. 1–28, www.betweenjournal.it.

On the nineteenth-century pornographic works of collectors like Ashbee, as well as later episodes in the history of twentieth-century censorship, see Walter Kendrick, *The Secret Museum: Pornography in Modern Culture* [1987] (Berkeley, CA, 1996). On the interesting deluxe editions of the De Vinne press, see Michael Koenig, 'De Vinne and the De Vinne Press', *Library Quarterly*, XLI/1 (1970), pp. 1–24. I have examined exemplars of the De Vinne Indexes held at the Newberry Library in Chicago.

The experiences of Congar, Chenu and the French Dominican 'Worker Priests' are recounted in Thomas O'Meara, 'Raid on the Dominicans: The Repression of 1954', *America* (5 February 1994), pp. 8–16, and documented in John Petrie, trans., *The Worker-Priests: A Collective Documentation* [1954] (London, 1956). See also Joseph Doré and Jacques Fantin, eds, *Marie-Dominque Chenu: Moyen Âge et Modernité* (Paris, 1997); Gabriel Flynn, ed., *Yves Congar: Theologian of the Church* (Grand Rapids, MI, 2005). On Küng and Schillebeeckx, there is Peter Hebblethwaite, *The New Inquisition? The Case of Edward Schillebeeckx and Hans Küng* (San Francisco, 1980), as well as Philip Kennedy, *Schillebeeckx* (Collegeville, MN, 1993), and Hans Küng's two volumes of *Memoirs* translated by John Bowden: *My Struggle for Freedom* (Grand Rapids, MI, 2003) and *Disputed Truth* (New York, 2008); a third volume has yet to appear in English.

CONCLUSION

For library practices concerning banned books at Laval University, see Pierrette Lafond, PROMENADE EN ENFER *Les livres à l'Index de la bibliothèque (fonds ancien) du Séminaire de Québec: prolégomènes à un objet oxymora*, MA thesis, Université Laval, 2011. Notre Dame's cage for prohibited literature was kept in the basement of what is now Bond Hall: Alex Caton and Grace Watkins, 'Echoes: Bound Volumes, Illicit Lit', *Notre Dame Magazine* (Autumn 2015), https://magazine.nd.edu. The Bibliothèque nationale de France in Paris still contains a section for pornographic and otherwise proscribed books known as *Enfer*, dating back to the early eighteenth-century royal book collection, as does the British Library; see Alison Moore, 'Arcane Erotica and National "Patrimony". Britain's Private Case and the Collection de l'Enfer of the Bibliothèque Nationale de France', *Cultural Studies Review*, XVIII/1 (2012), pp. 196–216.

The scholarship on modern censorship, whether Catholic or secular, is too vast to survey here. The same can also be said for the contentious topics of peer review and academic freedom, which academics (naturally) love to reflect on and debate from every possible angle. I will therefore conclude this section with no more than a small sample of recent publications on the latter topic which may be of interest to readers, along with the invitation to dig deeper into this fertile *terroir*: James Turk, ed., *Academic Freedom in Conflict: The Struggle over Free Speech Rights in the University* (Toronto, 2014); Akeel Bilgrami and Jonathan R. Cole, eds, *Who's Afraid of Academic Freedom?* (New York, 2015); Simon Springer, 'Anarchist Professor Takes on Hate Speech', *The Conversation*, theconversation.com/ca, 21 March 2018; Joan Wallach Scott, *Knowledge, Power, and Academic Freedom* (New York, 2019); and Henry Reichman, *The Future of Academic Freedom* (Baltimore, MD, 2019).

ACKNOWLEDGEMENTS

This project arose from research first begun thanks to Scott Van Jacob, a dear friend and brilliant academic librarian at the University of Notre Dame. Scott played a leading role in acquiring the Harley L. McDevitt Inquisition Collection (formerly assembled by the bibliophilic Porrúa family) for Notre Dame in 1997, the same year in which I arrived to pursue my doctoral studies at the Medieval Institute. Over the next few years Scott, along with my dissertation director, Olivia Remie Constable, and other ND mentors such as Sabine MacCormack and former Vatican Librarian Leonard Boyle, helped me to explore and come to grips with every aspect of this richly diverse yet all-but-unstudied set of texts. Thanks to their encouragement and guidance, I came to realize that 'the inquisition' was a much more complex, and in fact much more important, historical phenomenon than popular stereotypes would lead us to believe. Sadly Scott, Remie, Sabine and Leonard are no longer with us, but it is a comfort to me to know that they were able to see early fruits of the research they first set in motion over twenty years ago.

At St Thomas University and the University of New Brunswick I have found students who were willing to engage with inquisition sources of all types, in spite of their strangeness and apparent distance from topics they initially *thought* they wanted to study. Fellow professors on my own campus and elsewhere have also been most indulgent in hearing out my thoughts and arguments about even the most frankly obscure aspects of inquisition history and the history of book censorship. Special thanks to Jimmy Mixson of the University of Alabama, Gert Melville of the Technische Universität Dresden and Gary Waite of the University of New Brunswick for organizing conference sessions where portions of this book were first presented. Cheryl Petreman and Karim Baccouche provided research assistance in the early phases, and I am indebted to the students of History 3983 who gave excellent feedback on early drafts of several chapters. Generous access to the Archivio della Congregazione per la Dottrina della Fede and Biblioteca Apostolica Vaticana (Rome), Archivo Histórico Nacional and Biblioteca Nacional de España (Madrid), Bibliothèque nationale de France (Paris), Archivo General de la Nación (Mexico City), Newberry Library (Chicago) and the Rare Books & Special Collections Library at the University of Notre Dame was essential; thanks especially to Erika Hosselkuss and Sara Weber for assistance at the latter. Funding for research materials and travel was provided by the Social Sciences and Humanities Research Council of Canada, and St Thomas University. Warm thanks to the Document Delivery staff at University of New Brunswick Libraries, too, for always going above and beyond.

My thinking about the history of book censorship, and above all its implications for academic freedom in the modern university context, was honed to a finer edge in the political context of two terms as president of the Canadian Association of University Teachers (2014–16), and subsequent years of service on its executive commitee. Academics around the world benefit from the crucial advocacy work of the CAUT and its sister organizations, united under the aegis of Education International, and it was my privilege to meet and learn from many fine colleagues there. Vital struggles over the control of words and images continue today; this book is therefore not only an exercise in historical reflection but very much an expression of my conviction that university personnel, and the societies they serve, ignore legacies and echoes of inquisitorial censorship at their very great peril. It should be noted, however, that all errors, omissions and opinions contained herein are entirely my own.

Sincere thanks to David Watkins of Reaktion Books for his suggestion that I undertake this book in hopes of reaching beyond the narrow confines of a specialized academic readership, and for his patience with multiple pandemic-related delays. Deep gratitude also goes to John and Nancy Vose for their warm hospitality during a pair of invaluable writing retreats in the French countryside, without which this book would have been further delayed. But above all, I must thank Kim Vose Jones not only for her expert insights into censorship of art (as a professional contemporary artist) and literature (as a university reference librarian), but for her constant support. Along with our children Ryley and Owen, and our new grandchild Milo, Kim has always been a cheerful companion amid all the joys and sorrows, the delights and the frustrations, that academic research inevitably entails.

PHOTO ACKNOWLEDGEMENTS

The author and publishers wish to express their thanks to the below sources of illustrative material and/or permission to reproduce it. Some locations of artworks are also given below, in the interest of brevity:

From Isaac ben Moses Arama, *Akedat Yitzak* (Venice, 1546), photo Library and Archives Canada (LAC), Ottawa: p. 145; from Pietro Aretino, *Sonetti lussuriosi* (Venice, after 1537? – c. 1550), photo Sailko (CC BY 3.0): p. 187; Badische Landesbibliothek, Karlsruhe: p. 41 (Cod. St. Peter perg. 92, fol. 5r); with permission of Biblioteca Casanatense, Rome, MIC: p. 82 (Per est. 18.6/53r); © Bodleian Libraries, University of Oxford: pp. 88 (LP 88), 171 (MS Michael 276, fol. 14v); from Jules Bois, *Le Satanisme et la magie* (Paris, 1895), photo Bibliothèque nationale de France, Paris: p. 211; from *Le Catalogue des livres censurez par la faculté de theologie de Paris* (Paris, 1544), photo Bibliothèque nationale de France, Paris: p. 49; from *Cathalogus librorum, qui prohibentur mandato . . .* (Valladolid, 1559), photo University of Notre Dame, IN: p. 63; Gallerie dell'Accademia, Venice: p. 195; from Mario Guarnacci, *Vitae, et res gestae Pontificum Romanorum et S.R.E. Cardinalium*, vol. I (Rome, 1751), photo Getty Research Institute, Los Angeles: p. 85; Hesburgh Libraries, Rare Books and Special Collections, University of Notre Dame, IN: pp. 90, 119; from *Index auctorum et librorum, qui ab officio sanctae Romanae et universalis inquisitionis caveri . . .* (Rome, 1559), photo Österreichische Nationalbibliothek, Vienna: p. 61; from *Index librorum prohibitorum ac expurgandorum . . .*, vol. II (Madrid, 1747), photo Universidad Complutense de Madrid: p. 95; from Ramon Llull and Jean d'Aubry, trans., *Le Triomphe de l'amour et l'eschelle de la gloire* (Paris, n.d.), photo Bibliothèque nationale de France, Paris: p. 101; Loras College Library, Dubuque, IA: p. 229; Musei Vaticani, Vatican City: pp. 71, 92; Museo Diocesano Tridentino, Trento: p. 65 (photo Sailko, CC BY-SA 4.0); Museo del Prado, Madrid: pp. 37, 193; The National Gallery, London (on loan from Longford Castle collection): p. 53; National Portrait Gallery, London: p. 127; from *The New Testament of Jesus Christ* (Rheims, 1582), photo Boston Public Library: p. 126; from Onofrio Panvinio, *XXVII Pontificum Maximorum elogia et imagines* (Rome, 1568): p. 58; private collection: p. 81; Tambov Regional Art Gallery: p. 206; © The Trustees of the British Museum: p. 33; U.S. National Library of Medicine, Bethesda, MD: p. 163; photos Robin Vose: pp. 98 (courtesy Bibliothèque nationale de France, Paris), 156; Wellcome Collection (CC BY 4.0): p. 210.

INDEX

Page numbers in *italics* refer to illustrations.

Abelard, Peter 34–6, 43
Abreu y Lima, José Ignácio 214
Abu Mashar Jafar ibn Muhammad ibn Umar al-Balkhi 170
academic freedom 15, 51, 233, 238, 243
Accademia dei Lincei 166, 238
L'Action Française 216, 238
Acton, Lord (John Dalberg-Acton) 217
Aeterni patris 217
Africa, colonial censorship in 147, 150, 153, 198, 236
Agrippa, Henricus Cornelius von Nettesheim 162, *163*, 170
Akhenaten 27, 227
Alba, Duke of (Fernando Álvarez de Toledo) 66
Albert the Great 35, 160
Albigensianism *see* Catharism
alchemy 96–7, 160, 164
Alexander VII, pope 80, *81*, 112, 157, 196
Alexandria, Library of 28, 30
Alfonso de Zamora 145
Allen, William (cardinal) 125, 127, *127*, 137, 152, 154
Alloquentes proxime 219
Álvarez, Diego 79
Amari, Michele 209
amulets and talismans 32, *33*, 40, 159, 172, 193, 197
anarchism 214
anatomy 96, 168–9
Angelo of Clareno 39
anticlericalism 97, 172, 183, 185, 206, 213, 225
Antioch, library of 29–30, 34

Antwerp 66, 74, 87, 144, 170, 173, 200
Apocalypse of Chiokoyhikoy 147
apocrypha 31, 129, 132, 138
Aquinas, Thomas 11–12, 35, 78, 94, 112, 137, 160, 217–18
Arabic language texts 34, 36, 52, 55, 95, 128, 139, 143–4, 146, 148, 150–51, 153, 170
see also Qur'an
Aramaic 128–9, 142, 144, 146
Aretino, Pietro 186–7, 191
Arias Montano, Benito 66, 145
Ariosto, Ludovico 61, 185
Aristotle 29, 34–5, 43, 161
Arnold of Villanova 39, 43, 61
Ashbee, Henry (Pisanus Fraxi) 222
Asia, colonial censorship in 147, 149–54
astrology 22, 39, 159–64, 170, 177
astronomy 165–8, 209
atheism 22, 97, 172, 177, 207
Aubry, Jean d' 100, *101*, 104–5
Augustine, St 12, 32–3, 83
Augustinis, Thomas de 89

Bacon, Roger 160
Balzac, Honoré de 211
Barilli, Giuseppe 209
Basel, Council of 161, 185
Beauvoir, Simone de 211
Beccaria, Cesare 175
Beda, Noël 51
Beguins, Beghards 39, 42
Bellarmine, Robert 70, 72–3, 99, 138, 174, 237, 242
Bembo, Pierto 56, 59
Benedict XIII, pope 172
Benedict XIV, pope 92, 93–4, 96, 98, 107, 140, 151, 177, 196, 218, 242
Benedict XV, pope 219

Benedict XVI, pope 237
Bennazar, Pedro 117
Bentham, Jeremy 175
Béranger, Pierre-Jean de 212
Bergman, Ernst 220
Bernard of Clairvaux, St 35, 184
Bible, Douay-Rheims version 11, 125, *126*, 137–8
Bible, King James version 11, 125, 245
Bible, polyglot versions 66, 129, 131, 133, 144
Bible, Vetus Latina version 128
Bible, Vulgate version 10–12, 128, 131–3, 135, 137–8, 140, 145, 148, 152, 154, 208, 223, 245
Black Legend 166, 203, 237
Boccaccio, Giovanni 61, 184–5, 191, 201, 223
Bodin, Jean 170, 174
Bois, Jules 210, *211*
Borghini, Vincenzo 184–5
Bosseboeuf, Louis-Auguste 216
Bradbury, Ray 17
Brahe, Tycho 166
Brenz, Johannes 52
Broussais, François-Joseph-Victor 209
Bruno, Giordano 22, 111, 155, *156*, 157–8, 164–8, 176–8, 180, 224, 229, 235
Buddhism 151
Burke, Redmond 228
Bzovius, Abraham 101–2, 104, 107

Cajetan, Thomas de Vio 47, 56
Cala, Joannes 196
calificadores, calificatores see consultants
Calvin, John 47, 64, 78
Calvinists 9, 58, 87, 139, 155, 188
Campanella, Tommaso 178, 180
'cancel culture' 17
Carbonero y Sol, León 207
Cardano, Girolamo 158, 162, 165, 168
Carnesecchi, Pietro 56, 58–9, 63
Carranza, Bartholomé 59, 63, 69, 93
Castiglione, Baldassare 186
catechisms, missionary 148–9, 153
Catharism *37*, 38–9, 132

Cavalieri, Bonaventura 168
censors, Roman 29–30
Cervantes, Miguel de 182, 188, 201, 203
Chaillot, Louis 216
Charles V, emperor (Charles I of Spain) 18, 52, 59, 130–31
Chenu, Marie-Dominique 224
Chiari, Isidore 135
Cisneros, Francisco Jiménez de (cardinal) 144, 227
classical literature, censorship of 22, 61, 184, 186
Cleland, John 189
Clement VII, pope 56, 191
Clement VIII, pope 71, 73, 78–80, 84, 95, 107, 137–8, 145, 157, 164–5, 192, 194–5
Clement X, pope 86
Clement XI, pope 117, 139–40, 146, 151, 184
Coena domini 42
College of Santa Cruz de Tlatelolco, Mexico 149
College of St Alban's, Valladolid 118–19, 125
Colonna, Vittoria 56, 59
communism 214, 217
Comte, Auguste 209
Confucianism 28, 151, 154, 236
Congar, Yves 224
Congregation for the Doctrine of the Faith 23, 102, 105–6, 176, 224, 232–3, 235, 237, 244
Constantine, emperor 31, 128
consultants 23, 70, 78, 86, 94, 99, 102, 104–5, 107, 111, 113, 117–18, 120, 175, 238
conversos 46, 142, 147, 198
Copernicus 165–7
Coughlin, Charles Edward 220
Council for the Reform of the Church 57
Coverdale, Myles 129, 132
cultural genocide 19, 141, 148
Cum sacrorum 138

D'Annunzio, Gabriele 220
Dante Alighieri 43, 174

Darwinism 209
De auxiliis debates 78–9, 83–4, 95, 111–12, 167
De Vinne Press 222
Decree of Gelasius, the 32–3, 40, 42
Dee, John 164
Defoe, Daniel 188
Dei verbum 232, 240
Della Porta, Giovan Battista 158, 162
demons and demon-summoning 22, 32, 40, 43, 155, 157, 160–61, 164, 170, 172, 174, 177, 235
Diamper, synod of 151
Diderot, Denis 97, 173
divination 106, 114, 133, 160, 164, 168
Divini illius magistri 219
Dolet, Étienne 130–31
Döllinger, Johann Joseph Ignaz von 217
donec corrigatur 75
Donin, Nicholas 36
Draper, John William 208
Dryander, Johannes 168–9
Dumas, Alexandre 210–11
Dunoyer, Anne-Marguerite 202
Duvergier, Jean 84

economics, censorship of 175–6
edicts of censorship 9, 48, 50, 52, 54, 82–4, *82*, 86, 88–9, *90*, 91, 93, 98, 112, 118, *119*, 157, 164, 166, 175–6, 179, 217, 234
education reform, censorship of 214
Elizabeth I, queen of England 9, 64, 125, 164
Erasmus, Desiderius 52, *53*, 54–5, 61–2, 74, 129–31, 133, 153, 155, 184
erotica 182–4, 185, *187*, 189, 191–4, 220, 222–3
  see also pornography
Erotika Biblion Society 233
Espence, Claude d' 51–2
Estienne, Robert 130–31, 133, 135
Ethiopian books 131, 133, 139, 146, 150, 153
Ex corde Ecclesiae 233, 237
exorcism 172, 180
expurgation 70, 72–7, 79, 86–7, 89, 106–7, 110, 114–16, 118–19, 141, 145, *145*, 166, 168, 174, 178, 183–6, 188, 203, 208, 234, 236
Eymeric, Nicholas 32, 42–4, 54, 60–61, 69–70, 101–2, 104, 106, 116, 160, 164, 196, 226

Fagius, Paul 146
Farel, Guillaume 51
fascism 18, 22, 220–21
  see also Nazism
feminism 22, 221
Fénelon, François 96
Ferdinand VI, king of Spain 94
Ficino, Marsilio 162, 164
Fielding, Henry 189
'Fig-Leaf Campaign' 191
film 16, 219–21
Fiore, Joachim of 39, 42
Flaminio, Marcantonio 56, 59
Flaubert, Gustave 211
Fourier, Charles 214
France, Anatole 211
Francis I, king of France 48, 50, 131
Frankfurt book fairs 72, 108, 236
Freemasonry 22, 96–7, 213, 234
French Revolution 177, 189, 204, 207, 214–15, 225
Fuchs, Leonhart 169

Galilei, Galileo 22, *82*, 94, 111, 158, 166–8, 176–8, 208, 226, 235, 238
gallicanism 139, 215–16
geography, censorship of 176
Getino, Luis Alonso 218
Gibbon, Edward 173–4
Gide, André 211
Gnosticism 31
Goldsmith, Oliver 173–4
Gonzaga, Giulia 56
Goya, Francisco 192, *193*
Grafigny, Françoise 202
Greene, Graham 212
Gregory IX, pope 41
Gregory XI, pope 101, 107
Gregory XIII, pope 69–70, 73, 137–9, 146, 164
Gregory XV, pope 151
Gregory XVI, pope 208
Grotius, Hugo 174–5

Guanzelli, Giovanni Maria 75, 157
Guidetti, Giovanni Domenico 200
Gui, Bernard 40–42
Gunpowder Plot, the 119
Gutenberg, Johannes 46, 129

Hannot, Jean-Baptiste 89
Hansen, Leonard 100, 102–4, 115
Hayes Code 219
Hebraism, Christian 35, 66, 129–31, 142, 144–7
Hebrew language texts 12, 31, 110, 128–31, 135–6, 142–7, *145*, 153, 232
Heine, Heinrich 210
heliocentrism 94, 167, 169
Henry III, king of France 164
Henry VIII, king of England 48–9, 130
hermeticism 161–2, 164–5
Hessus, Helius Eobanus 130–31, 134
Hinduism 151, 154, 236
'historical Jesus' 208
history, censorship of 173–4
Hobbes, Thomas 174
homeopathy 209
homosexuality 181–2, 186
Hooke, Robert 238
Hugo, Victor 211
humanism 51, 56, 129–31, 142, 182, 184, 205
Hume, David 173–4
Hussites 44, 46, 129
Hypatia 30

idolatry 13, 147, 190, 198
Immaculate Conception, the 208
Immensa 111
imprimatur 104, 108, 233
In eminenti apostolatus 213
Index of Prohibited Art, the 194
Indigenous American cultures, colonial destruction of 18, 94, 96, 147–50, 152–4, 198
Innocent X, pope 84
Inter mirifica 223, 249
Inter sollicitudines 46–8, 65, 106
International Olympic Committee 15
Internet, the 8, 16, 228, 230, 240, 244

James, Thomas 87, *88*, 244
James I of England 11, 111, 125, 170, 245
Jansenism 83–4, 86, 93, 98, 105, 111, 139–40, 234
Jerome 12, 32, 128
John XXII, pope 40, 160, 174
John XXIII, pope 223
John Paul II, pope 233
Julius III, pope 59, 145
Junius, Francis 87

Kabbalah 21, 114, 142, 145, 161
Káldi, György 139
Kant, Immanuel 173
Kazantzakis, Nikos 221
Kepler, Johannes 166–7
Kimchi, David 142, 146
Knapp, William 222
Krapp, Andreas 200
Krestos, Se'ela 139
Küng, Hans 224

Lafontaine, Jean de 186, 201
Lambruschini, Luigi (cardinal) 204
Lammenais, Félicité de 205, 208, 216
Lateran V 46–7
law, censorship of 175
Lazarillo de Tormes 186
Le Maistre de Sacy, Antoine and Louis-Isaac 139
Lea, Henry Charles 222
learned societies 238–9
Lefèvre d'Étaples, Jacques 51, 65, 129–30, 132
Legion of Decency 219
Leibniz, Gottfried 96, 238
Lemos, Tomás de 79
Leo X, pope 46–7, 56, 106, 191, 245
Leo XIII, pope 206, 217–18, 242
Licet ab initio 57
Licet alias 74
Llull, Raymond 21, 39, *41*, 42–3, 61–2, 100–106, *101*, 116–18, 120, 153, 155, 162, 181, 242
Locke, John 174
Lollards 46–7, 129
Loyola, Ignatius 245
Lubac, Henri de 224

Lusitanus, Amatus 169
Luther, Martin 47–8, 52, 56, 78, 129–30, 132, 140, 146, 153, 230–31, 245
Lutherans 52, 58, 87, 134, 138, 173

McCabe, Joseph 222
Maccabees 29
Machiavelli, Niccolò 61, 74, 174
Maeterlinck, Maurice 211
Maimonides 36, 43, 141–2
Malingre, Mathieu 200
Malleus maleficarum 161, 170
Mariales, Xantes 112
Marot, Clément 131
Marracci, Lodovico 146
Marsilius of Padua 43, 174
Martin, Gregory 125
Martin, Jacqueline 221
Martini, Antonio 140
Mary I, queen of England 59
Mary of Hungary 51
master of the sacred palace 73, 75, 79–80, 83, 105, 108, 110–12, 157, 165, 237
materialism 173, 175, 177, 189, 207, 209, 215, 217
mathematics, censorship of 162, 168–9
Medici family 46–7, 56, 164, 166, 200
Medici *Graduale* 200
medicine, censorship of 168–9, 209
  see also anatomy; homeopathy
Melanchthon, Philip 52, 184, 200
Mendham, Joseph 222
Mercator, Gerardus 176
Mercier, Louis-Sébastian 179–80, 202
mesmerism 210, *210*
Michelangelo 191–2, 195
Michelet, Jules 209
Mill, John Stuart 174
Milton, John 188
Mirabeau, Count of (Honoré Gabriel Riqueti) 189, 223
Missale Romanum 112, 200
Miranda prorsus 221
Molinism 78, 83, 86, 98
Montaigne, Michel de 110, 186, 191, 201, 203

Montesquieu (Charles Louis de Secondat) 94, 174, 186
Monty Python 227, 240
More, Thomas 178, 180
moriscos 46, 143, 147, 151, 154, 198
Morone, Giovanni (cardinal) 56, 59, 63
Münster, Sebastian 130, 134
Murray, John Courtney 224

Nazism 14, 220–21
Neo-Platonism 161, 164–5
newspapers, censorship of 218
Newton, Isaac 166, 168, 238–9
Nider, Johannes 161
nihil obstat 108
Nobel prize winners 211
Nobili, Roberto 151
Noris, Enrico 85–6, *85*, 93–4, *95*, *119*
nudity 63, 181–2, *187*, 191–3, *193*, *195*

Ochino, Bernardino 50, 56–9
Officium ac munerum 218
Old Catholics 217
Olivi, Peter John 39, 42–3
opera 16, 212
Orientalism 153–4
Orwell, George 14, 17, 241
Osiander, Andreas 52
Ottaviani, Alfredo (cardinal) 223–4, 237
Ovid 30, 184

Pagani, Marco Antonio 200
Pagnino, Xantes 131, 133, 145
Paleotti, Gabriele (cardinal) 194
Palestrina, Giovanni Pierluigi da 200
Pallavicino, Ferrante 186
papal infallibility 22, 216, 224, 226, 242
Paracelsus 162, 170
Pascal, Blaise 84, 139
Patrizi, Francesco 164–6
Paul III, pope 57–9, 191, 226
Paul IV, pope 57–64, *58*, 66, 70, 87, 105, 135, 137, 145, 191, 195, 226, 241–2
Paul V, pope 78–9, 84, 151, 172

Paul VI, pope 223, *225*, 226, 232, 240
peer review 8, 16, 51, 75, 238–9, 242
Pelagianism 33, 85–6, 93, 119
Peña, Francisco 68–73, 79, 98–9, 102, 104–5, 164, 185, 226, 237, 239, 242
Pérez de Prado y Cuesta, Francisco 93
Petrarch 186
Pfefferkorn, Johannes 142
Philip II, king of Spain 51–2, 59, 61–2, 242
philosophes 94, 172, 189
Pico Della Mirandola, Giovanni 162, 164
Pius II, pope 70, 74, 185
Pius IV, pope 63–4, 66
Pius V, pope 57, 60, 66–7, 69, 74, 94, 136–7
Pius IX, pope 204–8, *205*, 211, 216–18
Pius X, pope 217, 219
Pius XI, pope 219–20
Pius XII, pope 221, 223
Pole, Reginald 56–9
political thought, censorship of 174–5
Pope, Alexander 188
Porete, Marguerite 39, 43
pornography 14, 20, 106, 186, 189, 191–2, 194, 222–3, 229
  see also erotica
Proudhon, Pierre-Joseph 214
psychology 209–10
Pufendorf, Samuel 174
Putnam, George Henry 222

qualificatores *see* consultants
Quanta cura 204, 206, 211
Quesnel, Pasquier 140
Quinzaine, La 221
Quiroga Spanish Index 76, 87, 113, 184
Qur'an 21, 36, 43, 114, 143–4, 146–7, 153–4

Rabelais 180, 182, 185, 201
radio 219–21
Rahner, Karl 224
Ranke, Leopold von 209
Raphael 46, 191
Rashi 142, 146
Raspail, Vincent 209
'realist' literature 211
recusants 9, 138, 237
Renan, Ernest 208
renegados 143
Republic of Letters 91, 116, 167, 238
Rerum novarum 217
Restif de la Bretonne, Nicolas Edme 189–90
Reuchlin, Johann 142
Reusch, Franz Heinrich 217, 222
Ribera, Juan de (archbishop) 149
Ricci, Matteo 151
Richardson, Samuel 188, 201
Risorgimento 214–15
Rituale romanum 172
Roche-Guilhem, Anne de la 202
Rojas, Fernando de 185–6
Rosenberg, Alfred 220
Rossetti, Gabriele 210, 213
Rota court 73, 94, 194
Rousseau, Jean-Jacques 97, 173, 189
Rubeis, Petrus Franciscus de 102–4

Sade, Marquis de (Donatien Alphonse François) 189
Sand, George 210
Sangro, Raimondo di, prince of Sansevero 96–7
Sartre, Jean-Paul 211
satire 22, 185–6
Saint-Simon, Claude-Henri de 214
saints, images of 13, 22, 190, 192–3, 196–7
Sandoval Spanish Index 76, 87
Satanism 210, *211*
Savonarola, Girolamo 47, 214
Schillebeeckx, Edward 224
Scientific Revolution, the 165, 170, 172, 234
Scot, Reginald 170
Scott, Walter 234
Scottus, Bernardino 62
Seyon, Täsfa 131, 133, 139
Silva, Feliciano de 186
Simons, Menno 48

Sirleto, Guglielmo (cardinal) 70, 71, 72–3, 137, 145, 237
Sistine Chapel 63, 191–2
Sixtus V, pope 71, 73, 107, 111, 137–8, 194, 222
Smith, Adam 175–6
smuggling 52, 87, 109–10
socialism 22, 209, 214, 217
Socrates 28–9
Sollicita ac provida 94–5, 218
Solomon, king (biblical and alleged magical writings of) 161, 170, 184
Sotomayor Spanish Index 76, 114
Spanish Armada, the 119, 125
Stendhal (Henri Beyle) 211
Sterne, Laurence 234–5
Sullivan, William Laurence 216–17
Susenyos I, emperor of Ethiopia 150
Swift, Jonathan 188, 201
Syllabus of Errors 204, 215

Talmud 21, 36, 42–4, 46, 59, 113, 141–2, 145, 147, 153, 237
Teilhard de Chardin, Pierre 209
television 220–21
Tintin 229–30
Tre Savi sopra eresia 109
Trithemius, Johannes 162, 170
Tunstall, Cuthbert 130
Turrettini, Bénédict 87
Tyndale, William 129–30, 132, 153

Ulenberg, Kaspar 138
ultramontanism 22, 215–18, 221, 226
Unamuno, Miguel de 211
Unigenitus 93, 140
Urban VIII, pope 84, 167
utopias in literature 178–81, 183, 186

Valdés Spanish Index 52
Valier, Agostino 72, 77
Vatable, François 51, 135
Vatican I 206, 217–18
Vatican II 207, 223–4, 226
Vatican library 70, 73, 86, 125, 145
Vergerio, Pier Paolo 56, 87
Verjuys, Joannes Baptista 100–104, 107, 114–16, 120
Vermigli, Pietro Martire 56, 59
Verona, Guido da 220
Veronese, Paolo 195–6, 201
Vesalius, Andreas 169
Veuillot, Louis 211
Victorines 35
Vigilanti cura 219
Vitoria, Francisco de 73
Voltaire (François-Marie Arouet) 97, 173, 198, 212

Wadding, Lucas 104
Walt Disney Company, the 15, 237
Weyer, Johann 170
Waldensianism 38–9, 46–7, 128–9, 132
William of Ockham 43, 174
witches, witch-hunts 47, 158, 161, 164, 170, 176, 197
Witte, Aegidius de 139
women writers 202, 210–11, 221, 244
'Worker Priest' movement 224
Wujek, Jakub 138
Wycliffites 44, 46, 129

Yerushalmi, Domenico 145, 146

Zapata Spanish Index 76
Zola, Émile 211
Zwingli, Huldrych 047